Art in the
Public Interest

Art in the Public Interest

Edited with an Introduction by
Arlene Raven

DA CAPO PRESS
NEW YORK

Library of Congress Cataloging in Publication Data

Art in the public interest / edited with an introduction by Arlene Raven—1st
Da Capo Press ed.
    "An unabridged republication of the edition published in Ann Arbor,
Michigan in 1989, with the substitution of several photographs"—T.p. verso.
    Includes bibliographical references, and index.
    ISBN 0-306-80539-1
    1. Public art—United States. I. Raven, Arlene.
N8835.A78 1993   93-2415
700'.973—dc20   CIP

First Da Capo Press edition 1993

This Da Capo Press edition of *Art in the Public Interest* is an unabridged
republication of the edition published in Ann Arbor, Michigan in 1989,
with the substitution of several photographs. It is reprinted by arrangement
with the author.

Published by Da Capo Press, Inc.
A Subsidiary of Plenum Publishing Corporation
233 Spring Street, New York, N.Y. 10013

Contents

Introduction

Arlene Raven
Photos and Photo Commentary by Robin Holland

Public art isn't a hero on a horse anymore. The bronze memorial, the most enduring public art form of the past century, gave way to large-scale abstract sculpture that flooded the public domain in the United States when the National Endowment for the Arts launched its art-in-public-places program in the 1960s. Then an explosion of new forms in the 1980s—as diverse as street art, guerrilla theater, video, page art, billboards, protest actions and demonstrations, oral histories, dances, environments, posters, murals, paintings and sculpture—radically changed the face of contemporary public art. *Art in the Public Interest* is devoted to these most recent forms of public artistic expression and to the critical issues raised by them.

Activist and communitarian, art in the public interest extends the modes of expression of public art of the past several decades. The new public-spirited art can, as well, critique (through its own approach and intent) the uneasy relationship among public artworks, the public domain, and the public. But the intersection of art and social issues in recent public efforts also presents knotty critical problems. A number of essays in this volume ask questions and examine the effects of socially-conscious art. How, for example, can we separate the good intentions of artists from the value of their work? The invention of new genres and artists' collaborations with nonartists seem, in addition, to defy existing standards. Since the audience for art cannot be quantified, measuring the achievement of these works even on their own terms remains difficult.

Does art that wants to do good do good? Is it fair to expect such work to be social work as well as art work? And does art in the public

---

Robin Holland's photographs and captions first appeared in *Village Voice* (3 May 1988).

interest really interest the public? As art critic Lucy Lippard states in "Moving Targets/Moving Out," "The great and still elusive questions surrounding public art are: Which public? Is there an exchange between art and audience?" In "Public Art from Public Sector Perspective," Wendy Feuer presents the question from the point of view of the art agency: "Should a state agency that serves such a broad spectrum of the population sponsor work that is esoteric, confrontational, or politically—or sexually—controversial? Is this type of work appropriate in an already overly stimulated environment?" Phyllis Rosser points out (in "Education through Collaboration Saves Lives") that the work of Tim Rollins and K.O.S., collaborative art projects that started in a Bronx classroom, is now represented by a SoHo gallery and sold at high prices. Can an art in the interest of the public be commissioned by corporations, funded by the government and sold in the art market?

Art historian Moira Roth chronicles performance artist Suzanne Lacy's spectacles in "Suzanne Lacy: Social Reformer and Witch." Lacy organized over four hundred black-clothed elderly women into a living *Crystal Quilt* in the glass-covered courtyard of a Phillip Johnson building in downtown Minneapolis in the spring of 1987. Several years of planning, funding, and organizing went into the afternoon performance. To what extent is Lacy responsible for what happens to her performers after the performance? Roth's article details the philosophy and planning process that separate Lacy's work from some spectacles. Still, such questions are appropriate, and Lacy herself asks them. Can artists work for the public by creating expensive productions—organized by elitist cultural institutions, seen by very small audiences, and finally chronicled as the latest feats of the artist? Are such artists merely ambitious media hogs? Lacy, in "Fractured Space," considers problems in producing public artworks with a strong accent on audience and community. She asserts that "Works of public art enter a pre-existing physical and social organization. How the work relates to, reinforces or contends with forms of expression of that community is a question that contributes to the critical dialogue."

The eighteen essays in this book neither dismiss art in the public interest as a subcategory of "real Art" nor offer only a sentimental advocacy. Instead, authors create a dialogue between respect for and even championship of an art that addresses the public interest in public and intellectual frameworks that can set these works into cultural contexts as well as critical perspectives. This dialogue is crucial not only for the future of public art itself but in the ongoing discourse among art, artist, audience, and society.

Writer/performer Linda Burnham's "Monuments in the Heart" chronicles performance and video experiments in community art since

WINDOWS

Most of New York City's windows showing art ("Windows on White," those at Franklin Furnace, the New Museum, Grey Art Gallery, etc.) are actual windows. But "10 on Eighty" (Eighth Avenue between 53rd and 54th Streets) is a series of showcases stuck into the ground-level west wall of the Municipal Garage, built in 1960 from plans by an architect with a fifties hangover. The shows change every two to four weeks. The installation in the photo, the "Alluvium Collectors," was done by BAT, an artists' group.

(All photos in this chapter are copyright Robin Holland)

1980. During the past decade, Burnham explains, community artists have been working all over America in unlikely grassroots territories from Alaska to the San Diego border to New York harbor. Their mission—creating their work in the public interest—has led them to aspire to reveal the plight and plead the case of the disenfranchised and disadvantaged, and to embody what they view as humanitarian values. A majority of the artists whose works are examined by Burnham (and, in fact, by this volume as a whole) came of age in the idealistic era of social protest of the 1960s. They were educated in the experimental seventies, when nontraditional approaches and media began to be widely taught in art schools. Awash in the permissive postmodern eighties, those who chose to work in public already understood that inventing forms and structures didn't mean searching for novel painting shapes—and that traditional arts could be put to new use in the public interest. Burnham claims that community artists' experiments in performance and video since 1980 have stretched the definition of community art "the way they stretched the definition of fine art in the seventies."

But the new forms of community art we see in the 1980s are defined even more by their methods than by their media. Artists who finally created groups with other artists and nonartists to carry out their projects first longed for communities that could enfold them, and an inclusive, experiential art. Working on site in small locales, clowns and puppeteers, shamans and laundry experts, directors, needleworkers, and trouble-shooters—artists all—they intended to create a parochial art in its best sense, an artistry that serves the territory of specific spiritual assemblies. Those incarcerated in prisons and hospitals; the elderly and teenagers; the displaced, homeless and unemployed; peace, healing, and labor organizations; race and gender-based groups became participating audiences and artistic collaborators.

Artists working in the public interest address a wide range of human concerns. Performance artist Rachel Rosenthal rejected toxic waste and embraced the animals and vegetables of the earth; Sisters of Survival artists collective renounced nuclear arms and swore allegiance to world peace; theater director Susan Franklin Tanner (TheatreWorkers Project) and The Waitresses performance group struck for wages, jobs, and freedom from harassment in the workplace; artist Charles Dennis (Hospital Audiences) hunted down medical malfeasance and searched for real healing. (See Burnham, "Monuments in the Heart.")

Artist John Malpede, a California Arts Council artist-in-residence in the Artists in Communities program, and individuals among the homeless of Los Angeles' skid row, have been performing original

COMMUNITY MURALS AND MEALS

"The Struggle Continues/*La Lucha Continua*" project, organized by Artmakers, created 24 murals in an open space in New York City running between 8th and 9th Streets at Avenue C. In September 1987, on the 9th Street side, Kalif Beacon, for whom sixties style—and, more important, sixties idealism—never became unfashionable, opened the Temple of the Rainbow soup kitchen. The food is prepared under a wooden awning, in 20-gallon pots set on a metal grating over open fires. Up to 1000 meals ("as much as anyone wants") are served each day. Contributions of money, food, paper goods, and time are welcomed.

GRAFFITI, SORT OF

The art world's delight in graffiti is ostensibly over, but judging by its continued proliferation on all suitable surfaces, the writers have not lost interest. In Prospect Park, New York City, a Haitian artist, Deenpa Bazile, carved faces in a tree stump. This is three-dimensional work, but it has the same immediacy and anonymity as two-dimensional versions. A park administrator spent a year tacking business cards to the stump before she made contact with the artist and commissioned a piece for "Branches: Artists Work with the Trees," at the Boathouse (30 April–4 July 1988).

theater works about their lives as the Los Angeles Poverty Department. (See Burnham, "Hands across Skid Row: John Malpede's Performance Workshop for the Homeless of L.A.") During the previous decade in Los Angeles, muralist Judy Baca created the Citywide Mural Project and art-directed a multi-ethnic crew of hundreds of youngsters and local artists in painting The Great Wall of Los Angeles, a redesignation of Mexican-American history and the longest mural in the world, in a flood control canal in the San Fernando Valley. (See Guillermo Gómez-Peña, "A New Artistic Continent.") Art collaborators Helen Mayer Harrison and Newton Harrisons' ecology-minded "Cruciform Tunnel"—an idea, then a proposal, arrived at through the Harrisons' Socratic dialogue, their model for discourse and method for developing their work— sought to rejoin two nature reserves in San Diego, California. (See Raven, "Two Lines of Sight and an Unexpected Connection: Helen Mayer Harrison and Newton Harrison.") On the San Diego–Tijuana border, Gómez-Peña and the Border Arts Workshop have been strik-ing a blow at Mexican-American myths and stereotypes originating at the geographical dividing line between Mexico and the United States, and redesigning the "artistic continent" of Chicano art. As "Mobile Image," according to Steven Durland in "Defining the Image as Place," Kit Galloway and Sherrie Rabinowitz created *Hole-in-Space: A Public Communications Sculpture* in 1980—a three-day, life-size, unannounced live satellite link allowing spontaneous interaction between the public on two coasts. Their use of satellite telecommunications allows "Mobile Image" to redefine the image as a real place that becomes the visual architecture for a live performance, the artist as a "metadesigner" who creates a context into which aesthetic and human content can enter.

Painter Eva Cockcroft chronicles the process of creating the La Lucha mural project she directed in New York City (twenty-six murals com-bining individual and collective works on four buildings surrounding a central plaza on New York's Lower East Side, addressing themes of intervention in Central America, apartheid in South Africa, and gen-trification in the local community). Mierle Ukeles has shaken the hand of every sanitation worker in that city, and designed a waste facility on the Hudson, during her ten-year partnership with the New York City Sanitation Department. (See Burnham, "Monuments.") Greenpeace unfurled a banner on the infamous New York City garbage barge in 1987: "NEXT TIME . . . TRY RECYCLING." Jeff Weinstein's "Names Carried into the Future: An AIDS Quilt Unfolds" takes a personal, experiential approach to The AIDS NAMES Project Quilt when the Quilt traveled to

MONUMENTS

In a city full of green horses and heroes (historical and winged) perched on pedestals and buildings, Michele Cohen, coauthor with Margot Gayle of *The Art Commission and Municipal Art Society Guide to Manhattan's Outdoor Sculpture* (June 1988), points to Augustus Saint-Gauden's collaboration with Stanford White, the Farragut Monument in Madison Square Park, as one of the finest. The Parks Department recommends John Hemingway Duncan's granite Soldiers' and Sailors' Memorial Arch at the entrance to Prospect Park in Brooklyn, with its three bronze groups by Fredrick W. MacMonnies and bronze reliefs by Thomas Eakins and William R. O'Donovan (*above*). The arch was completed in 1892 and its interior closed to the public until Prospect Park administrator Tupper W. Thomas invited the public in 1981. During June 1988 a six-person show called "Remember My Face," organized by Prospect Park arts coordinator Mariella Bisson, filled the arch's trophy room and each of the landings, reached by climbing one of the two decorated metal staircases that spiral to the top. Shown in the detail (*right*) is Gabriel Koren's *Self-Portrait 1, 2 & 3*. In the Anchorage (of the Brooklyn Bridge), another space that competes with its art for attention, an eight-artist show coordinated by Creative Time was also exhibited in June 1988.

New York. Originating in San Francisco, this monumental commemoration will (via television and travel to various U.S. locations) eventually be seen by a majority of U.S. citizens.

By defining their individual and cultural identities as well as producing end products, these collaborators and audiences are neither consumers of the works produced nor merely protestors of the wrongs they might want to right. Their creative process catalyzes reclamation and repossession of self, action in art/work and the building of community.

American history is full of artful images. Consider the dramatic, symbolic performance that inspirited protestors created when they crossed the Atlantic Ocean in 1620 in a lone vessel to form an ideal nation based on liberty and justice. More than one hundred years of community pageants and union marches—which merged diverse visual forms and involved large groups of artists and nonartists to confront pressing issues of the day—have provided sources and inspirations for current interdisciplinary spectacles, from Rachel Rosenthal's parade of animals to Sisters of Survival's marching nuns.

But public art still brings to the minds of many Americans an equestrian statue. In the United States, where "natural resources" can be code for patriotism and religion, outdoor sculpture has been traditionally associated with the large-scale "landscape gardening" of city parks (a movement inaugurated with Frederick Law Olmsted's creation of New York's Central Park in the late nineteenth century) as well as with city centers.

The individualistic conventions of twentieth-century modernism in the fine arts, including large-scale public sculpture, may not seem relevant to public interest. But, historically, there have been artists and movements that claimed to integrate aesthetic and social considerations and to serve their societies in some specific way. For example, the Russian Constructivists, artists working within the Russian Revolution in the beginning of the twentieth century and later at the German Bauhaus, provided a model of artists and art connected to their political contexts and to social change. Today in the U.S.A., however, art historian/critic Donald Kuspit cautions in "Crowding the Picture: Notes on American Activist Art Today" that activist art calling for social change may offer, instead, a new myth of conformity, "the same old lonely crowd in new ideological clothing." The complications and contradictions inherent in the intermixture of aesthetics and social issues, individual creative goals and outreach to audiences can be a clue to the troubling reception of American public and activist art in the past several decades.

Two periods in twentieth-century American history provided the conditions for a rise in the community arts. During the 1930s, and again in the late sixties and seventies, the desire for social change spawned public programs. Activity in the thirties, mainly New Deal employment for Depression-era artists, was centralized in the Works Progress Administration (WPA) and Treasury Section Art Programs. WPA easel and mural projects have left a legacy in contemporary two-dimensional public forms.

But public art changed altogether after 1966, when the National Endowment for the Arts' Visual Arts Program began its exploration of how to support the placement of art in public. The U.S. General Services Administration's Art in Architecture Program, inspired by a 1962 Kennedy administration directive fully activated in 1972, commissioned and paid for hundreds of sculptures for public places. In 1966, only a few public art programs existed in the United States, but in 1988 there were more than 135 funded state and local programs, as well as numerous efforts in the private sector. Storm King Art Center in Mountainville, New York, owns 115 large-scale modern and contemporary sculptures, displayed outdoors on its 400 privately purchased acres. On the C. W. Post campus of Long Island University a provocative Public Art Program has placed fifty-one pieces by forty-four artists (who loan the works long term) since 1985. First Bank of Minneapolis has challenged its employees and customers by placing controversial contemporary artworks in their workplaces. The Endowment itself has lent federal support to more than five hundred projects originating at the local and state levels since 1967. These have been located in every region of the country and in communities of all sizes (according to acting director of the Visual Arts Program Michael Faubion) "from Fargo, North Dakota to New York City," and ranged from "modest murals in city council chambers to monumental earthworks in reclaimed strip mines."[1]

Originally, the NEA's aim was to honor America's great artists. When Grand Rapids, Michigan, was awarded the first NEA Art-in-Public-Places Project grant, the city commissioned Alexander Calder's well-known *La Grande Vitesse*. But commissioning a sculpture for a city's public square now seems, even to the Endowment, artistically and politically naive as well as possibly imperious.[2] The "plunk" theory—a site is secured and a sculpture installed, thereby making it accessible to the masses—according to Suzanne Lacy, has given way to the more recent "chat them up" procedure: artists try their models out on the community, work with architects and city planners, and are somewhat receptive to public feedback, as long as artistic expression is not com-

IN THE PARKS

The Parks Department of the City of New York counts 1500 works of art under its jurisdiction. Of these, more than half are statues, monuments, memorial plaques, and historic structures (that aren't buildings). Some are works for children, such as Jose de Creeft's enduring *Alice in Wonderland* sculptures, at 76th Street near Fifth Avenue. Elizabeth Egbert's 1985 piece, produced by Cityarts Workshop (*above*), is for a playtime fueled by the contemporary fantasies of the He-Man and She-Ra generation. Called *Broadway Starship*, it's in Staten Island's Corporal Lawrence Thompson Park in West Brighton.

LOFTY
From Eighth Avenue in New York City and other viewing points on the ground,
Owen Morrel's 1981 *Boomerang* looks like an oddly configured satellite dish grafted
onto the south side of the old McGraw-Hill building. But to view Manhattan
climbing on *Boomerang*'s grate-work stairway, suspended 32 stories, is space-
walking: claustrophobic, acrophobic, and exhilarating.

promised. In an article devoted to comparisons between commissioned projects and grassroots efforts in Detroit, sculptor/writer Michael Hall states that "'Seeing' in the late 1980s (at least as it pertains to the perception of public art) has inclined almost everyone to reexamine the mythopoetic concept of the 'popular mind.'"

"Public art has descended from, but must not be confused with, large-scale outdoor sculpture, site-specific sculpture, and environmental sculpture," artist Scott Burton said in 1983.[3] Today there is no consensus about what public art should look like, or certainty about what a monument is. The public domain itself is more complex and less functionally stable than ever before. Public art has served concurrently as landmark, symbol, monument, functional element, architectural embellishment, isolated aesthetic object, and cultural artifact.[4] The Endowment's Visual Arts Program now funds performance, video, and other nontraditional as well as traditional public forms. Indeed many of the artists and projects addressed here have been funded by the NEA. But, using the example of Seattle, art critic Matthew Kangas argues in "Art in Public Places: Seattle" that for every success story, Seattle being "the biggest success story of all," there is "a failure, a glitch, a fiasco, or a tragedy" related to choice or the subsequent imposition of an art work in a public setting. The NEA has been instrumental in developing public art, and at the same time it has inevitably codified and limited the category.

It may not be surprising, therefore, that sources for the new public art—even sources of funding—lay outside of standard definitions. This fact also helps to explain the variety of works inside and outside of accepted definitions of art that are taken up here. In the sixties and seventies, the federal government invested in social programs directed at minority ethnic populations and the unemployed. The "counterculture," as well as the civil rights, peace, and women's movements, were strongly connected to cultural actions and artworks, sometimes made within their groups. Artists, as well, often participated in political coalitions, and their forms and content changed as a result of their participation. In the crucible of the late sixties, artist Allan Kaprow, the

---

MURALS
Architect Emery Roth designed 2 Broadway, New York City, to include a Lee Krasner mosaic mural. The untitled 1959 work, above the entrances, runs the length of the building's facade. Although Krasner had intended to work on the mosaic herself, union regulations reduced her role to that of a concerned spectator. The Pan Am Building, also designed by Roth, has a two-story Formica mural by Josef Albers, *Manhattan*, 1963.

PUBLIC DECORATIVE ART

Since 1977, a New York State law has required developers seeking zoning variances to conduct archaeological studies. 250,000 artifacts, donated by London and Leeds Development Corporation to the South Street Seaport Museum, were unearthed from the 75 Wall Street site. Those pictures here, collectibles of their day, circa 1810, were from a wealthy household.

UNDERGROUND ART

Long enlivened by graffiti (although New York City's MTA has another opinion of that form of public art), the subways housed eight completed, commissioned art works in 1987. Nancy Holt's *Astral Grating,* 1987 (*right*) lights a passageway linking lines at the Fulton Street stop in Manhattan. Four polychrome bronze reliefs, *The Open Secret,* 1984, by Houston Conwill, are installed in the 125th Street 4-5-6 station. The number 7 train's 61st and Woodside station features two porcelain and enamel murals by John Cavanagh, *Commuting/Community,* 1986, based on photographs. Rhoda Andors's *King's Highway Hieroglyphs,* 1987, can be seen by riders who use the D, M, or Q trains at that station. Two or three new pieces were slated for completion by late 1988.

And upstairs at ground level, since 1982, the Percent for Art Program has required 1 percent of the capital budget of each eligible city-construction project or substantial reconstruction be spent on art. The facilities that benefit include schools, firehouses, shelters, courthouses, prisons, and police stations. Four projects have been completed and more than a dozen are proceeding.

inventor of "happenings," and the late political activist Abbie Hoffman, were only two of many one could mention who approached the traditional form and content of the other's genre to such an extent that their innovative actions became (unintentionally) strikingly similar.

A number of the artists and writers contributing to *Art in the Public Interest* were members of groups like the Art Workers Coalition in New York or the Los Angeles Council of Women Artists, which formed in the late sixties and early seventies to demand more artist involvement in institutional decision-making, representation of minorities and women artists, and use of the influence of museums and funding agencies to change government policies on social issues such as the Vietnam War.

Explosively powerful artworks were made in conjunction with organized artists' activities, among them the notorious Art Workers Coalition's 1969–70 poster, *Q: And Babies?/A. And Babies.* The shocking color image of dead children in a trench reflected the furious passion of protest. Posters, banners, and street actions, documentary photography with captions, and realism predominated in socially-conscious artworks and actions. But during the next few years, these forms would change. The potential of Conceptual Art, a word- and content-oriented art movement raising ideas to a first creative priority, opened new possibilities for art and art criticism with a message. Earthwork artists responded to and incorporated the particulars of their sites (although these were not often in the public domain or accessible to the public), inspiring more sensitivity and play between artwork and environment.

It was clear by the early 1970s (and even clearer today) that existing art institutions could not and would not adequately meet artists' needs, much less represent their demands for social change. In response, artists created a large number of "alternative," artist-run institutions to meet their own agendas directly. Sometimes organizations were devoted to a variety of activities related to a particular gender or ethnic group (like The Woman's Building in Los Angeles, founded in 1973), inaugurated for a single purpose (co-op galleries, for example, for exhibition of member-artists) or reference group (such as the Foundation for the Community of Artists, begun in 1971 in New York). This tenuous network of individuals, institutions, and works forms the immediate historical context for the complex and ambitious projects that would be undertaken in the 1980s.

Some of the most radical and comprehensive artworks to emerge in the public interest began among artists working in these special-

BIG LOBBY ART

Anne Healy's *Slashing Tangents*, 1984 (*above*), commissioned specifically by the Prudential Insurance Company of America for the company's property, the Gateway Center on Mulberry Street in Newark, New Jersey, was reinstalled in June 1988. Most of the Prudential's 9000-piece collection is not as publicly available as the Healy but is hanging in its offices nationwide and in Canada.

Not designed for a specific space, often just hauled out of storage, lots of lobby art looks awkward and ill-used. Frank Stella's *Qua! Attacati La,* 1987, hung on just the other side of revolving doors at Saatchi & Saatchi's 375 Hudson Street headquarters in New York City, is swallowed up by a cavernous and sterile lobby. The piece belongs to Tishman Speyer, not to the widely publicized Saatchis.

BIG PLAZA ART

Big companies and big real estate developers in New York City tend to grace their plazas with museum-magnitude sculpture by major artists. Because (or maybe although) corporate self-aggrandizement has a bit to do with the commissions or purchases, much of the art is name-brand good. Isamu Noguchi's *Cube*, 1973, at 140 Broadway, sponsored by Marine Midland Bank, has a powerful presence, holding its own in a neighborhood of impressive architecture.

PRINTED MATTER

"Inserts," a project by Group Material, supported by the Public Art Fund, was a 12-page, 10-artwork supplement stuffed in copies of the 22 May 1988 Sunday *New York Times* bought in Manhattan from 23rd Street south and in selected neighborhoods in Brooklyn. The two pages in the photo are by, left to right, Barbara Kruger and Carrie Mae Weems. Some of the other eye-openers for brunchtime were provided by Louise Lawler, Felix Gonzales-Torres, Mike Glier, and Hans Haacke.

interest or coalition groups. They built an art from their experiences together that reflected the time and its issues. The women's movement in art proved to be particularly germinal. For example, in Los Angeles, The Waitresses, Sisters of Survival, Mother Art, and Feminist Art Workers—collaborative artmaking collectives—all originated at the Woman's Building and its educational component, the Feminist Studio Workshop, where artists had first formed a viable, ongoing community based on shared work and values. The distinctive art that emerged within the women's movement across the country combined personal and social issues, images and writing, performance and protest, intimate forms with public venues, and forcefully put forth women's concerns.

With the national economic reversals of the late 1970s, some institutions that had grown up and struggled during the decade to represent socially concerned artists began either to assume the institutional forms they had at first opposed or to fail. Funding had never been extensive, but at the turn of the decade funding drastically declined. Organizations had literally run on the energies of dedicated individuals who had often held other full-time employment in order to work for little or nothing in the alternatives they had created. In a drastically diminished American economy, the continued involvement of some movement leaders became less possible.

It is astonishing that many of the artworks described here, critical as they are of the status quo in the United States, have been funded at all, since private sector businesses and foundations as well as government agencies have never been enthusiastic about sponsoring their critics. But these triumphs are the more miraculous in the late 1980s. Significant declines of funding and funding agencies along with the demise of alternative, artist-instigated institutions created in the late sixties and seventies, as well as more than a decade of political conservatism, with drastic federal, state, and local cuts in social services, have made public interest art projects less likely to exist than at any other time in the last forty years. The disintegration of financial support in the eighties has made their work more difficult, but artists who are veterans of the protests of the sixties and the organization-building of the seventies have become more seasoned in finding cracks in the armor of resistance to social action/artworks and using the resources that exist.

All of the developments and alterations in the art world within American culture since the late 1960s are reflected in artworks in the public interest of the same period—even as they may be challenged and criticized—as the closest and most pertinent forces shaping their aesthetics, values, and methods. But this recent work is also grounded in the sturdy, if little recognized, heritage of American activist art that has persisted at the grassroots level with or without artworld stature or government support.

In some sense, all art is public art when it leaves the province of the artist. This fact was amply demonstrated in 1988 when David Nelson, an Art Institute of Chicago student, hung *Mirth and Girth,* a painting of Chicago's late Mayor Harold Washington in women's underwear, in a student exhibition. As AIC Graduate Division Chair Carol Becker recalled, *Mirth and Girth* triggered outrage and a sequence of events that fiercely engaged Chicago and, over the ensuing months, incited repercussions that spread throughout the national and international art communities. Nelson's educators may not ever have introduced considerations of content and audience; he was entirely unprepared for a confrontation with the multi-racial city of Chicago. Becker's "Private Fantasies Shape Public Events" not only describes events as they happened but speculates on why. She analyzes the social implications—including racism, sexism, and homophobia—of this surprising, significantly revealing microcosm of art and the public domain.

Does an artist have a responsibility to his/her audience as well as to his/her art? Richard Serra didn't think so. Robert Storr examines the complications engendered by Serra's *Tilted Arc* (1981), a GSA-commissioned work placed in the plaza in front of the Jacob K. Javits Building on Foley Square in New York City. In *"Tilted Arc:* Enemy of the People?" Storr relates that *Tilted Arc* was greeted with such hostility from those who had to look at it and walk around it that, after a lengthy process of petitioning and public hearings, its removal was recommended. "Trying to attract a bigger audience," Serra commented in a 1984 conversation with Harriet Senie, "has nothing to do with the making of art. It has to do with making yourself into a product, only to be consumed by people. Working this way allows society to determine the terms and the concept of art; the artist must then fulfill those terms. I find the idea of populism self-defeating."[5]

Serra's ordeal underlines the fact that installing or enacting artworks in the public realm does not automatically mean that monuments in town squares or corporation foyers are for or of the public. Yet we, the public audience, still expect civic commemorations to stand for their citizenry in some way recognizable to those represented. A small number of Vietnam veterans acted on this "right to representation" when they demanded and received a bronze statue of three soldiers realistically rendered by Frederick Hart to stand beside the black granite memorial tablet in Washington, D.C. The original chevron, a dramatic

PUBLIC PRIVATE
Some of the best privately owned work makes a public pit stop at the major auction houses before disappearing back into the private sector. Andy Warhol's estate, a collection that bizarrely includes what seems like all styles, periods, conditions, and category of valuable object, at Sotheby's in New York, attracted 10,000 during the first weekend viewing.

TILTED ARC
Richard Serra's controversy in Corten steel stood at 26 Federal Plaza in downtown Manhattan until March 1989, when, as a result of the public outcry provoked by the site-specific sculpture, the artwork was removed.

but nonrepresentational wall designed by Maya Lin, chronologically lists the names of American war dead in the style of a Greek epic poem. This memorial, widely understood and appreciated as a narrative but not as an image, didn't adequately embody the dead for all of the living. American culture's heterogeneous nature always makes such a consensus difficult and, sometimes, impossible, as controversies over the Vietnam veterans' memorial, Robert Arneson's Moscone memorial, and George Segal's Kent State University memorial illustrate.[6]

Lucy Lippard's description of the projects of the minimalists as grandiose and antipractical, and the conceptualists as ineffective in altering the urban environment points to a continuum of misses by public artists and the public. Public art in the United States since the sixties, Lippard says, "has been extraordinarily varied and vital; at the same time, it has also been extraordinarily elitist and boring." Much of recent art in the public interest cannot even confidently be identified as art. If advocacy/activist artists and their collaborators use as models not only traditional arts or community theater but telecommunications, scientific and anthropological research, art therapy and social work, have they crossed over to a new kind of social service or expanded the definition of art? And if they utilize propaganda and advertising techniques, are they in danger of incorporating the values and motivations of their forms? Michael Hall, looking into the condition of public art today, wonders if the whole enterprise, now largely based on postmodern imitation, may have slipped into kitsch.

The fact that art may be created to cause a social change for the better, of course, makes it neither politically effective nor good art. Do artists' projects, we must ask, wed the disciplines and issues that can empower through the creative process? And do artists working in the public interest produce credible, rich works of art that audiences who may not necessarily go to a gallery, museum, or theater can know? Audiences—which often have exceptionally high expectations of such art, matching artists' own aspirations—have not only frequently "failed" to get the message but have been offended, physically hurt, or psychically devastated by well-intentioned artists and their works.

Of artists engaged in public-spirited projects, most hope for a healing. But in the healing we always find the wound. Revealing the terrorist is terrorizing. Defending the defenseless, needy, and desperate may stir up a devastating disorder. To speak out as a victim, to step into the shoes of victims, or even stand beside victims to disclose the nature of an injustice, is volatile and possibly violating. Artists' portrayals of violence can evoke the brutality they want to heal. And if artist and art break the law or commonly accepted modes of morality,

BATTERY PARK CITY
On one drawing board or another for 20 years, New York's Battery Park City's master plan has included art since at least the 1979 proposal. Ned Smyth's *The Upper Room*, 1987 (*above*), is located at the Esplanade and Albany Street. Also planned are sculptures from R. M. Fischer, Richard Artschwager, Mary Miss, and Jennifer Bartlett, who designed an array of gardens.

can that art ultimately claim to have been made in the public interest? Helen Mayer Harrison, whose art in and for the environment with collaborator/husband Newton Harrison has been realized worldwide, mused that ''we cannot really know the consequences of our actions. That is why we need environmental impact studies, even on creativity.''

The powerful surge of buried feeling and discarded belief unearthed in witnessing the tormented and hopeless rise to speak out, live, and create may be crushing, but it can ultimately be inspiriting. And there have been some measurable good results. VITAL participant Bob Smith, for example, became the first developmentally disabled artist to win an NEA fellowship for independent video production. John Malpede won the Adaline Kent Award from the San Francisco Art Institute, and the critically acclaimed LAPD (some of whom are no longer homeless as a result of their work with LAPD) performed in residence at SFAI during March of 1988.

Attempting the improbable and unheard-of from the left field of human consciousness animates contemporary artists working in the public interest as it has animated all artists in all times. Artists of heart, many at middle age or maturity, already know that their endeavors are ''hopeless.'' Thus they have the liberty to recast events or create eccentric disentanglements for the knottiest practical enigmas. Their visions centralize archetypes, motifs, and people, to extend human potential and fulfill human aspirations. That can be a master/mistress-piece of work.

Notes

Special thanks to Linda Burnham for her ideas about and work on the new public art of the 1980s.

1. Michael Faubion, Foreword, in Stacy Paleologos Harris, ed., *Insights/On Sites: Perspectives on Art in Public Places* (Washington, D.C.: Parners for Livable Places, 1984), p. 9.

2. Kathy Halbreich, ''Stretching the Terrain: Sketching Twenty Years of Public Art,'' *Going Public: A Field Guide to Developments in Art in Public Places,* published by the Arts Extension Service in cooperation with the Visual Arts Program of the National Endowment for the Arts (1988), p. 9.

3. Scott Burton, ''What Is Public Art?'' *Design Quarterly,* No. 122 (1983).

4. Richard Andrews, ''Artists and the Visual Definition of Cities: The Experience of Seattle,'' *Insights/On Sites,* p. 18.

5. Harriet Senie, ''The Right Stuff,'' *ARTnews* (March 1984). See also *Public Art/Public Controversy: The ''Tilted Arc'' on Trial* (New York: ACA Books, 1987).

6. For a discussion of these and other projects, see *Insights/On Sites* and *Going Public.*

Art in the Public Interest:
New Public Art in the 1980s

1

Witness:
The Guerrilla Theater of Greenpeace

Steven Durland

There is an essential relationship between protest actions and images that—because such actions have not generally been considered in the arena of art and art history—has rarely been examined. According to Steven Durland, the late activist Abbie Hoffman claimed guerrilla theater as the oldest form of political commentary. Faithfulness to the nature and requirements of political commentary bears on why so many artworks in the public interest of the past two decades have not taken the traditional public art form of outdoor sculpture but have been, in- stead, live and performative. And their variety of forms considered marginal to the fine arts has made these art actions difficult to iden- tify and place in an artistic context.

    Steven Durland brings the guerrilla operations of Greenpeace—an organization not self-identified as an artists' group—into the history of protest theater. Durland also chronicles the largely unwilling but crucial partnership between actions for social change and the print and television media which publicize these novel and newsworthy efforts to a wider audience. Greenpeace has amplified the visual impact of its gigantic headline-banners aimed at toxic waste, nuclear issues and ocean ecology by (illegally) placing them in symbolic locales contain- ing existing public works of art, such as Mount Rushmore and the Statue of Liberty, or well-known public images such as the New York garbage barge. This linkage to older public sculpture brings the "installations" of Greenpeace more firmly into the history of public visual art as well.

This article originally appeared in *High Performance*, No. 40 (1987).

In 1968 a dozen members of the Yippie movement, led by Abbie Hoffman and Jerry Rubin, went to the visitors gallery of the New York Stock Exchange and threw money on the brokers below. "We didn't call the press," wrote Hoffman, "at that time we really had no notion of anything called a media event." But the press was quick to respond and by evening the event was being reported around the world. Within the month the stock exchange had spent $20,000 to enclose the gallery with bulletproof glass.

Hoffman continues, "A spark had been ignited. The system cracked a little. Not a drop of blood had been spilled, not a bone broken, but on that day, with that gesture, an image war had begun. In the minds of millions of teenagers the stock market had just crashed. . . . Showering money on the Wall Street brokers was the TV-age version of driving the money changers from the temple."[1]

In 1971 an ad hoc group of activists in Vancouver who for two years had been protesting American nuclear tests on Amchitka Island in the Aleutians without success, decided they too needed to ignite a spark. Their plan was to sail a broken-down boat named the *Phyllis Cormack* to Amchitka to "witness" the next bomb test. Hampered by storms and the U.S. Coastguard, they were forced to turn back, with expectations that their venture had been a failure. But thousands of supporters who had been following their efforts in the newspapers greeted their return and a second boat was immediately sent out. The second boat was still 700 miles from the island when the bomb went off and it appeared that all had been for naught. But as a result of the worldwide media attention the U.S. announced an end to tests on Amchitka and the island was restored to its prior status as a bird sanctuary. It was the first victory for Greenpeace.

For Hoffman and the Yippies their actions and the ones that followed were part of the long history of guerrilla theater, "probably the oldest form of political commentary," says Hoffman. "We would hurl ourselves across the canvas of society like streaks of splattered paint. Highly visual images would become news, and rumormongers would rush to spread the excited word."

ACID RAIN PROTEST, 1984
Robin Heid, of Denver, jumped from the 1100-foot smokestack of Gavin Power Plant near Gallipolis, Ohio, as part of a Greenpeace protest against emissions that cause acid rain.
(Copyright 1984 Hollis/Greenpeace. All Rights Reserved)

GARBAGE BARGE PROTEST, 1987
Greenpeace often tries to focus the public's attention with banners placed on significant places. Here, Greenpeace unfurled a banner on the infamous New York City garbage barge that traveled up and down the East Coast when no one was willing to accept the trash.

For the Canadians their Alaskan Sea adventure grew out of a Quaker belief called "bearing witness." A person who bears witness to an injustice takes responsibility for that awareness. That person may then choose to do something or stand by, but he may not turn away in ignorance. From this belief and a modest first adventure has grown the organization that claims over 1.5 million contributors and offices in seventeen countries. The organization's name was coined in preparation for that first adventure, *green* to signify the activists' conservation interests, and *peace* to signify their second goal.

The "actions" of Greenpeace have always been discussed in terms of the organization's ecology concerns, but it seems appropriate to include it in the history of protest theater, and in fact, Greenpeace might well lay claim to being the largest and most successful guerilla theater of all. During the past seventeen years they have conducted innumerable actions around the world and can take or share credit for such accomplishments as the reduction of international whaling by 84 percent, a ban on disposing of nuclear garbage in the Atlantic Ocean, the near elimination of mass slaughter of nursing harp seals and significant reductions in acid rain production, nuclear weapons testing and toxic waste disposal.

Of course Greenpeace is much more than a theater company, but its strength, and the element that differentiates it from other environmental organizations, is the impact of its visual and theatrical actions. According to Steve Loper, Action Director for Greenpeace U.S.A.,

> Greenpeace believes that an image is an all-important thing. The direct actions call attention to the issues we're involved in. We put a different point of view out that usually ends up on the front page of the paper. *Then* we have people who've done research and people who are lobbying so that once the attention is there it gets more done. We've embarrassed people for not doing their job, or we've called attention to facts that the general public wasn't aware of so they question their local politicians. If we just did research and lobbying and came out with a report it would probably be on the 50th page of the paper.[2]

Greenpeace focuses its efforts in three major campaign areas: toxic waste, nuclear issues and ocean ecology. It has been the organization's efforts to save the whales that has brought Greenpeace much of its attention. Since the initial exploit of the *Phyllis Cormack,* the organization has built an "econavy" ranging from converted fishing trawlers to inflatable rubber dinghies call Zodiacs. They have used their fleet to document and interfere with illegal whaling as well as toxic dumping and nuclear testing and transport on the seas. Their most famous vessel, the flagship *Rainbow Warrior,* was sunk in 1985 off the coast of New Zealand by French military intelligence. The *Rainbow Warrior* was in the Pacific to protest French underground nuclear weapons testing near the Mururoa Atoll. The incident created an international scandal for the French government, and in October 1987 an international arbitration tribunal headed by U.N. Secretary General Javier Perez de Cuellar awarded Greenpeace $8.1 million in damages from France for the sinking. Two French agents were sentenced to ten years in jail by the New Zealand court after pleading guilty to sabotage and manslaughter.

One of Greenpeace's more potent images was created in England in 1985 where internationally known photographer David Bailey directed a sixty-second film showing a glamorous fashion show in which one of the models comes out in a fur coat which suddenly begins spurting blood until the whole audience is splattered. In the final shot the model exits the ramp, dragging her fur coat and leaving a wide swath of blood behind her. The last image has also been produced as a billboard with the caption, "It takes 40 dumb animals to make a fur coat. But only one to wear it."

Greenpeace's actions frequently consist of plugging pipes that discharge toxic waste or climbing structures and hanging banners from such places as nuclear cooling towers, smoke stacks, buildings, and such famous symbols as the Statue of Liberty and Mt. Rushmore. The Mt. Rushmore action in October 1987 was an acid rain protest; the plan was to stretch a banner shaped like a gas mask over the mouth of George Washington. The banner said, "WE THE PEOPLE SAY NO TO ACID RAIN."

Local authorities interrupted the Mt. Rushmore action before it was completed but the image still appeared in numerous papers across the country and had its impact. "A symbolic image like Mt. Rushmore is a very powerful image," said Loper. "It lends a great deal of weight. It's almost like those Presidents against the Reagan administration. These people gave us this clean, beautiful country and we're not caring about it."

In 1984 Loper was involved in hanging a banner on the Statue of Liberty that read, "GIVE ME LIBERTY FROM NUCLEAR WEAPONS, STOP TESTING." "That picture went around the world," Loper said. "Every August 6th [the anniversary of the Hiroshima atomic bomb] the media is looking for an image that denotes protests against nuclear weapons. What we did in '84 was give them the perfect image. It was one of the most enjoyable I've done."

Greenpeace's actions often are directed at specific problems and specific companies. Loper helped plug an underwater pipe at a CIBA-

ACID RAIN PROTEST, 1987
On 22 October 1987, Greenpeace's protestors scaled Mt. Rushmore in South Dakota to protest the lack of strict U.S. government regulations on acid rain. The action was halted before the sign was fully unfurled.
(Copyright 1987 Townsend/Greenpeace. All Rights Reserved)

Geigy chemical plant in Lavallette, New Jersey, that was dumping over 200,000 gallons of chemicals a week into the ocean. ''A lot of toxic chemicals are odorless and colorless so it's hard to convince people they're dangerous,'' he said.

> But the effluent from CIBA-Geigy looked like spent motor oil. We brought big water jugs of it ashore where people were sitting or swimming or sunning. Their mouths just fell open. They knew just by looking that this stuff didn't belong in the water. A guy from the Chamber of Commerce tried to steal a bottle of the effluent. After the action an organization started in the community called Ocean County Citizens for Clean Water.
>
> Sometimes it seems like the government, the Environmental Protection Agency, is more like a defensive organization for the industry than it is a protection agency for people. For example, Dow Chemical in Midland, Michigan, has a risk assessment for the plant. Someone decides that it's okay, for instance, for five people or ten people in every million to die because the plant is there. That's not realistic in our opinion.

New York governor (and then presidential candidate) Mario Cuomo was the focus of a Greenpeace action last spring when it was learned that New York was going to permit Occidental Chemical to open an

---

A Not-so-Typical Day for a Greenpeace Activist

Being a Greenpeace activist means working for low or no pay, long hours, months away from home and possibly even time in jail. But nobody ever said it was boring. The following is Steve Loper's account of a 1986 action where Greenpeace sent a team onto the Nevada Test Site to prevent a scheduled nuclear test.

''We sent a team in a four-wheel-drive truck—two people from the American Peace Test, myself, Daniel Ellsberg and two other Greenpeace people. We planned to go in at night but things got mixed around and we went in around 6:30 in the morning. We drove in across the airforce base and over the mountain and into the test site.

incinerator in the Niagara region, an area already suffering from an overdose of toxic waste. "We're fighting to have people reduce the production of toxic waste at the source if it can't be dealt with," said Loper. "Currently there is no technology that does anything but put it somewhere else."

Loper and fellow activists climbed the state house in Albany at night and attached a banner that read "NIAGARA: STILL TOXIC AFTER ALL THESE YEARS. WHY, GOVERNOR CUOMO?"

"He was having a press conference," Loper said,

> and people were asking him "What's going on with Niagara? How come you're permitting this?" These are the kinds of questions we hoped to have asked. At the time he may have been a political candidate so he was in a position to have pressure affect him. He really got angry. He swore we were lunatics and equated us with Oliver North, but two months later we were invited by the governor's office to a signing of a toxic waste agreement at Niagara Falls. There's a grudging respect he's paying us.

Like the best guerrilla theater, the daring escapades and visual images take a backseat to results in the Greenpeace resume. "In some

---

"We were discovered about 7:30 by helicopters. They swooped down 50–60 feet from us and people jumped out and started running after us with M-16s. So we split into two teams. These guys were on top of us in half a minute screaming 'Stop or we'll shoot' but I kept running. They were yelling at me but there were two of them chasing us and they each grabbed one of our guys and I just kept going. I ran about 50 feet away and laid down by a tree. The hardest thing for them to do is find you if you're still because they don't know where you went and there's no trail to follow. They handcuffed the other guys and while they were moving them I climbed up in the tree and watched. They looked for two-and-a-half more hours.

"Finally I left my pack because it was heavy and headed for the test site about a mile away. I got about half-mile and changed my mind. I thought maybe I should get my pack and when I went back for it I was seen by these foot soldiers. They chased me and I got away from them twice. I just rolled under a tree and they ran right by me. The third time a guy with a .45 caught me and pointed it at me. I kept telling him I had a pack down there and I wanted to get it. He kept yelling, 'Shut up! Shut the fuck up!' I kept saying, 'Look, you can say that all you want, but I ain't going to shut the fuck up.' He was really mad that I wasn't

cases we do a protest and there's too much publicity on the protest itself—how high up we were, how we got there, how cold it was—so we defeat ourselves,'' said Loper.

> We try to downplay the thing we've done. We tell the media that our people are professional climbers, etc. What I always say after I come down is that it wasn't much of a chance I was taking because I'm trained, and the people who are taking a real chance without any choice are the people who are having all this toxic waste foisted on them. We try to get the light off the climb, or whatever we've done, and get it on the issue.

But Greenpeace often does get the attention on the issue and, according to Loper, they are suffering the results of their success.

> In recent years some of the things Greenpeace has done have caused retribution against us and I think that's a signal that we're being more effective. That includes prison terms and the sinking of the *Rainbow Warrior*. The more effective you are the more you piss people off. For instance the Mt. Rushmore climb wasn't successful in that we didn't get the whole banner up, but the event evidently went into three to four hundred papers in the United States including the *Washington Times,* the paper Reagan reads. Who's to say that he didn't say, ''Who are these little assholes?''

A Not-so-Typical Day (continued)

afraid of him. He had this gun pointed at me and in the movies it works, right? Then an older guy came down in the helicopter. He came over and was a lot more relaxed. He just smiled and said, 'Where you been hiding?' and I said, 'Well I was up the tree for a while, and then I was over here . . . '

"Anyway, the test was supposed to go off at a quarter to ten and they found me about 10:30. The test was delayed that day and it didn't go off the next day either. A lot of people claimed it was because I wasn't found. I don't know if that's true or not but it was delayed and it did get out into the papers that we had possibly delayed it and embarrassed them. It encouraged a lot more people to infiltrate the test site and they've been doing it ever since.''

Before we climbed Mt. Rushmore our lawyer's assessment was that we'd be fined $500 and that would be it. Then after we actually did it word came that there was high pressure from Washington to curtail our personal activities. The plea bargain the prosecution is offering right now is $250 fine and three weeks in jail.

What's surprising is that most people in the system that is prosecuting us support us. The policemen will tell you, "I think you guys are doing great. We respect what you did." The policeman in Albany who arrested us for the climb apologized the entire time for having to do it. Our banner was soaking wet because it rained that night. He took it out and told us, "We had it dried." We couldn't believe that.

There was a prosecutor on the East Coast who told the judge that he refused to prosecute the case because what we were saying was true. Then he walked over to the guy from Greenpeace who was on trial, handed him $15 for a membership and walked out of the courtroom.

Certainly, in Greenpeace's case, its protest theater is aimed at issues that are of concern to everyone, even the perpetrators. "I'm a philosophical person," said Loper,

and I don't feel that these are bad people. These are good people who are ignoring something that they know. The scientists and the government are telling them that what they're doing isn't hurting anybody and I believe they want to believe that. Anybody who's making money doesn't want to believe that they're hurting people. But somewhere inside themselves I think they know what they're doing is wrong. I think that's why when we do a protest so much energy is released because when we're down there plugging the pipes we're a part of them they've denied.

Loper finds Greenpeace's work helps empower the rest of the audience as well.

We always give people the feeling that something can be done. The power of individual action. When you go on the property of the company that's doing the damage and actually drape your feelings from their property it's a very distinctive defeat for them. It makes what you're saying true. The company is psychologically towering over those who would oppose it and this is like a slap in the face. It's motivating people to act. When we come along, a little three or four of us, take on a big company, it's giving the giant a whack on the nose. And it's a good thing.

In contemporary American culture the actions of Greenpeace, like the guerrilla theater of the Yippies and all effective creativity with a mission, are rarely considered art by those given to determining such matters. Interestingly, the more successful political theater is, the less important it becomes to those affected that it *is* called art. It certainly isn't a problem Greenpeace is worrying about. But as the function of art in our culture drifts steadily toward becoming investment commodity and entertainment, it might well be worth the art world's time to expand its narrow definitions to include activities that have a function more in keeping with traditional art values—creating images that have an impact on people's lives.

Notes

The author would like to thank artist and Greenpeace photo editor Jay Townsend for his efforts in supplying photos for this article.

1. Abbie Hoffman, ''Museum of the Streets,'' in Douglas Kahn and Diane Neumaier, eds., *Cultures in Contention* (Seattle, Wash.: The Real Comet Press, 1985), pp. 134–40.

2. Steve Loper, all quotes from an interview with the author, December 1987.

Names Carried into the Future:
An AIDS Quilt Unfolds

Jeff Weinstein

Jeff Weinstein demonstrates the humanizing quality of naming and the experiential nature of the Quilt in his first-person narrative about the NAMES Project. NAMES is the largest-scale quilt work in existence and, unfortunately, is still growing—each panel commemorating a person dead of AIDS. AIDS victims are celebrated as humans with personal and collective histories rather than as anonymous statistics.

The NAMES Quilt not only identifies individuals but gathers them and their loved ones together as a visible community. The elaborate ceremonies that accompany displays of the Quilt in various U.S. cities accent the important role of ritual as an educational and community-building component of today's public art.

"A gay man who writes about the Quilt must be writing, in part, about himself," says Weinstein. This author personally takes readers through the empowering process of confronting and overcoming fears, asking questions, and challenging the current state of affairs, through an active relationship with activist art. This massive contemporary artwork employs its act of naming as, ultimately, a catalyst for social change.

This essay first appeared as a cover story of the 21 June 1988 issue of The Village Voice, *a weekly newspaper in New York City with both a general and an arts-interested readership. It was meant to announce*

This article originally appeared in *Village Voice* (21 June 1988).

the appearance of the NAMES Project Quilt in New York to the general reader, explain its genesis and future, and, through description of the Quilt as an enabling focus of remembrance within communities, analyze the Quilt as an artwork within the realms of folk art, fine art, and public art. Because this article was purposefully shaped to fit into this multivalent context, I have left it in its original, "immediate" form.
—J.W.

All quilts tell stories. When I approach a quilt from a distance, its design predominates, and whatever meaning it has and response I have attach themselves to the surface's immediate beauty. In no sense is this a bad thing, but a quilt seen from far away necessarily flattens into a visual field. It becomes one work, a single achievement.

However, when I move closer, a quilt's parts begin to assert themselves. I can apprehend the integrity of each remnant and the taste that selected it. I can trace the handwriting of time that is its stitching, feel the ineluctable fitting of shapes, and muse, finally, over this quilt's particular history of use.

Quilts combine old use—tatters—with new use. Quilts have been multigenerational, local, socially tuneful, sometimes made by men. Traditional quilts are usually considered nurturing and communicating in general, personal and sometimes political in particular. All parts of them are impregnated with memory. They are always records of accomplishment, solo and mutual, and promises of continuity.

A quilt is a map of devotion to doing and using as well as to completion, and the coexistence of these ways of seeing results in the narrative pleasure of its art.

Yes, the quilt is art. It is not art that is defined by individual genius, the way modern sculpture and painting is supposed to be about genius. Even if one great quilt-artist "pieces" a quilt, the quilt still speaks of the value of the single part as it works within a corresponding whole. This is the pattern every quilt carries.

And, since art always acknowledges mortality (that is part of art's "purpose," its unavoidable end), a quilt must acknowledge death, too. Any quilt. Any quilt tells a story; any quilt acknowledges death.

San Francisco's NAMES Project Quilt actually sets out to tell stories— the saddest and most upsetting stories you ever want to hear. I first read about the NAMES Project a few weeks before the National March on Washington for Lesbian and Gay Rights on 11 October last year, where the Quilt, as an ongoing work, was first displayed. Those who returned from the march told me that they couldn't believe how moving it was to see, in bright, saturated colors, spread out on the same

AIDS QUILT
At Atlanta's World Congress Center, 29 May 1988, volunteers unfold each 32-panel block as the names on the panels are read off. By the time the ritual is over, the entire floor is a quilt.
(Copyright 1988 Robin Holland)

flat mall where they had so may times before gathered and embraced, a monumental realization of the names of those who have died AIDS-related deaths.

There were 1,920 panels in D.C., each one three by six feet. A few months ago the Quilt encompassed nearly 3,500, representing "approximately 13 percent of the deaths from AIDS or ARC," according to a NAMES project statement. "In other words, for each panel in the Quilt, 8 other people have died." As I write, there are 5,000 panels, as the NAMES Project becomes better known—and more names apply.

Those in Washington understood the Quilt's paradox: that it would almost certainly grow, and, terrible to think, become even more moving. How could you be profoundly affected by this work, by this undeniably beautiful work, and, at the same time, hope it would simply stop, vanish—or wish it had never existed at all? Sculptor Maya Ling Lin had left a small area in her Vietnam War Memorial for a last few names to be added. But that war is over. This one is not.

Next week, the NAMES Project Quilt, which has been touring the country since its Washington premiere, is coming to New York. It will be shown at Pier 92 from Tuesday evening, June 21, until midnight on Thursday, June 23; a New York quilt, comprising local panels that did not make it to the project's San Francisco workshop in time to be incorporated into the national work, will be displayed separately on the Great Lawn in Central Park as well as in a frieze around the Quilt at the pier.

This is obviously the reason for this report, but stories concerning art and death always result in more than descriptive history and a sympathetic version of the facts.* Intrusive commentary can't be helped: a gay man who writes about the Quilt must be writing, in part, about himself.

I wanted to learn what I could about the NAMES Project, spending time at the Lesbian and Gay Community Services Center in New York where panels were being made, traveling to Atlanta to see how a city prepared for and received its melancholy gift, because I was just plain tired of my fear, of the pervasive fact of it. Of course I'd had acquaintances and friends who died. Two of the men I have most loved and been loved by had died as well. It happened, continues to happen, and a receptive, open part of me had tightened and closed. Apparently, I was also afraid of my sadness—and I don't think myself the only one so afraid. Before I set out to write, I was warned over and over not

---

*There's already an excellent book, just out, about the NAMES Project and many of its personal histories: *The Quilt,* published by Pocket Books.

to fall into the trap of "sentiment," not to forget my common sense and my politics and my intelligence in the midst of some mindless, pathetic cloud. I was told, in effect, not to cry.

Sentiment. By sentiment my advisors meant emotion misdirected, emotion that did not match the event, emotion with the disco knob turned up. "Flaming queens," I remembered from the early days of gay liberation, were thought by their butch betters to exhibit similar qualities of embarrassing exaggeration.

Now, I am curious how these emotional experts can be quite certain they know the correct, modulated response to AIDS-related death. Should we put it "in proportion" because death is international? Not see the losses because loss was or will be, if we do our jobs right, preventable? Not comprehend the vicious untimeliness of a person just stopping, there, like that, or not feel the nasty twist for some of us because this illness and death seemed to—seems to—accompany the best parts of our hard-won love?

Get out your handkerchiefs.

At a 10 May 1988 New York press conference, the NAMES Project announced that at least twenty-five diverse AIDS service organizations in the metropolitan area, ranging from Gay Men's Health Crisis to ADAPT, the underfunded and far-seeing Association for Drug Abuse Prevention and Treatment, have joined to sponsor the Quilt. All Quilt-connected donations, individual and corporate, raised in New York (as in other cities) will be divided among groups that provide some form of "primary" AIDS care. The NAMES Project apparently acts as a catalyst, which had been foreseen, even planned.

Joe Papp spoke of "reading people through ceremony," and Mathilde Krim, looking battle-weary, juxtaposed individual loss with "collective impoverishment." A speaker wondered, because of the eclectic and inclusive nature of the Quilt, how anyone could deny support. A minute later we learned that four borough presidents had agreed to host the project; Ralph Lamberti, of Staten Island, would not.

Sunday afternoon, a month ago. The small room at the lesbian and gay center on West 13th Street, once a public school, was filled with donations: shelves of fabric remnants and colored thread, five sewing machines, a desk, phone, iron, and three large worktables. Whatever wall space remained was hung with finished panels: lessons, examples, inspirations. Sunlight poured in.

My first impression was entirely applicable, I soon discovered, to all the activity I saw spurred by the Quilt: slow exchanges of advice, definite but careful movement at and around panels and a balance of normally opposite feelings—grief and pride-in-work, for example—that together resulted in an almost utopian tableau of gratifying cooperation. I had virtually forgotten this sort of selfless promise, made twenty or so years ago.

Core volunteers, such as bobbin-maven Wes Cronk or clothes designer Mark Johnson, train other volunteers, who then pass skills back and forth. When someone comes in, with a sketch, an idea, or even just (just!) a name, the volunteers of the moment begin the somewhat delicate process of help, from providing space, material, and machines, to developing an apt design, to completing the panel later, by themselves. "Sometimes it's too difficult for the person to handle when someone's just died," New York Memorial Quilt coordinator Jordan Friedman said. Wes added that two hundred panels had been put together in the workshop so far but estimated that more than a thousand New York panels, made in or out of the workshop, would be ready by the time the national Quilt came to the pier.

As I was asking questions and taking notes, I started to cry. Nothing particular set it off, it just happened. Jordan (as well as the many others that afternoon who noticed it) smiled and said that everyone here cries, it comes in waves, can't be helped.

This was Margot Siegel's fifth week sitting at the machine. Brought in by an announcement in the GMHC newsletter, she had done "a piece of needlepoint for my friend—EL LAMPI—who had died, but when I come in here I sew on others." She had been working on a phoenix, and asked me, intently, if I knew what the promise of the phoenix was, what it meant.

College teacher Jim Morgan and his friend Karen Seitel were working on DR. TED, a Cabrini Medical Center doctor's gown with a Hershey bar in the pocket. "When he died," Karen said, "Jim had the idea of making a quilt. I couldn't sew before." She explained how they showed her how to use a chalk marker and set a bobbin. "Karen cut herself," Jim pointed out, "got blood on the doctor's coat, but we decided it would be a good thing to have."

"I'm Susan Gnoffo and this is Lamont Farrich, my brother's lover. I'm a teacher and he's a restaurant manager, he did the backing and my kids did the letters." DENNIS GNOFFO. They started three weeks ago, have spent two days in the shop, need at least one more day. Lamont finally said something: that Dennis "looked like a crow." He held up a small stuffed crow, they laughed, then soberly offered a snapshot. A very handsome crow. Lamont: "I'm glad I could share this with Susan. I've remained close with her, with the whole family."

Michael Jacobs, a graduate student, had bought the fabric yester-day: "A few of us have been talking about the design for weeks." I asked his partner, Phyllis Brachman, if she could sew: "Sew? I'm the kind of person who, when my hems come down, uses Scotch tape." They were planning a stage with parted curtains for JAY.

Dolores, a slight, carefully dressed person ironing in the corner, withheld her last name because she was on disability and thought they wouldn't understand. She looked up from her work, paused, and told me about her friend NICK GORE, a music teacher in the public schools she'd known for thirteen years; he lived on the same floor. "While he was sick he never admitted it—I played the game, pretending he was fine. I didn't realize how important Nick was to me until he died." She resumed ironing. The volunteers had finished her panel, but she wanted to spend more time at the workshop, "so they give me the easier jobs."

I went outside, into a small brick courtyard, to take a break and started talking with a leatherish guy who was holding a panel. Bob Wilson had the swagger, as it were, of a regular. He'd conceived thirty panels, most of them sewn up by volunteers. "Started with my lover, MIGUEL, which was the hardest. While I was doing it I kept looking at the back door 'cause I didn't want anyone to see my tears." Thirty panels. Why so many, Bob?

"Somebody's gotta do it."

I took a breath and mentioned that I hoped any writing I do about the Quilt "would be my panel." "Fine," he shot back, "but what's preventing you from doing a real one?"

They couldn't begin setting up the Quilt in Atlanta's World Congress Center until midnight because the previous rental was six hours late getting out. This was to be the largest manifestation of the Quilt, at least until it gets to Minneapolis. I should explain. Part of the Quilt's art resides in the organization of it. The NAMES Project staff knew, for example, that the Quilt's first outdoor showing (in D.C.) would also be its last: they couldn't again risk rain. Since indoor spaces come in different sizes, the already determined modular nature of the work allowed adjustment to almost any site.

It's surprisingly elegant. Each three-foot by six-foot panel is per-manently joined, by the San Francisco staff, choosing aesthetically or thematically, onto an eight-panel canvas square. Each of these squares is assigned a number. Later, at the site, four already chosen squares are fastened together into a square block of 32 panels. These blocks are the walk-around units the staff uses to map the protean Quilt into the specific sites. In D.C. the blocks were laid out into a monolithic mall-shape; in Atlanta they were diamonds, interrupted by the hall's columns. The blocks are also identified—A3, G6—to allow a viewer to find a name.

Yes, you may come to find a name. A computer has compiled all the panel names—with corresponding square-numbers—in alphabetical order into an ever-swelling national list. Visitors to the Quilt are handed this list, along with a map of quilt-blocks specific to that city and a table that matches name-numbers to each block. Look up the name, get the number, find the block that matches the number, find the block.

Staff and volunteers file in, dressed in assorted white. Some of the volunteers chat, others sit on the floor, bemused; they have come because they read about the Quilt, or heard about it from their gay or lesbian groups. Word "just got around." One fellow postered his workplace—Coca-Cola—so some of his colleagues are here with him. Those I see number a few dozen, but the head of volunteers says he has name tags for over eight hundred, to be picked up during the next two days. By the time the Quilt is dismantled, a city's isolated activists will have made connection.

At one a.m., piles of panels-on-canvas, like collapsed tents, are spaced equidistant on a portion of the floor. They do not look like much of anything, but lit, empty halls are built to anticipate. The staff begins to show volunteers how to unfurl and arrange their four squares, line up the grommets, and fasten the squares together with clear-plastic ties (called Bar-Loks) into blocks. These volunteers then teach others; it runs with an ease that I, who work in a small "organization," find novel and extremely satisfying.

To my amazement, a dance begins: each person takes a corner of the just-finished block, walks toward the center, and bends down. The block-square is now a smaller square turned sideways, a diamond, then a smaller square, then a diamond, folded at last into a laundry rectangle, which is carried in one person's arms and dropped onto a pile of similar condensed units that, overnight, have studded this public space, the way they have and will in dozens of halls and auditoriums. Grommetted white-canvas walkways surround them in a grid, and we see, at once, that last night's dance is to be repeated in reverse. More deliberately. As circles of volunteers, now performers, hold hands. As community figures from the Atlanta area read the names, one by one, that correspond to the names being unfolded. (Think of the personal engagement that such a rigorous, simultaneous structure evokes from all who participate.) This takes two, three hours, and, at its end, I finally comprehend what the NAMES Project means, why names must be spoken.

The reading of names is not new to religious or political events, which makes the Quilt even more complex, for it places it within their ken. What the reading of names does for me is fill out the artwork into something temporal, multisensual, communicative: a ritual. I had intended to interview those who came to view the Quilt. Eventually I did speak to some of them: one family that appeared miraculously unaffected was really here to see some sports event upstairs. But no one had much to say, beyond the obvious; most of those kind enough to talk to me, when asked about the Quilt's meaning or effect, could only generalize about the kindness they experienced in the project, the wellsprings of strangers' generosity, and the sadness. Perhaps this was to be expected, but I learned why in Atlanta: the Quilt spoke best.

If you listened you heard nothing but whirring ventilators and occasional sobs. Colors illuminated the spectators from the ground, making our motion even more theatrical and disquieting because we moved randomly at a speed unique to this event, slower than ambling, languorous even, the result of looking, reading, and moving on. Every time I lifted my head, at the others, I saw their heads bent. There were chairs near pillars, and near the chairs, a witty, even campy, Atlanta touch: pocket-packs of Kleenex in a line, tissue puffed out, waiting. Once in a while someone would sit down, or drop to the floor.

You can imagine, I think, the range of fabrics and styles of the panels. I wrote down almost everything that touched me. Panels were serious, flowery, affectionate—a zoo of teddy bears—and sexy. Panels for dead men, women, fathers, mothers, boys, girls, infants. For lovers and friends. For gay, not gay. An entire block of names from Black and White Men Together (I hadn't known there were so many far-flung chapters). Superb traditional quilters, graphic artists, and tyros made the panels—names carried into the future, tenderly and democratically, by images.

In black block letters on a medieval "unicorn" fabric used for other panels: DAVID R. In blue-crayon script:

from Alaska, loved flowers and wanted to open a flower shop but he managed a bank instead (you know how life can be) well he was positive (?HIV?) and full of love, then his health slipped and he met a blond. They robbed the bank of $60,000 and went to LA, the blond lost all the money in Vegas, David visited Hawaii, where he was very happy, then his health got worse, he went to NYC, was in tremendous pain, the first two nights he attempted suicide with pills but failed, then succeeded with a plastic bag. 1987

In red crayon at the bottom, almost rubbed out:

David I still love you if it means anything anymore.

And what about anger? This is the unstated question. Count the names that would fly off the Quilt if our murderous government did what governments are supposed to and valued its people enough to. . . . Who were those who died doubly miserable, forcibly excluded by bigots and fools from the necessary protection that is sometimes called love? What good is this expensive Quilt to them?

The Quilt began as an idea and had a creator, San Francisco gay activist Cleve Jones. Ideas are usually transient, but this one can be placed: at the November 1985 candlelight procession that commemorated George Moscone and Harvey Milk, and the cardboard placards, fastened to the stone wall of the Federal Building, that spelled the names of those who had died of AIDS. "Those placards didn't look like a quilt, really," Cleve says, "but when I said the word *quilt*, it evoked such . . . powerful, comforting memories."

He developed a picture in his mind of almost exactly how it would look: "There had to be enough angry gay men with sewing machines out there who would be willing to create these things as banners." His influences? Some could be expected, such as the quasi-collaborative nature of Judy Chicago's *Dinner Party,* as well as Chicago's employment of traditional media in the service of contemporary feminist art. But Cleve also cites the sensual fabric of Christo's marathon *Running Fence*—and Christo's statement that the logistics of putting up something of that scale is as much a part of the work as the work itself. The Vietnam War Memorial? Cleve was prepared to dislike it, for he was raised a Quaker and mistrustful of any glorification of war, but the names pulled him in, changed him. Cleve, by the way, doesn't consider himself an artist.

By making the first panel for MARVIN FELDMAN, his most loved friend, Cleve found that he banished cynicism and paralysis. Then, when I offer that some have criticized the Quilt as passive and sentimental, he becomes very angry: "They can call it anything they want, but every time the Quilt is displayed we generate hundreds of brand new volunteers, people who have never taken part in AIDS-related work who go on to more. Anger? Anger cannot be sustained."

May I tell you what I have learned from this?

That tears aren't idle, and I'm glad for them. That most of us need help to grieve widely, need some structure to allow a private and paradoxical "binding together." This structure was the ritual I saw in Atlanta but also the ongoing activity in the workshop in New York.

That the "individual" is neither the antagonist to, nor merely a part of, the "whole." It is point of view, or scale, that distinguishes these functions. I agree with Cleve: some memorial behavior is heartening, and the deed of making something—of art, I could add—is that heart's blood.

3

Hands across Skid Row: John Malpede's Performance Workshop for the Homeless of L.A.

Linda Frye Burnham

John Malpede, a New York performance artist at mid-career, faced a dilemma. His colleagues were acting in clubs—the most popular stage for performance art of the 1980s—and making their art about the media, a focus Malpede considered removed from everyday reality and incapable of encompassing a genuine social role. He chose to leave New York, the privacy of his studio and the artistic control of individual performance work to collaborate with Los Angeles' homeless both as a paralegal specializing in homeless outreach and as the creator/director of his performance workshop, LAPD (Los Angeles Poverty Department).

Linda Burnham's essay documents LAPD. Composed of homeless transients on Los Angeles' Skid Row and other artists, LAPD has, in less than a decade, become an award–winning troupe. Simultaneously, everyone involved in its creation, including Malpede, has undergone profound personal transformations. Malpede's full-time involvement on Skid Row makes his work more measurably effective and widely relevant than it could have been as an artist's interpretation of a social problem through an individual product. The LAPD process has also extended the definition of improvisation to accommodate the diverse,

This article originally appeared in *The Drama Review* 31, no. 2 (Summer 1987). Copyright 1987 New York University and the Massachusetts Institute of Technology. Reprinted by permission of the author and The MIT Press. Epilogue is rewritten from an article originally in *High Performance*.

often unpredictable group, including role-switching to cover absent or incapacitated players and incorporation of the directorial voice within the production.

In a filthy, baggy, mismatched suit and broken glasses mended with tape, he climbed the platform and put his mouth to a giant megaphone aimed at Manhattan, the world's most expensive real estate. In a hesitant monotone he began reading something that sounded suspiciously like Whitman's "Song of the Open Road," but . . . different.

> Alight and foothearted [*sic*] I take to the open road.
> Healthy and free, the world before me,
> The long brown path beating me wherever I choose.
> Henceforth I ask not good fortune, I myself am no good.
> Henceforth I whimper no more, no mas, no more, need
>   nothing.
> Done with indoor, outdoor, side door, and rear door
>   complaints, complaints, complaints.
> Strong and content I grovel the open road.
> All seem beautiful to me.
> I can repeat over and over to men and women, you have done
>   such good to me that I would do the same for you.
> I will cut myself for you as I go.
> I will scatter myself among men and women as I go.
> I will toss a new gas and roughness among them.
> Whoever denies me, it shall not butcher me.
> Whoever accepts me, he or she shall be blistered and shall
>   blister me.

So began *Olympic Update: Homelessness in Los Angeles,* John Malpede's contribution to New York's 1984 Art on the Beach Festival. Malpede is an artist who, like many others, was touched by the desperation of the thousands of homeless children, women, and men in America. But instead of going back to his East Village studio to work alone, honing his career, he went to California in 1984. There he began work on Skid Row, both as a paralegal specializing in homeless outreach and, starting in October 1985, as the creator/director of his own performance workshop for the transients who sleep on L.A.'s sidewalks and live on mission food. He spends at least fifty-five hours a week on Skid Row—that's 5th Street, sometimes called "The Nickel."

Life on the Nickel

"Sound off! Don't go off!" the flyers read. "Free street theater/performance workshop for Skid Row residents. Be in the workshop and develop your own creative material that will be performed in the neighborhood and broadcast on the radio."

"I was scared," says Malpede. He feared the workshop would be ignored but found he had "tapped into an energy that had been hanging there. Once the space was provided they flooded it with ideas" (Durland, p.11).

What Malpede hoped to create was a space in which the homeless might be able to communicate. Malpede had become involved when he visited L.A. earlier that year, right before the 1984 Olympics, and saw L.A. police on horseback stopping, questioning and harassing some of the 15,000 transients who congregate in a ten-block area in the heart of the city.

The *L.A. Times* quoted Capt. Billy Wedgworth, commander of the police department's central area: "We have increased the intensity of everything we do. We're trying to sanitize the area" (Roderick, 2:1).

Malpede began researching homelessness in L.A., deciding to use the material in his performance work. He attended meetings of the County Board of Supervisors and introduced himself to the activists of H.O.T. (the Homeless Organizing Team) and the lawyers of H.L.T. (the Homeless Litigation Team), who were directing a two-pronged effort to ease the stringent conditions of California's "workfare" program and raise the monthly General Relief stipend. Instead of presenting the courts with complex legal briefs, the lawyers were using a revolutionary method to put forth their cases: testimony by street people describing the desperate conditions in downtown hotels, the rapes, the robberies, the impossibility of survival on a $228 monthly General Relief check. Gary Blasi, an attorney for the Legal Aid Foundation of Los Angeles and a leading advocate for the homeless, calls this "bringing the ugly reality of the streets and alleys into the courtroom." "Life on the streets," he says, "is completely incomprehensible to most judges" (Clancy, 5:1).

Malpede, who had long been using storytelling in his performance art pieces, was enormously affected by the power of this testimony. As a result, his *Olympic Update* was not a rant against the rich or the police but rather a series of rambling, wacko-poetic speeches touching on the pain and bewilderment he saw among the people of Skid Row. His speeches were interspersed with actual recordings of street people testifying before officials about their lives. He went home to New York to perform the new piece but was determined to go back and settle in L.A.

When he did return in November 1984, he found H.O.T. setting up a Tent City on the square opposite City Hall. He was there during Christmas, while the population of the settlement swelled, and he was there when ten of its residents were arrested in a sit-in at a Board of Supervisors meeting. They said they couldn't leave because they had no place to go.

Malpede hung out at the Inner City Law Center (ICLC) at 6th and Gladys and watched a shantytown spring up on a nearby children's playground, next to the Catholic Worker's Soup Kitchen. He became friends with the thirty people who collected there over the next four or five months, including their leader, Ted Hayes, who at first impressed Malpede as "a maniac in flowing robes." Hayes talked to Malpede about his vision of community. He saw the people on Skid Row as isolated in the extreme—from society and from each other. He wanted a place for them to live together where they could become resocialized. The place became widely known as "Justiceville." Even though the owner of the lot gave his permission for it to remain, Justiceville

---

from
Olympic Update: Homelessness in Los Angeles

John Malpede

(MoTo appears over hill looking stately, dignified, wearing sportscoat, slacks, and tie. From a distance his clothing looks clean, but up close it's filthy. He's carrying a megaphone and a large ghetto-blaster wrapped in foil and a clear plastic garbage bag. He goes up the ramp to the giant megaphone. He puts down the megaphone and the blaster on the platform and begins to talk thru the giant megaphone. His style is oratorical, as if addressing a political convention. He begins by reading from Whitman's "Song of the Open Road," which he alters as he reads.)

[. . .]

was eliminated by the city for "health violations." Malpede remembers staying up all night with Justiceville citizens, then watching the bulldozers flatten their homes the next day. "It was a blow to the solar plexus," he says (Burnham, Interview).

According to a spring 1986 survey by the L.A. County Department of Mental Health (Decker, 2:1), the average age of a homeless person on Skid Row is forty, near Malpede's own age. More than half are Black or Latino, and half are addicted to drugs or alcohol. Many suffer from severe mental illness. Few of the needy receive any care at all because of the lack of facilities—and often because of their inability to reach the few facilities there are.

They sleep in cardboard boxes, all-night movie theaters, mission beds, and substandard flophouses, often staying awake all night for fear of attack. A quarter of them carry knives in plain view—big ones.

The survey revealed some of the isolation typical of these people. Sixty percent have never married, 25 percent are estranged from their families, and 40 percent told the researchers they had had no contact with friends within the last month.

In the greatest contrast with the average L.A. resident, 14 percent

---

(MoTo unwraps the ghetto-blaster, picks it up, and turns it on. It plays the "Olympic Fanfare" [made famous by ABC] and then "The Star-Spangled Banner." While the national anthem is playing, he wraps up the blaster and descends the ramp with it and the small [i.e., normal sized] megaphone. At the foot of the ramp the performer becomes MoTo's friend who hurriedly moves toward the audience. His hurried manner suggests a concern with the pacing of the entire presentation. At the end of "The Star-Spangled Banner" he turns off the tape and begins to talk to the audience in a low-key, conversational though presentational manner.)

FRIEND MoTo and me, we just came from Los Angeles. And on behalf of the City of Los Angeles, home of the '84 Olympics and the homeles capital of America, MoTo and I have been asked by the L.A.O.O.C. (the Los Angeles Committee for the Organizing of Olympics) to travel this land during the Olympics and tell the people of our land with this Olympic Update Report. And they asked us to do this. And they paid for us to do this. They gave us bus tickets to travel America and come here. They gave us one-way bus tickets. They paid for them. And this is called Greyhound therapy.

We were in Los Angeles for the Olympics. What the Olympics were like, the Olympics were like the movie

have suffered during their lives from schizophrenia, 35 times higher than the overall county population, while another 11 percent have been diagnosed as manic-depressive, 18 times the average. The survey estimated that a third are severely and chronically mentally ill, with even more who are anxiety-impaired or suffering from personality disorders. Of these, only 4.4 percent received inpatient care during the six months prior to the survey. Sixty percent of those interviewed claimed to have had serious health problems within the last month.

The average day on Skid Row can be bleak. Less than a third of the people eat three meals; 24 percent live on one meal or less. For shelter they alternate between the street and the missions, averaging ten days on the pavement each month. One third were physically assaulted within the last year and another third were robbed. While a third of them are believed to be eligible for disability benefits, only 9 percent receive them, with another 9 percent receiving welfare. The application process was deemed "fraught with problems" by the researchers.

Malpede found a job as a paralegal with the Inner City Law Center (ICLC), the only free law center on Skid Row. The center, founded and

---

Olympic Update (continued)

Blue Thunder. Blue Thunder was in Los Angeles. And just like in the movie there were super helicopters, like blue thunder, from the L.A.P.D. Skywatch watching down from the sky. There were Olympic helicopters everywhere. All over the city. The skinny ones—not the puffy helicopters that are round like balls, but the long ones like blue thunder, that look like giant grasshoppers and can see thru walls. They can point right at you, and they know how cold or hot you are. And they can find you and shoot you down just because you're warm, thinking the wrong thoughts. (And you thought there weren't any more of them because in *Blue Thunder* Roy Snyder [sic] shot them down with an old-fashioned bubble helicopter, and got the tape to the TV station that showed how they were going to look thru walls and go into your mind and read it even when you were sleeping.)

But now there are Olympic helicopters and they fly over the city and sit on the sides of skyscrapers like the 17-year locusts—like when the 17-year locusts came and covered all the trees in Ohio. And now the Olympic helicopters, they sit on the sides of the buildings reading thoughts and looking for terrorists. And the L.A.P.D. they come down into Skid Row Park at 6th and Gladys, across the street from the Hospitality Kitchen and the Regal Hotel, and they make everyone lie down on the ground with their

directed by Nancy Mintie, grew out of a Catholic Worker facility and functions as a friendly neighborhood drop-in place. Some of its funding comes through an advocacy grant from the Liberty Hill Foundation, raised by John Malpede. In his day job at ICLC, Malpede and his partner, activist Carl Graue, spend all day on the street taking declarations from the homeless to be filed with H.L.T. lawsuits. Meanwhile, using his talents and experience in performance, plus an artist-in-residency grant from the California Arts Council, Malpede has established a performance workshop, now held every Wednesday night and Saturday afternoon.

A formidable effort. But as of September 1986, the news was very good. Thanks to the legal efforts of Malpede and his associate, General Relief had been raised from $228 to $247 a month, the first increase in five or six years. "Not a lot," says Malpede, "but at least it's more than the rent in a downtown hotel ($220–240 a month). And it adds up to about 8.1 million dollars a year, every year. Hands across America raised about $16 million, but this is literally a handful of people who did this" (Burnham, Interview).

Equally important to Malpede is the progress, both creative and

---

heads behind their hands. And they talk thru their walkytalkies to the Olympic helicopters. And the Olympic helicopters read the minds of the people lying on the ground, and they signal the L.A.P.D. and the L.A.P.D. take them away. They take them away and they put them in jail so that we can have the Olympics.

spiritual, of the LAPD, the Los Angeles Poverty Department, a fluc-
tuating group of about fifteen people between the ages of twenty and
fifty who have remained with the performance workshop since its
beginning in October 1985.

While two or three still sleep on the street, the financial picture
has improved for LAPD members. Some have steady work and four are
considering getting a house together. Some do drift away into jail or
mental hospitals or simply into the ozone, but others are showing an
interest in listening and talking instead of ranting and raving, and two
who might be called mentally disabled are on their way to getting Social
Security disability benefits, a long and tortuous journey within the
catch-22 of L.A.'s relief system: to get it you have to be sane enough
to say you're crazy and make it through the application process.

Workshop: Erecting Monuments in the Heart

My first experience with LAPD came in February 1986 when I attended
a workshop at LAMP (L.A. Men's Place, a facility for mentally ill men).
LAMP is a tiny, shabby storefront, little more than a spot where am-
bulatory schizophrenics can hang out and feel safe during the day. At
night they bed down in cardboard, huddled up against the building
as if it were home.

Malpede's group usually works at the ICLC, but there was a meeting
there that night, so LAMP took the group in. Since the workshop is
always open to anybody, this meant LAMP clients were welcome. As
I was introduced to the LAPD members, I noticed a disheveled young
man, wrapped in some passionate, furious world of his own, stalking
around the edges of the group shouting, whispering, singing, and
reciting his world view. The workshop was unperturbed. "I'm over-
whelmed by their ability to tolerate different kinds of people," Malpede
told me later. "They'll listen to people who talk extremely slowly, lose
track, etc. It's a humanizing fact of life on Skid Row."

While I shook hands with Sunshine, Tania, Frank, George, Joe,
Marlon, and Chris, Mark, the roaming commentator, provided an under-
tone of dislocated irony for the proceedings.

"It's only been a day!" he yelled as people shed their coats and
talked excitedly with Linda Sibio, LAPD's assistant director, about her
efforts to find them a regular rehearsal space. Sibio is a wild-eyed young
woman on a motorcycle who also works for performance artist Rachel
Rosenthal and appears with The Actor's Gang, a local theatre group.
She is an energizing, driving force in LAPD but gets in tussles with the
men when they display attitudes she thinks are sexist or uncooperative.

Currently she runs the workshop's talent shows every Saturday at Thieves' Corner (the corner of 5th and Wall), a job that takes muscle and moxie. "Last week I saw a murder across the street from the talent show," she told me. "It's real serious down there."

Sunshine, a handsome, thirtyish man who looked unusually drowsy, recruited people for a later reading of his play. I was introduced to him, and he immediately cast me as a fifty-year-old Black wino.

We listened to an audio tape of Joe and Frank appearing with Malpede on a Pacifica station radio show. Malpede did his "creating a community" speech, followed by the two workshop members singing their song "We Will Rob You" (to the tune of Queen's "We Will Rock You": "Take all your money/ run down the street/ spend all your money/ with the people we meet/ We will we will rob you"). The song tells the story of being robbed of money and clothes outside a check cashing place, then being arrested for indecent exposure.

Frank's voice told of his experience with LAPD as "a place to sharpen your tools." He talked of his background in street-corner rap singing in the sixties in Philadelphia. Growing up in juvenile homes and jails prepared him to survive on the "mean streets." He became the "Poet Lariat" [sic] of his neighborhood by telling stories on street corners about movies he had seen. His rapping became more sophisticated and is now the rich, rocking, dirty "Bad Boy's Badass Song," with images of Fat Daddy "dressed like a jitterbug" and Black culture "taken by the Beats in their goatees and tams."

When the tape was finished, Marlon, an older man with a truly weathered face, produced a poem he had been "writing all my life." "I erected a monument in my heart," he said, "to a friend I lost in the sixties," apparently to drugs. While the poem displayed no particular poetic skill, the pathos of the situation and the sincerity of the speaker carried the moment.

George, a young man who often accompanies Malpede on his daily rounds, told stories of his 108-year-old grandmother. The stories shape and change each time he tells them—because he can neither read nor write.

After a noisy break, during which Mark announced, *"I was there in '59 when they dropped the big comic book!"* we regrouped for Sunshine's play. Sibio and I found ourselves miming the surreptitious lighting of a joint while waiting in the dinner line at the mission. After that a scene by Joe about "falling in love on Skid Row" featured Tania, dressed in a Gucci sweatsuit. (She announced she was engaged to Sunshine, who woke up right away.) In the scene, Tania had lots of boyfriends who had schemes to make money, including cheating on welfare. There were heartbreaks and salvations. It was followed by a spontaneous critique during which I questioned the motivation of one of the characters who was "saved by Jesus." The group explained to me the phenomenon of becoming "Bible-struck" while hanging around the missions, a condition far beyond redemption and closer to insanity.

After the plays had been read and avidly critiqued (with minimal direction from Malpede), we settled into a discussion about the purpose of the workshop. "I'm not here just to write plays!" Frank said, "I'm not here to waste time and have friends. I want to make social change!"

"*Rosewater Foundation, may I help you?*" offered Mark. "*Go ahead and kill yourself. $250.*"

Joe talked about a party that George had thrown the other day. "It was about celebrating that we have a community. We're so isolated that we're isolated from ourselves. It was about what's here on Skid Row."

"*The crash of '29 came early!*"

Frank: "I see this group as people with different philosophical ideas. We could come together like they did in the nineteenth century to smash slavery. We could take the things we don't like and smash them down."

"*When we turn on that TV we better be damn sure we know what we're doing!*"

Malpede: "We could be building some bonds together to make meaningful statements, like for changes. Stick together and not drift away."

"*We're a pre-teen world!*"

The workshop finished up with a rendition of "Out on My Own," a song that has almost become the LAPD theme song:

> Out on my own
> Livin' alone
> Nowhere to go
> I really want to grow
> The County was there
> They gave me the air
> It opened up my door
> Now I can go for more
> I knew it wouldn't be easy
> I knew it would be hard
> I kept on stickin' to my guns
> I'll make it to the stars.

Looking over my notes from that workshop, I wondered if I hadn't stumbled on a script from *Cagney and Lacey* or some other issue-oriented TV show where the characters talk about values all the time. But Malpede assured me that they often talk about community, that the attitude is an offshoot of Justiceville and really is the prevailing climate of the LAPD.

In Performance: *South of the Clouds*

Because they have no permanent playing space, LAPD performances of skits, monologues, and songs have taken place on street corners, in mission lines (where performers have been asked to clean up the language), at parties, in art lofts and art spaces, and in local downtown theaters, usually with Malpede as organizer or director, not as performer.

Most rewarding for the group so far was *South of the Clouds,* part of a weekly performance series held throughout July 1986 at the Boyd Street Theater in the heart of Skid Row.[1] Directed by Malpede, the piece was a series of monologues by the group's members, based on an acting exercise in which Malpede asked them to recall an action that makes them feel good when they do it (partly, he says, to help them recognize that they can produce that good feeling when they want to). Finding and doing the actions produced writing that delved into interesting conflicts for each actor, illuminating the interior life of damaged but hopeful and talented individuals.

"My criterion for people being in that show," Malpede said,

> was the people who had gone beyond themselves, who had found that kind of conflict, or that kind of subtext. They'd gone beyond themselves and discovered something new in the workshop around that material.
> What I was saying about socialization relates to the monologues in *South of the Clouds.* At the point we did that show, not everybody was capable of ensemble work, and with monologues everybody went away with a little piece of something they could do, a self-affirmation. I'd like to see the group work toward ensemble work, because if they could do that, they could function in society, maybe. It's close to the way interaction works. A monologue doesn't require active interaction.

It had been five months since I attended the workshop when I saw *South of the Clouds.* While I recognized some faces, I was struck by the polish and creativity of the group—and amused by their bios in the program.

Frank Christian was listed as having "attended every reform school in Philadelphia and also has an M.A. from the University of Michigan."

For the acting exercise, he had chosen a routine from his days as a boxer. While he moved around the stage with the grace of a dancer, bobbing and weaving, jabbing and punching at the air, he recalled the night he lost the will to fight and looked into his opponent's eyes and saw "Martin Luther King and his Poor People's Campaign."

Jim Brown "attended a number of universities around the U.S., eventually receiving a B.A. in history and an M.A. in political science after completing his military service. After a stint in US QMC Pusan, Republic of Korea, he became a union organizer, sometimes guest of mental institutions, part-time jock, and insurance salesman. He is now an itinerant hobo." Brown recreated a sandlot baseball game from his youth "between the White Plains Road Wops and the Jerome Avenue Jews" that spun out in all directions to create a picture of "growing up in white-ethnic urban-America." He performed it with considerable force, wielding an imaginary bat and circling the bases, sometimes regressing into racial ranting, sometimes forgetting his lines and having them tossed to him from offstage. Over the four weeks of the show, Brown, pushed by Malpede to learn his lines, pulled his act together and simultaneously created solid changes in his off-stage life. Malpede feels Brown is one LAPD member who has made remarkable progress.

A Change of Heart

A Monologue by Frank Christian

(A middle-aged man in red trunks, black boxing shoes and gloves skips onto the stage shadow-boxing. He kicks his legs out after knee-bending several times. He bobs and weaves his head from side to side as he shuffles to a nearby wall. When he gets about four feet from the wall, he begins to punch it with the eight-ounce boxing gloves he is wearing.

After several minutes he turns, bobs, and weaves to a brick column and throws punches in rapid succession. He then dances to the center stage bouncing from one foot to the other with both hands raised. He is imitating a fighter who is being announced by the referee; not an ordinary club fighter, but a champion.

Robert Clough chose washing and wringing clothes as the feel-good activity to use for his monologue, which was transformed into revenge against his father for abusing his mother. Clough talked out his memories as he mimed wringing the wet clothes. After the first performance, Clough disappeared and his piece was performed by another member, along with explanations about Clough's whereabouts according to the latest rumor: "He's in San Francisco having cosmetic surgery." The truth finally surfaced: Clough *was* in San Francisco, detained in a mental health facility after a fight in a Tenderloin hotel where he broke all the windows. Malpede conceded he may never know why Clough departed the show, and Clough is so delusional when he's off his medication that he may show up again and not remember where he went.

The flamboyant Pat Perkins, the only white woman in the show, used blues singing to give an account of a youthful infatuation with a Black musician, her admiration for his music, and her eventual loss of his love to another woman.

In one of the evening's most moving pieces, Joe Clark and Kevin Williams enacted a scene that had really happened to one of them while preparing the show: a drunk at a bus stop had mistaken Williams for

---

He comes to the center of the ring and touches the imaginary gloves of his imaginary opponent. He throws four stiff jabs at the invisible opponent; the last one hits the brick column with a bang. At this point he sticks his tongue out at this viewless adversary, stalks back to his corner, and taunts him as he sits on his stool. We see him taking instruction from his trainer. He responds to his coach by shaking his head and pointing his thumb at the other corner, shouting verbal abuse at the other fighter.

As the bell rings for round two, he runs over to the fighter's corner and hits him with twenty-seven punches, just as he gets off the stool he is sitting on. All of a sudden things change.

He starts to hold on. We see his head snapping back several times from a number of punches. He grabs for his opponent to hold on, but is beaten down to the canvas from against the ring ropes. He sits there with his mouth opened in agony and humiliation. After several minutes, he rises, comes to the center of the stage, and begins to speak.)

CHRIS COLT   That was eighteen years ago, but it seems like yesterday. Place: Trenton, New Jersey. 1968 Golden Gloves Championships. Me, Chris Colt, versus Gypsie Joe Harris, the Philadelphia Buzz Saw. *(He throws a right hand and bobs when he says, "me, Chris Colt," and puts his balled*

his son and Williams had used the opportunity to play out a scene between himself and the father who had abandoned him as a child, playing into the old drunk's fantasies.

Not Just Playin'

The workshop has a certain notoriety in Los Angeles, particularly
because homelessness and performance art are both currently in the
media spotlight. There have ben writeups about the group in the *L.A.
Herald Examiner,* the *L.A. Reader,* the *L.A. Weekly, High Performance,*
the *Wall Street Journal,* and the *Village Voice* (see references). Most
reviews have been favorable, but usually they focus on the social
phenomenon of the workshop, rather than on the work itself. These
press notices have made some celebrities and opened some doors. Frank
Christian told Malpede that when he applied for a security job, he was
hired because his future employers recognized him from the paper as
an LAPD member. On several occasions members have been saved by
their celebrity from being rousted by the cops, which is a real payoff
in their lives. As for attitudes on the street, Malpede says, ''I think

---

A Change of Heart (continued)

fists on his waist sides.) In the first
round, I was feeling good, like a Pall
Mall should, solid? We came out,
touched gloves, and circled each other
feinting, but without throwing any
punches at all.

I throw two lefts and a right to
his shaven head. The punches landed
but slide off his greasy bald head.

He kept moving in throwing zip-
ping lefts and rights to the body and
my head. I caught most of the punches
on his elbows and arms, spinned Gypsie around, threw two left hooks and
a right hand. Gypsie's knee buckled,
but he kept coming in, throwing
round-house lefts and rights, missing
me by a mile.

I stuck my tongue out at him. I hit

Joe Harris with four left jabs and
laughed at him as I went back to my
corner. I threatened Gypsie from my
stool and I told my trainer Gypsie was
one piece of cake.

As the bell rang for the next round
I ran to the corner of Gypsie and hit
him with a barrage of punches. Then
disaster struck. I began to hold on. The
crowd said, ''What's happening to
Colt? You hurt or somethin', man?''

Gypsie noticed too, and hit me
with all kinds of punches as I covered
up. Finally, I sagged to the canvas from
a punch combination.

Why? Why did I stop fighting?
Huh? I had a change of heart, that's
why. For four weekends, I was helping Martin Luther King's group with

people are getting to be respected and well-known for what they're doing. Since we've gotten all this stuff in the press, they're taking us more seriously. Before that they thought we were just playin'."

At this writing, LAPD has more dates at the Boyd Street Theatre coming up (21 November 1986–2 January 1987), as well as *Condo Thieves' Corner,* an outdoor installation project funded by the National Endowment for the Arts (25 and 26 October 1986). For this show they plan to set up a huge cardboard stage for performances by themselves and others from Skid Row and the L.A. artist community.

Among the most satisfying results of all this activity is the request that LAPD serve as the advisory board for the Inner City Law Center, providing information and feedback about the center's interaction with the community and the needs of people on the street. One of the first things the group brought to the center's attention was the need for some kind of protection around the check cashing centers on the first and fifteenth of the month, when relief checks are issued. "It's really dangerous down there," says Malpede. "It's easy to tell who's vulnerable, and the vulnerable get hit." Especially with the cocaine epidemic burning its way across America's cities, the atmosphere is becoming so violent in central L.A. that murder is always in the air.

---

the Poor People's Campaign in Resurrection City, Washington, D.C. Those people were putting their bodies on the line, man, can you dig it? Huh!!

They came from everywhere to D.C. Some by hitchhiking with their transistor radios blasting to Dylan's "Like a Rolling Stone." People young and old; most left, some right, some black, some white. Father Groppi from Milwaukee and his sidekick, Sweet Willie Wine, and many others. The march, dedicated now to the recently slain King, Medgar Evers, Viola Liuzzo, the Italian Filly with Balls, a Chicago housewife who went down south for others' civil rights and got wasted, man. Damn!

The Kennedy boys! Scottsboro boys! Yeah! Yeah! Yeah!

I ain't lost my heart, man! I can still fight, but I'm fightin' a different way now. Like the two white dudes from Harvard and Yale. They dedicated their lives to human rights, when they were young. Now they live in fatherless black homes among the rats and roaches. I lost my bigotry when I saw them trying to get love from the litttle black children that they didn't get from their parents.

You see, man, while their parents were jet-setting around the world, they were in private institutions all alone. One of 'em said he was sexually abused there, man. They were in prison, too; but they had more food and clothes than me.

Art at the Pressure Point

John Malpede, forty-one, artist, white, New Yorker. His job at ICLC is the "first real job" he's ever had, "with a regular paycheck and insurance and everything." He lives about two miles from my studio, where I interviewed him in August 1986. His roommate is a social worker at LAMP; they live on a hill in a funky clapboard house that has been burgled twice. Between my place and his lies Skid Row, which he keeps referring to as "down there," as though it were a sump, a vortex, or black hole pulling L.A. down at its center. Though his house has no yard, at least he can walk out in his bathrobe and get the paper in the morning, a welcome change from living in New York's East Village, "surrounded by concrete, no matter what."

Malpede went to graduate school at Columbia University, not in art or theater, but in philosophy. Much of his theatrical experience was in street theater, working with the Bread and Puppet Theatre and with his own groups under the auspices of city grants. They were "sent to the inner city like cultural kamikazes" to perform in parks, on the street, at Coney Island. He took workshops and classes in dance, voice and contact improvisation.

A Change of Heart (continued)

For the first time, solid, I saw Whitey as a victim and right then and there, solid, I dedicated myself to the whole human race, to prove I's mystical. Can you dig it? Hoo!!

Now my body's on the line too, Dudes, and I'm still fightin'. But there is one thing I won't fight no mo' for; I won't fight no mo' for trophies that rust.

While working briefly with dancer Barbara Dilley at the Naropa Institute in Colorado (1975), he met a group from New York called Central Notion Company, and when he returned to New York, he worked off and on with them. Through improvisation with the company he and performance artist Bill Gordh discovered the personae of Dead Dog and Lonely Horse, a man/dog (Gordh) and man/horse (Malpede) who palled around, improvising on the street and in any interesting location they could find, and eventually opened something of a detective agency in Manhattan. Audience members could make appointments with them and witness a performance by hanging out with them in the office or on the street. I met them about this time (1978) when they came to perform in L.A. The pairing was a remarkable collaboration in terms of exploring unknown performance realms, and Lonely Horse's soulful boniness seemed to fit Malpede's long, tall frame and his hesitant, big-eyed, companionable generosity.

Malpede hit the performance art circuit alone in 1980, working in New York, Los Angeles, and other cities at art spaces like the Kitchen and LACE (Los Angeles Contemporary Exhibitions). He has received artist's grants from the National Endowment for the Arts and the New York and California Arts Councils, plus two residencies at the Blue Mountain Colony in New York, where he had the space to develop his ideas. Performances often took a talk show or monologue format and examine the nature of performing, the passing of information, and, more and more, the plight of America's outcasts.

By the time Malpede came around to *Olympic Update: Homelessness in Los Angeles,* he was completely radicalized. Performing in the character of the dissociated and suspicious poetic genius MoTo, and switching to the character of MoTo's street friend who told stories about him, he created a stream of consciousness about the condition of living on the street, outside of society. Malpede's colleagues in performance art were flocking to the clubs and making art about TV and the media, but Malpede saw a social role for art. "It's really sad," he told Jacki Apple in the *L.A. Weekly,* "when the main focus of the art world is television. It just shows how removed from reality we've all become" (21).

He chose Los Angeles for his project because the situation with the ICLC doesn't exist in New York, but also, as he told the *Village Voice,* "I don't think I could have done this work in New York, not because the work can't be done there—it can—but because I couldn't have allowed myself to do this instead of trying to get in the BAM Next Wave series" (Solomon, 12).

His workshop participants are glad he did, and are fully aware of the changes the workshop has wrought in their lives. Joe Clark observes that the work with the LAPD "can increase your self-esteem incredibly, and it fills the need to describe and make sense of your world." They are aware of Malpede's commitment and recognize him as a part of Skid Row. Joe notes: "The workshop couldn't happen if John were just an artist coming down to Skid Row a couple times a week like the strangers who show up on Christmas, give you a meal, and never care about you again" (Solomon, 12).

In some ways, Malpede *is* one of them. Skid Row is embedded in the center of the downtown art community, which ranges from Broadway to the border of East L.A. Many artists live on Main Street, on Wall, on San Pedro above the pawn shops and "art" theaters, and often swap stories with the denizens of the inner city. In private moments, those struggling for recognition in painting and performance art betray fears that they will wind up on the streets pushing shopping carts full of junk till the end of their days. When you're forty and you've never had "a real job," maybe the one thing that separates you from the totally destitute is the spiritual enrichment of a life in art.

Malpede is a handsome, friendly person whose manner is somehow both vague and direct. His mind seems to run at several different speeds

---

Afternoon Seance: Bronx River Parkway

A Monologue by Jim Brown

Afternoon seance. Bronx River Parkway. Bronx River Park. Sandlot baseball, pre-junior high school. Real Americana. As umpire an ex-cop who worked for the Police Athletic League, retired because of an injury, Italo-American, who also coached the other team—the White Plains Road Wops, the Dagos, the Guinnys, vs. us: the Jerome Avenue Jews, the Kikes, the Mochis. He's gonna umpire from behind the pitcher, rather than like normal people, from behind the catcher. In typical ass-backward Guinny fashion. North Bronx, heart of urban America's fastest and most competitive city. Bronx as Iowa. Twelve and a half miles from Columbus Circle, same as living in Dubuque, Des

at the same time, and conversation can drop off in the middle of a sentence as if he is listening to something else, maybe a different drummer. Yet he is one of the few people I know who seems to genuinely enjoy making eye contact with people.

When we talked in August [1986], his California Arts Council grant as artist-in-residence had just been renewed for another year and I asked him how he felt about that.

MALPEDE It seems like we're right in the middle of doing it. It seems like it's not at an ending point. It's not a lifelong thing. I am going to do it only as long as it's interesting. It's not always fun. Day to day it's not fun. Sometimes I am killing myself. That's why I don't want to do the talent shows on Saturdays. I want eventually to pass this whole thing along to the people in the workshop.

BURNHAM Are you getting more cynical and depressed? Are you more hopeful about life in general?

MALPEDE All of the above. It's hard not to be cynical sometimes. It's also really nice to be in a place where you feel like you can really make

---

Moines, Clinton, Iowa. Playing catcher. Typical sandlot baseball. Many errors. Mucho and macho runs scored. My team bitching as if they were feeling a witch's tit in freezing North Bronx weather.

Bronx River Park. Bronx North. In the days immediately preceding the end of World War II. Fiorello H. La Guardia Mayor of The City of New York. F.D.R. President. In those naive days before oral sex à la France, Goldfarb's imported pornography (supplied by Frank Squillanti's North Bronx pornography cellar). Avid consumers included the Bronx County D.A.'s office, the Manhattan, New York County, D.A.'s office, the Mayor's office, the largest accounting office in the world, and presidential and vice-presidential candidates.

At bat five times. Hit the ball once. A base hit. The umpire three times in a row called runners safe at home plate when every player on the field knew the runners were out. My team decided that they wanted me to bait the umpire, as one of us usually did, which sometimes caused a big rumble, face-to-face fist fight. I refused which bugged the shit out of both teams. The umpire, in true Board of Dis-Education, Police Athletic League fashion thought that he would get me to react to such nonsense. My teammates, I used the word advisedly, were unusually docile waiting for a confrontation. They never got the scenario.

a difference. It's nice to get paid for something that is at a real pressure point. You really feel like you can do something. I also feel that, in terms of my art, *Olympic Update* was an overtly political thing, but it was in a context that didn't really have any oomph. The context my art is in now, it's able to have much more impact in the arena it's concerned with. That was a sort of unknowing intent of mine all along.

BURNHAM   How do you feel this relates to your art? Are you talking specifically about directing this show, or do you see social community organizing as the same as performance art?

MALPEDE   No, I don't. I'm too East Coast for that. I think that when you write a script or something, that's art, and when you create social change, that's something else. That's just an East Coast way of looking at life. But I think there is a place in which those things intersect, like the outdoor installation idea. That's an idea that has more of an intersection, maybe. Also, *South of the Clouds,* that came out of an acting exercise, so that seems like art to me. That was definitely art.

BURNHAM   What do you think their essential view is of what's going on in the workshop? Is it really communication or are they hoping to

---

Afternoon Seance (continued)

Score tied at 16-16 going into the ninth inning. Bronx Park North and south of the clouds. In the days before the realization that Harry's Homo Heaven, Amazon Annie's and Liza and Lizzy the Lez'es running wild were real. Tom Sawyer and Huckleberry Finn grew up in rural and semi-rural America, vicinity of Hannibal, Missouri, in the quarter of a century immediately preceding the irrepressible conflict: The Civil War, 1861–1865. Seventy-five percent of the population rural and agricultural. Studds Schwartz and Vinnie Pistocchi, North Bronx Central. Seventy-five percent of America Urban in the months immediately preceding the end of World War II. Tom Sawyer and Huckleberry Finn: White, Anglo-Saxon, Protestants. WASPS. Puke. Schwartz and Pistocchi: third generation Southern and Eastern European immigrants. The salt of urban America. America's forgotten non-Catholic, white ethnics. Spat upon despised and above all feared. Jews too competitive. Italians don't want to play against a stacked deck. North Bronx Central calling. "Hello operator, I haven't been in the Bronx in a long time. Is there still an exchange Oldenville Seven? There is? OK. Thank you, operator." Calling Oldenville Seven. Seven. Seven point seven. Seven million Italians, seven point seven million Jews arrived in the years after the great Civil War, or as my southern

gain skills they can use to make a living? What do they think they're doing?

MALPEDE   Some of them have professional ambitions. There's a lot of community concern about communication, but there are also some ambitions, which are unrealistic. How many people do their first performances in a real theater and then get it written about in all the papers in town and all that? So they think, well, if this happens this month, then by next month—

BURNHAM   *Miami Vice!*

MALPEDE   —at least I should be earning my living as a performance artist by next year. They don't realize that there are only about ten or twelve people around who do that. Nevertheless, the people have a lot to communicate and there is a lot of talent there, not necessarily the kind that can be packaged in Hollywood.

BURNHAM   Do you think they view it as therapy?

MALPEDE   No, and I don't either. I regard it only as art. But it is therapeutic. It creates a better life, a more social, better life. And that's

---

friend, who I met in the service, would say, "the War between the States."

Playing baseball. Last of the ninth. We've been playing for four hours, it's getting dark. It's drizzling and getting cold. Score still tied. Two outs. Our second baseman, Monty Horowitz lines a double. He's on second base. I'm up. The first pitch is way outside. Wait. That goddamn Guinny umpire called it a ball anyway. I can't believe it. A boff fangool. Kush mere und tuckas a rinde. OK. Here comes the second pitch. It's way outside again. Strike two! The Guinny bastard. I get it. I better hit the next pitch or he's gonna call me out and call the game on account of darkness. I'm cold, shivering. OK, pitch the ball wop. Pitch the ball. I've been trying to hit it over the right field wall all day. Look at 'em. Look. The right fielder. He's eatin' a big Guinny grinder out there. Look. The center fielder and the left fielder are eating them too. Big Guinny grinders. You know provolone cheese, Genoa salami, and peppers. Now the umpire's sharing one with the third baseman. I can't believe it. Let's go. Pitch the ball wop. Here it comes. Bam. Batting right handed I hit the ball off the freakin' fence. There goes Monty Horowitz. He's rounded third. "Slide Monty Horowitz. Slide!" That's it! We win it. We the Jerome Avenue Jews, the Litvaks, beat them the wops, the Sicilianos.

Nude swimming in Van Cortlandt

another thing that's been really amazing, with Jim Brown in particular, the baseball player in the show. He used to get thrown out of everywhere. He still gets in a lot of trouble, but he used to get thrown out of LAMP all the time because he was so obsessive and crazy that he would make everybody else crazy. He'd just incite people to riot. And you couldn't really talk to him. He could only talk obsessively about a few things. Molly Lowery, who runs LAMP, was saying to me the other day that it's amazing the difference in him since the show. He's really, really different. The last couple of days he's been hanging out with another guy who used to be a writer for *Sanford and Son* and *The Jeffersons*, a very intellectual guy, and Jim is, too. He hasn't been able to engage in conversations with people—two-way, give-and-take. And now he's beginning to do that. I'm really pretty impressed by the power of art, I have to say.

BURNHAM   Are you still as involved with the group on an individual basis? You were lending them money and going out with them to events. Is that still happening? Did you get your heart broken, as predicted?

Afternoon Seance (continued)

park. Mirrors under girls' dresses to see if they wore pink panties. If they wore pink panties them girls were for real. If they didn't wear pink panties, then maybe they were a little on the strange side. Growing up in white-ethnic urban-America.

MALPEDE   A number of times. Sometimes it feels like a house of mirrors down there—you don't know what's true and you'll never know. It depends on how you hold it. Basically I don't give things away looking for them to come back, because then I'd be setting myself up to be bummed out.

BURNHAM   There must be some people who look upon you as some kind of patsy.

MALPEDE   What's interesting is it's a whole reverse psychology. For a lot of people, if you get somebody to give you money, then they're a chump, right? They do it because they think they're doing you a favor, and you make them feel like they're doing you a favor, but in fact you're regarding them as a chump because they gave you something. It's like everything gets twisted.

BURNHAM   Is there anything that's changed about your life as an artist?

MALPEDE   The points where it gets most interesting to me are when it seems like I'm changing. And I'm definitely continuing to do that. At this moment I'm more aware of the constant side of me. But about two weeks ago, I was really moved by—I forget the particular circumstances, but it was really me changing. That is the most interesting, when I'm not just finding out about other people's lives.

Epilogue: The Real Deal—
An Update on the Los Angeles Poverty Department

Since I wrote *Hands across Skid Row,* a lot has happened to LAPD. It's been written about heroically, granted handsomely and presented with awards. But most interesting are the changes—artistically and personally—in the group and its members.

What began as a gathering of the curious and the homeless who responded to Malpede's flyers handed out on the sidewalk is now an intimate conglomeration of inner-city denizens—artists, drifters, singers, actors, writers, lovers and fighters well acquainted with life on the street.

As I write this, John Malpede's California Arts Council residency at Inner City Law Center has reached the end of its three-year contract, but the project is progressing full steam ahead.

When we left LAPD in the pages of *The Drama Review,* they had finished their first production, *South of the Clouds.* One of the monologues from that show went on to fame when Jim Brown (now known as Jim Beame) won a creation/performance award from the *L.A. Weekly*. The paper featured the group on its cover, interviewed Beame, published a story called "Homelessness—How It Happened to Me" by Pat Perkins, and called LAPD "The World's Best Theater of the Homeless."

Next came *Condo Thieves' Corner* at the corner of 5th and Wall in the heart of Skid Row: a talent show in the neighborhood with cash prizes. A giant "cardboard condo" was designed as the stage, and local musicians, comics, dancers and solo performers appeared both weekend days. The event seemed to please the locals and many downtown artists and LAPD members took part also. Artist Lin Hixson helped with the coordination.

About this time Linda Sibio departed to work with artist Rachel Rosenthal, and soon after I came aboard as administrator to write grants and book performances. I wanted to help if I could, and I was in something close to awe over Malpede's staying power, patience and fortitude. I wanted to better understand his method.

The next production was the perfect opportunity. *No Stone for Studs Schwartz* was a group improvisation based on a long, rambling

---

from
Olympic Update: Homelessness in Los Angeles

John Malpede

(*Ascends platform as MoTo, who again addresses audience thru giant megaphone.*)
MOTO   Peter Ueberroth, president of the L.A.O.O.C., Peter Ueberroth said to me, "This is going to be the greatest Olympic games of all time. But to have the greatest Olympic games we must sanitize the city. We must put up pastel banners all over the city. We must make the city smile. But to do this we need you, MoTo. We cannot do this without you MoTo." And I said to Peter Ueberroth, I said, "Peter, your shit stinks like everyone else. Your shit stinks like everyone else. Your shit, it stinks like everyone else!" And he said to me, "MoTo, yes it's true, my shit stinks like all the rest.

story by Jim Beame—the saga of a small-time union organizer fleeing the Mob from New York to the Caribbean, with side trips to Vietnam and Israel. Packed with characters and incongruously emphasized facts, the "script" skates from one reality to the next—from the Catskills to L.A.'s Union Station where Schwartz is murdered. It's nearly impossible to follow and when Malpede told me he was going to try to perform this idea, I questioned his sanity.

For one thing, the cast was enormous, and there was no way everybody would show up for rehearsals, much less be in town for the performances. Secondly, few could be counted on to remember their lines, and there were a lot of seriously underdeveloped "actors" in the group. Here's where Malpede's method comes in. It's elastic. He had already told me, "It's all in how you hold it." What he meant was the expansion of the idea of performance to make room for a story and cast as wildly diverse as this one. True renegades one and all, some are legally considered mentally disabled and others are just ornery.

Jim Beame was to play Studs Schwartz. Beame had changed enormously since we met him, and was now personable, intelligible and compliant, if still a bit distant. He still tended to wander from the "plot"

It stinks like all the rest only worse, MoTo. Only worse. Only you know that MoTo. Only you know how it stinks only worse. You don't have to smell it but you do, MoTo. You don't have to carry it around and smell it but you do. You don't have to carry it around and smell it but you do. You don't have to carry it around and smell it but you do. You doo-doo. Doo. You doo-doo you." And Peter Youand-both, he put his arm around me and he drew me close to his side and he handed me a bag of the most nasty and blackest shit I'd ever seen. Black and knotted shit. Knotty twisted shit in a baggy shit, swimming in its own drips. Its own hardness and its own drips. All knotted in a baggy. And

Peter Tubbermouth, he said to me, "MoTo, I'm counting on you. All of America is counting on you. You must take this blackest of shits and you must carry it thruout this great land of ours. You must carry it across this country from California to New York, as the Olympic torch is being passed from hand to hand and carried from New York to California. You must take it in your hand and you must hold it high. You must take this shit in hand and hold it high. This Olympian task, this Herculean task, I entrust to you and you alone, MoTo. To you and you alone. And I took the bag from him and said, "Peter, you are full of shit." I took it and I said, "Peter, you are full of shit." I took it and I said, "Peter,

so Malpede stepped in as his "alter ego," shadowing Beame, mirroring his body language and voice, and keeping the show on track by directing it from within:

"Enough about Richard Nixon! Get back to the story." "Louder and funnier!"

And it was funny. As the show evolved from its maiden run at the Boyd St. Theater on Skid Row to various appearances on the road, it mutated hilariously. Improvisation took over, with the cast goofing on each other constantly. Individual quirks were skewered, relationships were exposed and a real comedic timing was developed.

The set was a map drawn on a drop cloth, to keep the plot on line. Furniture was imaginary. The speed of the action varied in the extreme; sometimes it went by so fast that musical numbers like "Hava Nageela" and "Back to Back, Belly to Belly" took only seconds.

Most interesting of all, everybody learned each other's lines so they could trade characters if they were needed to fill in during periods of absence or incapacity. Gender and race were no bar to these exchanges, and they finally became so interesting, and then so much fun that role-switching is now a regular part of every production and workshop. Any

---

Olympic Update (continued)

you are full of shit!" And he cried.

(MoTo descends platform, Performer becomes MoTo's Friend.)
FRIEND   All over America everybody wants to talk to MoTo. We go downtown. The seats are soft and green carpeted. Everything is cool like the walls. People talk. We wait for MoTo's turn to talk. *(Friend punches in tape excerpt of [L.A.] County Supervisor Edelman's [July 1984] Hearings on the Homeless.)*
ELLA GRAHAM   My name is Ella Graham.
EDELMAN   G-r-a-h-m?
GRAHAM   G-r-a-h-a-m. I have a place to stay but I'm still homeless. I've been on Skid Row in Los Angeles for a year

and a half. I been assaulted twice. Both times the attacker had knives. I had my room broken into, my food stamps stolen. I called the police and they said if I didn't see the person who'd broken in there was nothing they could do except take the report. I have to carry a pair of scissors everywhere I go for protection. And the police tell me not to leave my room after dark because it's so dangerous where I live. I pay $220 a month for rent for a room ten by ten. And I have to share the toilet and shower with 79 other rooms, even with prositutes gays and anything else. The toilet rooms are always filthy and the shower is so nasty I feel dirtier after I get out of the shower than

given actor might play, within the same production, a large male mobster, a thin black female bar singer and an elderly Latino hotel manager, slipping in and out of dresses and slacks almost at will.

Schwartz was a big hit with audiences and critics. The *L.A. Herald Examiner*'s Richard Stayton said, ''For sheer danger and dramatic power, no actors on a local stage can compare.''

Schwartz was a very male-spirited piece because most of the people in the group were men. Skid Row is arguably the most sexist spot in America. At best, women are disregarded in the group. I once gave a lecture in workshop about the history of L.A. performance art, and the very word ''feminism'' drew boos and missiles. In *Schwartz* women were given bimbo roles.

Most women didn't stay long, except Pat Perkins, one of the original members, possessed of real stubbornness. The other was Elia Arce, a Costa Rican filmmaker and former member of Bread and Puppet Theatre, who showed up at *Condo* on a pair of stilts.

Arce and Malpede eventually became roommates and partners in life. Now attending UCLA Film School, she is a real comedic talent and has added much to performances and to the direction of the group,

---

when I got in, because they've got feces on the walls asnd all like that. And when I complain to the manager she says if I don't like it to get out. So I have a place to stay, but I'm still homeless.

EDELMAN   Tell us where this building is that you live.

GRAHAM   I live at 816 East 6th Street in room 107. I lived in room 107 since last March.

EDELMAN   O.K. Thank you. Let me ask. . . .

GRAHAM   It's the Regal Hotel.

EDELMAN   The Regal?

GRAHAM   Regal.

EDELMAN   It doesn't sound too regal.

GRAHAM   It isn't. *(She giggles.)* It's anything but Regal. *(Friend stops tape.)*

FRIEND   People talk. We wait for MoTo's turn to talk. We wait so long for MoTo to talk. Sometimes MoTo has to wait so long. So long.

[. . .]

FRIEND   They make MoTo wait so long. It's not fair. They make him wait so long, he gets upset. MoTo gets upset. Sometimes then I read him his favorite letter from this year and it smooths him. It smooths him. *(Friend takes rumpled paper from his pocket and reads it. He reads it to MoTo on platform, as if MoTo were standing poised to speak.)*

FRIEND   *(reading letter):*

due to her experience in Central American theater communes. Often members are temporarily sleeping or permanently living in their house. He lends money and they respond to suicide threats. Arce tried recruiting women to the workshop but with small success.

Then came Jazzmin, a resident of the Skid Row hotel Pat Perkins stays in. A woman with a great deal of street experience, Jazzmin is a natural clown and storyteller for whom LAPD has become a real artistic vehicle. Capable of doing a monologue that will keep an audience in stitches, Jazzmin (Janet Solis) has no theater experience except the theater of the Skid Row streets.

Physically she's astounding. Tipping the scales at over 200 pounds, she refers to her racial type as ''gumbo''—Black, Chicano, Indian and other strains. Far from a ''victim'' of homelessness, Jazz is a woman who, as she tells it, found freedom and power on Skid Row.

When Jazzmin came to LAPD, the first thing she did in workshop was a monologue with the thesis that God created woman so far superior to man that He had to put a curse on her. That and a monologue on sex on Skid Row were too much for some of the male members and they departed.

Olympic Update (continued)

Dear George,

Forgive me for not calling you MoTo, but when you and my mother were married and we were all living in Pontiac, we kids always called you George. In truth I feel like calling you Dad, because that best expresses what you mean to me.

You have no idea what it means to me to have found you again after all those years when we didn't know whether you were alive or dead. So many times during those years I wanted to tell you how unfair I thought the family had been to you about my mother's death. But, I never thought I would get the chance to do so.

I can truly say that being with you was the most meaningful experience of my life. I will cherish it always. I wish I could have convinced you to come back to live with me and my family. Please know, George, the door is always open.

I've enclosed a small check which I hope you'll accept. And Dad, please be careful of it.

I love you, Dad,

Larry

(Friend ascends platform, and becomes MoTo. MoTo talks.)

MOTO Mr. Chairman, my name is MoTo. The cars go by, I see them. They stop at the corner. They roll up their windows. They lock their doors. I see them. Their mouths say, ''they're

Jazzmin's presence was influential, and made the group more attractive to women. The work began to change from aggressive, conflict-
oriented, violent scenes to more emotional and introspective content,
especially feelings about making performance together.

A few months earlier, Kevin Williams, a young unemployed steelworker
and formerly homeless, had been appointed assistant director. He was
central to the project that followed *Schwartz,* an LAPD collaboration
with artist Susan Franklin Tanner's TheatreWorkers Project. Tanner was
mounting an interdisciplinary production called *S.E.L.A!,* which stood
for South East Los Angeles. TheatreWorkers Project was a performance
group of older unemployed steelworkers, and this piece was to dredge
up the lost histories of L.A.'s dying industrial sector. For the piece
Williams wrote and directed a video play, called *What Do We Do,* about
the divisive effects of unemployment upon a group of people who frequent the same neighborhood bar. A California Arts Council
multicultural artistic assistance grant provided us with help from filmmaker Javier Serrano, who loaned video equipment, shot the piece and
worked with Williams in the editing process.

---

homeless because they want to be
homeless.'' I see them. I don't hear
them. I see them say that people
are homeless because they want to be
homeless. That people are homeless
because they choose to be homeless.

Mr. Chairman, people are not
homeless because they choose to be
homeless. They are homeless for many
reasons of mind and money, but they
are not homeless because they choose
to be homeless.

If no one chooses to be homeless,
then anyone could be homeless.
Thank you, Mr. Chairman.
*(Descends platform and again
becomes Friend.)*
FRIEND   And now MoTo and I, MoTo
must get his rest.

For the following project we cooked up *LAPD Inspects America.* Workshops had been stalled for several months. Various men in the group had brought in fully scripted plays they wanted done, but none of them would fly. They proved impossible to cast—nobody would cooperate.

This was the summer of 1987 and homelessness was in the spotlight. The Pope was coming to L.A., and ironically the city's modest cathedral, where he would be staying, is located next door to the Union Rescue Mission. This was a good excuse for the mayor to order more Skid Row "sweeps." Street people were ordered off the streets at night, a cardboard village on Towne Street was flattened and a sort of concentration camp was opened up on the banks of the L.A. River. The river is actually a concrete drainage ditch, and the camp was dusty and desolate.

After the Pope left, the camp was dismantled and the people turned back to the streets. Many of them moved to Santa Monica and Venice Beach.

LAPD Inspects America started as an investigation of gathering places like these. The group interviewed homeless people on video and audiotape and some of that material was worked into short improvisational exercises on the Venice boardwalk—for instance, two actors panhandling each other for hours on end next to a Men Working sign that fluttered in the rain.

We decided this would be an interesting traveling project, and I wrote a few proposals to visit homeless encampments, do talent shows and interviews there, interact with local social service agencies (Malpede and LAPD board member Carl Graue are both full-time field welfare specialists for Legal Aid) and produce a performance using this material in a local theater or artspace.

Our first chance to try this out came in San Francisco. John was honored for his art career with the Adaline Kent Award at San Francisco Art Institute. The award included a stipend and a month in the gallery at SFAI. Malpede spent both on LAPD.

The month became a "residency" during which the whole gang went to San Francisco. They created an environment in the gallery: a theater made of orange netting, a stage made to look like a Roach Motel, and a display of mounted depositions by mental health professionals and welfare recipients about the horrors of trying to get financial aid from the state and county. The entire group stayed for a performance of *Schwartz,* and a contingent remained to create a new piece. There were talent shows in Boedekker Park in the Tenderloin district to recruit new performers from San Francisco's homeless, workshops at SFAI, a symposium on homelessness featuring local activists, and some performances of the new work, *LAPD Inspects America: San Francisco. Inspects* is still in progress. It is an autobiography of the group, vignettes about the process of creating the residency itself.

The piece as performed in San Francisco and Los Angeles centers mostly on the rigors, disasters and frustrations of traveling with Robert Cloud (not his real name, for reasons of privacy), one of LAPD's original members. Robert is a young Black transvestite with an array of mental and emotional problems and, at that time, an attraction to drugs. Much of the residency was taken up with chasing and "sitting on" Robert. His frequent clashes with students at SFAI produced some insights into contemporary racism. His brushes with the law and forays into the underground kept everybody hopping.

In the performances Malpede played Robert's alter ego, as he had with Beame in *Schwartz,* and as it turned out John played the part alone more often than not, flopping about the stage in a wig, makeup, dress, pantyhose and Robert's voice, smoking ferociously and announcing, "I can do anything I want because I'm a world traveler and John's the biggest chump in America."

A huge backdrop of San Francisco, showing sites important to the action, was painted by SFAI student Nancy Yeo, who later dropped out of school to follow the group to L.A. Social researcher Kristen Kann was also attracted, as was itinerant actress Jenny Bass, who had worked with performance artist Lin Hixson in Chicago. We also acquired Debbie Winski, a political activist from Los Angeles, who became the group's caretaker.

The S.F. piece went through a phase in which a number of Tenderloin people joined the workshop and created a musical about a woman who was "turned out" (became a prostitute) to support her drug habit. Nearly all of them departed before the show, and that whole saga became part of the "script."

Jazzmin was an important part of the birth and direction of *Inspects.* Her contributions, hilarious as they were, always probed the experience for meaning. LAPD was becoming a force of change in her life, and she wanted the performance to reflect that. The more she talked about her feelings, the more the others did too.

Jazz was brought to S.F. on one occasion to "sit on" Robert because only she could handle him. The conflicts everyone felt about Robert and his disruptions became paramount. Ambivalence about the energy he demanded was rampant. A focal scene in the performance depicted Julious Jenkins (played by Arce) proclaiming his mixed feelings about working with Robert: "Robert Cloud is the smallest piece of whale shit on the bottom of the ocean, but even a piece of whale shit has to have a bottom of the ocean to stand on and I say LAPD is it! He stays." (The reason Arce played this scene is that Jenkins ultimately refused to be part of a show Cloud was involved with. In this case a very short female with a Central American accent played a very tall Black man in a flashy wardrobe.)

The moments of growth and revelation came fast and furious as the group lived and worked together during the San Francisco, L.A. (Boyd Street Theater) and San Diego (Sushi, an artspace) residencies. Emotional and sexual alliances were struck and a quasi-familial glue began to take hold. (During one late-night bull session we decided we were a cult.)

Individuals experienced transformations of character and celebrated them on stage. (Ed Rodriguez became "Reverend Chill," adept at "casting out the anti-Elvis.") In San Diego, Arce took over Jazzmin's monologue about Robert, sanity and a sense of "belonging" discovered in LAPD, but in her hands it transmuted to a pronouncement about her own experience, as a Spanish-speaking alien, of the multiple realities of American life.

Jazzmin was going through her own crises at the time. From a free spirit, the queen of Skid Row, she was suddenly transformed into the mother of three teenage girls when her daughters, who had long lived with their grandmother, turned up on her doorstep at the Haskell Hotel. Several hair-raising months later, all three were in residence in a nice little house at 3rd and Union, LAPD having scraped together some cash and a cosigner for the lease. Periodically, Jazzmin drops out of the group to deal with motherhood, the latest crisis being her fifteen-year-old's escape from the family, romance with the "dope man," witness of a murder, and finally, pregnancy. In six months Jazzmin endured more stress and heartache than any of us, including D. J. Smith, who suffered a major accident and knee surgery. The group remains Jazzmin's emotional mainstay, and she let us know it. We help keep her welfare worker in line and the child endangerment people off her back and she, in turn, throws barbeques in her backyard and keeps us laughing.

The sort of information collected by LAPD during its inspection is not what most people expect to hear. Some critics call the work too personal and not political enough, forgetting that the personal *is* political. The stuff of these personal lives is part and parcel of the politics that rules over them. As *LAPD Inspects America* puts it, "You want the cosmetic version or you want the real deal?"

The real deal isn't often a bleeding heart approach to the problems of the poor, and usually something of a surprise. In San Diego, for instance, Lenora Hills surfaced in a workshop at Rachel's, a local women's day shelter. Lenora is a striking young Black woman dressed to the nines, but inexplicably living in a halfway house. Her version of the hardships involved in being homeless in San Diego revolved around the "discrimination" she experienced in all the women's shelters, which she claims are run by lesbians. "I like dick!" she proclaimed righteously in her own defense.

Lenora joined the cast for rehearsals and performances as did "The King of Balboa Park," an itinerant and charismatic storyteller who appeared during a rowdy, friendly parkside LAPD Talent Show. His story of his friend Felix and the local police closely paralleled stories of Robert and was full of irony.

Robert, meanwhile, was embroiled in his own police story. It was a raw sequence of events that proved the final straw. There was an increasingly visible drug addiction, a stabbing incident, a trip to a halfway house, arson, parole violation and finally incarceration. Throughout this Robert received as much sympathy and aid as his dispirited friends could muster, but one of the most pressing ramifications of this situation was his absence from the performances.

In the San Diego version, John performed Robert so convincingly that he was interviewed *as Robert* by three young art students during the intermission. Not until Act II, when John snatched the wig from his head and did a monologue as himself, did they realize who he was.

Besides the belly laughs, LAPD touches most seriously on some of the toughest subjects of our time: racism, homophobia, sexism, betrayal, loneliness, confusion, and pain. It's a constantly shifting panorama of improvised scenes, encompassing virtually any issue that comes up during the process. This is Malpede's generous, lightly held method for creating a theater that is big enough for its subject, that can accommodate the concerns and abilities of a family of desperados like these. (Negotiations are being conducted to take the residency to New Orleans, Tucson, Atlanta, New York, Detroit and again to San Francisco and San Diego.)

At this writing (November 1988), perhaps seventy people have moved through the group, with about ten to twenty now attending the twice-weekly workshops; some have remained with the group since the beginning—fairly astonishing given the transience of Skid Row. The racial mix is about 50 percent Black, 35 percent white, 15 percent Latino. Some have had stage or art-school experience; most have none. About half are on government benefits of some kind. On average one or two participants are temporarily sleeping on the street or in cars; another

10 percent live in Skid Row hotels. In the last year, some of the money earned in performance has been donated by the group to a fund to help provide individual members with the crippling security deposits required to rent decent housing.

While there have been dozens of rave reviews and grants for LAPD, there have also been bad reviews, skirmishes with the law, serious illnesses, angry departures, and long periods of confusion and desperation. (Most recently one longtime member was critically disabled when he was thrown from the sixth-story window of a downtown building, and another departed to live with her parents after losing two of her sisters in a plane crash.) Maintaining a life in art certainly isn't easy under these circumstances. But what probably keeps most hanging on is the excitement of change, of transformation. There's no question LAPD offers its members something essential. The basic issue of street life may not, after all, be hunger, but freedom. And that's a basic issue of art life too. Because Malpede has the nerve to leave the door always open, LAPD offers an experience of real artistic freedom, especially sweet when so far freedom's been just another word for nothing left to lose.

Note

1. *South of the Clouds* was part of a group of theater pieces billed together as *Outcasts.* Also included were *December* by Matthew Ghoulish and *The Magician* by John O'Keefe.

References

Apple, Jacki. "Where the Sidewalk Ends," *L.A. Weekly,* 4–10 July 1986: 21.

Bebb, Bruce. "*Outcasts:* Good Intentions as Theater," *Los Angeles Reader,* 27 June 1986: 11.

Burnham, Linda Frye. Interview with John Malpede, August 1986.

———. "Los Angeles Poverty Department," *High Performance* 9, no. 3 (1986): 76.

Clancy, Frank. "Lawyers Team Up to Fight for the Homeless," *L.A. Times,* 18 September 1986, sec. 5:1.

Decker, Cathleen. "Skid Row—Living on a Dead-End," *L.A. Times,* 2 May 1986, 2:1.

Durland, Steve. "Hot Shorts," *High Performance* 8, no. 4 (1985): 11–12.

Fox, Mary Jo. "Outcasts," *L.A. Weekly,* 27 June–3 July 1986: 59.

Hughes, Kathleen A. "Street People Find a Home in the Theater," *The Wall Street Journal,* 22 July 1986: 28.

Lynn, Maude. "Theater Is Their Home," *L.A. Weekly,* 20–26 June 1986: 30.

Roderick, Kevin. "Horse Patrols Ride Herd on Transients," *L.A. Times,* 21 July 1984, sec. 2:1.

Solomon, Alisa. "Unaccommodated Men—And Women," *The Village Voice,* 20 May 1986: 12.

Stayton, Richard. "'Outcasts' Hits Home with Skid Row Actors," *Los Angeles Herald Examiner,* 27 June 1986: 36.

4

Two Lines of Sight and
an Unexpected Connection:
Helen Mayer Harrison and Newton Harrison

Arlene Raven

Helen Mayer Harrison and Newton Harrison's installations contain a variety of artworks that together document projects the Harrisons have carried out in cities, rural regions and even in bodies of water all over the world. Their two-decade artistic collaboration and much longer marriage is their basic model for discourse. As two voices, they engage in Socratic questioning that becomes a method for developing their works.

In presenting their projects, the Harrisons wish to open their discussion. Their documents in art spaces stand for the sites they describe and also become sites in which a significant interchange can take place. Conversation that reestablishes human exchange about the social and physical environments is the primary aim of the Harrisons' work.

This article describes the approach the Harrisons take as artists, an approach that differs from those of other professionals who tackle environmental problems. Helen and Newton Harrison use the artist's tools of myth and metaphor. Their eco-feminism and eco-aesthetics, as well as their New Age optimism (that transformation of the environment and human consciousness is necessary and possible) are philosophical underpinnings for works that have had practical applications and measurable impact on their sites. They have reclaimed waste land, saved a species, halted erosion. They have worked with city governments and planners to enact transformations that are unique to their vision. Their imaginative solutions to ecological problems have sometimes succeeded when planning professionals have failed even to apprehend that a

---

This article originally appeared in *High Performance*, No. 40 (1987).

problem existed. Although they have made what can be called prod-
ucts, their work rests in a process of mutual thinking and imaginatively
engaging with and in the world.

Introduction

What is art in the environment supposed to be or do? Can such art just
sit there, surrounded by nature? Or hang in galleries in the art environment and simply refer to ecological issues? Does environmental art have
to be ecological? If so, what—in practical terms—does that mean? By
what standards should it be said to have accomplished or not accomplished its purpose? And by whom? Art critics, environmentalists,
scientists, or the public?

Helen Mayer Harrison and Newton Harrison make no claims to
answer these questions, to fit into any established categories of art and
environment, or to fulfill any standards but their own. They insist that
their work, at its core, shifts fundamental designs in human perception and calls an observer to participate in recreating a dynamic, healing balance between nature and people. The Harrisons are artists who
rediscover and recreate physical, social, philosophical and mythic
environments—with artistry, originality, and exemplary integrity.

I.

Helen Mayer Harrison and Newton Harrison began a conversation in
1970. After eighteen years, their discourse continues uninterrupted.
Mutual thinking, the basis for all of their collaborations, contextualizes
works to such an extent that they titled a recent interview about new
projects, "Nobody Told Us When to Stop Thinking." They embark
" . . . **when we perceive an anomaly in the environment that is the
result of opposing beliefs or contradictory metaphors. It is the moment
when belief has become outrageous that offers opportunity to create
new spaces, first for the mind and thereafter in everyday . . . always
compose[d] with left-over spaces and invisible places.**"[1]

II.

> We did a work for an exhibition called "Land Art" . . . at Bard College . . . we took
> a look at the coffee pot. You know, we like good coffee. It was so encrusted with
> salt from the drinking water you could hardly believe it. So we developed a work
> about cleaning the water. The ironic part of it was that the water purification would
> be done right there in the gallery. Therefore, the only place on campus where you
> could get pure water would be in the art gallery.[2]

The Socratic dialogue which distinguishes the Harrison relationship appears as myth and metaphor in their work. *The Lagoon Cycle,* created over a period of twelve years, opened at the Los Angeles County Museum of Art on November 18, 1987. It is a poetic meditation, asking questions and mulling over these questions together as "Lagoonmaker" and "Witness." As Carter Ratcliff observed,

> One meets the Witness and the Lagoonmaker in the introductory panel of the Cycle. That is the first of numberless occasions for wondering to what degree the Witness is Helen Mayer Harrison and the Lagoonmaker is Newton Harrison. . . . From the start the Lagoonmaker and the Witness treat large questions of creation and self-creation, will, and belief and action. . . . The Witness and the Lagoonmaker have learned to improvise. As they create the Lagoons through which they travel, they accept the "discourse of lagoon life" as a metaphorical guide. Or at least they struggle toward that acceptance. If our culture undertakes the same struggle and accepts the same guide, perhaps we'll find ways to adapt even to ecological disaster. Our adaptation may even be, in the Harrisons' word, "graceful."[3]

But the relationship of Harrison to Harrison is also a concrete comradeship within a marriage that has endured thirty-five years. Domestic, everyday. And an intriguing aspect of the two personas of *The Lagoon Cycle* is their clarifying fidelity to aspects of male and female, nature and culture. They weave their colloquy to reconnect these personas and thus initiate a healing that stands against the antagonism of mechanistic culture for unruly nature. As metaphor and example, their collaboration also reconsiders the plunder of world ecology and the fissure between men and women. Their eco-feminism and -aesthetics spring from this point of departure.

III.

In light of their unusual approach to artmaking on the one hand, and their commitment to artistic identity on the other, the Harrisons' view of the function of art in contemporary society is complex. For Helen, **"The structure underlying our work is different because the assumptions underlying our work are more complicated."**[4]

Referring to a historical example, Newton reasoned that "if you go to look at the Parthenon, you see a truly astounding work of art. But those artists were totally at the service of the culture's imperialistic impulses. If I took the Parthenon as a model, I'd say it was the job of the art to glorify that culture."[5]

"Conversely," Helen adds, "earlier art was probably at the service of religious cults or impulses, although we can only theorize what such impulses might be that could lead to such diverse expressions in time

THE FIRST LAGOON: THE LAGOON AT UPOUVELI
This image, from *The Lagoon Cycle* originated in 1985 at the Johnson Museum of
Cornell University, Ithaca, New York, and was installed most recently at the Los
Angeles County Museum of Art in 1987.

The Lagoon Cycle is a narrative installation that features seven lagoon projects
described in maps, drawings, and photographs created by Helen Mayer Harrison
and Newton Harrison. The images contain handwritten texts that trace the
processes and consequences involved in the projects.

The Lagoon Cycle is named for the esturial lagoons that are endangered
everywhere. The lagoons are used as a metaphor for life itself.

The story is that of two characters called the Witness and the Lagoonmaker who
begin a search for a ''hardy creature who can live under museum conditions'' and
become transformed by their search.

(Photo copyright: Harrison)

and space as fecundity figures like the Venus of Willendorf or delicately carved miniatures like the head of Our Lady of Brassempouy or the Bulland Vulture figures of Catal Hayük or the covered skull from Jericho with its inlaid cowry shell eyes.''

Commenting on modernism, Newton said, ''Art, like all aspects of modernism, is fractured, bifurcated and rebifurcated, in little bits and pieces. We have decorative art, deconstructionists, Duchamp leftovers. Various forms of realism, conceptualism. Our work is influenced by all of them. In truth, we go back to the story of the place's becoming and if we can be part of that story, enhance it. I don't know or care if that is 'far out.'''

In contrast to current emphasis on product, he explained that

> **I don't think about our art as product at all. As a guiding thought, ''product'' is counterproductive.** Every once in a while we will make an array of images. We hope people buy them. But generally we make installations which stand for the place and as meeting ground for discourse, which are models for how to perceive and enact our work. We pack our ''products'' in boxes and tubes and hope some day somebody will put them up somewhere. But the most important parts of our work are nonproducts. In the reshaping of a place, our work exists in bits and pieces of the planning process of the place. In a gallery, those parts are attributed to us. But when enacted in the real environment, we become anonymous. We are both bigger than our plan, and more anonymous.

Helen Harrison underlined that, in contrast to city planners, the two had no vested interest in nor any sense that they must choose between loyalty to either art or the environment. ''One of the things that happens to people, even the best of the planners, is that they have a vested interest in getting *something* done.''[6]

Rather, the question of conflict ''comes up when money is made available,'' said Newton. ''We will take that project over a little better project which is unfunded. And that's the only conflict—when someone else is trying to modify our participation.''

The Harrisons have been compared and contrasted in almost every interpretation of their work to earth artists, survivalist artists, conceptual and performance artists, and even the Hudson River School of landscape painters active in the nineteenth century, and earlier twentieth-century social realists. Musing about Michael Heizer, Helen admired ''the vast energy put into those early big cuts and shapes in the desert that are inherently gestural, simply primary structures in another context. They are transactional with museum spaces, not with the earth. They are involved primarily with forms.''

In ''Earth Art: A Study in Ecological Politics'' (*Art in the Land: A Critical Anthology of Environmental Art,* edited by Alan Sonfist),

Michael Auping says of Heizer: "Heizer has often argued that it is naive to criticize his work from an ecological standpoint, given the fact that modern industry is rearranging the landscape on a scale that dwarfs any of his endeavors."

Quipped Newton: "No art is as intrusive as a freeway intersection. I'd love to see Heizer take up 10 percent of Los Angeles. I'd vote for him."

"Christo's contribution was to 'redefine how big you can get,' added Helen. "His *Running Fence* didn't do more to the environment than a picnic. The ecological balance can readily restate itself. James Turrell makes a very small move, not taking your now for granted. That's economy of means at a very high level."

IV.

Cruciform Tunnel is a work of art that proposes one single move that will engender three consequences of simultaneous value to the urban and natural communities within the boundaries of the city of San Diego.

If a tunnel is cut under Genesee, reconnecting the presently divided canyons, and this tunnel is constructed in such a manner as to permit a bicycle path, the intermittent flow of water, the movement of small game, and of people on foot, these remarkable opportunities emerge . . .

The Harrisons have an idea for San Diego, where they live and work. *Cruciform Tunnel* would extend under Genesee Drive, rejoin two nature reserves (the Torrey Pines Reserve and the UCSD nature reserve), the Penasquitos Lagoon and the Pacific Ocean. Water from the UCSD campus would now be channelled to the Penasquitos Lagoon. And a new bicycle path from their campus at UCSD to Sorrento Valley would be created.

Cruciform Tunnel is, indisputably, ecological art—art concerned with (improving) the environment. But the Harrisons are not primarily motivated by the need for a bicycle path or even increasing the overall ecological value of the site for *Cruciform Tunnel.* Nor are they mainly concerned with the aesthetics of the tunnel or the resulting beauty of the landscape, though these might be desirable and even necessary results of their work. Rather **"We go to a place, anywhere!, and engage in the story of the place. We make a representation of the story, of its own becoming. We add a story to it. Our work is, as best we can make it, the poetry of the whole."**

Newton Harrison's explanation of concerns is headily abstract, and poetic itself. Yet the Harrisons' works have practical applications, require careful research and have often had a measurable impact on their sites. How do their concerns differentiate their works from standard ecological research?

"When did standard ecological research," responded Newton, "begin with a medical metaphor, turn itself into poetry, turn back into a proposal, shift into a performance, and then begin a process of nagging a city council? Standard ecological researchers made a series of experiments with canyons of San Diego. We then did a work based on this research, and proposed *Cruciform Tunnel*. A lot of our work depends on illuminating ecological research by others, which sits in limbo, in an untransformed state."

V.

"We have also done standard ecological research," said Newton. "For the Second Lagoon ["Sea Grant," for which an artificial environment for crabs was constructed], we did environmental and habitat studies, as well as observed and concluded through observation that cannibalism [in crabs] reduces itself when the environment is complicated."

Our 1973 Sea Grant crabs laid out experimental grounds [for the development of a commercial aquaculture system for the crab]. Our method is available and can be used. We believe in theoretical research. Although our work points in certain theoretical directions, we haven't engaged in theoretical research.

> **But**
> **the tank is part of an experiment**
> **and the experiment is a metaphor for a lagoon**
> **if the metaphor works**
> **the experiment will succeed**
> **and the crabs will flourish**
> **after all**
> **this metaphor is only a representation**
> **based on observing a crab in a lagoon**
> **and listening to stories**[7]

However, when it becomes necessary to do original research, we can and have. Nonetheless there is a big difference between original research and a work of art and our focus is on the work of art. But we define art broadly.

VI.

The fluidity of professional roles and tasks with which the artists are able to move through researching, planning, proposing and carrying

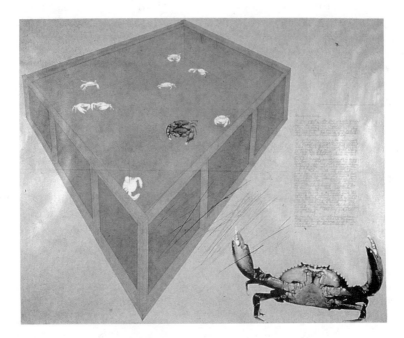

THE SECOND LAGOON: SEA GRANT
But
the tank is not a lagoon
nor is it a tidal pond
nor does the mixing of fresh and salt
waters
make it an estuary
Filters are not the cleansing of the tides
water from a hose is not a monsoon
lights and heaters are not the sun
and crabs in a tank do not make a life web
— The Witness
text from ''The Second Lagoon''
(Photo copyright: Harrison)

IMAGE FROM BARRIER ISLANDS DRAMA, 1983
Barrier Islands Drama (Wenger Gallery, San Diego, California) describes in ballad form the destruction of the fertile mangrove nurseries by the encroaching Australian pine, introduced into the Sarasota, Florida, area in 1938. The mangrove and the pine are metaphors for attitudes toward the land and the environment.

Spoils Pile was a 40-acre reclamation project at Artpark in Lewiston, New York. The Harrisons collected topsoil and organic matter in autumn to make soil and later plant a meadow (a three-year project). After 3,000 truckloads were gathered and half the area was covered, the directors of Artpark stopped the project because it was too large.

Meditations on the Sacramento River, the Delta and the Bays at San Francisco argues that over time a land division system, which destroys topsoil, and a river-polluting system have been invented to develop the Central Valley of California for industrial farming. The Harrisons see the system as exploitive and self-cancelling, with a dust bowl the outcome.

—The Lagoon Cycle
texts from the chronology by Ann Trautman

(Photo copyright: Harrison)

out their projects in their own minds has very often become problematic when the process of their work is thrust into the nuts-and-bolts world of sponsors, agencies, sites and workers. When the Harrisons attempted to make earth and plant a meadow on top of forty acres of rock pile—according to them, **"a physical act of reclamation,"** called *Spoils Pile* (1977) and planned for the refilled old canyon quarry at Artpark—they were forced by Artpark authorities to stop after twenty acres were covered with soil, ostensibly due to the (too large) scope of their project.

Meditations on the Sacramento River, the Delta and the Bays at San Francisco (1977) was based on the same principle of reclamation. Said Newton, **"We made a work projected to impact the level of public awareness."**

"Our work was an extended argument in many media," added Helen, "from billboards to posters to radio and newpaper spots, to a museum mural. Heads of environmental agencies later quoted our own words in the newspapers without crediting us."

In 1982, they created *Thinking about the Mangrove and the Pine* (their working title for *Barrier Islands Drama*), a site-specific work for the John and Mable Ringling Museum in Sarasota, Florida. They considered the pines that were brought in from Australia to Florida for

---

The Harrisons' Text:

1983
At first seeing herons feeding in a little river next to the Performing Arts Center only blocks from downtown, we realized that this river, despite all odds, was still alive, so we wrote

To the Mayor and the City Council:
Can it be you have forgotten your
    river?
There appears to be no comment
    on it in your city plan
This river, the Guadalupe River,
    which meanders neglected . . .
Be
Cleansed by greater releases at its
    headwaters, dredged
Where silt build-up

decorative purposes. The pines had unbalanced the native ecology, taking up mangrove root and sun space. As the mangroves disappeared, the pines took over water's edge.

> Take Longboat Key, for instance
> Where
> That pushy shallowrooted immigrant
> That exotic and graceful pine from Australia
> Colonizes behind that oceanic nursery of mangrove roots
> When
> Displacing the mangrove
> Gaining water's edge
> It topples in the wind[8]

How can their voices be consistently aligned with their values when they are not in complete control of the process by which their projects are realized? In fact, they cannot. Also, as Helen noted, "We cannot really know the consequences of our actions. That is why we really need environmental impact studies, even on creativity."

Has damned the flow, have its
  ecology restored, its bridges
  restated,
A serpentine walkway designed for
  its banks and extensions
Made to the
Refugia area wherever there is
  vacant land
"The refugia will be to the city as
  the hedgerow is to the field"

1987
Finally we saw the new plan for the river and realized that, although they had taken our language of meander and park and refuge, the city had decided that they could do that and still put the river in concrete. Thus where the herons used to feed be-

came concrete platforms with steps and trees planted in neat holes and we wrote

To the Mayor and City Council:
Can it be you have forgotten what
  a river is?
There appears to be no space for
  one in your plan for water
  features
Therefore we propose
That
In the last available space for a
  park in Silicon Valley
The space between the railroad
  tracks
And the airport
Between the Guadalupe Express-
  way and Coleman Avenue . . .

VII.

I was in Sao Paulo putting up a piece in the last Biennale when someone told me there was a place nearby where babies were born in the usual numbers but some of them without brain parts. I asked the obvious and he said it was the smog. I was told that in Cubatao life was cheap. People told me that the city was surrounded by multinational chemical companies where the chemical outfall into the bay and nearby canals was so bad that the surface of the water caught fire last year killing many in the adjoining favella. I asked if there were environmental laws and he said there might be.

—text from *Breathing Cubatao,* a work by the Harrisons

The Harrisons' art participates in the "New Age" and in its optimism that transformation of the environment and human consciousness is necessary and possible.[9] With eco-feminists and environmentalists, they reexamine the European scientific revolution and simultaneous rise of our modern market culture. But while utilizing contemporary technology, they question the model of the cosmos as a machine rather than an organism, a (machine) model which has for centuries sanctioned, de facto, domination over nature and women. The existence of the Harrisons' work calls for the contributions of the "fathers" of

---

The Harrisons' Text (continued)

Let a new riverbed be cut
A new meander for the Guadalupe
    waters
That replaces the length of river to
    be put in concrete
Let the old channel remain as now
    planned for flood control
But let this new section of river be
    the meander and the refugia
That the old river once was and
    could again be.
"Again the refugia will be to the
    river as the hedgerow is to the
    field."

modern science—Francis Bacon, William Harvey, Rene Descartes, Thomas Hobbes, and Isaac Newton—to be reevaluated in light of the mechanistic roots of their modernism. Most important, the Harrisons' work both presents and suggests alternative organismic paradigms which must temper the catastrophic contemporary consequences of the long-running machine age if humans and nature are to survive and thrive.[10]

VIII.

Baltimore Promenade *consisted of mural-size photographs of the area with text. An organized walk on December 13, led by the mayor of Baltimore, other officials, and the president of the Maryland Institute, dramatized the Harrisons' proposal.*

—text from the chronology by
Ann Trautman, "Baltimore Promenade,"
Maryland Institute, College of Art

Their particular blend of aesthetics and politics evolved from their working process and their focus on conceptual, artistic and ethical issues. "**[A]n aesthetic exists always in interaction with, and in commentary on, a larger social context. . . . [T]o isolate an aesthetic and attempt to make it unrelated to other things is impossible.**"[11]

With their connections between their aesthetics and the social context for producing art in mind, it seems natural that the Harrisons would name as imperialist and unjust the disruption of social intercourse and physical movement as artistic "problems" to be confronted. Their propensity for making and altering maps—appropriately enough, a preoccupation of visual artists during the Renaissance—can also be traced to their aesthetics, from which originates the impulse to restore the relationship between the physical ground and the humans inhabiting that ground. They want to create actions that not only stand beside but work to undo domination and manipulation of nature in the service of man-made hierarchical systems.

The environments for their environmental art are, therefore, the human and societal environments, in a dialogue with physical environments. The Harrisons are never motivated by a sentimental love of trees or animals or unspoiled rivers, but of justice, balance, good sense and people. When addressing problems of city planning in San Jose, Atlanta or Baltimore, they observe when basic human activities—in these cases, walking—have been disrupted because urban planning served other needs. They unearth the cultural values embedded in systems of domination that make "other needs" priorities, rather than simply battling in the realm of politics and law.

In the service of their central concern—reestablishing discourse—through their central method—opening dialogue—they proposed a promenade for Baltimore based on their conviction that

> a promenade is both an activity and a place, a stage on which people in a community meet and mix. . . . A promenade is marked by people physically tuning to common movement and rhythm. A promenade is an activity common in all urban ecologies, a basic homeostatic or self-regulating mechanism by which the community as a whole maintains awareness of the well-being of the individuals who comprise it, and by which the sense of community is reaffirmed collectively.[12]

The city's Baltimore Harbor Project was already established when the Harrisons took up their analysis. They proposed connecting the Harbor Project to the city's cultural center in one direction, and to a park, which already existed, in the other. As Susan Platt put it,

> They visualized this connection by simply pointing out that, by means of two twenty-minute promenades, people could move out of the self-contained nucleus of the harbor, surrounded by its eight-lane noose of highways, to the surrounding city. All that the artists suggested was a walk that made use of the city as it already existed—they simply drew a line on a map to mark the walk. The total cost to the city was that of moving one bridge and adding a stoplight, and the result was "Baltimore Promenade/a concept for making a Baltimore walkable (again)/a proposal inviting involvement and action."[13]

And, as Helen Harrison says, "The ideas about redevelopment that we had went into the city plan and are occurring in city time—that is in scores of years—but they are happening."

IX.

If one accepts (and I do) the fully artistic and fully ecological nature of the art of Helen Mayer Harrison and Newton Harrison, then they are legitimately creative resources for identifying the most pressing environmental concerns and suggesting the opening phrases of our communion with our earthly surroundings.

"We have focused a fair amount on water," they said. "Water is a very critical bio-indicator. If water remains pure, and rivers are maintained, then many other good things happen. Pollution into oceans can be reduced, for instance. One can just as well spend time on trees. Or the stork, as we did in Kassel [Germany, for Documenta 8, 1987]."

We're really not messianic. We're just two people putting one foot in front of another, asking for reasonably ethical behavior. We've empowered *ourselves* through our work. And our greatest concern is establishing models wherein *anybody* can start *anywhere* and radiate out change and transformation by engaging the discourse. The most important thing is to begin anywhere, and get cracking.

Notes

1. Statement, *Helen Mayer Harrison and Newton Harrison: New Projects*, Grey Art Gallery, New York, March 17–April 18, 1987, reprinted in ''Nobody Told Us When to Stop Thinking,'' *Grey Matters: The Quarterly Bulletin of The Grey Art Gallery and Study Center* (New York University, N.S.) 1, no. 2 (Spring, 1987).

2. Helen Harrison, statement, paraphrased in *Grey Matters*.

3. Carter Ratcliff, ''A Compendium of Possibilities,'' *The Lagoon Cycle* (Ithaca, N.Y.: Herbert F. Johnson Museum of Art, 1985), p. 13.

4. Helen Harrison, *Grey Matters*.

5. Newton Harrison, interview with Arlene Raven, October 1987. All quotations of Newton Harrison and Helen Harrison unless otherwise cited are from this interview.

6. Helen Harrison, *Grey Matters*.

7. Text from *The Lagoon Cycle* by Helen and Newton Harrison.

8. Text from *Barrier Islands Drama* by Helen and Newton Harrison.

9. See Linda McGreevy, ''Improvising the Future: The Eco-aesthetics of Newton and Helen Harrison,'' *Arts Magazine*, 62, no. 3 (November 1987): 68 for a discussion of ''New Age'' philosophies and the therapeutic aspect of the Harrisons' work.

10. See Carolyn Merchant, *The Death of Nature: Women, Ecology, and the Scientific Revolution* (San Francisco and New York: Harper & Row, 1980).

11. Newton Harrison, interview with Michael Auping, in *Common Ground: Five Artists in the Florida Landscape* (Sarasota, Fla.: The John and Mable Ringling Museum of Art, 1982).

12. Helen and Newton Harrison, from their statement about *Baltimore Promenade*.

13. Susan Platt, ''Helen Mayer Harrison and Newton Harrison: An Urban Discourse,'' *Artweek*.

5

A New Artistic Continent

Guillermo Gómez-Peña

The art of American "minorities" such as Mexican-Americans, Guillermo Gómez-Peña's subject, has more often than not existed outside of galleries and museums. When an exhibition by Chicano artists does appear on the American artistic landscape, artworks are often distorted by their context.

Even in advocacy criticism over the past quarter-century, Chicano art, like Black art or feminist art, has been considered as a subcategory of (already marginalized) socially conscious art. But outside of an Anglo-American-centered conceptual milieu, the kinship between Chicano/Latino art and Latin American cultures of liberation can be seen and appreciated. Explaining "indigenismo," Gómez-Peña describes the alliances among Chicanos, American Indians and Mexicans as the basis for a transcontinental grassroots consciousness manifested in a unified artistic expression.

Gómez-Peña redesigns the "artistic continent" of Chicano art by offering information that changes perceptions of avant-garde developments in socially based art. He demonstrates with the example of post-modernist artistic practice that Latino, Mexican, and Chicano artists led North American and European artists but were not credited for their leadership because criticism is blindly centered in North America and Europe.

Gómez-Peña's investigation suggests a restructuring of history and criticism. He makes a convincing case for reseeing criticism as well as

This article originally appeared in Spanish in *La Opinion* (Los Angeles) (November 1985) and *El Mexicano* (Baja, California) (November 1985). An extended and updated version was commissioned by *High Performance*, No. 35 (1986), which version was also published in the catalogue of the "Made in Aztlan" festival of Chicano Arts (Centro Cultural de la Raza, San Diego). The Introduction appears here for the first time.

art from an antiracist, anticentrist view. His is a cautionary perspective even in this book about art in the public interest with a North American focus, yet his position is inclusive. "Anyone, including the Anglo-Americans and others who share the dream of a continental culture," Gómez-Peña writes, "can be part of it."

My original impulse to write this text was to instigate a dialogue between alternative art practitioners and writers from Mexico and the Chicano milieus of the U.S. Today in 1989, four years later, a lot has been accomplished and many writers and artists from both countries have been exploring meticulously the dark areas I was merely pointing at. What four years ago was just theory is now a cultural reality.
                                                                —G. G.-P.

Chicano art has been mostly understood as an isolated phenomenon with its own foundation, processes and dilemmas, a flaming entity that burns as a reaction to mainstream Anglo culture, but seems to float independently from Latin American contemporary art.

In 1986, it is necessary to begin the epic enterprise of placing it within the large-scale artistic map. But in order to achieve this, we must first uncover its relationship with the larger Latin American culture.

This text by no means attempts to accomplish this purpose. I am neither a critic nor an historian. I am merely an instigator, and these words are meant to trigger the curiosity of others who are better equipped to link, redefine, compare and explain. The design of a new artistic continent is urgently needed. For now, I am hoping to detect certain correspondences and parallel attitudes between the Latino artists of both Americas.

The artistic processes that Chicano, Latino and Mexican arts have experienced touch the North American–European networks only tangentially. With the exception of those of us who have spent a long time working within a North American–European context, "postmodernism" seems a meaningless term.

The leap from modernism to postmodernism was also that from the concept of the artist as a bohemian to the artist as a social thinker; from the microcosm of the studio to society; from art as unigeneric to interdisciplinary, and, most important, from culture as a static, self-contained system to a dynamic one encompassing multiple territories of thought and action (semiotics, politics, social anthropology, media, education, etc.).

When the New York and European art worlds were making this leap, Chicano and Latino artists didn't participate formally in this historic breakthrough. Why? Either it wasn't a culturally relevant leap to make (our intellectual needs were other at the time), or it simply wasn't available to us. One had to be a student of an exclusive art school, subscribe to specialized art magazines, or live in New York.

A curious fact is that Chicano and Mexican artists, with no exposure to the winds of the avant-garde, much less to the radiation of Western rationalism, had already been involuntarily practicing techniques, methods and attitudes that strongly resembled those of the newly discovered *"ismo."*

Verbigratia: The concept of "deconstruction" (to break down structurally a specific tradition and to reorder its parts) had long been practiced by artists who, utilizing the traditions of Mexican folk art (*retablos, altares, milagros*[1] toys, miniatures, etc.), had "recontextualized" them and imbued them with wild pop culture iconography. We must remember, for example, the work of Mexican artists Jesus Reyes and Benjamin Serrano, who were using mass cultural imagery long before Warhol and Oldenburg decided it was all right to do it.

Intrinsically postmodern techniques, like the "pastiche" and the juxtapositions of borrowed texts and images, had also been used by *artistas graficos* who were responding to a tradition that had long before discovered these modes. The obvious example is Posada, Mexico's top nineteenth-century engraver.

The streets of Latin American cities and Chicano barrios have always operated as "free stages" for para-artistic events of an interdisciplinary nature that strongly resemble what we now call "performance art."

Though not always consciously, many Chicano, Latino and Mexican artists have often thought of the artistic métier as a means to paint or sculpt society. They have also conceived of public spaces as a context for creation and substitutes for the "gallery system." Joseph Beuys and Allan Kaprow weren't the first artists to come to those realizations. For us, the role of the artist commonly extends beyond the formal art world; for example, in an attempt to codify the memory of post-revolutionary Mexico, the mural movement of the 1930s was carefully orchestrated by Minister of Education José Vasconcelos, who was himself a poet and a philosopher.

Artists functioning as intruders into the mass media, as counter-cultural journalists, organizers, educators, proponents of debates, utopian activists, cultural topographers and/or spokespersons of their entire communities, are frequently found in Chicano and Latino America. And their actions are not exactly considered "avant-garde." They are

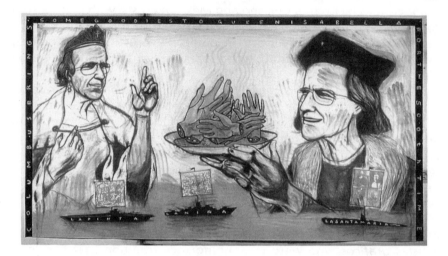

merely responding to a tradition that considers art as an intrinsic part of life, and culture an ongoing process of negotiation.

These forms of "involuntary postmodernism" should be acknowledged as such by North American–European critics. Now that "postmodernism" is just another identified *ismo,* and its history is being written, it appears to be absolutely necessary to redefine its parameters.

In the mid-to-late sixties, Chicano artists working in various media began forming groups like the Mexican American Liberation Front (San Francisco Bay Area), Teatro Campesino (San Joaquin Valley) and Toltecas en Aztlán (San Diego). For them, art and political activism were either equivalent or complementary, and their objectives were mostly outside the parameters of art: access to education, support of the Farmworkers' movement, protection against police brutality and participation in the larger political process, to name a few.

Parallel to this, Mexico City was experiencing perhaps its most drastic transformation of consciousness since the Mexican revolution. The student movement of '68 began a new era in our understanding of "the public sphere," radicalizing the intellectuals and making the arts an important territory for political debate.

In both *Califas*[2] and Mexico, artists were utilizing their art forms (posters, banners, impromptu murals, mimeographic prints, songs, and guerrilla theater skits) to distribute new ideas in rapid and effective ways.

These parallel attitudes weren't purely coincidental. Nor is it enough to say that "change was in the air." The fact that Mexico City and Berkeley were two of the main nerve centers of student activism clearly shows how both *Califas* and Mexico, in their quest to dismantle authoritarianism, were undergoing a similar process of reevaluation of social and cultural values.

In the early seventies, many Chicano artists became involved with the American Indian Movement. In San Diego, some even travelled to the Hopi Reservation and began designing alliances with their "red brothers," who became their pre-Hispanic avatars. These alliances included both an agenda for political unity and self-determination and a quest to revive and maintain pre-Hispanic art forms.

COLUMBUS BRINGS SOME GOODIES TO QUEEN ISABELA FOR THE 500TH TIME
Enrique Chagoya, 1992
Charcoal, pastel and acrylic on paper, 5′ × 9′

This *indigenismo* (movement toward sympathy with indigenous peoples) was criticized by other Chicanos who believed that the true fighting grounds were the cities, and by the Anglo mainstream who thought of *indigenismo* as just another B-culture branching out of the hippie movement.

Once the *indigenismo Chicano* became consolidated, some of the people involved realized it had been a useful step to structure the cultural self and took off into an uncertain modernity. As of now, a few remain completely involved.

At that time, what very few people understood about *indigenismo* was its innovative nature. By recognizing the Chicano condition in the light of that of American Indians, and by extension their Mexican *compadres* (the *concheros*[3]), they created the basis for a true transcontinental consciousness at a grassroots level. This consciousness didn't acknowledge the existence of the border, nor the European-derived governments and mainstream cultures of the U.S. and Mexico.

An inevitable analogy comes to mind. Since the late fifties, the leading writers of the so-called "Latin American Boom"[4] had been speaking of *pan-latinoamericanismo*. Inspired by the old dreams of José Martí and Bolívar, they proposed an all Latino-mestizo culture beyond geopolitical boundaries. This culture was founded upon the premise that all Latin American countries share a pre-Hispanic past, a history of double colonization, a language and the recognition of a common continental rival: the bitter heritage of the Iberic tyrannies meticulously intertwined with the history of multinational North America. What these visionary writers overlooked was the fact that Chicanos and Latinos in the U.S. were also connected to these principles.

Today, when we attempt to define a contemporary Latino consciousness and culture, we must acknowledge *pan-latinoamericanismo* and *indigenismo* as being both seminal and integral concepts for artists working on both sides of the border. We must also realize that the issue is no longer an ethnic or nationalistic one. Anyone, including the Anglo-Americans and others who share the dream of a continental culture, can be part of it.

The situation is critical and unavoidable: Latin America lives and breathes in the United States and vice versa. And this is a demographic, economic and cultural fact. Whether we want it or not, the edge of the border is widening, and the geopolitics are becoming less precise day by day.

The term *grupo* or *colectiva* defines a group of artists working in different media with similar goals, operating in mostly public or nonspecialized spaces upon the premises of collective/collaborative creation.

This concept flourished in Mexico City during the seventies, and there it soon became the most significant artistic contribution of the decade. The most influential *grupos* were *Suma, Peyote y la Co., Proceso-Pentágono,* and *Tepito Arte Acá.*

Parallel to this, *grupos* were also emerging throughout *Califas.* Some like Asco (Los Angeles) and the Royal Chicano Air Force (Sacramento) were interdisciplinary. Others like Self-Help Graphics and the East Los Streetscapers, both from Los Angeles, were dealing mainly with the visual arts.

What amazes me is—and members or exmembers of *grupos* from both sides of the border have confirmed—that the Chicano and Mexican *grupos* weren't really familiar with one another. They may have known of each other's existence, but never established any sort of ongoing dialogue that could explain their similarities.

We must also remember that it was during the seventies, and thanks to the *grupos,* that more contemporary media and genres like performance art, video, installation, book-art, mail-art and sound-art became popular in both *Califas* and *la capital.*[5]

This makes me think that our contemporary responses to society and culture on both sides of the border correspond. Yet, we cannot explain these correspondences as being symptomatic of the overall Western art process. If on one hand it is true that the use of the new media was first pioneered in Europe and the U.S., its interrelated use by the *grupos,* for social and political purposes, is *sui generis* and cannot possibly be explained in the same light. Here we have an artistic lagoon that needs to be carefully explored.

The similarities between the Mexican and Chicano artistic manifestations of the past fifteen years are too many and too obvious to be disregarded as pure coincidence.

Verbigratia: The original Chicano *teatros—Campesino, La Esperanza* and *Mestizo*—were aesthetically and ideologically akin to *Cleta* and *Mascarones* from Mexico.

The Mexican *Neográfica* (mimeographic prints, xerox, rubber stamps and manipulated media images) shared materials and intentions with the early work of Chicanos René Yañez and David Avalos.

Chicano filmmakers like Jesus Treviño and Gregory Nava, in their attempt to make meaningful independent films that explore the condition of Chicanos and Latinos in the U.S., aren't totally disassociated from Mexicans Renato Leduc, Eduardo Maldonado and Nicolás Chavarría.[6] Again, both contingents seem to know very little about each other.

The incredible number and diversity of murals in the Chicano barrios can only be paralleled with the hundreds of regional murals generated by the Mexican H_2O Project.[7]

Syncretic altars that attempt to combine differing beliefs, folk-inspired objects with political subtext and mixed-media constructions inspired by current pop culture and mass-media events, are found on both sides of the border.

When photographers Lourdes Grobet and Graciela Iturbide portray the tragic/comic souls of Mexican people living on the cultural fringes, they are involuntarily sharing an aesthetic sensibility with many Chicano photographers documenting the crevices of barrio life.

Los Lobos' new wave *norteño* sounds and Arizona artist Larry Yáñez' *punkarachi* music parallel the Mexico City *charrock*[8] and the eccentric blend of *tambora*[9] and jazz that can be heard in the grotesque Tijuana bordellos.

The colloquial poems of Chicanos José Montoya, Juan Felipe Herrera and Luzma Espinoza could very well be in the same anthology that includes some of their Mexican, Brazilian, Cuban and Argentine contemporaries.

The highly stylized, bicultural performances of my own troupe, *Poyesis Genética,* which combine magical realistic imagery with multimedia technology, relate to the theatrical experiments of the Brazilian troupe *Contadores de Historias.* Again, the impulses, sensibilities and intentions are similar.

Certain similarities can be explained by the fact that some of these artists have worked on both sides of the border. Others still are to be studied.

The geopolitical wound called "border" cannot stop the cultural undercurrents. In its quest to produce art and criticism that don't acknowledge the existence of the border, the San Diego–Tijuana-based Border Arts Workshop (BAW/TAF), integrated by Chicanos, Mexicanos and North Americans working in an interdisciplinary manner, becomes symptomatic of today's desperate need for true intercultural communication. The "artistic border" is artificial. It shouldn't be there, and it is up to us to erase it.

The strength and originality of Chicano-Latino contemporary art in the U.S. lies partially in the fact that it is often bicultural, bilingual and/or biconceptual. The fact that artists are able to go back and forth between two different landscapes of symbols, values, structures and styles, and/or operate within a "third landscape" that encompasses both, gives them an obvious advantage over other artists. A "border consciousness" necessarily implies the knowledge of two sets of reference codes operating simultaneously. The challenge is to fully assume this biculturalism, develop it and promote it. Synthesis has always engendered original fruits and it is only from the space within synthesis that one can critically oversee its various components and develop innovative formats to express them.

Here the important questions are: How can we identify true bilingualism, biculturalism and biconceptualism? How can we determine what is a true artistic synthesis versus an incongruous mumbo-jumbo? What is the difference between biculturalism and cultural schizophrenia? These concerns are textually or subtextually palpitating in the work of most Chicano/Latino artists working in the U.S. And those who choose not to deal with them are sadly condemned to alienation or, even worse, to complete acculturation.

Within the political arenas of Mexico and Latin America, there has always been space for artists and intellectuals to assume leadership and utilize their metiers as catalysts for public debate.

Here there is a very clear similarity between the Mexican and Chicano cultures. Where else can we find political leaders mingling, collaborating and interacting daily with their artistic counterparts, or avant-gardists also being political celebrities? This quintessential Latin American phenomenon, in which political and artistic thought and discourse are inevitably intertwined, remains alive in the Chicano communities.

It is not by coincidence that Chicano poets Alurista and José Montoya, visual artist Rupert Garcia and theater director Luis Valdez were also shapers of political consciousness. It is also perfectly logical that Mexican writers Carlos Fuentes and Homero Arijdis were also ambassadors; that Felipe Ehrenberg's mural and alternative press workshops across the country were realized through the Mexican Ministry of Education, and that Argentine novelist Ernesto Sábato became the head of a commission to investigate the crimes of his country's militia. Furthermore, since the Mexico City earthquake, many respectable artists, writers and musicians, Ehrenberg and Carlos Monsiváis among them, have assumed leadership of consciousness and action in the painful process of the reconstruction. Two cities have to be rebuilt. One that we all share and another within each of us. Aware of this, Bay Area Chicano artist and entrepreneur René Yañez has joined this epic crusade, fundraising for *la reconstrucción*.

In all these cases, art and politics are two sides of the same coin, *binomios,* as Ehrenberg would say. In all these cases, the concept of the artist's métier is much larger and more open-ended than that of mainstream artists in the U.S. and Europe.

Chicanos have consistently experienced a triple form of discrimination: economic, racial and artistic. And because of this, they have developed what we call in Spanish *arte contestatario.* This art is meant to reply to and question the surrounding "other," the one on top. And because this "other," the U.S., is the most dominant culture in the world, the intensity of the Chicano reply has been exponential. As a result, new creative paths have been discovered.

It is precisely in the recognition of being *contestatario* and alternative that Chicano/Latino art in the U.S. has discovered its kinship with the Latin American cultures of liberation. And at the same time, these cultures have found in the Chicano artist not only a distant friend, but a vanguard voice that can warn them in advance. This mutual recognition is certainly the most solid foundation for the birth of a pan–Latin American art movement that doesn't stop at the Rio Grande, but continues north to the *Nuyorrican barrios* of the East Coast and beyond into the European Latino milieu.

With this understanding, we must design a new map that portrays Latin America, as well as the Latino region of the U.S. and Europe, as one immense sociocultural entity that could very well be networked.

The two conferences that occurred, first in Havana, then in Mexico City, under the title of *Diálogos de las Américas (1981–82),* included the participation of intellectuals and artists from throughout the continent. There a very serious problem arose: our artistic continent has been clearly sliced by an ideological knife, and it would be very naive to think that either side will give any ground for the sake of utopian *panamericanismo.* In the political context, the supporters and detractors of power, and the enemies and sympathizers of political change, cannot simply sit together at the same table to chat like old friends. The same goes for those in the art world who defend the European concept of "universality of art and culture," and those who are aware of its sociopolitical implications and differences. These polemics will never be resolved, but what realistically may happen is that the polarization can reach the point of open cultural warfare. And those artists who sincerely strive for a culture that is from, for and about this continent, will inevitably exclude those who interfere with the realization of this ambitious goal.

There are a number of people working in both Americas who have assumed the responsibility of becoming "cultural ambassadors" without official representation. Tomas Ybarra-Frausto, René Yañez, Felipe Ehrenberg, Carlos Fuentes, Shifra Goldman, Margaret Randall, Helen Escobedo, Ariel Dorfman, Fernando Alegría and Eva Cockcroft, among others, are constantly travelling between the two Americas and coasts, spreading information and weaving binational networks and projects.

The main project demands a new definition of the artistic continent and a brand new set of relationships between its parts. And certain magazines such as *Mutantia* (Buenos Aires), *La Regla Rota* (Mexico City), *La Línea Quebrada* (Tijuana–San Diego), *High Performance* (Los Angeles) and *Contact II* (New York) are certainly doing their bit.

Today [1986], the main concern seems to be networking beyond the border. For the various Chicano/Latino communities in the U.S. (which suffer the horizontal isolationism of North America), the grand challenge is to establish an ongoing dialogue with the larger Latin American arts community. And for the Anglo-American intellectuals and artists, it seems necessary to carefully reexamine their own history in order to recapture the various "cultural strata" (indigenous, Black, Mexican, Anglo-Saxon, etc.) that compose and energize their multilayered culture.

Never before was this concern so vividly expressed by artists, and never before were the means to realize it so concrete and available.

We are now witnessing the creation of axes of thought. By "axes" I mean both an exchange of information and artwork (for instance, this article would never have been possible ten years ago), and the design of travelling routes for artists and intellectuals.

The main "axes of thought" still incomplete, temporarily broken, or simply lacking are those between Tijuana and San Diego and therefore between Alta and Baja California; between Mexico City and Los Angeles, and between Mexico City and New York (direct or via Tijuana–San Diego). Other networks between Mexico and the various cultural centers throughout the Southwestern United States are still to be realized.

The link with Mexico City is of utter importance, for only through *la capital* can the linkage be made with Caracas, Sâo Paolo, Bogotá, Lima, Buenos Aires, Managua, Havana, Madrid, Barcelona, etc.

In this new artistic topography, the Tijuana–San Diego border, being the main junction between the two Americas, as well as the most vulnerable political, economic and cultural zone, becomes a strategic spot for exchange, experimentation and confrontational dialogue, and perhaps in the near future, the very cardinal center of this axis. Few

ALTAR

Amalia Mesa-Bains

This altar by Amalia Mesa-Bains represents the traditional Mexican home altar that Chicanos utilize as a point of departure for the elaboration of very complex visual languages.

places in the world reflect so vividly the contradictions of two worlds in permanent conflict as does the Mexican-American border region.

These are the challenges of a new generation of artists and cultural activists: to redesign our continental map, to rebaptize it in our own terms, and to express it in completely new ways. We must invent new languages capable of articulating our unique circumstances. Nationalism, provincialism, political/aesthetic conservatism and ethnic resentments are but a few of the tremendous number of obstacles we have to sort out before we can find the real shape of the continent's consciousness.

Notes

1. Small offerings in the form of hands, arms, hearts, etc. Small naive paintings that express gratitude to a saint.

2. Chicano slang for "California."

3. Mexican ritual dancers who are holders of pre-Hispanic music, dance and poetry traditions.

4. Carlos Fuentes, Gabriel García Márquez, Julio Cortazar, Juan Rulfo and others.

5. Mexico City.

6. Leduc, Maldonado and Chavarría are the best independent filmmakers of Mexico City. Leduc's *Reed México—Insurgente* and *Frida* and Chavarría's *El Niño Fidencio* are masterpieces of Mexican cinema.

7. Felipe Ehrenberg's regional mural project. Since the late sixties, Ehrenberg has been a pioneer of avant-garde thought in Mexico.

8. A blend of rock-and-roll and mariachi music.

9. Traditional Big Band music from the state of Sinaloa.

6

The La Lucha Murals: Making a Political Art Park

Eva Sperling Cockcroft

Eva Cockcroft describes the 1980s community mural movement as sup-
porting a noncontroversial realism that wasn't much different from
elitist high art. In response, a group of downtown New York artists
banded together as Artmakers, Inc. (an artist-run, non-profit, politically
oriented community mural organization) in 1983 to create forceful,
community-generated public murals.

Without pay, and with donated materials, they painted the "La
Lucha Murals"—twenty-six individual and collective works on four
buildings around a central plaza on New York's Lower East Side. Their
themes were intervention in Central America, apartheid in South Africa,
and gentrification in their local community. The interweaving of these
three issues came out of the 1980s climate of greater political sophistica-
tion and a coalition mentality that emphasized the universality of "la
lucha" (the struggle).

"Painted images cannot stop wars or win the struggle for justice,"
Cockcroft writes, "but, they are not irrelevant. They fortify and enrich
the spirit of those who are committed to the struggle and help to
educate those who are unaware."

The community mural movement began in the late 1960s out of a desire
by artists, caught up in the social ferment of that period, to create art
that dealt with issues and communicated to ordinary people. Early community murals, although varied in style, were political in nature. They
formed part of the more general social struggle.

This article originally appeared in another form in *Community Murals* (Winter 1985).

By the mid-1970s murals had become an accepted form of neighborhood improvement, with established techniques for community involvement and regular funding. The location of the murals in poor communities, accessibility of subject matter and environmental improvement had become sufficient justification for their existence. Controversial or political themes were discouraged.

After 1980, with the popularity of photorealism and neofiguration in the art world—rather than the esoteric abstractionisms of the 1970s—the division between elite and popular forms became less important. Accessibility of meaning was no longer a problem since most painters (unlike sculptors) entering public art, whether working for big commissions or community organizations, tended to work in realistic styles. Additionally, during the Reagan years, the local community organizations that sponsor a muralist's work in the neighborhoods, rather than pushing the artists toward bold statements, demanded instead that the work avoid all controversial subjects.

This was the situation in 1983 when a group of artists, including Joe Stephenson and me, formed Artmakers, Inc., as an artist-run, nonprofit, politically oriented community mural organization. Both Stephenson and I had been involved in the mural movement since the early 1970s. We had begun painting murals out of political and artistic convictions during a period in which, more often than not, the politics of the artists and the aroused communities coincided. We were frustrated with the blandness of most currently funded community art—a frustration that was fueled by the knowledge that political murals had been painted in Chicago and San Francisco.

Artmakers painted a small collective mural for Emmanuel Day Care Center on 6th St. between Avenues B and C in 1984, but our first major project was the La Lucha Continua/The Struggle Continues political art park in 1985. The La Lucha project represented a return to beginnings, to the organic feeling of the early mural movement—and the youthful romanticism of working without getting paid.

The La Lucha park consists of twenty-six murals painted on four buildings around a central plaza—La Plaza Cultural—between 8th and 9th Streets at Ave. C in New York City's Lower East Side, twenty-four of them in 1985. More than thirty artists painted over 6,310 square feet of murals, some as high as forty feet, on the themes of intervention in Central America, apartheid in South Africa, and gentrification in the local community.

The project was organized by Artmakers in conjunction with Charas, Inc., a neighborhood housing and cultural organization, and carried out with donated materials. Grassroots fundraising in the political art community was used to pay the necessary cash expenses like scaffolding and insurance. Both artists and organizers donated their time. The total cash outlay came to no more than $3,500, although the budget for such a project, were the artists to be paid and supplies purchased, would come to more than ten times that amount.

La Lucha began shortly after the massive ''Artists Call against Intervention in Central America'' and ''Art against Apartheid'' exhibitions. It seemed essential that the project deal with at least those two issues. The third issue, the housing struggle, or gentrification as it is called, was the most important issue in the local neighborhood. The equivocal position of artists in the gentrification of the Lower East Side, coupled with the East Village gallery scene and Mayor Koch's use of artists' housing as an opening wedge for real estate interests, had created an awareness among artists of their role. Two shows sponsored by the political art organization, PADD (Political Art Distribution/Documentation), demonstrated the high level of artists' interest and activism around this issue. In addition, it seemed important both educationally and politically to link these three struggles together in order to emphasize the fact that they are the same struggle against the same enemy. The universality of this struggle for freedom and social justice was emphasized in the project by the use of the words ''the struggle continues'' in many different languages as a logo to both frame and separate the individual murals.

In mid-April of 1985, Artmakers sent out a call for ''artists of conviction'' interested in painting political murals to attend an open meeting. These and other artists recruited from the Art against Apartheid group and the local community formed the core of the project. The group was mixed, including minority, political, graffiti and East Village artists. A majority were women. The artists became the driving force for the project and provided the energy that made it possible. Design proposals were submitted and approved by a committee composed of Artmakers, Charas and other concerned community people.

Once the designs were chosen, determining their exact location was the next challenge. This was a problem far more complex than simply arranging an exhibition, since it required the approval of building owners and community gardeners (there were two different garden groups on the site) as well as the agreement of the artists. In addition, it was important politically that each of the issues should be visible from every major viewpoint.

The biggest problem was with the owners of 8BC, a trendy nightclub which owned one of the buildings. Initially, the club owners were enthusiastic about the project, but, after they saw the designs, it became clear that there was a large gap in taste between them and the more explicitly political artists. A compromise was worked out in which the west wall of their building would be painted by a group of four artists associated with the club while the murals facing the club (on a buiding they did not own) would be chosen jointly from our designs. In return, the east wall of the club would be curated entirely by Artmakers, subject to the approval of the neighbors who had planted a garden in that area. Unfortunately, only one of the artists chosen by 8BC completed his mural: Luis Frangella painted a large head in the corner of the building.

Two subthemes that appeared when the designs were selected were feminism and police brutality. Rikki Asher, who painted her wall in July because she was leading the Arts for a New Nicaragua brigade of muralists, which painted three murals in Nicaragua in August, brought together the cultures and women of Central America and Africa in her design. Susan Ortega, one of the organizers of the Art against Apartheid exhibitions, portrayed South African women marching against apartheid, while Betsy McLinden used two symbolic female figures as agents for self-determination in the three regions.

The police brutality theme was explored in three murals dealing with the story of Michael Stewart, the young graffitist arrested and killed by police earlier in 1985. Seth Tobocman, a political illustrator and creator of World War III comix, created a dynamic image of confrontation between a youth and a mounted policeman—a local reference since Tomkins Square park, only a block away, is patrolled by cops on horseback. Etienne Li told the story comic-book style in panels, while Chico, a local graffiti writer turned artist, used spray paint to create a subway scene. After the police officers were acquitted in 1986, these images became a focal point for dissent. *Daily News* columnist Jimmy Breslin used the murals, which he called ''walls of sorrow,'' to express the anger of minority people toward what they considered to be a racist verdict.

The keynote mural, thirty by forty feet, which I directed, dealt with gentrification and was designed and painted by a collective group of eleven artists, many of whom also painted individual murals. An earlier mural on the same wall by Freddy Hernandez of Cityarts Workshop had been destroyed in 1981 when the landlord tarred the wall. Hernandez' work, which showed images of Chinese, Latino and African culture, reappears in the new mural in a scene of artists painting on a building.

The issue of permanence was one that we considered carefully before deciding that this would be a project with a limited life span— probably no more than three to five years. There was no guarantee that the buildings now standing would not be destroyed and new ones built within five years since the entire area was in flux. More importantly, the direct issue orientation of the work meant that it could easily become dated if, for example, apartheid were ended or Hispanics totally displaced from Loisaida. Also, several of the walls, including that for the big mural, were covered with tar, the worst possible surface on which to paint since it expands and contracts more than even the most flexible paint. For painting on the tar surface we followed the lead of graffiti writers, using a thin layer of oil enamel which would be absorbed into the surface. In this way we hoped to avoid peeling, although we knew that some minor cracking (as in old oil paintings) would be inevitable after the first winter.

The design collective decided on the basic composition—a crystal ball showing the future in the center surrounded by a series of vignettes representing the current reality and ranging from negative to positive. After the images were chosen, different artists sketched each of them. Keith Christensen worked up the homeless family and shark-wrecker-limo scene; Marguerite Bunyan, the evicted family and the fire escape scene; Etienne Li, the sweat equity workers and the cultural center; Joe Stephenson, the solar rooftop: Rikki Asher, the market; and I, the crystal ball images and general composition. The idea for the police figure came from a drawing by Judith Quinn while the brick patterns were contributed by Therese Bimka. In the painting process some of the original artists dropped out and others joined in: Karin Batten, Camille Perrottet, and two art student interns, Robert Brabham and Dorianne Williams.

Beneath the large mural are five smaller murals: an image of Nicaragua by Karin Batten; a root image containing the names of local grassroots organizations by Keith Christensen with a background by Anthony Buzco; an image of African liberation by Cliff Joseph in which the flag becomes subtly organic with a red sky, green jungle, and within the black, the mass of the people rising; an image of equality and freedom by Camille Perrottet represented by naked children playing with a ball; and a symbolic image of the Puerto Rican liberation struggle by neighborhood activist and muralist Maria Dominguez showing a folkloric mask in front of a death's head with red, white and blue ties around the staff.

Perhaps the most popular of the murals among local residents is *The Final Judgement,* a collaboration by Robin Michals and Kristin Reed in which the jury that judges the arms merchants below is composed of portraits of neighborhood characters as well as world leaders like Nelson Mandela and Daniel Ortega. On the same wall is an image of South African liberation by Leon Johnson, himself from South Africa, symbolic dancers on a rooftop by Leslie Lowe, an exquisitely colored semiabstract rendering of marchers at rest by Noah Jemison, and a ceramic piece by Argentine-born artist Dina Burstyn. The ceramic, composed of separate pieces of clay mounted in a circle and signifying the endurance and break-up of the ancient Meso-American culture, is mounted on a rough cement section of wall, itself a contemporary ruin.

The end wall of this building was marred by a large and elaborate dog cage built of chicken wire and poured cement which appeared suddenly one night shortly before we began painting. The antigentrification mural, designed by Nancy Sullivan and Janet Vicario and painted by Nancy Sullivan, had been given that spot. Nancy Sullivan, herself a Lower East Side dog-owner, integrated the cage into the design and added a painted image of the dog.

The garden wall, on the east side of 8BC, contained some of the most negative and therefore controversial images. In addition to the murals mentioned earlier, there is a scene of the struggle against gentrification by neighborhood artist, Willie Birch; Sandinista guerillas at rest during a lull in the fighting in Nicaragua by Marilyn Perez; the *Tomb of the Disappeared* painted in slashes of vivid color by Pat Brazill; and a marvelously complex and detailed gentrification octopus by Noel Kunz.

An all-day dedication fiesta was held to celebrate the completion of the murals and present them to the community. The program included performers representing the African, Latin, and political themes of the murals, two salsa bands, Neo Mnumzana, UN representative of the African National Congress and Roberto Vargas, cultural attaché of the Nicaraguan Embassy, poet and activist Bimbo Rivas, and Chino Garcia, president of Charas. Hundreds of people, a mixture of the political art world and local community, attended.

The dedication did not signify the end of the project, but only the beginning of the second phase. For the people in the local community, the images created beauty in their daily environment and provided a focus for discussion and education. Once the images had been created, however, they could influence a far greater audience than the limited number of people who live nearby or visit the site. We know that photo exhibitions and slide shows of the project were seen in New York, Seattle, Paris, and Ireland, but we are unable to keep track of all the photographers who visited the site. Color postcards of seven of the images were printed and distributed widely outside New York City. Press coverage has continued on a fairly regular basis. In 1988, for example, La Lucha was included in stories about public art in the *Village Voice* and *New York Times*. Over the years the mural images have been used as backdrops in films, videos and fashion spreads as well as being the subject of at least two videos by independent filmmakers.

PUSH CRACK BACK
Artmakers, 1986,
Acrylic, 15' × 40'. Artists: Eva Cockcroft, Keith Christenson, Cliff Joseph, Joe
Stephenson, Eric Stephenson, Camille Perrottet, Sarah Kleeman, friends and
neighborhood residents. The mural is located on 142nd Street between Amsterdam
Avenue and Hamilton Place in New York City.
(Photo by Eva Cockcroft)

There have been a number of changes in La Lucha since 1985. There are new fences dividing the area and when a gallery bought the nightclub in 1986 and repaired the building, Chico's mural was moved and two new murals added: a ceramic mural by Therese Bimka, *One among Many*, about the "disappeared" in Guatemala and a collaboration between Joe Stephenson and me, *The Border*, about the plight of migrants crossing the U.S.-Mexican border.

In 1987, the planning board approved a plan for low-cost senior citizen housing at this site. This is supported by many community residents (including our cosponsor, Charas) who fear that if they reject this option, the land might eventually go to luxury-housing developers. Others have demanded the retention of this area as green space and the preservation of the murals. The latter group have set up a tent on the lot. In conjunction with the squatters, a soup kitchen for the homeless was set up in the area in front of the collective mural for about a year. Artmakers has not taken a public position on this issue, but we do point out that we never anticipated that the murals would last for longer than five years.

Building on the experience of collaboration gained in the La Lucha project, Robin Michals and Kristin Reed did a new mural in 1986 containing portraits of neighborhood children, *The Enchanted Garden*, only a few blocks from the first. The experience of collective work led to another Artmakers project, an anti-crack mural at 142nd Street between Amsterdam Avenue and Hamilton Place in West Harlem by a group of artists mainly from La Lucha, including Keith Christenson, Camille Perrottet, Joe Stephenson, Cliff Joseph, Sarah Kleeman and me. *Push Crack Back* attempts to encourage community action by depicting Malcolm X encouraging the efforts of community people to stop the advancing "crack train" which is filled with casualties of the drug. The crack train is decorated with graffiti painted by local teenagers.

In the tradition of La Lucha's combining of collective and individual artworks into a single large project, in 1988 Artmakers undertook the installation of a nineteen-artist project, *The Changing Face of SoHo*, in the Broadway/Lafayette subway station. This installation includes nine individual pieces, a collective ceramic piece and a collective mural. All the artworks deal with the increasing gentrification of this one-time factory area, which has forced artists out of the spaces they renovated.

Hopefully, the La Lucha project can serve as the model for many more political art projects in other cities and countries. Painted images cannot stop wars or win the struggle for justice, but they are not irrelevant. They fortify and enrich the spirit of those who are committed to the struggle and help to educate those who are unaware.

7

Education through Collaboration
Saves Lives

Phyllis Rosser

Art in the public interest has been self-conscious about wanting to educate participants and the public. It seems appropriate therefore that many projects have included children. Phyllis Rosser tells about three artistic collaborations—Tim Rollins + K.O.S. in the Bronx, New York; John Kavalos and white, upper-middle-class students in New Jersey painting murals in suburban malls; and Doreen Nelson's "City Building Education" curriculum in Venice, California—that actually began in classrooms and developed as a part of the three instructors' innovations in the education of their students.

The character of the contemporary public art that resulted demanded a process that was often antithetical to standard art training (or any other training) in schools. The problems contemplated and solutions found were not hypothetical or removed from the lives of the children and the communities surrounding their institutions. Children addressed real dilemmas and interacted not only with homogeneous companions in their classrooms but with a variety of people in their larger environments.

Empowering students to learn by doing unleashed potential and revealed intelligence previously unrecognized by the school systems. Tim Rollins and K.O.S.' work has also been recognized as viable in the international art market. Rollins and K.O.S.' decisions concerning their art world success have become a part of the practical art-educational process Rosser addresses.

Tim Rollins was annoyed when he found someone had painted in the book he was reading out loud to his remedial reading class. Then he saw its artistic potential and mounted the pages for display in the classroom. This marriage of text and image inspired other students to create a large cooperative painting of the images they had been drawing while listening to him read. From this inauspicious beginning was born the artistic collaboration known as Tim Rollins + K.O.S. (Kids of Survival) which has now earned widespread critical recognition and financial success as well as educational kudos.

As a painter working in New York City's "Learning to Read through the Arts" program in 1980, Rollins used classical literature like *Moby Dick, Frankenstein, The Scarlet Letter* and *Amerika,* rather than "embarrassing primers" to teach dyslexic and emotionally troubled Black and Hispanic students in special education classes at Intermediate School No. 52 in the South Bronx. While he read, all the students drew images from events in their own lives that corresponded with the stories they were hearing, a method they called "jamming." (Art critic Lawrence Rinder compares this to the early twentieth-century Surrealist technique for capturing imagery from the subconscious mind called "automatic writing.")[1] Relating the stories to their daily lives not only helped them understand the work but also allowed them to express and deal with what was happening in the "real world" outside the classroom in a way that most school activities never permit. Reading about Hester Prynne in *The Scarlet Letter* reminded them that they were labeled underprivileged, disadvantaged and low-income by the people in power, says Rollins. They were impressed with Hester's transformation of the shameful "A" into a symbol of pride, like a "superhero," and created a collaborative *Scarlet Letter* painting in which large red and gold "A"s in different styles were painted over the Hawthorne text.

Rollins found a number of his students were "enormously artistically talented, with an intelligence that wasn't being served because it didn't measure well on standardized English and Math tests."[2] Drawing awakened their interest and facilitated the learning process. He says many of them now read classical literature because they enjoy it. Carlos Rivera remembers Tim noticing his drawings and encouraging him to join his art class. Although Carlos was dyslexic, Rollins says he produced highly accomplished drawings by avidly copying the work of Grunewald, an activity supposedly beyond his low attention span. Carlos feels this saved his life and says, "As long as Tim's alive, I'll always be there."[3]

In 1981, when gallery owner Ronald Feldman asked for recommendations of new, young artists' work for The Atomic Salon exhibition, Rollins mentioned a collaborative classroom painting, "Hypocenter: South Bronx," that his students had just finished. To his amazement it was included in the exhibition. "There it was, hanging next to Warhol

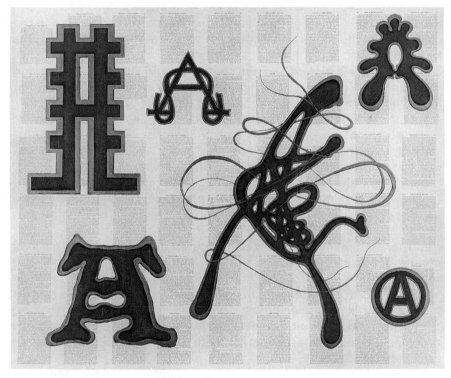

HESTER AT HER NEEDLE
Tim Rollins + K.O.S.
Watercolor, charcoal and bistre on bookpages on linen, 108″ × 140″.
(Photo courtesy of Mary Boone Gallery, New York)

and Guston,'' he says.[4] The students were so encouraged by their nearly instant art-world recognition that Rollins founded the Art and Knowledge Workshop and K.O.S. (Kids of Survival). Today, twenty teenagers, ages thirteen to eighteen, attend the after-school workshop to produce serious collaborative art based on great works of literature. Since 1982, these paintings have been exhibited internationally and bought by prominent collectors like S. I. Newhouse and Charles Saatchi. In 1988 they were shown at the Walker Art Center in Minneapolis and the Jay Gorney Gallery in New York's SoHo art district. They are in the collections of the Museum of Modern Art in New York, the Philadelphia Museum of Art and the Dia Foundation.

But art world success has generated a certain amount of anger and skepticism within the art community, which cynically suggests that Rollins embarked on this work to further his artistic career. Or that he's selling short his political activism (he cofounded an advocacy group for socially committed art in the East Village as Group Material) by accepting huge sums of money for this work. Rollins admits that success has been problematic but says his goals remain revolutionary. Money from sales is put into a non-profit trust fund to be used mainly to found a school that will provide a new model for learning by using a broad curriculum of interdisciplinary studies focusing on the fine arts. He believes that letting students express their feelings, discover their creativity, and relate classroom activities to their experience in the community unblocks the learning process and gives them the ability to change their lives.

The Art and Knowledge Workshop's collaborative creative process has stayed close to the model developed in the remedial reading classrooms. After reading and analyzing a book together, students fasten all the pages to a support to create a grid-like background (which can be as long as fourteen feet) for the artwork that is painted on top. Individual images drawn during the reading are discussed, edited, combined or elaborated to create a group visual response to the literary work, which may take years to work out. Students also visit galleries and museums to gain inspiration from the way artists through history have treated similar themes. Grunewald's *Isenheim Altarpiece* and Peter Magubane's photographs of South African Blacks struggling against apartheid provided inspiration for the images of wounds used in the painting of *The Red Badge of Courage,* which also expressed the experience of violence and survival in the South Bronx.[5]

The collective's style has evolved, according to critic Lucy Lippard, from ''raucous figuration to subtle metaphor and abstraction.''[6] Earlier layering of individual symbols like the exuberant golden trumpets of Kafka's *Amerika* have been replaced by collectively-chosen single images in paintings with a minimalist look.[7] In *The Whiteness of the Whales; Monstrous Pictures of Whales* based on *Moby Dick,* a field of translucent whiteness suggests an omnipresent power reminiscent of Rothko. But Rollins has been criticized for ignoring his students' ethnic roots by working in traditional establishment styles. Defending the choice, he claims his stylistic preferences are mediated by his collaborators' experience—the violence and alienation in their community. Lippard concurs, saying their work "epitomizes everything that is best about the art of this decade, i.e.: it is a hybrid, disturbingly familiar and simultaneously jolting and not post or neo anything."[8]

Despite art world success, the true value of this collaborative work is in saving adolescent lives—taking potential dropouts and helping them learn through self-expression. And the benefit spreads to the artists' families and friends as they become involved in this artistic enterprise and offer suggestions and support. By working cooperatively to connect what happens in school to what happens outside, students realize their experience and concerns have value—and historical relevance. Creating art about their experience that is taken seriously gives them self-respect and confidence, making them not only valuable community members but also possible agents of change.

It is too early to assess the long-range community impact of this work on its participants. But in the short term, older students have rejoined the Art and Knowledge Workshop as staff members and five former students are attending specialized art schools, including a top art college where tuition is paid by the Workshop Trust Fund. Meanwhile, Rollins is broadening his activities to involve a larger segment of this South Bronx community. Using funds from the National Endowment for the Arts and the Art and Knowledge Workshop Trust Fund, he is collaborating with two hundred neighborhood parents and children to create twelve paintings that will replace the ads in their Longwood Avenue subway station for a year.

While Tim Rollins + K.O.S. sell their paintings to art world denizens, John Kavalos collaborates with white, upper-middle-class, suburban New Jersey teenagers to make murals for people who rarely buy serious art. In 1985, he worked with a group of ten volunteer students who designed and painted large murals in the middle of three busy shopping malls for the sole purpose of teaching the public and the painters what art is and how it is made. Upon completion, the murals were removed from the malls, with sections given to each of the student painters.

"One elderly Italian man came to the Echelon Center Mall (near

Camden, New Jersey) every day to watch us work," says Kavalos. "When we were taking the mural apart, he said a prayer of thanks ending with 'God Bless You' and made the sign of the cross over us. It was very moving. Perhaps we reminded him of his childhood or the Italian fresco tradition."[9] Teenagers came to watch or taunt their painter friends but sometimes ended up volunteering for the project. And many people, particularly senior citizens, returned daily, not only to watch but to offer comments and artistic advice.

Kavalos decided, after receiving an MFA from the Tyler School of Art and a Yale at Norfolk Painting Fellowship, to work in arts education and to teach students that anyone can express themselves artistically. He gave art history lectures (with slides and books) and "learning by doing" painting instruction to student painters and mall audiences in Woodbridge and Cherry Hill, New Jersey, as well as Echelon, under the auspices of the Rouse Corporation's Art-in-the-Marketplace program and New Jersey State Arts Council's artist-in-residence program. Rouse Corporation's Director of Art-in-the-Marketplace Becky Hannum saw the project as a way of creating a sense of community in the malls. Although hiring painters to demonstrate the artistic process is not a new idea (Diego Rivera was hired to paint murals for visitors to San Francisco's 1930s World's Fair), Kavalos found the average mall-goer could identify more easily with teenage painters than adults. "They would think to themselves, 'if they can do it, so can I,' and the pop culture images students chose from the 'surrealist realism' of rock music albums and MTV were more accessible."

The murals had to be large enough and interesting enough to grab the public's attention away from the visual hype of mall advertising. Two parallel walls were constructed in the Echelon Mall, and the public was enticed to walk through by the drama of the scene—a comic book rendition of an amusement park shooting gallery. Figures in bright, primary colors appeared to be aiming pop-guns at the viewer as they sighted targets on the opposite wall. In the Cherry Hill Mall, the mode was more introspective. Students painted bold, larger-than-life portraits of themselves standing in their favorite environment that invited the viewer into their world in a personally revealing but powerful way. In the Woodbridge Mall, students created minidramas with themselves as the characters, either relaxing in a medieval tavern or eating hamburgers in a 1950s restaurant—settings they felt were appropriate for a mall surrounded by highways. Large plywood cutouts dominated the space with a Red Grooms–like playfulness. "Only a few of the students who worked on these projects had recognized artistic talent and none of them had mural experience," says Kavalos, "so I had to teach them how to paint and how to communicate in a public space. The final products were of very high quality. I would rate them as comparable to junior year college work.''

''It's not easy to paint yourself with a mirror on your hip while a whole community watches you,'' says Hannum. ''It takes a lot of guts.''[10] ''Trying out new ideas and failing, and having art work critiqued in full public view, was high-level risk taking for a teenager,'' says Kavalos, ''especially with viewers offering suggestions as you worked.'' But, unlike school, the students had some control over their own learning as they made collective design decisions and interacted with the public.

Making art in the public eye and garnering adult respect and approval was empowering for the students. Dave Schuman, now a sophomore at the University of the Arts in Philadelphia, says, ''I loved working big and having it seen by other people.''[11] Colin Throm, a second-year student at Rutgers, agrees: ''It was the first time I did an art project that had anything professional about it and that was displayed in a public space.''[12] His artistic experience has been so enriching that he switched majors from pharmacy to art this year. Hannum notes that the collaborations created ''new communities.'' Parents who brought their children to paint became friendly with one another and ''some students enjoyed working as a team so much that they signed up for a second year.''

For Doreen Nelson, the people who lived in the towns where she taught became both subject and participants in her teaching of creative development. In Venice, California, Chicano parents came to the beach to watch their third-graders redesign their community for a hundred years in the future. ''Teaching originality,'' says Nelson, ''is teaching alterations and I was showing that you can take something you know (like sand) and make something different—not sand castles as we usually do—but design a whole city, if you choose.''[13] She invited younger brothers and sisters to work along with her students and found that parents joined in.

In 1969, Nelson designed a curriculum called City Building Education—with third through sixth graders from a low-income, ethnically mixed neighborhood in Venice—which she hoped would teach them to envision and create future environments. ''I had served on the Los Angeles Goals Committee and found that most adults didn't have the problem-solving ability or even the interest to imagine the future. I wanted to see if children could do it by learning the mental processes used in creative thinking and problem resolution rather than having them memorize information that would be obsolete in twenty

VENICE, CALIFORNIA
The Oakwood area of this city as redesigned in 1970 by students from grades 3, 4, 5, and 6.
(Photo courtesy Doreen Gehry Nelson)

years. I believed creativity and inventiveness weren't magical gifts bestowed on a few artists and scientists but the result of mental processes which could be drilled like the times tables."

In contrast to traditional elementary school curricula, City Building Education allowed students to relate what they were learning to their lives outside the classroom by having them map their community, analyze what was good and bad about it, and conduct neighborhood polls of what people would like to have in their environment. These activities provided a familiar context for creativity and a way to understand how their community was organized to meet human needs. In the final phase of City Building each student was given a parcel of land to develop. Then the class collaborated in building a large scale model of their future town, incorporating the individual structures designed by each student. The fundamentals of creative design, model building and city planning were taught during weekly visits by architectural consultants, which included her architect brother Frank Gehry and volunteer architecture students from the University of Southern California and the University of California at Los Angeles. Nelson found that all the "basic skills" could be taught for the activities of planning a city. Math was learned for measuring and map making, reading was taught with list making and categorizing and written reports were required for most activities. (Although originally designed for elementary school students, the curriculum has since been taught in high school, college and even graduate school courses.)

Nelson discovered her economically underprivileged young students were capable of mastering complicated skills supposedly beyond their learning level—like using a protractor and compass—when it was presented in a useful context rather than the abstract way new skills are normally taught. Freed from the usual classroom art projects of historic dioramas and stage coach models, they were also capable of making impressive design and planning decisions. The large (twenty-by-twenty-foot) scale model of Venice-redesigned-for-the-future inspired school neighbors Charles and Ray Eames to help Nelson obtain funding from the National Endowment for the Arts to implement City Building Education in other Los Angeles classrooms.

Nelson's desire to empower her students in the political aspects of environmental change also attracted parental interest. Parents from the seemingly apathetic minority community accompanied their children on field trips to City Hall where they observed and sometimes participated in Planning Board meetings. The City Hall sessions helped students create their own planning board whose members approved the final designs for the model city.

Her friend, sculptor Claes Oldenburg, sent one of her classes a drawing of his own future plan for Venice—five huge ice bags sitting on the beach. "I don't want to make you feel bad," said one girl in a thank you letter to Oldenburg, "but if we did all ice bags for a city it would be boring."[14] This was exactly the kind of environmental information and initiative that Nelson was working toward.

For Halloween, students made "costumes" of everyday objects—telephones and toothpaste tubes that were big enough to wear—and created a parade with this family of objects. These "object transformations" provided training in a mental habit that Nelson feels artists use to encourage intuitive leaps. To demonstrate how artists tranform everyday objects, she had the children work on an art project using canvas and protractors at regular and enlarged scales. They traced the protractors, cut out the canvas shapes and painted them. Then Nelson took them to an exhibition of Frank Stella's Protractor Series (1969) at the Pasadena Museum of Art. Afterward students met Stella, showed him their art work and said, "You stole our idea."

"City Building is a system," says Nelson, "that provides teachers with methods for helping students have creative insights. They begin teaching transformation with simple changes like making something small bigger; then they interconnect the simple changes by transforming the city. The final model becomes the culmination of all these teachable lessons, connecting the various transformative processes that invoke intuition." The model buildings inspired by this training in transformation often look like fish or flowers rather than the traditional geometric architectural shapes. The final cities are full of brightly colored fantasy structures that give a lively sculptural quality to the model but bear little relationship to the current environment—because the point of the training is to develop creativity, not to come up with practical architectural design solutions to planning problems. Even though creativity is the goal, some class inventions do have futuristic possibilities like a mass transit system called "Scooter Tubes" which moved people around the city in life-sized versions of the department store pneumatic tube.

Scale models of future cities designed by City Building students have been exhibited widely—from a furniture store in Saugus, California, and several Los Angeles public libraries to the Smithsonian Institution, the Southern California Institute of Architecture, the University of California at Los Angeles, and the Rotunda of Los Angeles City Hall. Nelson says adults are astounded by this work. They often respond by wanting to join in, to "help" the students redesign their community. In 1986, she supervised the building of a thirty-by-fifteen-foot model city at the Walker Art Center in Minneapolis, in conjunction with an exhibition of Frank Gehry's architecture. One hundred fifty parents and children of all ages participated in the project, along with local art teachers, architects and staff members of the Walker Art Center.

"Designing buildings for use in the future gives children a lot of freedom," says Nelson, "they can bring their own space-age fantasies into the classroom without fear of criticism because there are no wrong answers in a future context. As the model city develops, students take charge of the classroom, allowing the teacher to step out of the central authority role and become an advisor." She has found that empowering students pays off. A junior high school principal called her to ask "what is this program that produced all the leaders in my school," and another principal from a school near Watts found her students were more committed to their work because "it wasn't phoney; it's part of an end product." City Building students have scored consistently higher on standardized reading and math tests and entered gifted high school programs even if they did not have gifted I.Q.'s. Twenty-eight-year-old Lisa, a prize-winning creative writer in high school, told Doreen in August 1988 that the program empowered her to become a writer. "What's remarkable," says Nelson, "is that she remembers everything that happened in that fourth grade classroom, and it's the only thing about her schooling that she remembers. These were profound experiences for my children, in the way that art is profound."

City Building Education programs have been conducted throughout the United States and Europe. The most intense work has been done in the Los Angeles County Schools, and until 1988 it was part of a teacher training center for all grade levels at the ABC Unified School District in Cerritos, California. Nelson currently uses City Building to teach architecture and design to liberal studies, general education, and architecture undergraduate and graduate students in the College of Environmental Design at California State Polytechnic University in Pomona, California. She continues researching creativity with City Building at the Open School in Los Angeles, under the auspices of Apple Computer's VIVARIUM research project.

She says, "My program isn't practice for a life that will begin for students some time in the future; it's about future life as they imagine it right now." This key ingredient of empowerment is present in all three projects discussed here. Students do work in the real world which receives adult recognition and respect. This builds self-confidence and self-discipline. As knowledge of the world is enhanced, the mind seems more open to academic learning. Stanford professor of education and art Eliot Eisner says, "The images around us, the forms we see in our art and the vernacular forms of our culture—our manners, architecture, dress, rituals, and ceremonies—provide potent prototypes through which we classify, compare and appraise the qualities of the world we encounter. . . . Knowledge of forms is as important as knowledge of causes."[15]

Learning by doing, working collaboratively and relating one's experience to life in the community also seem to build self-confidence. Students feel more connected and important to their community as they represent their lives in it but are also part of the audience, of the community which shapes those lives. As one City Building student said, "When you build a city, you see how important your job is and everyone contributes. I guess I realized I'm not just a nothing person."[16]

Notes

1. Lawrence Rinder, *Viewpoints: Tim Rollins + K.O.S.* (Minneapolis: Walker Art Center, February 1988), p. 2.

2. Joseph Dimattia, "Tim Rollins' Survival Course," *Artpaper* (February 1988): 11.

3. Sara Kent, "Bronx Break," *Time Out* (London) (September 1987).

4. Rosetta Brooks, "Tim Rollins + K.O.S. (Kids of Survival)," *Artscribe* (May 1987): 41–47.

5. Lawrence Rinder, *Viewpoints: Tim Rollins + K.O.S.* (Minneapolis: Walker Art Center, February 1988), p. 2.

6. Lucy Lippard, "Reading from Reality" (Philadelphia: Lawrence Oliver Gallery, 1987).

7. Waldemar Januszczak, "Artful Dodge in the Bronx" *Arts Guardian* (London), (September 1987).

8. Lucy Lippard, "Reading from Reality" (Philadelphia: Lawrence Oliver Gallery, 1987).

9. All quotations from John Kavalos are from conversations with the author in August and September 1988 unless otherwise noted.

10. Conversation with the author, September 1988.

11. Conversation with the author, September 1988.

12. Conversation with the author, September 1988.

13. All quotations from Doreen Nelson are from conversations with the author over the past twelve years unless otherwise noted.

14. Letter from Venice, California, student to Claes Oldenburg, property of Doreen Nelson.

15. Eliot W. Eisner, "The Primacy of Experience and the Politics of Method," *Educational Researcher* (June/July 1988): 16.

16. Doreen Nelson, *City Building Education: A Way To Learn* (Santa Monica, Calif.: Center for City Building Educational Programs, 1982), p. 64.

8

Public Art from a Public Sector Perspective

Wendy Feuer

"Should a state agency that serves a broad spectrum of the popula-tion sponsor work that is esoteric, confrontational or politically—or sexually—controversial?" Wendy Feuer, director of Arts for Transit of the Metropolitan Transportation Authority in New York, writes about the art in the subways program—an example of publicly supported public art—from her point of view as a member of an overseeing agency. Feuer describes several MTA programs in which professional artists, community groups and art institutions bring visual art, dance, music and performance to the underground.

The process of commissioning and installing a work of art in a public facility is long, complex, often unwieldy and sometimes antithetical to artists' creative processes. And reactions of transit riders to the MTA's Percent for Art offerings (paid for with their tax dollars) have not been uniformly positive. Still, the possibility of enhancing urban life remains in the public interest and spurs agencies to continue the discourse with the broadest of public audiences toward mutual challenge and satisfaction.

New York would not have its riot of tall buildings or a street life so spectacularly vibrant, gritty and dense without its subways. Their labyrinthian complexity rivals the human circulatory systems—a profusion of arteries and synapses working 'round the clock, twitching even the little toes of the city that never sleeps. . . . Not counting buses or com-muter rails, New York's subways alone move 3.7 million people a day on 7,043 trains traveling through 463 stations across 230 miles of tracks. More than 23,000 people run

> *the New York City system, including 6,500 train operators and conductors, 3,800 token sellers and 11,500 maintenance workers—a city within a city.*
> —Jim Sleeper, in *Washington Post,* 24 April 1988

Given the organic relationship between New York City and its subway,[1] it is not surprising that the cultural life that flourishes in galleries and museums and on concert stages has mushroomed underground. Yet the differences in these environments have, by necessity, resulted in the development of unique processes and produced a distinctive genre of public art.

New Yorkers have adorned their underground world with ornamental designs from the start. August P. Belmont, Jr., the banker who financed the Interborough Rapid Transit Company (IRT)—the first subway line—was said to have been especially proud of the decorative elements in the stations, for which he had budgeted $500,000. In a modest but quite successful way, the IRT's architects, principals in the firm of Heins and La Farge, combined textures of materials and colors to create a unique design vocabulary in the stations, some of which are now New York landmarks. While all stations had certain common features, distinctive elements were added to give each station its own identity. The designers used individualized faience and mosaic plaques to provide important visual clues to the millions of immigrants who were entering the city around the turn of the century. These were people who could not read English but for whom mass transit was vital. A colorful faience plaque with a relief of Robert Fulton's steamship, the *Clermont,* informed people that they were at the Fulton Street station of the Lexington Avenue line and the image of Columbus' flagship, the *Santa Maria,* told people that they had arrived at 59th Street and Broadway, better known as Columbus Circle.

Thus when the first and second segments of the subway system were opened in 1904 and 1908 respectively, the artistic aspects of the stations were given special praise. The stations were considered "delights to the eye," and the city was congratulated for its contribution to "Civic Art."[2] It was this commitment to the high standards for design, set early in the century, that was obviously and sadly lacking in the work on stations for most of the rest of the century.[3]

Much has been written about the deterioration and near collapse of New York's underground system in recent decades. The decline, which began in the 1960s, hit bottom in the early 1980s. Trains derailed on an almost monthly basis. Frequent track fires added to the unreliability of riding by subway. And the graffiti covering almost every train, inside and out, was a final indignity for riders who had no choice but to use mass transit. Many of the people who did have a choice deserted public transportation and returned to their private cars and taxis, which increased the traffic congestion and pollution above ground, choking the life out of the city.

Because the city's future depended on getting people out of private vehicles and back on mass transit, in 1981 politicians and transit officials put together a plan to rehabilitate the transit system.[4] The Metropolitan Transportation Authority began what has since grown into a $16.3 billion, ten-year Capital Program, a herculean effort to reverse the decay that had permeated all aspects of the subway, bus and commuter rail systems. In the beginning, a majority of the funds went to fixing the tracks, and purchasing and rebuilding rolling stock, the fibers of a system that binds the New York region together like a patchwork crazy quilt. When clean trains began to arrive in stations on a regular basis, the deplorable condition of the stations into which they arrived became more evident.

The Authority recognized that passengers spent a great deal of time in the stations, either rushing to catch trains or waiting for them; it was clear that the waiting experience, as well as the riding experience, had to be improved. Thus they embarked upon a program to upgrade, restore and modernize stations. Consistent with many other public works projects around the world, one percent of the construction budget for station improvement projects was dedicated to permanent works of art.

The Arts for Transit office was established in 1985 by the MTA, to oversee the Percent for Art program and develop other programs with the goal of bringing art prominently back into the TA's underground city.[5] It has a broad mission to install both permanent and temporary visual art projects, as well as produce dance, music, and other types of performances. The work is created by professional artists, art students, graphic designers, community groups, and cultural institutions.

Since 1981, eleven site-specific works have been installed in subway stations. They exemplify the extraordinary diversity of styles and media in which artists are currently working and function in a variety of ways within these most visible, most busy, and unfortunately most abused of public settings. For example, Rhoda Andors created porcelain enamel murals, titled *Kings Highway Hieroglyphs,* that work as aesthetic objects in the Kings Highway station in Brooklyn and have an iconographic relation to the function and location of the facility. The murals are situated at the entrance to the station with beach-related symbols on the side of the mural next to stairs to the Coney Island–

KINGS HIGHWAY HIEROGLYPHS
Rhoda Andors, 1987
Kings Highway Station, Brooklyn, New York. Commissioned by the Metropolitan
Transportation Authority Arts for Transit office; owned by the New York City Transit
Authority.
(Photo courtesy Les Stone)

bound train and symbols of work on the side leading to Manhattan. These contemporary symbols of travel, local scenery, and other objects, all done in a hieroglyphic motif, provide subtle directional signals as they make a playful reference to place. They are, in a sense, an update of the subway's original faience plaques—on one level telling people where they are, on another telling them where they are going.

David Wilson's *Transit Skylight* visually complements an architectural element of the station. He designed and fabricated a zinc-glazed polycarbonate piece that was installed in the skylight of the Newkirk Avenue station control house.[6] Similarly, Steve Wood created organic, underwater motifs, *Fossils,* for 180 bronze tiles that were inlaid throughout the platform walls of the 137th Street/Broadway station. The bronze tiles are the same size as the ceramic tiles and embellish an otherwise plain wall. It is a powerful work that, upon installation, changed the atmosphere in the station.

Valerie Jaudon and Ray Ring created works that serve functional purposes. Taking off from her geometric style of painting, Jaudon designed *Long Division,* a work of art that doubles as railings that separate the paid and unpaid areas of the 23rd Street/Lexington Avenue station while Ring designed *Clark Street Passage,* a multicolored, geometrically patterned terrazzo floor for the Clark Street Station in Brooklyn.[7]

The process of commissioning and installing a work of art in a public facility, such as a subway station, is complex and often unwieldy. Many people with diverse concerns are involved with the creation of that single piece of art. As a result, the completion of a project sometimes seems a small miracle. An overview of the TA's process for station modernization projects will reveal the complexity of a system that, surprisingly, has had excellent results.

The Stations Department of the New York City Transit Authority maintains subway stations and chooses the locations for rehabilitation. Once sites are identified, a scope of work is developed by the Engineering and Construction Department with input from Track and Structures, Systems Safety, Revenue Control, Electrical/Mechanical and other departments. This scope will include structural and electrical work as well as architectural finishes, such as floor and wall treatment and lighting. The Transit Authority then may put the job up for competitive bidding (when selection is based on cost only) or may request proposals (when selection is based on criteria including qualifications and past experience, conceptual approach and responsiveness to project, and cost). A committee chaired by a representative of the Materiel Department weighs all the criteria and awards the contract. Either way, the

LONG DIVISION
Valerie Jaudon, 1988
23rd Street/Lexington Avenue Station, Manhattan. Commissioned by the
Metropolitan Transportation Authority Arts for Transit office; owned by the New
York City Transit Authority.
(Photo courtesy Les Stone)

architect or engineer capable of proposing the best design may not get the job.

The Arts for Transit staff begins to select an artist for the station after the design consultant is hired; a panel of art professionals, along with representatives from the sponsoring department of the TA, the architectural consultant firm and the community is convened.[8] The panel is given a tour of the site (or is shown slides) and is introduced to the preliminary design plan. The community that the station serves is described, and limitations on materials are reviewed.

The panel is asked to be sensitive to riders who spend part of each work day in the station year in and year out. The purpose of the art in relation to the community of riders, the community above, the system as a whole and the station design are also discussed. By and large, most panel members (who for the most part are also mass transit riders) seem to believe that the art in the subway should be challenging and contribute to an overall improved atmosphere. Slides by twenty to thirty artists are shown, and the panel usually narrows the field to up to five artists who are asked to develop proposals.

While a limited competition is the most frequent method of selection, Arts for Transit continues to experiment with approaches to reach both new talent and artists experienced in the public art field. For example, in 1988 a national competition was held to select three artists for the Herald Square subway complex project. Nearly five thousand announcements were sent to individuals and organizations across the country; over seven hundred artists asked for guidelines for which they paid a ten-dollar fee. About 150 proposals were received and reviewed by a five-person panel.[9] Sometimes selection is less exhaustive; after reviewing slides to select artists for nine stations on Metro-North's commuter line, the panel made their final choices for the commissions, subject to their review of proposals.

Artists have had a variety of responses to the request for a proposal when they know it will be judged against other proposals. Some feel that the decision should be based on their previous works, finding even a limited competition demeaning. Others enjoy the edge of competition and appreciate the chance to develop a new concept which they may apply elsewhere if their work is not selected. More often than not, panels prefer to review several proposals. They argue that even if an artist's work is well known, one can never anticipate how she or he will respond to the site. In addition, an artist's work that is successful in a gallery setting may not translate well to a more vulnerable and widely accessible public setting. It is, therefore, beneficial to the project to have several site-specific proposals from which to choose.

Each artist is given the same background material that was shown to the panel. They are allowed approximately two months to develop a preliminary design proposal, for which they are paid between $500 and $1000, depending on the size of the project. The full panel, including the consultant designers, representatives of the TA and the community, is reconvened for the artists' presentations. All who are present are encouraged to ask questions and participate in the discussion. One panel, after almost six hours of deliberation, decided that no art would be selected for the site. This was a difficult decision, but an honest recognition that under some circumstances art may not be appropriate for a project. More often there is consensus on the proposal that will work best for a station. The interaction of professionals bringing different points of view to the issues, while not always smooth, ultimately enriches the process. Since the panel's decision is advisory rather than binding, alternates are sought when there may be serious questions about the technical or budgetary feasibility of the recommended proposal.

Once an artist is selected, a contract is drawn up and must be approved by the MTA Board. The artist's lawyer often has a number of changes, and negotiations about issues such as copyright, ownership of models, payment and work schedules, indemnification and warranties are resolved before a contract is signed. This can take from three months to a year or more. For example, it took well over two years to select artists for the Times Square station.

The experiences of David Wilson and Valerie Jaudon illustrate the unpredictability of moving from contract to completion. Wilson, who created a zinc-glazed polycarbonate skylight for Newkirk station, early on provided the Transit Authority with materials that were tested for their ability to withstand freeze and thaw cycles, as well as fire. His final designs were reviewed and approved by the Transit Authority and the art panel. The artist assembled his work and TA workers easily installed it about twelve months after the contract was signed.

Designing, fabricating and installing Jaudon's piece—sixty linear feet of railing ranging in height from nine feet to over eleven feet—was a more time-consuming process, slowed down by the obstacles that can arise when working on functional elements. The artist's earliest idea was a simple one: to design a modular unit with a pattern that could be repeated indefinitely. When the work was installed, the patterns would connect to create "a larger esthetic whole." The feeling would be "both architectural and human, with reference to the elements of the subway and the city, doorways, stairs and passages."[10] The artist understood that she would have to comply

TRANSIT SKYLIGHT
David Wilson, 1988
Newkirk Avenue Station, Brooklyn, New York. Commissioned by the
Metropolitan Transportation Authority Arts for Transit office; owned by the
New York City Transit Authority.
(Photo courtesy Les Stone)

with Transit Authority standards for railings which stipulate that openings cannot be wider than five inches at any part. Budget also steered the design of Jaudon's artwork. When she learned from the ironwork company manufacturing the railings that the cost rose for each cut and weld, she had to simplify her proposal substantially; fortunately, she was able to retain the feeling of the original patterns. The practical aspects of installation, including a floor that slanted, beams needed for attachment that were in different planes and conduits that might snake through the art, quickly negated the possibility of one modular unit. Designs had to be reworked several times before they were reviewed by the art panel and TA departments. Construction continued in the station while the technical aspects of the art component were resolved. This took several years. Once the problems were solved, full-size design drawings were presented to the fabricator within months. The company that was selected by the MTA through the competitive bidding process did an excellent job—which is not always the case.[11] Four months later, the work was installed, with the artist overseeing installation. The project took more than five years from selection to installation and many more administrative hours than the Wilson piece. Part of the problem was typical of precedent-setting projects in which people are wary of new ideas. The work in situ goes far to set a tone for the station that was lacking before Jaudon's piece was installed.[12]

The whole notion of selecting by committee an artist who then works (or, as the case may be, doesn't work) with an architect selected by another committee may seem antithetical to creativity and overall good design. The public process thus might be seen to compromise the creative process. Yet the MTA's Percent for Art program has produced a body of art that has a positive, though often subtle, influence on the underground environment. A busy traveler who walks on Ray Ring's floor probably doesn't see it as art. Even Rhoda Andors's murals may not be experienced separately from the station itself. While this may diminish the importance of the work from a traditional critical perspective, it does not detract from the profound effect the work has on individuals. Though the underground milieu—a closed utilitarian space—restricts some avenues of creativity, it challenges artists to reconceptualize the environment. Art in the subway can reinterpret spaces for the thousands of people who pass through every day; it has a different goal from work created for a gallery, museum or even privately owned public setting. Thus it would be a mistake to judge the work using all of the same criteria that exist for other types of art. In an underground setting, the art must stand on its own merit as well as speak to the larger urban issues of creating a sense of place in what is often perceived as a hostile environment.

Some Arts for Transit projects have a broad social role. One program, Creative Stations, encourages community organizations to make aesthetic improvements to their local stations. The artworks are by and about the communities. The MTA provides matching grants of up to $5000 to support these temporary art projects. Applications are sent out annually to selected groups to solicit proposals. Each year five to ten projects in the metropolitan region are selected by an independent panel of art professionals.

In the Stilwell Avenue station, the last stop on the Brighton Line and gateway to Coney Island, artist Kristi Pfister worked with youngsters from the community in putting together her project. She placed a sixty-nine-foot wooden wave, punctuated by beach scenes, high on the station wall as a greeting to visitors who reached their destination on the B,D,F,N,M or Q trains. At the Bleeker Street station, Artmakers (an organization dedicated to community-based art) coordinated the work of nineteen neighborhood artists for a multimedia display about the changes taking place in SoHo. The art is located in an area where passengers transfer from one line to another, and provides information about life above that people might never experience.

Creative Stations is a modest program, intended to send a message to local riders that the station is an integral part of the larger community. Arts for Transit's goal is to install the best community art possible without adding visual clutter to an almost saturated environment. The office, however, must be sensitive to the comments and criticism of elected officials and the approximately 150 legally constituted oversight bodies. Some organizations, if they are not selected as part of the Creative Stations program, will use political influence to try to implement their subway station project. To circumvent this problem—which could jeopardize the artistic integrity of such a program—the Arts for Transit office has targeted its mailing list to community-based arts organizations and stipulated that other community groups hire a professional artist to implement their project.

While Percent for Art works with professional artists and Creative Stations solicits proposals from community groups, a third program, Exhibition Centers, works with another of the region's many cultural layers, arts organizations and institutions. Institutions that may be known in a particular neighborhood or by a particular constituency and would like to expand their base of support are invited to participate. An exhibit in a busy station gives the organization an opportunity for publicity not otherwise affordable and provides access to a public not otherwise reachable. Passengers passing through the station or waiting for a train can see a small exhibit and learn about a cultural resource. For example, the Bronx Museum created an exhibit of photographs and text to publicize a major initiative to make the Grand Concourse "grand" again.

Stations have provided an excellent showcase for performing artists. These artists, in turn, have helped to reverse negative public perceptions of the spaces. In discussing a group of musicians in the Times Square station a writer for *The New York Times* commented, "In the audience was someone who had, for about the 75th time this year, just given up on New York. It was too crowded, too dirty, too difficult. . . . But, the malcontent reflected, living in a quieter, easier place would mean not hearing Andean musicians on the way to work. She decided to give the city yet another chance" (*The New York Times*, 20 November 1988). About three months earlier the same paper wrote, "On the stuffy platform, a man plays an electronically amplified flute, a noise that invades every corner. The music is Mozart; the flautist, first rate. Why is it so offensive?" (*The New York Times*, 2 September 1988). While there are dissenters, the public response to music in the transit system has been encouraging. Surveys have found that passengers enjoy music; it makes them feel more comfortable and perhaps a little safer.

Performers probably have used subways as stages since subways were created, and so it might have seemed redundant to start a program to harness the street talent that would have performed anyway. But the overwhelming response by musicians to a call to audition for the Music under New York program (MUNY) negated this thought. Over a hundred performers were auditioned in the first year, sixty were selected to be part of the program, and thirty regularly participate. Part of the attraction for musicians is the legitimacy that comes with being in designated locations with an identifying banner that sets them apart from the multitudes of vendors and panhandlers that operate underground. The other part is the appreciative audiences. Musicians have said that playing in the subway is better than performing in clubs. The benefit is mutual, as many passengers are surprised by this unexpected entertainment. The program allows music to reach nontraditional audiences as it provides a venue for less traditional music.

The performance programs have brought up interesting issues about public sector art. In 1985, for one of its first programs, Arts for Transit worked with Franklin Furnace Archives to host "Live from Underground," a four-day festival of dance, music, performance art and video events that explored the interactive quality of art in the mass transit system. Performance and video artist Barbara Hammer encouraged riders to talk to each other and share their experiences and thoughts about their rides. Yoshiko Chuma and the School of Hard Knocks developed a site-specific dance program and Bob Goldberg and the Brooklyn Academy of Noise produced a sound piece for the stations.

Janus Circus's creation, *Watch the Closing Doors,* spurred conflict among the sponsor, the MTA and the artist. Proposals were solicited by Franklin Furnace; a committee selected the groups to participate. While the MTA was part of the selection committee, it did not see the actual programs until the opening performance. Janus Circus put on a farce that included a mock hold-up in a fully graffitied train as well as a scene with a man dropping his pants. The MTA felt uncomfortable with the material as it was counter to all efforts being made to improve the system's image. MTA asked the group to delete these scenes or tone them down, but the performers felt this was censorship and continued to perform the piece unchanged. Program goals, since this incident, have been made more explicit from the outset to avoid similar situations.

It is inevitable that such conflicts will arise when artists work with a large bureaucracy. Yet these disagreements raise questions that are fundamental to the *publicly supported* public art field.[13] Should a state agency that serves such a broad spectrum of the population sponsor work that is esoteric, confrontational, or politically—or sexually—controversial? Is this type of work appropriate in an already overly stimulated environment? What is the responsibility to people who have not paid to see art but have paid to be provided with transportation services? Is the art doomed to mediocrity? When evaluated by traditional standards of art criticism, the work will be seen as falling short. The public sector imposes a different set of demands on the artist: the art must speak to the multiple populations that avail themselves of the MTA's services. This does not mean that the power of a work must be diluted. The constituencies that would like the work to be political, confrontational, abstract, ethnic or experimental are all among the many constituencies that should be heard. The work in a system as large as New York City's should be challenging, abstract, representational, thought-provoking, decorative, informational, beautiful. A system with 466 stations and 3.6 million weekday riders can hold, indeed cries out for, many different visions. Budget, passenger flow, noise levels, durability are added to the more usual considerations of artists when embarking on a project. This does not mean that the work produced in such an atmosphere, whether visual or performing, cannot be held up to high standards; it simply means that the standards must factor in different considerations.

Notes

1. Jim Sleeper, "The Subway as City: An Underground Overview," *The Washington Post* (24 April 1988). Sleeper's article conveys the rough-and-tumble experience of NYC's subway system. Some of his facts have been updated. In 1988, 3.7 million

people rode in just over 6000 subway cars on weekdays, the highest level in thirteen years. There are now 466 stations, with three added December 1988; three more will be added in 1989. The 230 miles refers to route miles; there are 705 track miles.

2. New York City, Landmarks Preservation Commission, *Designation List 129,* LP 1096, 23 October 1979, p. 10, quoting "The Old Rapid Transit and the New," *Real Estate Record and Builder's Guide* 74 (24 October 1904), p. 896.

3. The BMT was built in 1918, and the IND (the Independent line, so named for its independence from private interests) was put into operation in September 1932. The IND is the plainest of the lines, with little evidence of the attention to detail and delight in craftsmanship of the earlier lines. New York City became the sole operator of all subway and elevated rail lines in 1940. Through the years, platforms were extended to accommodate longer trains. None of the additions were done with regard for the original materials.

4. In the mid-1960s, the Metropolitan Transportation Authority (MTA), a state-chartered public benefit corporation, was created to oversee much of the mass transportation in the metropolitan region. The MTA sets policy for a number of operating agencies—the New York City Transit Authority (TA), the Long Island Rail Road (LIRR), Metro-North Commuter Railroad (Metro-North), the Triborough Bridge and Tunnel Authority and the Metropolitan Suburban Bus Authority (MSBA). Its funding comes from fares and tolls, federal, state and local governments, the sale of bonds as well as revenues from advertising and real estate.

5. The Arts for Transit office also administers programs for MTA's other agencies, but this article is mainly concerned with the TA.

6. A station control house is an unattached street-level facility that houses the token booth and waiting areas with the tracks below. Most entrances to subway stations are cut into the sidewalk or occur within buildings.

7. Richard Andrews, "Artists and the Visual Definition of Cities: The Experience of Seattle," *Insights/On Sites* (Washington, D.C.: Partners for Livable Places, 1984), pp. 17–27. Andrews includes in this very informative article what he sees as the functions of public art in the experience of a city.

8. Richard Posner, "Essay," in Robert Jensen, ed., *Architectural Art: A Discourse* (New York: American Craft Museum, 1988), pp. 15–19. There is an ongoing discussion in the public art field about whether it is more beneficial for artists to collaborate as equal members of the design team or work with architects to create work for a specified site. As a result of recent successes in collaboration, we are seeing more willingness to work in this way. An underground bus and trolley system in Seattle, currently under construction, will provide an excellent case study for the team method. Some artists continue to prefer to work autonomously, however, and marriages of artists and architects have been known to be disasters. While collaborations may work in some cases, they should not be dogmatically insisted upon for all cases; each project should be analyzed on its own merits.

Just as there are different approaches to the role of the artist in a project, so there are many approaches to artist selection. For example, Boston creates an advisory group and art panel for each project. The advisory group includes representatives of the business and residential communities, the Community Development

Office and the Historical Commission; the art panel is made up of three arts professionals. The advisory group describes the station and its social and physical context and makes suggestions to the panel. The art panel makes the final decisions. In the MTA's program, only the art professionals and a representative of the TA are voting members. The community representative and architectural consultant do not vote.

9. The Herald Square Art Competition utilized architectural, rather than art, competitions as a model. Instead of sending slides of past work, artists were asked to develop proposals for designated sites in a station. The sites—one including a large area of the station—were identified by an advisory committee. A separate art panel reviewed the anonymous proposals until the final cut. Though very labor-intensive, the competition advisor and the Arts for Transit office believe artists were selected who may not have otherwise been considered, and in spite of the extensive guidelines necessary in a single-tier competition, many artists, including those with extensive public art exposure, submitted very sophisticated proposals. A report on the competition will be available in September 1989.

10. Letter from Valerie Jaudon, artist for 23rd St./Lex station to Jennifer McGregor, New York City Percent for Art Coordinator, 18 July l984.

11. Arts for Transit prefers to have the artist responsible for fabrication, thus avoiding the necessity of competitively bidding the work. In cases when an artist is inexperienced with a material and afraid of liability, the commissioning agency takes on the responsibility. Brussels, which has an extensive art program in its underground system, in many cases takes over execution of the work to contain costs.

12. Wendy Feuer, "Down the Tube—A Rapid View of Underground Art" *Stroll* 6/7 (June 1988): 84–85. The author notes that artists "cannot improve a bad station design." When the station design is neutral, the artwork increases in importance, as was the case at 23rd Street.

13. As director of the Arts for Transit office, I receive many requests to sponsor art projects in the system. Mostly we cannot support these projects because of lack of funds. Fewer are rejected because of their potential to elicit controversy. While the office may not be in a position to sponsor such work, there is no prohibition on an artist or organization from raising funds on their own to realize the project. Even before the office was established, this was the case with Les Levine's "WE ARE NOT AFRAID," subway advertising cards that appeared several years ago. The work was paid for by the National Endowment for the Arts, the Lower Manhattan Cultural Council, the Public Art Fund and the artist. More recently, Alfredo Jaar bought all of the advertising space in the Spring Street IND station with the help of the New York State Council on the Arts. He installed photographs of workers in South American gold mines with the price of gold posted next to the pictures.

9

Suzanne Lacy: Social Reformer and Witch

Moira Roth

Suzanne Lacy, one of the most prominent performance artists work-ing since the late 1960s, has produced large-scale spectacles with social agendas throughout the 1980s. Lacy's working method is designed to involve large groups of participants (such as elderly women or African-American women) and even larger audiences. She creates film, video, audio and print documents to further broaden her constituency, and her work has attracted widespread media attention that has produced local and national print publicity and television coverage. The nature of Lacy's work and all spectacle that courts media, on the one hand, and proposes advocacy of the disadvantaged and social change, on the other, raises questions that Lacy has put to herself and that Moira Roth grapples with in this article.

Image is paramount in Lacy's performances. Her overall design, theme and colors are always tightly controlled. The visual aspects of her performances are beautiful in the traditional artistic sense and unify their diverse elements. But Lacy's assessments of her work are based on the quality of experience for participants and audience, and the "staying power," the longer-term impact, of her work.

Roth's discussion of the witch and shaman brings to the fore Lacy's contribution as not only social action or networking but, in addition, as a redefinition of the male-apprehended shaman into the terms of female power. Roth also delves deeply into the personal, historical and mythical underpinnings of Lacy's work absent from most discussions.

This article originally appeared in *The Drama Review* 32, no. 1 (Spring 1988). Copyright 1988 New York University and the Massachusetts Institute of Technology. Reprinted by permission of the author and The MIT Press.

The apprehension of all public interest work may be, without such explorations, sanitized and stripped of richness.

The Social Reformer

> As political people, feminist performance artists were in-
> terested in social change outside this [Southern Californian]
> feminist circle; they became more subtle in the way they
> communicated to an audience. Simultaneously, their vision
> of who the audience could be grew larger.
> —Suzanne Lacy, quoted in *Artforum,* November 1980

In the summer of 1982, Suzanne Lacy was in San Francisco producing *Freeze Frame: Room for Living Room,* one of her huge visionary pieces. It involved more than one hundred women: groups of old black church women, old Jewish women, prostitutes, young professional women, bridge players, nuns, pregnant women, Chicana artists, teenagers, disabled women and many others. Commissioned by the San Francisco International Theater Festival, *Freeze Frame* was staged in an expensive, elegant furniture showroom. It attracted a large audience (as diverse as the performers) who gathered around to listen to the women as they sat at tables and on sofas, chairs and beds, talking amongst themselves about survival—emotional, financial, and political.

In the fall of that year, Lacy, who had returned to her home in Los Angeles, wrote to me in La Jolla about the painful stresses of her private life, ending her letter with: ''I need some vision, some exciting image to go for . . . or is that possible in flat, burnt-out Los Angeles? I constantly think about a hundred or two old women in white, standing on the cliffs and by the side of the mountain, sitting on the beach around white tablecloths, telling each other secrets: 'Whisper, the Waves, the Wind.' Right down the street from your house! Secrets about dying?''[1]

Two years later, after a year of intense organizing in the local community, Lacy created the brilliant, sunlight image of her *Whisper, the Waves, the Wind,* in which over 150 white-clad women from a wide variety of cultural, racial, and class backgrounds and ranging in age from sixty to ninety-eight sat on a La Jolla beach at small, white-covered tables.[2] On the cliffs above, one thousand people watched and listened to the women's prerecorded voices as they told secrets about dying and living. Lacy followed this first Whisper Project with an even

Moira Roth

Because artistic projects of such unusual scale and range of subject
[matt]er have not been done before, Lacy's work calls up several ques-
[tions]: What is the impact of these enormous tableaux and pageants,
[and] how can we judge them? Immediately after *Freeze Frame* in 1982,
[she] and I—talking intensely, arguing and speculating—wrote our
[resp]onses to the event. Mine was an account of the genesis of the piece
[for] the *Village Voice*.[5] Lacy composed an intriguing speculative and
[self-]critical essay for the *New Art Examiner*[6] in which she analyzed
[wor]k that had enthralled her since 1977. She postulated three ways
[of m]easuring the "success" of her work, which I find singularly useful
[as g]uides. These were, first, to examine the quality of the performance
[expe]rience for participants and audience; second, to evaluate the
[pote]ntial of these networking performances as models that can be ap-
[plie]d to other issues and circumstances; and third, to assess the life span
[of t]he processes set in motion by the performance.

[R]egarding the first criterion—the quality of the performance ex-
[per]ience for participants and audience—Lacy's work, for the most part,
[has] been successful.[7] Many people, both audience members and par-
[ticip]ants, have described informally (in conversation and in written
[resp]onse) the impact of these performances, whose poetic and pas-
[sion]ate images, live verbal exchanges and collaged sound tapes have
[offe]red powerful visions of women's communities and networks while
[allo]wing space for individual voice and experience.

[L]acy's response to her second criterion—the potential of these net-
[wo]rking performances as models—was crisply to the point. She wrote
[tha]t while her performances offer information on such things as the
[me]ans by which access to the media can be gained, they do not fully
[fun]ction as models for work concerned with more overtly political
[iss]ues, such as abortion rights. Lacy reasoned that specific "political"
[iss]ues have an unfortunate "way of polarizing people, and part of the
[str]ategy of eliciting participation from broad constituencies is in find-
[in]g issues that are not divisive. This is a major dilemma for me: the
[th]emes of my networking performances appear, of necessity,
[da]ngerously 'liberal,' rather than dangerously 'radical.'"[8]

[A]s to Lacy's third criterion concerning the life span of the processes
[se]t in motion by the performance, this too has proved problematic, at
[le]ast up until the 1987 *Crystal Quilt*. Lacy had been disappointed by
[th]e lack of "staying power" of her performances in their geographical
[si]tes. She wrote of her 1980 experience in New Orleans as an example
[of] this.[9] In the context of Lousiana's nonratification of the ERA, Lacy
[h]ad staged *River Meetings,* a theater evening which included
[d]ramatizations of "the lives of women in the Delta," poetry readings

WHISPER, THE WAVES, THE WIND
Suzanne Lacy
Over 150 white-clad older women sat at tables on the beach in La Jolla, California,
sharing secrets about dying and living.
(Photo courtesy Liz Cisco)

more ambitious work in Minnesota in the spring of 1
Minnesota Project produced a "living quilt" in the v
courtyard of a Phillip Johnson building in downtown
Crystal Quilt, performed by more than four hundred ol
women, drew an audience of several thousand.

Central to Lacy's thinking and to the structure of
art are her collaborations with Leslie Labowitz, an ai
who studied with Joseph Beuys in Europe in the mid-
and Lacy worked together for several years beginnin
Labowitz contributed street theater events to Lacy
organizing feat, *Three Weeks in May,* a three-week exa
protest about the incidence of rape in Los Angeles.[3]
Lacy and Labowitz produced the first in a series of colla
In Mourning and in Rage, in which women costumed i
and made to appear seven feet tall, surrounded and s
crowd of black-garbed women, appeared on the st
Angeles City Hall. There they each spoke briefly, addre
media's sensational coverage of the Hillside Strangler
more generally, the nationwide outbursts of violence a
Working together, Lacy and Labowitz produced other a
events and founded Ariadne: A Social Network, an org
served to bring together women in the arts, media and
who were committed to feminist issues. In a series of ar
together and separately, the two women refined their i
ing media and the successful structures of action-orien
performance.[4]

Since 1977 Lacy—working out of the context of the
tions with Labowitz, Susan Stone and other feminists—h
series of spectacles across the country. In these works and
longed and intense networking which produced them, Lac
turned from her earlier focus on specific feminist, action-or
to more general concerns with women's histories and comm
has moved from city to city establishing the connections r
produce ambitious large-scale works such as *The Internati
Party* (San Francisco, 1979); *Making It Safe: A Project on Viole
Women in Ocean Park* (Ocean Park, California, 1979); *Rive
Lives of Women in the Delta* (New Orleans, 1980); *Tree: A Pe
with Women of Ithaca* (Ithaca, New York, 1981); *Freeze Fra
for Living Room* (San Francisco, 1982); *Immigrants and Sur
Angeles, 1983); *Whisper, the Waves, the Wind* (La Jolla, 1984)
Madonna (Los Angeles, 1986); and The Whisper Minnesota P
Crystal Quilt (Minneapolis, 1987).

THE CRYSTAL QUILT
Suzanne Lacy, 1987
430 black-clad older women form a living quilt in the Phillip Johnson-designed IDS
Building in Minneapolis and, toward the end, applaud their audience.
(Photo courtesy Peter Latner)

and a gigantic potluck dinner attended by some five hundred women from all over the United States. Lacy left the city with ''a feeling of certainty that there was real energy afoot among women there and that this performance had helped crystalize it.''[10] Various subsequent projects had been proposed—including the beading of a tapestry of names signed at the dinner—but, after several meetings, the New Orleans planning committee ceased to convene. There was a similar lack of follow-up action in Ithaca after the 1981 *Tree*,[11] an event attended by one hundred women, fifty black and fifty white, in response to the region's historical connections to the 1848 Seneca Falls Women's Rights Convention, the underground railway for slaves and the feats of Harriet Tubman. Lacy's estimation regarding the dearth of responses to her projects was similarly borne out in San Francisco, where *Freeze Frame* failed to generate further activities in the city, and again in La Jolla after the Whisper Project.

So what are we left with? We are given vast pageantlike gatherings of women celebrating their differences, their commonalities, their survival, and their wisdom—performances with enormous poetic impact but hollow in terms of action-oriented resonance. Yet perhaps these performances inspire their participants and audiences with feminist visions that help sustain feminist energies and hopes. Surely that is a great deal for an artist to offer. And yet I sense that to Lacy, who was trained in radical feminist circles and whose earlier work had been action-oriented, these later networking performances appeared insufficient on a certain level because of their lack of concrete impact. I feel it was partially Lacy's driven, self-critical assessment of the ''success'' of her work that drew her to the highly supportive environment of Minneapolis, where she created the networks and series of events of The Whisper Minnesota Project, which led to her May 1987 *The Crystal Quilt*, the most extensive of her large-scale pieces, and perhaps her grand finale in this genre.

The Crystal Quilt audience of several thousand looked down from balconies on the ''living'' quilt of Lacy's four hundred black-costumed older women performers from throughout the state of Minnesota. After a ceremonious entry and unfolding of black tablecloths to reveal red and yellow cloths, the women sat at tables in groups of four, talking among themselves while they slowly arranged and rearranged their hands in unison on the tablecloths. The audience looked down on this spectacle and listened to Susan Stone's crystal-clear, taped collage of Native American and Hmong (Cambodian) songs, thunder claps and bird cries, combined with prerecorded conversations by some of the performers. As in the La Jolla *Whisper, the Waves, the Wind*, the Minnesota women spoke of their experiences of aging, death, life, and history.

Unlike any other networking performance by Lacy, The Whisper Minnesota Project not only promised but already has generated further actions. A group of *Crystal Quilt* performers have begun "Speak Outs" on the subject of older women, which they plan to take to small communities throughout the state. Sponsored in part by the Marquette Banks Minneapolis, a photo exhibition of *The Crystal Quilt* by seven well-known photographers will circulate throughout the state. And in Washington, D.C., the National Council on Aging has expressed an interest in hosting a roundtable discussion on the project. It is too soon to assess the ramifications of The Whisper Minnesota Project/*The Crystal Quilt,* but its potential is enormous and exciting.

There are several explanations for the more pragmatically successful outcome of this two-year project in Minnesota. First, the state justifiably prides itself on its support of the arts and its investment in civic concerns. Accordingly, there has been far more interest and community support than there was for the Californian Whisper Project. In Minnesota, Lacy's project was viewed as a novel catalyst for focusing on older women, whose interests were already a deeply felt concern. Second, the two-year piece was far more rooted in existing local and state organizations than any previous Lacy pieces had been. From the beginning of the project, Lacy and her coworkers had been closely associated with and strongly supported by many state and educational organizations, including the Minnesota Board on Aging, the Minneapolis College of Art and Design, the Hubert H. Humphrey Institute of Public Affairs (affiliated with the University of Minnesota), and with private organizations such as the feminist theater At the Foot of the Mountain, whose Phyllis Jane Rose was the associate director of the Whisper Minneapolis Project. Third, for the first time Lacy had sufficient staff—both paid and volunteer—some of whom have continued since May 1987 with follow-up work. Fourth—and this is hard to prove but I know it is a significant factor—there is now a "critical mass" of Lacy's performance work, especially with the combined weight of the La Jolla and Minneapolis performances.

So far I have described Suzanne Lacy, the charismatic creator of nationwide pageants and analytic writer on feminist performance art theory: Lacy, the social reformer/critic. There is, however, another way to look at her. Among the many personae she has adopted is one that brings her close to the often-taboo situation of the witch in Western culture. Historically, the witch has been the carrier of much that could not be spoken: she has embodied what is most terrifying about female consciousness and female sexuality.

The Witch

I was interested in taboo topics even before I was working with art. It's an interest in the macabre, the underbelly of society, the dark side of life. It is related to a certain kind of female spirituality. I've been interested in witches since I was eight. That esthetic is something I can trace back through childhood, including dreams that I later pinpointed as Dracula or vampire dreams. I was reading about the witchcraft trials at 12.
—Suzanne Lacy, Interview with Ruth Askey

In the Spring of 1980, I interviewed Lacy just after she had finished *River Meetings*. As we spoke of the California feminist art movement, and her past and present work, she said that "the conflict that I think is always present in my work, and I am sure a lot of other artists must feel it too, is the need to make a very private gesture or symbol manifest in the world. . . . You shouldn't censure the visions as they emerge. I know that for me the image comes first; the idea originates in the shower, on the freeway, floats in the air. And then there is the honing of it, which is a combination of esthetic and political processes."[12]

Such images—unruly, often coarse, violent and initially uncensored—have always pressed upon Lacy's imagination. She is fascinated by raw animal carcasses and entrails, by livers, lungs and hearts, all of which she used as ingredients in early performance pieces. The story of Dracula and the Gothic horror of Mary Shelley's Frankenstein inspired her two *Monster Series* pieces (1974–75). Lacy's sustained interest in "the macabre, the underbelly of society, the dark side of life" was dramatically apparent in her 1976 *Falling Apart* series (black-and-white photos of Lacy's nude body flying over the ocean were cut in two by roughly torn colored photographs of raw animal entrails) and in the narratives and illustrations for *Three Love Stories*, a self-published 1978 artist's book that includes photos of animal brains and lungs and a bottled raw animal heart.[13]

A vivid picture of the intense and obsessive young Lacy emerges in Judy Chicago's account[14] of *Ablutions,* a 1972 collaborative performance by Chicago, Aviva Rahmani, Sandra Orgel and Lacy. (This was basically the first time Lacy was involved in the creation of a performance.) In *Ablutions,* nude women plunged into blood, egg yolks and clay, and later were bandaged and roped. A devastating tape of women describing their rape experiences accompanied the performance. Lacy took one of the few active roles in the piece, nailing raw animal kidneys to the walls and tying them with a rope pulled so tightly "that the blood ran out of the meat and down the wall." She and another performer then walked round and round the performance space, "tying everything up neatly, like some obsessive housekeeping duty, until the performance area was like a spider web."[15] The content and imagery of *Ablutions* provide a vivid picture of the charged ambiance—Judy Chicago's Fresno Feminist Art Program and its later manifestation at Cal Arts in Los Angeles—which shaped Lacy's earliest work.

One of Lacy's most dramatic uses of animal carcasses was in *There Are Voices in the Desert,* a 1978 Las Vegas performance created in the context of *From Reverence to Rape to Respect,* a ten-day collaboration with Labowitz. Prior to Lacy's performance, women had written on the walls of a small white room with a three-foot entrance (specially constructed for the piece in the University of Nevada Gallery) about their experiences of sexual violence. On the night of the performance the audience entered this space, its floor covered with dirt and rocks, and listened to the taped sounds of desert winds blowing. Jeff Kelley published a vivid account of his experiences of this astonishing piece:

> One entered the room, encountering against the rear wall three lamb carcasses suspended as if dancing, embellished with pink and white Las Vegas showgirl plumage and beads draped over their fresh meat. Like horrid puppets, the carcasses were at once dancing and hanging by necks wrenched in the moment just before death. Lacy sat above the entry, naked, almost spiritual in presence, the antithesis of Las Vegas meat. She placed necklaces around the necks of the viewers, symbolically linking them with the adorned lamb carcasses.[16]

Were these animal carcasses and entrails mere Gothic obsessions to be superseded by Lacy's later (more mature?) public images and concerns? Or do they continue to be essential underpinnings and metaphoric substructures within her current pageant work? A revealing clue can be found in Lacy's employment of animal carcasses in her first 1976–77 experiments using her own body to think about aging— the focus of her large networking performances since 1983.[17]

Between August 1976 and November 1977, Lacy, then in her early thirties, produced a trilogy on aging: *Inevitable Associations; Edna, May Victor, Mary and Me: An All-Night Benediction;* and *The Bag Lady.* In *Inevitable Associations,* she sat for four hours in the lobby of the Los Angeles Biltmore Hotel while a Hollywood makeup artist made her look old. Lacy was then joined by friends of hers, real older women who clothed her in black, similar to their own dresses: "I had an incredible feeling of uniting with them in a matriarchal connection. . . . They called up associations of witchcraft, death, wisdom, and fear."[18] The second event of the trilogy, *Edna, May Victor, Mary and Me: An All-*

Night Benediction, was staged in a private room of the Los Angeles Hilton Hotel and accompanied by taped conversations among three old women. Lacy herself sat as an old woman surrounded by memorabilia (of Edna, an older woman friend of hers) while on the bed lay a large lamb carcass which Lacy periodically covered and uncovered during the all-night performance. Recorded by a closed-circuit video camera, the night passed; in the morning Lacy briefly traded places with the lamb.

In another piece of this period, performed at Mills College in Oakland, California, Lacy appeared—old, gloved and hatted—awkwardly walking and clutching a handbag as she cradled the bandaged carcass of a lamb in her arms. The title of this 1978 piece is intriguing: *The Lady and the Lamb or The Goat and the Hag.* The "lady and the lamb" has a ring of Christian decorum to it, whereas the use of the word "hag," derived from the Greek *hagia* and originally meaning "a holy one," conjures up both the pagan crone and contemporary feminist associations. In her various manifestations, the hag appeared in German mythology as the Hag of the Iron Wood, and was worshiped as a goddess by the Saxons and Danes.[19] As for Lacy's use of "the goat" in her title, there are references in the records of French witchcraft trials to a Devil-lover of the witch who would appear disguised as a goat.[20]

What does Lacy know of such history? Certainly she has always expressed an interest in it. And there was much talk about it in her immediate circle in Los Angeles. The first issue of *Chrysalis,* the Los Angeles-based feminist publication whose editors were among Lacy's closest associates, appeared in 1977 containing extracts from Deena Metzger's *The Book of Hags* and from Susan Griffin's then-unpublished *Woman and Nature: The Roaring inside Her* (1978). In the article's introduction, Griffin stated that the patriarchy has always "regarded and treated women and nature in the same way."[21] Griffin's texts consist of a highly graphic and disturbing juxtaposition of the history of scientific discoveries with witchcraft, poetic speculations on the nature of the mule, the horse and the lion; and a section on "the old woman" describing the passage of life imprinted on her body.

Lacy's work has always recognized such archetypal connections, though not necessarily in a scholarly way. As an intensified focus on older women—their bodies, their psyches, their lives, and the ways they have been socially marginalized—replaced Lacy's earlier use of animal entrails and carcasses, her work has become accessible to larger audiences. Old women, as Griffin suggests, are our repositories of experience and knowledge, a resource vastly underutilized today in American society. Lacy's work with older women and witches also needs to be considered in the light of recent feminist writing about the closely related figure of the crone.

The Crone

> The "Thousand-Named Goddess" . . . was the first Holy Trinity. Her three major aspects have been designated Virgin, Mother, and Crone; or, alternatively, Creator, Preserver, and Destroyer. The same trinitarian pattern can be traced in all the Goddess figures of India, Arabia, Egypt, the Middle East, Aegean and Mediterranean cultures, and among the Celtic and Teutonic peoples of northern Europe.
> —Barbara G. Walker

In her 1985 book, *The Crone*,[22] Walker traces the history of the most powerful of the three personae (Vigin, Mother, and Crone) of the many-named great Goddess. The Virgin and Mother aspects of the ancient Goddess were subsumed by Christian ideology but that of the Crone— the Queen of Shades, Goddess of the Underworld, Lady of the Night— was not (except in the Gnostic-Christian Great Mother Sophia). At first, the Crone was "diabolized" in the form of the medieval witch: old women were the most frequent victims of medieval persecution of witches. Later she was almost entirely suppressed in Western cultures. Walker argues that "such archetypal connections must be considered in any serious effort to trace to its roots the combination of sexism and ageism that makes elder women the invisible citizens of the modern world."[23]

Walker's study of the Crone (together with Lucy R. Lippard's *Overlay: Contemporary Art and the Art of Prehistory* [1983], Susan Griffin's *Woman and Nature* [1978] and other feminist revisionist scholarship on the meaning of medieval witches) provides a rich array of poetical insights into the mythic and ritualistic aspects of Lacy's performances. Walker describes the "ceremonies of blood" in prehistoric matriarchy (the reading of entrails and the pouring of blood into sacred cauldrons) and the sacred poetry of the Scandinavian oracular priestesses (the *sagas*). Particularly germane to Lacy's color symbolism is the fact that in both northwestern Europe and southeastern Asia there were three colors associated with the female trinity: white for the Virgin, red for the Mother and black for the Crone. These colors appear frequently in Lacy's work. Red—which, for example, in the case of the Indian goddess Kali is symbolic of "blazing energy and passion"—was predominant in many of her early pieces. The red-stained, moaning nude women who crouched harpy-like above a ledge next to the winged, skinned lamb carcass in *She Who Would Fly* (1977) and the red-and-black garments of *In Mourning and in Rage* (1977) are two examples of this predilection. In 1984, Lacy chose white for the participants' clothes and for the tablecloths in *Whisper, the Waves, the Wind*. She followed this in 1986 with *The Dark Madonna*[24] whose dazzling white tableaux—created by (primarily) Black, Chicana and Asian women wearing white clothes and posed on white pedestals— were transformed after dusk by black-garbed women. Finally, in *The Crystal Quilt* (1987), Lacy turned bluntly to black, the color of the Crone. This was a controversial decision in Minneapolis: Lacy and Miriam Schapiro, the painter who had designed the "quilt" of the performance piece, maintained that they chose black (together with red and yellow tablecloths) for formal reasons, whereas many of the participants and most ardent local supporters of the piece argued that black was too closely and too negatively associated with death and mourning. For example, Elva Walker, president of the statewide Board on Aging and a great supporter of Lacy's project, commented to me wryly some time before the performance that it would "take pure genius not to make it look like a funeral procession." No one, as far as I know, referred to the ancient associations of black with the Crone.

Certainly there have been no references to the curious parallel between the titles of the La Jolla and Minneaplis spectacles and a medieval German legend cited by Barbara G. Walker in *The Woman's Encyclopedia of Myths and Secrets* (1983). Walker wrote of the Triple Goddess, who "presided over a land of the dead called Wisperthal (Valley of Whispers) centering on an enchanted Hall of Mirrors—perhaps related to the fairytale Crystal Mountain. Three innocent youths once trespassed in the valley, met various aspects of the Goddess as three beautiful maidens, three terrible hags, and three black death-ravens. They barely escaped with their lives from the eerie place and vowed never to return."[25] I quote this not to suggest a literal illustration of this old legend by Lacy, who indeed told me recently that she was unaware of the story, but rather to emphasize again the unconscious affinities between Lacy's imagery and old legends, myths and rituals.

Recent discussions of Lacy's work generally contain no reference to subjects such as the Crone and the Witch or to the kind of powerful, discomforting ideas that they conjure up. Why the dearth of awareness and/or recognition of these foundations in Lacy's art? I suspect that they would greatly hamper the increasingly broad appeal of her spectacles—most dramatically apparent in the statewide interest in her Minneapolis project. Lacy herself makes less reference to this material than she once did; the art writers most interested in her work now are usually concerned with its overt political aspects; and the journalists who wrote so many articles on *Whisper, the Waves, the Wind* and *The Crystal Quilt* may be unaware of this material. I have recently come to feel, however, that it is important to put this material back into the discourse surrounding Lacy's art. To ignore it is to allow a too simplistic, decorous and sanitized reading of her work.

The Anatomy Lesson

> *By the body of this old woman we are hushed. We are awed. We know that it was in her body that we began. And now we say that it is from her body that we learn. That we see our past.*
>
> —Susan Griffin

This passage comes from "*The Anatomy Lesson* (Her Skin),"[26] in Griffin's *Woman and Nature,* the beginning of a poetic discourse on the body of the old woman, which Griffin followed by "*History* (Her Hair)," "*Memory* (The Breasts)," "*Archives* (Her Vulva)," "*Letters* (Her Clitoris)," and "*Records* (Her Womb)"—a visceral reading of history and memory akin to Lacy's.

From the time of her undergraduate and graduate work in pre-med studies, zoology and psychology, Lacy has been drawn literally and metaphorically to the "anatomy lesson" inherent in women's bodies.[27] Indeed, between 1973 and 1976, Lacy created a photographic series entitled *The Anatomy Lessons,* which developed out of a general interest in medical history and a public slide-lecture she gave on the history of medicine in which she compared historical illustrations to certain performance art works. The photos in the *Anatomy Lessons* included images of Lacy eating different parts of a chicken (*Wing, Arm, Breast, Leg*) and as an energetic cooking instructor—a mad, knife-brandishing Julia Child, using parts of a lamb carcass to explain *Where the Meat Comes From.* Lacy once said of her *Fourth Anatomy Lesson*'s imagery—a pool with bags of guts floating over her nude body—that she associated it with giving birth, and, generally, with women's spirituality: "I've long thought that women's spirituality is rooted in the physical and that women will transcend through the body, whereas the male form of transcendence is through idea, it is more of an ethereal transcendence."[28]

Simplistic and crude as these *Anatomy Lessons* were, they graphical-
ly illustrate Lacy's consistent preoccupation with, as she once phrased
it, "being inside a body which changes and grows infirm."[29] Tied to
this conviction that the body is a "time bomb" and, again, deeply
rooted on an almost visceral level is Lacy's recognition of and longing
for "loosening the physical boundaries of the flesh, hence of the
identity."[30]

At the heart of Lacy's early work as well as her current pageants
is her dual need to experience and to become one with "the other."
This desire appears clearly in work after work in which she reaches out
powerfully, poetically, analytically and often almost greedily to understand and sometimes literally experience (witness her performances as
an older woman) the bodies, lives, and convictions of women profoundly different from herself in race, class, age and lifestyle. The verbal exchanges and the appearances of the seventeen *Freeze Frame* groups
in the San Francisco furniture showroom were probably the most dis-
tilled and concise of Lacy's many dramatic presentations of the lives
and beliefs of radically diverse women.

I remember as I moved from one *Freeze Frame* group to the next—
each so visually distinct, so deliberately stereotypic in dress—listening
to a disabled woman speaking of being labeled mentally defective
because of her cerebral palsy, to a young Asian-American woman
describing her six-foot-tall grandmother in China; to ex-psychiatric in-
mates raging against public attitudes toward mental illness; to bridge
players (including Lacy's own mother) discussing their long-term friend-
ships; to prostitutes recalling their childhoods; to radical Chicana artists
and corporate women analyzing the ways they had been stereotyped;
and, finally, to Mrs. Cohen in the older Jewish group announcing the
almost immediate arrival of her one hundredth birthday. These women
sat in their respective groups, coming together only at the end to turn
as one group and face the audience as they spoke briefly in unison—a
sound like that of a river or of wind blowing through the trees.

Freeze Frame appears to be light years away from such early works
as the *Anatomy Lessons*. Instead of raw guts, we now witness the
spilling out of secret, often painful experiences; instead of silent raw
lungs, we now hear women's voices; instead of raw hearts, we are now
offered the passions of women's experiences; and instead of raw entrails from which to read auguries, we now can envision, through Lacy's
spectacles, communities of women in the future. But is this really so
different?

The Spectacle

Every genuinely shamanic seance ends as a spectacle unequaled in the world of daily experience. The fire tricks, the "miracles" of the rope-trick or mango-trick type, the exhibition of magical feats, reveal another world—the fabulous world of the gods and magicians, the world in which everything seems possible . . . *where the "laws of nature" are abolished, and a certain superhuman "freedom" is exemplified and made dazzlingly* present.
—Mircea Eliade

The term "spectacle" has been much bandied about in performance circles (as has "shaman"). Indeed, spectacle performance might be seen as constituting a genre—with Robert Wilson as its most brilliant and long-term exponent. Spectacle performance artists employ many traditional theatrical devices, such as scripts, extensive rehearsals and elaborate lighting, costuming and staging, to create their "Theatre of Images" (Bonnie Marranca's term)—theater which is presented remotely, grandly and expensively in large spaces to large audiences. Such spectacle performance is dramatically different from earlier performance art which, especially on the West Coast, was committed to privacy and intimacy—of content, audience and space—and to nontheatrical modes of presentation. In some ways Lacy's recent work still relates to this earlier performance sensibility, but in many other ways the grand, public scope of her events is akin to this new genre. Yet one can also argue that her spectacles and certain aspects of her modes of experience can be profitably placed within a shamanic tradition (Lacy has often spoken of her fascination with the trickster tradition)—if it is at all possible to speak of shamans, and female ones at that, in this society.

For both performer and audience there were moments in *Whisper, the Waves, the Wind* and *The Crystal Quilt* when, through the magic visual "tricks" of the dazzling spectacles and the voices of the old, white-clothed women on the beach and the black-clothed women in the crystal court, another world was revealed. This was a world akin to the shamanic one that Eliade described, a world in which *"everything seems possible . . .* and a certain superhuman 'freedom' is . . . made dazzlingly *present."*[31]

In contemporary American thought, the witch is still denigrated or trivialized (except in radical feminist circles) whereas the shaman has been romanticized and, accordingly, has become a rather popular subject. Though in reality shamans were frequently tricksters and sometimes almost mad, current American and European scholarship often offers a somewhat simplistic reading of shamans as benign healing figures situated at the center of their societies. Thus the shaman has earned a good reputation; the witch has not. Nevertheless, there are many parallels between the roles these two have played. Why has the shaman attracted so much more serious scholarly attention than the witch? Is this because most shamans, with rare exceptions (in Korea, for example), are male, whereas witches are almost exclusively female? Surely, the construction of the male shamanic healer in contemporary Western scholarship must be read in part as a measure of the continued downgrading of female power. Is it possible that Lacy's work not only demands recognition of the taboo witch but also might lead us to redefine the shaman's role in terms of female power?

Notes

1. Personal correspondence with author, 1982.

2. The film, *Whisper, the Waves, the Wind,* by Kathleen Laughlin and Suzanne Lacy (1986), combines footage of the performance with a filmed sequence of a reunion one year later by some of the main organizers.

3. Lacy compiled a fascinating, self-published account in an edition of ten of *Three Weeks in May* (1978), which details through chronologies of the process, correspondence with city officials, press releases, newspaper cuttings, etc., her brilliant organizational skills and modes of working, already firmly established by 1977.

4. Coauthored essays by Suzanne Lacy and Leslie Labowitz include: "Evolution of a Feminist Art: Public Forms and Social Issues" *Heresies* 2, no. 2 (Summer 1978); "Mass Media, Popular Culture, and Fine Art: Images of Violence against Women" *Social Works* exhibition catalogue, edited by Nancy Buchanan, The Los Angeles Institute of Contemporary Art (September-October, 1979); "Two Approaches to Feminist Media Usage," *Proceedings of the Caucus for Art and Marxism,* College Art Association (January 1979); "Feminist Artists: Developing Media Strategy for the Movement," in Frederique Delacoste and Felice Newman, eds., *Fight Back* (Minneapolis: Cleis Press, 1981); and separate articles in which they explore shared ideas.

5. Moira Roth, "A Family of Women?" *The Village Voice* (A Special Supplement, "How They Make It, Three Artists at Work," 28 September 1982), pp. 71–74.
   I have written extensively on Lacy, including reviews of *The International Dinner Party* in *Art in America* (April 1980) and of *The Crystal Quilt* in *High Performance* 10, no. 3 (1987) and in *Art in America* (March 1988); sections in "Toward a History of California Performance: Part Two," *Arts Magazine* (June 1978); and in *The Amazing Decade: Women and Performance Art in America, 1970–1980* (Los Angeles: Astro Arts, 1983), which I edited and for which I wrote a long essay on women's performance art, including one section devoted to Lacy.

6. Suzanne Lacy, "Speak Easy," *New Art Examiner* (October 1982): 7, 9.

7. Obviously, it is hard to estimate such reactions. Lacy has conducted interviews and keeps a lot of written responses. I myself have witnessed most of these major works

over the last ten years and so have a firsthand sense of the reactions. Of course, there have also been criticisms, including expressions of discontent among some of the participants and complaints by the members of the audience ranging from gripes about not being able to see the event clearly enough to criticisms of style, content and intent.

8. Suzanne Lacy, "Speak Easy," p. 7.

9. Ibid., pp. 7, 9.

10. Ibid., p. 7.

11. See Suzanne Lacy, "The Forest and the Trees," *Heresies* 4, no. 3.

12. Moira Roth, "Visions and Re-Visions," *Artforum* 19, no. 3 (November 1980): 43.

13. In a phone conversation with Lacy on 7 August 1987, she said that what she described as her intense "interest in evil" during this period was expressed in two ways: in her private works on vampires and monsters, etc.; and, on a more public and sociopolitical level, in *Three Weeks in May* and *In Mourning and in Rage*.

14. Judy Chicago, *Through the Flower: My Struggle as a Woman Artist* (Garden City, New York: Doubleday & Company, 1977), pp. 217–19. Chicago does not refer to Lacy by name but Lacy is, in fact, the "fifth woman" in Chicago's description of *Ablutions*.

15. Ibid., p. 219.

16. Jeff Kelley, "Rape and Respect in Las Vegas," *Artweek* (20 May 1978); p. 4.

17. Lacy had been emotionally and artistically drawn to older women before 1977. The *Menopause Tape* (1972), made while she was a student at Cal Arts, recorded conversations with postmenopausal women.

18. Interview with author, Encinitas, California, 3 November 1977.

19. Barbara G. Walker, *The Crone: Woman of Age, Wisdom, and Power* (New York: Harper & Row, 1985), pp. 53–54.

20. Margaret Alice Murray, *The Witch-Cult in Western Europe* (Oxford: Clarendon Press, 1971), p. 68.

21. Susan Griffin, "Women [sic] and Nature: The Roaring Inside Her," *Chrysalis*, No. 1 (1977): 55.

22. Barbara G. Walker, *The Crone*, p. 21.

23. Ibid., pp. 37–38.

24. *The Dark Madonna*, sponsored by the University of California, Los Angeles Center for the Study of Women and the U.C.L.A. Wight Art Gallery, was a three-part event. The first section was a two-day symposium (*not* about Lacy's work) on "The Dark Madonna, Women, Culture and Community Rituals" (8–9 November 1985); the second section consisted of a series of private meetings among Los Angeles women to discuss racism; and the third was Lacy's *The Dark Madonna*, performed in the Franklin D. Murphy Sculpture Garden of the U.C.L.A. campus on 31 May 1986.

25. Barbara G. Walker, *The Woman's Encyclopedia of Myths and Secrets* (New York: Harper & Row, 1983), p. 1075.

26. Susan Griffin, *Woman and Nature: The Roaring Inside Her* (New York: Harper & Row, 1978), p. 209.

27. See the interesting array of articles in *Representation,* No. 17 (Winter 1987), a special issue devoted to The Cultural Display of the Body and Abigail Solomon-Godeau's "The Legs of the Countess," *October* (Winter 1986).

28. Interview with the author, Encinitas, California, 3 November 1977.

29. Moira Roth, "Visions and Re-Visions," p. 43.

30. Ibid., p. 43.

31. Wendell C. Beane and William G. Doty, eds., *Myths, Rites, Symbols—A Mircea Eliade Reader,* vol. 2 (New York: Harper & Row, 1976), p. 282.

10

Defining the Image as Place: A Conversation with Kit Galloway, Sherrie Rabinowitz and Gene Youngblood

Steven Durland

Kit Galloway and Sherrie Rabinowitz, as Mobile Image, have created projects using satellite telecommunications for over a decade. Steven Durland believes that "they combine the technological and sociological possibilities of 2-way communications with artistic sensibility to create elegant models of the way things could be." The ego-identified art product must, Rabinowitz and Galloway feel, give way to the task of creating a context for two-way communication if an authentic environment for art and for life is to be achieved. As "metadesigners," they approach the image as a place—a real place where artists and artworks can have new power and meaning. Their use of technology and of satellite telecommunications in particular, also raises new questions and sets fresh criteria for their unique form of artist-generated public-interest art.

Durland's article is in the form of a conversation with Galloway, Rabinowitz and Gene Youngblood, an expert on art and new technology. The choice of this format is especially appropriate, because conversation is the high level of communication that defines good art for the three interviewees.

Scale is possibly the most important aesthetic and political feature of their work. The skills and equipment needed for work in their form and on their scale are out of the reach of the great majority. But, Rabinowitz remarked, "the only real power is to work at the same scale

---

This article originally appeared in *High Performance*, No. 37 (1987). The Addendum appears here for the first time.

that contemporary society is working on. If you don't create on the same scale that you can destroy, then art is rendered impotent."

The context that Mobile Image wants to make available on a much wider scale someday could serve other artists, whose political-issue work could become content. This truly alternative environment and an inclusive participation by artists and others to determine what will be communicated together make the Mobile Image vision highly political and potentially powerful. Their work takes the art/life dichotomy squarely onto the side of life. And although Satellite Arts Project, Hole-in-Space *and* Electronic Cafe *may now seem futuristic or fantastic, Rabinowitz and Galloway envision their next work as taking place entirely in participants' present tense.*

Since meeting in 1975, Kit Galloway and Sherrie Rabinowitz have focused their collaborative art career on developing new and alternative structures for video as an interactive communication form. Under their organizational moniker of Mobile Image, the pair have created three major works, *Satellite Arts Project* (1977), *Hole-in-Space* (1980) and *Electronic Cafe* (1984), as well as numerous smaller projects. Their sophisticated knowledge of satellite telecommunications had made them sought-after consultants in the field and their research has resulted in numerous contributions to the technology. They combine the technological and sociological possibilities of two-way communications with artistic sensibility to create elegant models of the way things could be. These "models," a term they prefer to "artworks," serve not only as a vision of how telecommunications could serve humanity but also put forward some provocative notions of the future and function of the artist.

Gene Youngblood has been a writer, lecturer and teacher on the subject of art and new technology for seventeen years. In 1970 he authored *Expanded Cinema,* the first book about video as an artistic medium. Today he is considered one of the most informed and articulate theorists of media art and politics. His theory of the "creative conversation" is an inspiring vision of the role of the artist in society.[1]

Youngblood is a faculty member at California Institute of the Arts, where he teaches the history and theory of experimental film and video. He is currently collaborating with Rabinowitz and Galloway on a new book titled *Virtual Space: The Challenge to Create at the Same Scale as We Can Destroy.* According to Youngblood, *Virtual Space* will examine the political, philosophic and aesthetic implications of the communications revolution.

In addition to their contributions to *Virtual Space,* Rabinowitz and Galloway are developing a composite-image performance between dancers in the Soviet Union and the United States. A second project-in-progress, *Light Transition,* will use satellite television images to sync contemporary technology with natural systems and ancient technology such as Stonehenge. Critical moments of sun/moon intersection, etc., will appear for twenty seconds every half-hour on a cable TV superstation. "This project will be more poetic than our others," said Galloway. "It's basically a celebration of earth's systems and human-made technological systems. We hope to create a project in which both systems reflect the elegance of the other."

In early March I visited the Mobile Image studio in Santa Monica and listened in as Rabinowitz, Galloway and Youngblood discussed the work of Mobile Image and its implications for the future of art and communication.

SHERRIE RABINOWITZ   When Kit and I first met it was in Paris. I'd been invited over and I was introduced to him as the person who knows everything about *ze video* in France, in Paris.

KIT GALLOWAY   Bit of an exaggeration.

SR   Before we met I was working in San Francisco and helped start Optic Nerve, a group there, and Kit was working in Europe with the Video Heads. Both of us through our experiences had come to two realizations. One is that the power of television is its ability to be live, to support real-time conversation independent of geography. Number two was a sense of the way television is experienced, the way it's taken in, this wash of images with nobody really remembering the context of any particular image. Television is an image environment and that's how you have to understand it. Making tapes didn't make sense because it wasn't affecting the context or the environment.

Kit had become interested in satellites, in '73, '74. When we met we put our ideas together and developed the track that we've been on ever since.

KG   Living in Europe I could see what effect television was having on different countries, reading all the material at UNESCO back when satellites were beginning to appear and were seen as a weapon against illiteracy. I was seeing how most of the world apart from the United States had an international policy for telecommunications. But the United States, under the guise of "free flow of information," was putting forward a policy of first-come, first-served, screw you if you can't get up there and park a satellite.

ELECTRONIC CAFE
Kit Galloway and Sherrie Rabinowitz, 1984
Mobile image with the prototype for the *Electronic Cafe* sites.
(Photo courtesy Bob Chamberlain)

SATELLITE ARTS PROJECT:
A SPACE WITH NO GEOGRAPHICAL BOUNDARIES, 1977
In collaboration with NASA, the world's first interactive composite-image satellite dance performance. Using the U.S.-Canadian CTS satellite, dancers located 3000 miles apart at NASA Goddard Space Flight Center, Maryland, and the Educational TV Center, Menlo Park, California, were electronically composited into a single image that was displayed on monitors at each location, creating a "space with no geographical boundaries" or virtual space in which the live performance took place. Performance includes the first satellite time-delay feedback dance; three-location live-feed composite performance; flutist Paul Horn playing with his time echo. July performance and three-day performance in November.

HOLE-IN-SPACE: A PUBLIC COMMUNICATION SCULPTURE, 1980
A three-day, life-size, unannounced, live satellite link allowing spontaneous interaction between the public on two coasts. Video cameras and rear-projection screens were installed in display windows at Lincoln Center for the Performance Arts in New York and The Broadway department store, Century City, Los Angeles. Each screen displayed life-size, full-figure images of people on the opposite coast. There were no signs or instructions. Passers-by drawn to the windows discovered an open channel through which they could see, hear and talk with people on the other coast almost as if they were standing on the same street corner.

ELECTRONIC CAFE, JULY–SEPTEMBER 1984
Called "One of the most innovative projects of the Los Angeles Olympic Arts Festival," officially commissioned as an Olympic Arts Festival Project by the Museum of Contemporary Art (MOCA), Los Angeles. *Electronic Cafe* linked MOCA and five ethnically diverse communities of Los Angeles through a state-of-the-art telecommunications computer database and dial-up image bank designed as a crosscultural, multilingual network of "creative conversation." From MOCA downtown, and the real cafes located in the Korean community, Hispanic community, black community and beach communities of Los Angeles, people separated by distance could send and receive slow-scan video images, draw or write together with an electronic writing tablet, print hard-copy pictures with the video printer, enter information or ideas in the computer database and retrieve it with Community Memory keyword search, and store or retrieve images on a videodisc recorder which held 20,000 images. *Electronic Cafe* ran six hours a day, six days a week for seven weeks.

I was aware of the imbalance and I got more and more interested in television and its technology as a communications medium. We started looking at ways of using international satellite transmissions. There were no interesting ideas in the mountains of UNESCO documentation. We looked at the idea of collaborative performances between artists in different countries meeting in this composite-image space we had conceived, mixing the live images from remote locations and presenting that mix at each location so that performers could see themselves on the same screen with their partners. That became the premise of the work and experimentation we wanted to do.

In '75 NASA announced that they were accepting proposals from public organizations to experiment with their US/Canadian satellite. They were trying to drum up some public support by providing access. So we hopped on a Russian liner and landed in New York and in a couple of months had secured NASA underwriting for a project that was going to last for about a year, a project that to date is probably the most intensive look at the interactive potential of human communications, and satellite time delay problems.

SR   It's still the most sophisticated. And it's only been in the past few years that people have come to appreciate what it is. It's still not been duplicated.

HIGH PERFORMANCE   How did your projects develop?

KG   We came back here with the idea that we would work domestically, doing model projects, and then, when we had the credentials, to move out internationally.

SR   We did a number of projects—large-scale ones like *Satellite Arts, Hole-in-Space* and *Electronic Cafe* and smaller ones that had a different intensity, laboratory things.

KG   The first project was called *The Satellite Arts Project.*

SR   When we first did *Satellite Arts,* nobody was interested in satellites; everybody was interested in, I don't know, video art. It took a long time. And now others have caught up. We always approached the image as a place. To our way of thinking, the essence, the magic, is this ability to carry a living event and then interconnect with satellites to connect places over vast distances. When we started, and even now, there was no aesthetic approach to this. Businesses used teleconferencing, but the aesthetics of what that connection is, is a whole new reality that hasn't been explored. In a sense it's a metadesign. It's looking at the live image in telecommunications as part of a grander structure.

KG You just don't go out, which is relatively easy to do, and rent satellite time and do something that would be of any significant contribution outside of the context of ignorance. There's a great context of ignorance both in the industry and in the art world as to the intrinsic nature of this medium. We focus on the living event, not being too concerned with whether it's artlike or not. We don't produce artifacts, we produce living events that take place over a period of time, to facilitate a quality of human-to-human interaction.

GENE YOUNGBLOOD When video first started there were three directions that it took, all simultaneously. One was "artist's video," that is, people like Bruce Nauman and Vito Acconci, who came from the art world, using video to document their art practices. Then there was what is called, for lack of a better term, "electronic video," that is, the exploration of the essence of the medium, represented by people like the Vasulkas. Then there was "political video," guerrilla television and so on, which was essentially a documentary tradition. But that excluded this whole other world of live interconnection, which is what Kit and Sherrie represent. It's an important direction.

KG Other artists have accessed satellite technology but look at what Douglas Davis has done with his access, or Nam June Paik more recently. Doug's pieces have been very sort of "artist using a satellite with a written scenario," like a theater piece that is all scripted out and some interaction is then portrayed during the access of this technology. It's still held within the context of control.

GY Spectacle.

SR One of the essences of our work is scale. When you galvanize that much technology and that many resources, it's not like an artist working in a garrett. As soon as you work with telecommunications, a satellite's part of your structure, as is the society around you. You have to deal with NASA and Western Union to access your satellite time. You have to deal with where the satellite comes in, you have to deal with the real thing, and it's expensive. So the idea of doing something that's self-focused just doesn't seem to be a very ecological, political use of the medium. You can't deal with this technology without dealing with it politically.

GY It really pushes up against a question of how far an artist is willing to go in the direction of not being an artist, giving up the ego identification with the product. That's a central issue with all this. Everybody knows that people in power can use this technology to put on a spectacle; we see it every day. So the fact that an artist could raise the money to do this is not really a revelation. It doesn't constitute a revolutionary use of the medium. But if somebody were to set up a system and then turn it over to people, like Kit and Sherrie do, nobody else does that, nobody. So who in our society is going to do that? The artist as traditionally understood won't do it.

So we need a new practitioner, who does what I call "metadesign." They create context rather than content. An artist can enter the context they create and make content, which will now be empowered and revitalized in a way that it could never have been empowered before without the context that these people set up. To me, this is the new avant-garde: the collaboration of the metadesigner and the artist. One not being enough without the other, each needing the other and together constituting a whole new force. A context is created that can be controlled by the people who constitute it. Those people might be artists whose work would then be given an autonomy of context, which it dearly needs, which the whole modern history of art is screaming for. So this is where it gets important.

HP I'm very intrigued with this idea of using art to empower other people instead of using it to empower yourself.

SR I don't see the way we create our pieces as based solely on the fact that you have to empower people. The way we embrace the issue is pretty classically art. If you define the aesthetic of the medium by defining what the essence and integrity of that medium is, then good art—in the sense of telecommunications—means that you create a situation that has to be some kind of communication between people in order to maximize what that technology can do. If you're just scripting from one side to the other side, you don't need a satellite, you can run two tapes. There has to be that quality of tension that defines what communication is, that higher level, which would be, as Gene points out, the conversation. And unless you create that tension in the work, then you're not really looking at the qualities of the medium, or the qualities of the art.

HP Were you aware of a television program called "The People's Summit" that featured a live studio audience in Seattle hosted by Phil Donahue meeting with a live studio audience in Leningrad hosted by Vladimir Posner?

KG The Phil and Vlad show.

SR That's who we're starting to work with now, those and others. Not Donahue.

KG   We believe very much in the principle of informal networking, which is aligned with the new phenomenon of citizen diplomacy. Now when you put that in the context of a nationally-rated syndicated program like Donahue, then again it becomes a spectacle, and it's not really an informal network. When that happened I felt that it was very much a disaster, ill-conceived, ill-executed. The consequences were not all that good. Yet in a context of ignorance even a gesture in that direction is somewhat healing, or an improvement over what existed before.

SR   Everybody, including the Russians, is ready for something more interesting, more cultural integration between the United States and the Soviet Union and also cultural integration between all of us and the electronic culture.

HP   On the order of *Hole in Space*?

KG   There's interest in that. Our work with *Electronic Cafe* was carried to the Soviet Union. They looked at what we did here in Los Angeles as an international model for crosscultural communications systems. I could show you newspaper articles from *Pravda* where they took the concept and totally embraced it. They made an Electronic Cafe in Moscow, did some slow-scan and voice-only connections with San Francisco.

SR   One of the things we're working towards now is the composite-image performance similar to what we did in '77 *(Satellite Arts).* We'll have performers in the Soviet Union and performers in the U.S. meet in this composite-image space, this virtual space with no geograpical boundaries, and in that space they'll perform together and dance together. Dance and performance doesn't need to be translated. When you start communicating and being able to touch and join bodies, it creates a whole other context.

KG   All this sounds very strange, very experiential, but if you do this, you realize the communication's power of being able to mix space or exchange spaces.

GY   People have kind of a phantom limb sensation, it's actually visceral.

SR   The video image becomes the real architecture for the performance because the image is a place. It's a real place and your image is your ambassador, and your two ambassadors meet in the image. If you have a split screen , that defines the kind of relationship that can take place. If you have an image mix or a key, other relationships are possible. So it incorporates all the video effects that are used in traditional video art, but it's a live place. It becomes visual architecture.

KG   A lot of work was done discovering things like reversing the scan on the image so that when the dancer moved to the right, the image moved to the right instead of the left, and all the special technology that surrounded the performers to facilitate this interaction. A lot of research and development went into how fast movement or activities could take place with the satellite time delay being present.

GY   It needs to be pointed out that they're doing the same thing that other people have gotten international recognition for in video, the Vasulkas for example. Most of their life has been this kind of research and development. They enter the digital domain and find out what's possible and they're internationally renowned for doing so. Kit and Sherrie are doing the same thing. These are new frontiers and you can't just step in and make art automatically; first you have to research and find out what's there, what's possible, what are the consequences. I think it's interesting that everyone recognized that as a value in video, but it has not been recognized so much in telecommunications. Nam June and Doug Davis just step in and make precious works of art immediately and there's no sense of exploration or research and development.

KG   Nam June did *Good Morning Mr. Orwell.* He took a lot of the work from *Satellite Arts* without discussing it with us and gave us a credit on the end. He had Merce Cunningham in some studio in New York stumbling in front of a TV monitor that hadn't had the scan reversed, making a fool out of himself by his standards, certainly.

GY   This addresses the post-modern notion that what artists do now is not attach themselves to any particular medium. They just float amongst whatever mediums are appropriate to whatever they want to say. However, when it comes to creating on this kind of scale, you can't do that. There is only a limited set of technologies that operate at that scale and if you want to do something meaningful, something new, you have to know that tech, you have to get access to it over extended periods of time, you have to devote your life to it. You cannot come in as a dilettante or aesthete.

KG   We're not about the whole "access" mentality, which often doesn't really cultivate work. It's like running out, driving a stake in uncharted territory and saying I was here first.

SR   The art world in general is pretty impotent. I think part of the reason is the whole sense of scale of contemporary society, the scale at which we can destroy ourselves, the little chips that hold how many pieces of information we don't even know, genetic engineering. Really, all the new technological developments are out of human scale. The more that we explore space, the more we feel lonely. It seems to us that the only real power is to work at the same scale that contemporary society is working on. If you don't create on the same scale that you can destroy, then art is rendered impotent.

GY   This is what I meant earlier about the metadesigner and the artist together. The artist is the one who can make the most powerful, the most moving representations of our life situation. Yet the forms that have traditionally been available to the art world just don't meet the scale of the problem. This raises the question of what is political art. My own opinion is that there is no such thing as political art. There is art about political issues. But only situations are political, only circumstances are political. So if you set up a space bridge or a hole in space or an electronic cafe as a situation, as a circumstance that spans boundaries of people, and then you put those poignant, powerful representations of the artist in there, then you've got both: art that addresses a political issue within a political situation. The whole thing becomes highly political and powerful.

HP   Do you grapple with the issue that some peple bring up, such as Godfrey Reggio, the director of *Koyaanisqatsi,* that technology is inherently evil?

GY   To me it's beneath an answer actually. It's like this book, *Four Arguments for the Elimination of Television*[2]—remember that book? These views are what is called "vitalism." It's like saying in protein there is life. It's voodoo. It doesn't contribute anything constructive to what we have to do.

KG   It doesn't contribute anything; in fact, it's backpedaling. The fact is if we don't learn how to use this technology to manage the human and material resources of this planet we're screwed. End of story. Fade to black.

HP   What are your realistic goals with this technology?

KG   We're not going to realize our vision in our lifetime, I don't have that much expectation, but somebody has to be creating models to liberate people's imaginations so they can apply them to hope and the possibility of redefining these technologies. We've gotten to a point where we've realized the limits of models. We want to take the revolution into the marketplace. We've designed a cost-effective, kickass, multimedia, crosscultural teleconferencing terminal that will allow communities of common concern to link up and evolve collectively.

HP   Are you talking about providing a set of instructions? Are you talking about providing actual hardware?

KG   We're looking at turn-key hardware solutions. There have been all these attempts at networking crossculturally but all of them take place using a different set of technologies. Some are cost effective, but most are made by the teleconferencing industry that's marketing to the Fortune 500, so the markup is like tens of thousands of dollars over the value that's really in the box. We see the possibility of creating a turn-key system that would create a compatability standard for a multimedia teleconferencing terminal that provides fax, slow-scan, full-motion video, written annotations on pictures, pictorial data management, text conferencing. We can see putting that together at a price that would fall into the small organization price range. That's what we're looking at right now. The creation of a pilot network is our first priority because people must have the opportunity to experience systems like this or like *Electronic Cafe* to fully realize the indispensable value of technology such as this.

SR   The whole nature of this so-called information and communications society is really dependent on people synthesizing and being creative. It's almost as if capitalism and communism are turning in upon themselves and possibly meeting in a new place. It's determined in part by the progression of the technology, which is becoming decentralized, which is becoming dependent on creating this information economy. How do you create information? When you get right down to it, information is based at some point on somebody's discovery or somebody's synthesis or somebody's research and development.

GY   I'd like to address this. We've been talking about the communications revolution. People take this in one of two ways: either it's some kind of sixties, hippie, utopian idealism or it's a marketing scam by industry—you know, "The communication revolution is here, and our product. . . . " There has been no middle ground discourse between those extremes. I would just like to point out that any interesting thing that people like Kit and Sherrie would do with this technology would by definition have to be a model of what a communications revolution would be like if there were one. McLuhan said, "The medium is the message." What's the medium? Depending on who you talk to, the medium is television, the medium is this and that. But I always understood it this way: the medium is a principle, it's not a piece of hardware. The medium is the principle of centralized, one-way, mass-audience communication. We happen to do that through broadcast TV, but you can do it through cable TV, you can do it through the telephone lines. That's the medium, and that medium *is* the message. It determines that what will be said over a centralized one-way, mass-audience communications system will have to be said within a very narrow framework of what is possible, what will be accepted by such a mass audience. That is the medium. A revolution would be to invert that principle through whatever technologies permit you to invert it: a decentralized, two-way, special-audience system. Art-world theorists who criticize anyone who talks about this would have you think that this all was attempted in the sixties and failed! This is bullshit! The only thing that happened in the sixties is that we got the vaguest notion that this was even something important to think about. We woke up in the sixties and now we're starting to take the first steps to see what direction that inversion might lie in. Do we think it'll happen? That's completely beside the point. The point is that this is the only meaningful thing to do with our lives because we know that no other institutions are capable of addressing the problem.

KG The trouble is there haven't been enough participants to make a major shift that would land on the cover of *Time* magazine. What we've been trying to do is to get it out into public spaces so that people participate in these environments. We create the context and invite people to come in and do their laundry, hang up their clothes, live there for a while and see what it's like. To begin to recognize the value of it and to acculturate it for a period of time. Redefine themselves through it.

SR In an art context what we've been doing is perfectly logical. If the art world has problems with it, it's because that logic challenges the validity of the art institutions for this new practice in contemporary society.

First you look at communication and then you look at the aesthetic quality of the communication. As soon as you do that, and you're true to your art form and your art logic, not worrying about whether it fits in a gallery or on a shelf, then you very naturally put one foot in front of the other and get to these places. The art logic just marches you right out of the art institutions into life.

HP What about the communications possibilities of videotapes now that everybody's got a VCR?

KG The great thing about tape rentals is that they're just knocking the side out of broadcast television and cable. It's just knocking them for a loop.

GY   Mailing around personal videotapes and the home VCR network is revolutionary, but the real issue is to have an alternative social world that doesn't stop, that is continuous the way television is. Television is a social world, it's there twenty-four hours a day, it has a history. They're called series, you know. The news develops a history: "You know what happened yesterday, here's the update," and so on. So it's a world. The point is to have this alternative social world that's always there and never stops and is always validating itself as a possible social world. And then alongside of that are all these other supplementary "periodic" media. I can go to the store and get a tape just the same as I can go to the store and get *Mother Jones* or *Newsweek*. But if it were *only* these periodic media, this would not constitute an alternative social world of any significant power. So they're complementary.

HP   The *Electronic Cafe* ran for over seven weeks. Why couldn't it have just kept running indefinitely?

KG   Nobody wanted it to come down, but we couldn't perpetuate it because it was not cost effective. We put it together with available technology and it wasn't the system to perpetuate. Now we've got a system that's cost effective.

SR   One obvious idea that we've thought about is a new electronic museum. It's a way to link people, places and art works in this new environment.

GY   *Electronic Cafe* created this new inversion of the art and life situation. The longer it ran, the more it just became life, right? In a sense you could say the less it became art, the more it became life. Or the shorter it ran, the more it became art, but the less it would be doing what it ought to really be doing, which is becoming life.

KG   Just look at this as interaction with a system. It's looking at creativity applied across the boards and at different levels. Even though *Electronic Cafe* had to go away, it's successful in that it empowered people in those communities with enough experience to describe what is desirable or what they would want as a system. It's politically hot, culturally hot. It created a lot of travel, an exchange between these communities, and used Los Angeles as a global model. When you look at the archiving aspect of it, this is important because the face of Los Angeles, the demographics, the dynamics of it are so wild that the face of history is going to change so fast that there's not going to be much of a record of it. But when you have environments where people can come and register their opinions and ideas and show their stuff and accomplishments—little kids breakdancing—whatever it happened to be, all that can be there to be looked at under the context of a social space, it's not private.

The other aspect of *Electronic Cafe* that was very important was that it created a public space in which one could participate in telecommunications anonymously. You could be among people without anyone knowing how many kids you have, how many points you have, what your income is. It was like a public telephone booth. It wasn't the privacy of your own home, where there's a wire right up your consumer tract. It was a place to present your ideas, register your opinions anonymously. You didn't have to sign your name. The artifacts you created—pictures, drawings, writing, computer text—either independently or collaboratively could be, if you desired, permanently stored in the community-accessible archive. People could have access to opinions without being monitored. There always exists the possibility of being monitored when it's in your home. A "commons" was created that was very important in terms of the freedom and what gets to define our personal freedom in this electronic space.

GY If this isn't political, I don't know what is. They gave people a living experience of one of the hottest political issues of our time—how can we move into electronic space and still be anonymous? Are we going to be anonymous? Is anyone even talking about that? Has the issue even come up? No. You gotta join The Source, you got to give all your data to Compuserve. Anonymity is a possibility that could just vanish, except for those people in East L.A. now who've had that experience, who are therefore much hipper than probably most of the consultants to AT&T who never thought. . . .

Addendum

Shortly after this article was originally published (April 1987), Kit Galloway and Sherrie Rabinowitz began working with the La Villette museum in Paris to develop an "Electronic Cafe International." The project, certainly their most ambitious to date, will establish Electronic Cafes in Paris, Los Angeles, Moscow, and Tokyo. The couple have been working on a study commissioned by La Villette that will be completed in October 1988, and they are hoping to have the cafes up and running by the end of 1989.

Their goal is not to create a short-term telecommunications "artwork." They anticipate that much of their energy will go into maintaining the original four sites and getting other locations involved in the project as well, in hopes that it will take on a permanent life of its own. "We are trying to establish a de facto standard that others can build on," said Galloway, "whether they just start with a computer and modem and send text or they're fully video and graphics capable."

"We will be initiating projects to illustrate the possibilities of the system, such as composite image performances," said Rabinowitz. Groups or individuals in Fresno, California; Telluride, Colorado; Santa Fe, New Mexico; and Seoul, South Korea, have already expressed strong interest in joining the proposed network and many others are expected to follow.

"However," said Galloway, "we don't want this project to be married just to an art world environment. We intend it to reach out to the world community. Artists may find it as a way to do new art, or create different ways of collaborating, but we also want to have people doing 'people' work."

The pair feel that by establishing this international network and a set of standards for telecommunication, they may, if enough interest is generated, be able to convince a major retailer to develop affordable systems that could become available to the public. Already people at the La Villette are proposing to establish an Electronic Cafe based on Galloway and Rabinowitz' first model that would connect the various ethnic communities of greater Paris. A businessman in Seoul has already gone out and bought a restaurant and trademarked the name "Electronic Cafe" in anticipation of establishing a site there. "If we can just reach a point where it becomes potentially feasible for anyone to participate, then anything can happen," said Galloway.

In addition to the Electronic Cafe International, the pair have also been approached by a group to create a "Hole-in-Space" between Moscow and Washington, D.C., and another group has inquired about setting up the same thing between Tokyo and Los Angeles. Even the industry has recognized their innovative visions. *Telespan,* the in-house newsletter for the telecommunications industry, recently gave them their annual Pace Award for ten years of leadership in the field of teleconferencing.

Notes

1. Youngblood discusses the creative conversation thus: "To create new realities, we must create new contexts, new domains of consensus. That can't be done through communication. You can't step out of the context that defines communication by communicating; it will only lead to trivial permutations within the same consensus, repeatedly validating the same reality. Instead we need a *creative conversation* that might lead to new consensus and hence to new realities, but which is not itself a process of communication. I say something you don't understand and we begin turning around together: 'Do you mean this or this?' 'No, I mean thus and such. . . . '

During this nontrivial process we gradually approximate the possibility of communications, which will follow as a trivial necessary consequence once we've constructed a new consensus and woven together a new context. Communication, as a domain of stabilized noncreative relations, can occur only after the creative but noncommunicative conversation that makes it possible: communication is always noncreative and creativity is always noncommunicative. Conversation, the paradigm of all generative phenomena, the prerequisite for all creativity, requires a two-way channel of interaction. That doesn't guarantee creativity, but without it there will be no conversation at all and creativity will be diminished accordingly." Excerpted from ''Virtual Space: The Electronic Environments of Mobile Image,'' by Gene Youngblood, *IS Journal* 1 (1986).

2. Jerry Mander, *Four Arguments for the Elimination of Television* (New York: William Morrow, 1978).

11

Monuments in the Heart: Performance and Video Experiments in Community Art since 1980

Linda Frye Burnham

Linda Burnham identifies a diverse group of mid-career performance and video artists working all over the U.S. in a new genre of community arts. Their dynamic experimental projects are carried out where they live and in partnership with inhabitants—both individuals and institutions—of their communities. Working in prisons, hospitals and homeless shelters has not only transformed participants and produced innovative artworks that confront the most serious current social problems. The structures invented to carry out work also bring to the fore vital information about the issues addressed that has been previously ignored and misconstrued.

Burnham notes that some historians believe that humans are again moving toward a partnership society of freedom and peace that has not flowered since neolithic times. ''Monuments in the Heart'' are models for the coming era.

The title of Burnham's article is taken from a remark by a homeless man in John Malpede's performance workshop, who said he had been writing a poem for years as a monument in his heart to a friend who died as a result of drug abuse.

This article originally appeared in another form as ''Tracking a New Wave of Socially Committed Art'' in *American Theatre* 5, nos. 4–5 (July/August 1988). *American Theatre* is published by Theatre Communications Group. Reprinted by permission of the publisher. The article ''What's Up?'' was adapted from the article ''Mending with Tape,'' which originally appeared in *L.A. Weekly* (3–9 July 1987).

It's a rainy winter day on Venice Beach near Los Angeles. The biting wind bellows the makeshift tents and dropcloth shelters grouped on the sand. Hundreds of destitute people huddle over small fires plotting their next move in the relentless search for safety, warmth, food and work.

Only feet away on the boardwalk, two men, one black, one white, take turns panhandling each other. Nearby a collapsible "Men Working" sign shudders in the blustering storm. They work this way for almost an hour, observed by clutches of passers-by. Not many know it, but this is a performance art experience by John Malpede and the Los Angeles Poverty Department. They are carrying out their mission to manifest in performance the character of their community: the growing homeless population of the United States.

Two thousand miles away from Los Angeles, four hundred older women gather in the vast, glass-roofed courtyard of a building in downtown Minneapolis, there to create a "crystal quilt" of moving imagery for an audience of three thousand, while the women's recorded voices speak of their lives and bodies, of aging and history, of civic and personal concerns. Nearby stands the performance's director,

Susan Franklin Tanner and TheatreWorkers Project

Susan Franklin Tanner, an actress and lifelong political activist with experience in Washington D.C.'s well-known Living Stage Theatre Company, created TheatreWorkers Project to examine issues around labor and to give voice to working-class nonactors. The first project she tackled under this banner involved a multiracial group made up mostly of older male steelworkers from southeastern Los Angeles. These half-dozen men were among the two thousand workers who were forced into early retirement when the Bethlehem Steel plant in Vernon shut down in 1982. "Lady Beth" was one of three hundred factories shut down in Los Angeles County over the last

artist Suzanne Lacy, who has shaped the artistic, social and political dimensions of the three-year Whisper Minnesota Project.

In a California men's prison, video artist Gary Glassman moves easily among his students, framing and focusing a narrative piece the men are creating about their lives as incarcerated humans. They talk of fear and suspicion, love and hope as Glassman helps them learn to control the images that tell their story.

And as far away from these three happenings as it is possible to get in the U.S., performance artist David Wheeler and a band of Eskimo children probe the boneyard outside their isolated village in the wilds of Alaska, looking for the perfect piece of antler or bone from which to fashion a puppet. Together they will make a puppet play about the social impact of a new road planned for the village. Tomorrow a field trip will take them to Nome, where the children will view the only tree they have ever seen.

These four artists have something in common with:

Branda Miller, who has taught boys on probation how to make music videos about life in their California juvenile court school; and with—

---

few years, when imports and lack of modernization caught up with them.

In their fifties and sixties, most of the men in Tanner's steelworkers group receive a retirement pension of around $500 to $700 a month, with one man receiving no pension at all. "Each man has his own story," says Tanner, "where he came from, how he got to where he was going, who he was with and why he was doing what he was doing."[2]

Beginning with journal sessions ansd theater exercises, she asked the men to explore the feelings they had about their jobs and the machines they tended, searching for tactile images and emotional links. After several false starts, the group began, with the assistance of Tanner and other artists like playwright Rob Sullivan and musician John Coinman, to shape a performance piece from these images and finally not only staged the play—*Lady Beth*—in Los Angeles at the Ensemble Studio Theater (premiered March 1986), but in September 1986 took it on the road to the suffering communities of the "rust belt" cities of the northeast with the help of rock star Bruce Springsteen. The cast members, many of whom had never traveled outside Los Angeles, were moved to find that audiences of other unemployed workers shared their feelings about their lost jobs and atrophying hometowns. The tour included a visit to Capitol Hill in Washington,

Charles Dennis, who has formed a New York theater company that includes the elderly and mentally ill adults who are his students in a program called Hospital Audiences; and with—

Guillermo Gómez-Peña and Emily Hicks, who, in the Border Arts Workshop, make performances about biculturalism with artists and others at the San Diego–Tijuana border; and with—

Kit Galloway and Sherrie Rabinowitz of Mobile Image, who create interactive video satellite links between pedestrian populations as distant from each other as Moscow, Paris, New York, Los Angeles, Tokyo and Seoul; and with—

Alan Dachman and his Project VITAL, which has trained developmentally disabled adults in Chicago to produce TV programs for cable systems, create prize-winning video art, and serve as professional video technicians; and with—

Susan Franklin Tanner, whose TheatreWorkers Project gives unemployed Los Angeles industrial workers the chance to tell the story of their dying hometowns.

In projects like these all over America, performance and video artists are stretching the definition of community art the way they stretched

---

Susan Franklin Tanner (continued)

supported by Congressmen backing legislation that would require early warning about plant closure.

The piece, staged as a dramatic reading with Coinman's music, specifically identifies each of the performers—Cruz Montemayor, Hermes Pais, Frank Curtis, Tony Garcia, Richard Carter and Lloyd Andres—offering their payroll badge numbers, their specific jobs, their tenure and the amount of their pensions, as well as the anger and sorrow they felt when their labor community was shattered. "Some lost all of their possessions, their families, and had to go back where they came from with nothing but memories," says the script. "Never has leisure created such impatience. Damn this devil! It has forced me into

the straitjacket of unemployment."

In a documentary about the group produced by L.A.'s public television station, KCET, the members spoke of their excitement at being able to formulate their ideas and communicate about the central experience of their lives, their longtime service at the steel plant.

Cruz Montemayor worked at the plant as a pit boss for thirty-seven years, living alone nearby, and was pensioned at $722 a month. "By doing this," he said of TheatreWorkers Project, "I consider I'm contributing something for this time I'm supposed to be on this earth." Montemayor died in 1987.

Frank Curtis, now working for Pacific Bell, observed: "When I saw

the definition of fine art in the seventies. In an exciting movement that seems to signal a trend, mid-career artists are creating dynamic experimental projects in the communities where they live, and involving the inhabitants of those communities in the artwork itself, bringing art making to many who have never experienced it before. Just as importantly, these projects are breaking silences, freeing voices and providing a focus for information that has been overlooked, misinterpreted and even suppressed by other information systems. These intriguing projects are being carried out in prisons, in hospitals, in schools, in community centers, on Skid Row, in homeless shelters, in soup kitchens, in AIDS hospices, in refugee asylums, in protest groups, in environmental study coalitions, in free law and health centers, in retirement communities.

Many of the artists creating them are between thirty-five and forty-five, a generation that emerged in the late sixties and set out to change the world—and in the process established performance and video as the front guard of seventies and eighties art forms. In the barrier-smashing fever of revolution, the seventies became a laboratory for experiment in which almost any proposition was tolerated. Perfor-

---

Bethlehem Steel was going to close . . . there was a lot of anger. I could stand on the corner and scream—but so what? Well, I finally got to tell that story. I finally got to also talk about my whole life and what is the kind of person that works in these places and I think that's important."

Tanner said of the experience, "I believe that a new kind of bond has been formed among these men. They are more articulate. They are braver. And they have done a great service to humanity by creating this work of art that reflects the plight of thousands and thousands of their fellow workers. They feel less isolated and I think it has changed their lives."

Talking of her own experience,

Tanner said, "It allowed me as a woman in this industry, who started out really as an actor, to go into being a producer and create projects that I care about, that are meaningful to the world. And this is like a godsend because it is so rare that you do that."

The group's second production, *S.E.L.A!*, was an interdisciplinary collaboration with Los Angeles musicians, video, film and performance artists, using a variety of media to probe the constantly shifting, "invisible" identity of L.A.'s southeastern industrial sector. Through weeks of research, the group sifted little-known facts about the cultures that had settled in the small communities, and then were blown away by the winds of economic change, leaving behind, for instance,

mance, in particular, questioned the boundary between art and every-day existence; video approached an examination of the media as a force in every facet of contemporary life.

In many ways the eighties gave rise to a new renaissance in which barriers of all sorts—definitional, cultural, historical—went down, seemingly forever. Art was redefined; disciplines crossed again and again; new cultural influences flooded in as women and immigrants and ethnic minorities made themselves heard.

At the same time, many artists were deeply involved in civil rights work, the women's movement, labor organizing, antiwar protests. They found no conflict in a dual role as artist and socially involved citizen. As they entered their middle years, however, many did find themselves in conflict with the increasingly materialistic careerism of the eighties art world, with the gallery as hideout and the museum as bastion of culture. Out of personal need, some turned to working in partnership with social institutions and ad hoc community groups. In embarking on this journey they are searching for nothing less than the function of art in contemporary life.

New performance and video artists are moving directly into the heart of the extreme social problems that cause so much despair in our

---

Susan Franklin Tanner (continued)

a body of Latino rock-and-roll songs in the twentieth-century hit parade.

Tanner is also working on performances with workers in the year-long Hormel meatpackers strike in Austin, Minn., and with female dock workers and the Skid Row Elders' Council in Los Angeles. Also under the Theatre-Workers aegis she organized a seminar on art and money, as well as a lobbying effort to support greater city funding for the arts in Los Angeles.

time: homelessness, unemployment, AIDS, the growing elderly population, longing for peace and disarmament, the isolation of city dwellers
and more. Their markedly unconventional approaches underscore their
conviction that art is part and parcel of everyday life and politics, that
human development is based on creative exchange, that the crossing
of social currents and diverse cultures is essential to the survival of the
race.

For many more who are watching, working with and learning from
these pioneers, the job of the nineties will be to make work that reflects
their personal and aesthetic concerns, and at the same time addresses
a timely social and political agenda.

The partnerships created in these projects are surprising, forging
new links among art, commerce, industry, media, health care, labor,
social service and more.

For instance, when John Malpede, as a California Arts Council artist-
in-residence, decided to form a performance troupe from among the
people on L.A.'s Skid Row, he did it in partnership with the Inner City
Law Center, a free law clinic where he works as a rights advocate for
the homeless and those on welfare. The workshops and resulting performances touched not only the art audience and the homeless, but
the welfare advocacy community as well. And in the process, works like
*Condo Thieves' Corner, No Stone for Studs Schwartz, South of the
Clouds* and *LAPD Inspects America* raised the issues surrounding
homelessness to national public view through notice in the mass
media—and raised the self-esteem and self-knowledge of the participants in the way only successful art making can do.

Susan Franklin Tanner, also a CAC artist-in-residence, partnered
with the Steelworkers Oldtimers Foodbank, a union entity struggling
to feed its unemployed members in the shadow of a shut-down
Bethlehem Steel plant in southeastern L.A.

In another interesting partnership, Gary Glassman's prison video
workshops linked the California Arts Council with the State Department
of Corrections, and the project's videos have been shown on national
television. Alan Dachman's Project VITAL (Video Induced Training and
Learning) is located at Little City, a large Chicago facility for the retarded
and developmentally disabled, adding a completely unforeseen dimension to Little City's services to that population; American Cablesystem's
public access channels serve as project partners.

Suzanne Lacy, for *Whisper Minnesota*, partnered with a variety of
arts and social service agencies statewide because she wanted not only
to involve the state's older women in art making, but also to serve as

a catalyst for social action by and on behalf of those women. She created a web of activities that crossed the whole state, linking arms with the Minnesota Board on Aging, the Minneapolis College of Art and Design, the Reflective Leadership Program of the Hubert H. Humphrey Institute on Public Affairs and Minneapolis First Bank.

David Wheeler's partner in his Eskimo puppetry workshops is the Alaskan Arts Council; at home in New Orleans he and his art-therapist wife Kathy Sanderson compare their methods in community art and art therapy at a local hospital. Galloway and Rabinowitz, in their satellite video link-ups, have partnered with such diverse organizations as Jet Propulsion Laboratory, the Olympic Arts Festival, NASA Goddard

---

What's Up?

with
Branda Miller and Peter Brosius

In the spring of 1987 a circus came to Los Angeles. In the center ring was an act that had never been tried before, a balancing act between the Juvenile Court, nine "juvenile delinquents," a video artist, a Chinese-Korean-American blues singer and the Mark Taper Forum. The act is preserved in an award-winning thirty-two minute videotape about teenagers, *What's Up?*

Alistair Hunter, a career administrator in the county's juvenile-court school system, has long struggled to establish the arts in the system's curriculum. After years of experience in bringing working artists to the juvenile halls, probation camps, group homes and community centers that contain and educate 50,000 troubled kids each year, he's convinced that the art experience provides what they need most: help in learning to think critically, behave ethically and communicate with the world they will face when they are released from the shelter of the juvenile court.

Peter Brosius agrees. Brosius, director of the Mark Taper Forum's

Space Flight Center, Lincoln Center, the Corporation for Public Broadcasting and the French Ministry of Foreign Affairs.

One of the riskiest and most innovative partnerships occurred when Branda Miller and Peter Brosius piloted their theater/video project at a juvenile court school in suburban Los Angeles, with the goal of proving the usefulness of the arts in school curricula—in this case adding to the experience of troubled teenagers the power of mastering media techniques.

And the story goes on, as other artists take steps like that in other directions.

Mierle Ukeles has an ongoing relationship with the New York City

---

Improvisational Theater Project, has spent his career making theater with ghetto kids, and has worked extensively with Hunter in the court school system. Together they hatched a project for the school where Hunter is assistant principal, Masada Placement Day Center School. The plan was to select a group of students to spend eight weeks with artists from the Taper, making videos about their lives.

At that time, Masada served eighty-eight white, black and Latino young men, fifteen to eighteen years old, all of whom were on probation, living away from their families in licensed group homes. A menacing restlessness bubbled beneath the surface; the teenagers strained at their leashes, anxious to get out and live on their own. It was Masada's complex assignment to restrain them and "emancipate" them at the same time.

Brosius brought Branda Miller aboard as the project's video artist because of her unorthodox approach to documentary video. Miller is a friendly, articulate woman who is both artistically sophisticated and street-

wise. Her curator's statement for the "Surveillance" exhibition she mounted at LACE Gallery in 1987 found her quoting social philosopher Michel Foucault and crafting theory about the politics of technology. Her tape *L.A. Nickel* views life on Skid Row from the window of her studio at 5th and Wall. An Emmy winner who sometimes works as an editor for the movie industry and such mammoth corporations as AT&T, Miller also understands life on the street.

Brosius envisioned using Miller's technique for the project: "Instead of doing a simple documentary, I wanted to just sort of jump over to graduate school, have it be an art experience about collage, montage, juxtaposition, disjunctive storytelling, image work. I liked Branda's use of sound texture, the use of looping, repetition. I wanted to work in that vein."

Using as a model her tape about a day in the life of a group of teenage girls, *That's It, Forget It,* Miller made a working outline that allowed for maximum student input. Appropriately styled much like a music video, the

THE SOCIAL MIRROR
Mierle Laderman Ukeles, 1979–83
Commissioned by the City of New York Department of Sanitation, this 20 cubic-yard garbage truck is covered with hand-cut and fit-tempered mirrored glass with Plexiglas mirror strips.
(Official photo of the City of New York Department of Sanitation. Courtesy Ronald Feldman Fine Arts, Inc., New York)

AMERICAN DINING: A WORKING WOMAN'S MOMENT
Jerri Allyn, 1987
An art installation in restaurants including jukeboxes and placemats. Shown here are the artist and waitress Carmen Decena in Gefen's Dairy Restaurant, New York.
(Photo courtesy Marty Heitner)

Sanitation Department. Her ten-year *Touch Sanitation* project, designed to illuminate the system that takes care of the city, had her shaking hands with every single sanitation worker in New York, as well as directing a ballet of garbage barges and mirrored sanitation trucks. Her current *Flow City* project features a design for a part of a permanent waste facility on the Hudson River that will bring citizens into the heart of a waste processing plant through a tunnel made of recycled trash, onto a glass bridge over incoming barges and face to face with a video wall that brings the Hudson inside the facility.

Donna Henes leads a never-ending quest for world peace, engaging street passers-by in her *Chants for Peace/Chance for Peace* celebra-

---

What's Up? (continued)

tape collages the everyday sights and sounds of the students' lives and subtly combines them with insights gleaned from the soul-searching theater exercises of Peter Brosius, with all the choices made by the students themselves. "I set up a very defined and controlled structure for freedom and anarchy within it," said Miller. "It's a balancing act. I believed in the boys, that their choices would be the strong ones. That's what you see on the tape."

They decided that the autobiographical tape would have three parts: where I come from, where I am now and where I'm going. Parts 1 and 3 would be montage segments constructed by the whole group. Part 2 would be a series of individual statements, one by each young man, in which he could say or do whatever he wanted, chroma-keyed into a background chosen by him and underscored with music he made himself.

Brosius spent the first month on storytelling, exercises, improvisations.

"The focus," he said

was to get personal information, images, dreams, fantasies, role-playing. The goal was moments in your life when you learn something about being a man. The goal was to get them to tell their stories in ways that might be new. I don't think any of us were prepared for the stories of the violence that has happened to the kids, for the kind of family crisis they'd gone through. A third of the guys, their fathers were Vietnam vets who were in rough shape because of the war and had taken it out on the kids in different ways. Some people go through that and they don't end up running away or doing drugs or joining gangs. Some people do.

At first the students were reluctant to open up, to expose their inner life to teachers and classmates, who they knew would see the tape. Much of the credit for the candor that poured forth in workshop goes to Gary Wong, a painter also known as blues musician Charlie Chan, brought in by Miller because she felt he would

tions in which the public joins her in making "streams of conscience," or streamers with peace messages in many languages. Her "celestially auspicious occasions" on the solstices and equinoxes celebrate the seasons in public and unite strangers in rituals. She plans an international simultaneous spring equinox celebration by satellite. Henes also serves as a "town artist" of sorts for Rosendale, New York, where she has organized "light parades" involving all the citizens and every agency of city government.

Dee Dee Halleck of Paper Tiger Televison works with Deep Dish TV, a cable access distribution project for a series of grassroots videos exploring national issues from community perspectives.

---

have an important rapport with the students. "There were talks in that room," said Brosius of Chan's influence, "about what it means to be an artist, that were very beautiful and touching—things I don't think these kids get a chance to hear a lot." Chan found it "an invaluable experience. I wanted them to see they have choices. They're stuck where they are. It was wonderful and heart-wrenching. Fights almost broke out, but that's a sign that something volatile is going on."

"The way they approached it just opened everybody up," said seventeen-year-old Tom (real names and identifiable photo images are not used here, in accordance with Juvenile Court regulations). "People were getting deep. Guys I'd known for six, eight months were telling stories I just could not believe—a macho athlete telling about the time his dad stuck his hands in boiling water."

Segments of the soundtrack, from workshop recordings, reveal the oblique angle from which the exercises allowed the students to tell their stories, sometimes in the third person, as if describing a movie:

> It's about a guy who lived a hard life from the beginning. . . . Father's an alcoholic, mother's an alcoholic, they're two people trying to come to grips with their disease. All the time they are trying to find themselves, they are forgetting about their child. . . . He shuts out the world, he goes into his own private world, he don't talk to nobody, just sits in his room all day, just staring at the wall, thinking how the hell did I get here, how in the hell is this happening to me?

And so on, with stories about child abuse, death in the family, "gang-banging," getting arrested.

If opening up their feelings brought a volatility to the workshop, the skills they developed put the power of technology into their hands. With the guidance of the artists, plus sound engineer Dan Birnbaum and professional cameraman Jim Backus and musician Mitchell Oda, the students recorded workshops, collected sounds from their environment,

Cheri Gaulke, a performance artist, partnered with the Women's Graphics Center in Los Angeles to offer the Postcard Project, free workshops where participants of all races choose a woman (or female myth) important to their lives and design and print an edition of a postcard honoring her.

Jerri Allyn designed a graphics project in public diners across the country examining labor and the metaphor of service, *American Dining: Labor in the '80s.* Jukeboxes played audiotaped narratives and songs that explored working for a living, while placemats decorated with riddles challenged diners. Allyn also was a member of the Waitresses, a team of artists and waitresses who performed in restaurants and

---

What's Up? (continued)

logged twelve hours of sound and edited it to ten minutes, made video shot sheets, shot and edited the visuals and created the soundtrack at Chan's Riffraff Studio. The students made all the choices that make *What's Up?* a portrait of life at Masada.

It's a hip, salty, image-packed picture, funny, poignant and crackling with street talk. The tape is strong, something the artists are very proud of. In 1988, *What's Up?* received awards from the Atlanta Film and Video Festival and the Sony/AFI USA Film and Video Festival, with several of the student videomakers on hand to receive the prize: video equipment that they donated to Brosius' theater project at the Mark Taper Forum. As a result of the experience, some of the students are talking about art as a life's work. Several have gone on to community colleges.

"It's been a mind blast," said eighteen-year-old Dennis, "coming in here and getting on these machines. Putting out what you want and for how long. You know, *you got that moment.*"

"I learned more in one week than I learned in two months in computer trade school," said Jim, who wants to produce records.

"I've learned to express how I feel, communicate with my peers," said Tom, "because of the way these people opened up. Maybe it was just the situation that popped the cork. It was a real experiment."

The California juvenile court school system recently made important decisions to incorporate the arts in the curriculum, far surpassing the regular public school system in arts programming.

At this writing, Los Angeles is going through an intense period of youth gang warfare, with the police claiming helplessness. Local leaders feel that society needs to reach out to these young people and show them the future is worth living for. In the case of the artists, students and administrators involved in *What's Up?*, steps have been taken in that direction.

parades. In addition, with Cheri Gaulke and others, Allyn created the Sisters of Survival, a group of five women dressed in brightly colored nun's habits who appeared in public performance at sites in America and Europe important to the cause of disarmament.

Michael Kearns gathered thirteen people with AIDS and their significant others to create *AIDS/Us,* a performance piece in which they told their stories. The play gave birth to Artists Confronting AIDS, an L.A. coalition of artists involved in a variety of touching projects. There are now many AIDS-related arts groups throughout the country, such as ACTUP (AIDS Coalition to Unleash Power), who work with people with AIDS to draw attention to the issues surrounding the disease.

These artists have not abandoned their own personal work as video and performance artists; they continue to craft artworks that speak to their artistic concerns. But they profess an equally intense dedication to their community activities and have simply created an extra parallel workload that strains an already difficult existence.

The benefits of these projects to the participants are obvious. Each artist mentioned here has stories of lives touched and changed by the projects they've initiated. Just as important are the changes wrought in the artists themselves, as they incorporate in their lives the knowledge gained from working in socially strained situations.

Perhaps what these artists are proving about the function of art is that it is a vehicle for spiritual and social transformation. A positive experience with art making is something that is no longer considered essential to the educational system in the United States, yet the transformative effects of such experience are demonstrated time and again through art projects in our social institutions, our neighborhoods and our public communications systems.

The fact that these activities are going on record as "art" and not "social work" may be more significant than we know. As the saying goes, life is short and art is long. We are learning much about human history through its artifacts, and lately some of those discoveries have extremely important implications. Art historians, along with archeologists and cultural anthropologists, are today uncovering evidence about human nature that overthrows the basic definition of humanity as characterized by war, slavery and domination. Through evidence left by artists, they are describing a neolithic prehistory of partnership, freedom and peace. Scholars like Marija Gimbutas and Riane Eisler believe we are coming around again to a partnership society.

Like neolithic art, our contemporary art will leave a record of peaceful cooperation, sharing and social progress through partnership, thanks to people like the artists mentioned here and their students and colleagues.

Note

1. All quotes in this section are taken from a televison documentary about
TheatreWorkers Project, "Steel Life Drama," produced by Peter Graumann for California Stories, a production of the New and Current Affairs Department of public television station KCET in Los Angeles, first presented May 2, 1987.

12

Moving Targets/Moving Out

Lucy R. Lippard

*Lucy Lippard, long a champion of socially concerned art and author of a collection of essays on the subject (*Get the Message: A Decade of Art for Social Change, *E. P. Dutton, 1984), comments, as the eighties end, on a crosscultural, crossdisciplinary trend that began on the out-skirts of the art world ten years ago and is now gaining force.*

Lippard's approach to thinking through the effectiveness of art on the American political and cultural margin is inclusive. Art that is thoughtfully constructed as appropriate for large or small audiences, well-funded or grassroots projects, art in the streets or in museums, may be equally able to be politically effective and a benefit to the public interest.

In several short pieces, Lippard considers a number of multileveled public artworks by artists as diverse as Nancy Holt and Adam Purple. She reviews the history of Group Material on New York's Lower East Side and the dilemmas facing the community-based artists' collective now. She chronicles the controversy that shook San Diego when David Avalos, Louis Hock, and Elizabeth Sisco placed "Welcome to America's finest tourist plantation" posters on city buses. "A progressive artist's job," Lippard states, "is . . . to produce an image that expands the public's expectations of what they may get from public forms, to pro-voke thought, and help people look around them with fresh eyes." World War 3 Illustrated, a comic magazine published by Peter Kuper and Seth Tobocman since the turn of the decade and the Reagan ad-

This article is composed of four articles previously published: "Mixed Messages from Public Artists," *Village Voice* (2 October 1984); "One Foot Out the Door," *In These Times* (8–22 July 1986); "Moving Target," *Zeta Magazine* (June 1988); and "Drawing the Battlelines," *Zeta Magazine* (September 1988). The Introduction appears here for the first time.

ministration, is "more than a magazine, less than a movement," an original activist publication that is the "small form" of art in the public interest Lippard advocates.

The great and still elusive questions surrounding public art are: Which public? Is there an exchange between art and audience? From the grandiose and intentionally unrealizable "projects" of the Minimal era, the earthworks in generally inaccessible locations, and the nearly invisible alterations of the urban environment of the conceptual period, to the community mural movement and guerrilla performances in the streets of the sixties and early seventies, to the rise into the public art domain of women artists (who brought a very different approach to their interactions with place and people), to the resurrection in the late seventies of street art inspired by ghetto graffiti and the Left, public art in the United States has been extraordinarily varied and vital; at the same time, it has also been extraordinarily elitist and boring. As the eighties end, a crosscultural, crossdisciplinary trend that began on the mainstream margins a decade ago seems to be gaining momentum. The relationship between art and environment, art and context, artist and audience remains at the heart of any public art that's worth its turf.

Sometimes the public interest is better served by art that isn't a giant space invader. Sometimes the art is small in scale and the audiences are gigantic. Sometimes the audiences are small but affected by the art in a big way. Sometimes the exchanges take place in (gasp!) a gallery or even a museum. A social-change artist must be ambidextrous. S/he must be able to think on two fronts, to understand dual coding and act in dual contexts, taking into consideration who the art is for, where it is, and what s/he wants to accomplish by putting it there.

The real challenge lies outside conventional venues—not only outside museum gardens, but outside of bank plazas and civic spaces. I've selected the four short pieces below for reprint, rather than longer, more theoretical pieces I've written on public art, because I hope to suggest the diversity of means by which artists can affect the public—from vast, well-funded projects to inexpensive independent actions. I am only scratching the surface. In the last few years many artists who show primarily in the mainstream have branched out to work on billboards, subway and bus posters, with public slide and film projections, in banks, schools, and union halls. Artists are performing in hospitals and senior citizens' homes as well as in the streets and at demonstrations. Many of them are learning to adapt their work to different contexts just as they would make alterations for different mediums.

As art moves out, it is taken for granted as a public presence. Yet I know of no art schools in this country whose students work consistently in the public domain, and consequently each artist has to experiment and develop a sense of public effectiveness, public responsibility, public response for her or himself. I look forward to the time when the techniques, tactics or strategies of public interaction are given the respect that making it into a gallery is now.

Beauty and the bureaucracy have as much trouble coupling as all the rest of us. There is a mutual distrust and impatience between artists and officialdom that stems from the former's social naiveté and the latter's innate conservatism. Artists tend to delude themselves about the effect and communicability of their offerings and patrons prefer blandness. Good intentions notwithstanding, the term "public art" covers a multitude of economic and aesthetic sins.

Still, over the last two decades, some progress has been made, often by the combined forces of ecological activists and artists with something to say. During the seventies, a good many sterile, unloved objects were plunked down in city spaces. But the cranky, hybrid views of Robert Smithson also found fertile ground, and amid the monstrous aluminum chatchkas are an increasing number of artworks that insist on a place *and* a voice.

Some are ephemeral, like Joyce Cutler Shaw's giant ice-sculptures (for example, *Survival* outside the UN), accompanied by a flight of messenger pigeons; or Olivia Gude's and Jon Pounds' stencil images and historical quotations commemorating the Pullman strike. Some are concerned with getting the word directly *out*. On 5 November [1984], a large electronic sign on a semitruck travelled through New York City with a computerized running "Message Board" of words and images from a mixture of citizens, reminding people of their lives under the reign of Reagan and urging them to vote. Instigator Jenny Holzer, whose own art often takes this form, was inspired by her stint on the Spectacolor light board at Times Square (now in its third season), where Jane Dickson and the Public Art Fund have programmed intermittent "Messages to the Public" from artists. For the last presidential election, Holzer handed out brochures ("Jesus Is Coming to New York on November 4") at Grand Central Station, warning passersby about the millions of new fundamentalist voters.

Out on the nation's highways, Lee Nading, based in Bloomington, Indiana, has been traveling around the U.S. for more than a year painting pictographic images at environmental sites where nature, culture and technology are up against one another. Each white oversized graffito recalling Native American iconography is unique. "Rising" birds (facing right) are painted where natural values are reasserted; "falling" birds (facing left) where they are in peril. Nading paints hit-and-run, but hopes local sympathizers will maintain his acrylic images. *The Trail of the Rising and Falling Birds* ("A Message Art Project") is perceived by the artist as a step toward a social art that develops from vision to slogan to canon to ideology to politics to action. As a peripatetic *brujo,* Nading has "jinxed" sites such as "the Los Angeles Aqueduct, for robbing the desert for years and pools" and paid homage to "the spirits over the Old Spanish Trail," the United Farm Workers, and the Tahachapi Mountains "for surviving Los Angeles smog."

Some public works are, or would be, very substantial. At Max Hutchinson [fall 1984], Athena Tacha, who has an impressive record of public commissions across the U.S., showed models and drawings for her "Massacre Memorial" series. Enlarged photos and factual texts have been sandblasted onto elaborate labyrinthine and/or stepped monuments. Aware that all good memorials are as much about life as about death, Tacha has derived her forms from patterns in nature (lava flows, leaf veins), hoping that their familiarity will help communicate the grim social realities of the Holocaust, Hiroshima/Nagasaki, or Central America.

The more permanent public art must offer an experience that is intimate, complex and enduring, as well as decorative and acceptable to its sponsors. Nancy Holt's *Dark Star Park* in Rosslyn, Virginia, just across the Potomac from Washington, and Adam Purple's *Garden of Eden* on New York's Lower East Side are both examples of independent action by artists, one with public support, one without.

Holt, a highly successful landscape sculptor, was selected to make an object to be placed in a small park that didn't exist yet. After visiting the site, she had bigger ideas and got herself designated park designer. The whole 29,000 square feet became a work of art, and she also worked with the architect of the new office building at its core. *Dark Star Park* was inaugurated in June after a five-year process. It is, most visibly, a series of spherical forms that play against one another, a number of tall poles and the shadows of both, and against a grassy mound with tunnels, a round reflecting pool, a traffic island, and the new building.

Holt's work always incorporates time as well as space. *Dark Star Park* is sight-aligned so that viewers can relate the forms, testing their perceptions of distance and scale from varied vantage points. One day a year the shadows cast by poles and spheres line up with the asphalt paths. That's on August 1 (at 9:32 a.m.)—the day when William Henry Ross acquired the land that became Rosslyn—thus merging linear historical time with the cyclical time of the sun.

Public art in any form requires extraordinary patience and persistence. Audience is the least of the problems. Red tape and officialdom are the most. (Witness Betty Klavun's disastrous experience with her sculpture/play-lot in the Bronx, abandoned by its sponsors despite community popularity.) Adam Purple (John Peter Zenger II), a self-described Zen/Taoist/anarchist, has been locked in combat with the New York City Housing Authority since 1982, when the NYCHA announced its intention to develop "lower-income" housing on the site of his *Garden of Eden,* constructed independently in 1974 on five vacant lots on Eldridge Street.

Purple's persistence has become as legendary as the garden itself. No hokey, down-home intervention into urban decay, the *Garden of Eden* is exquisitely designed and planted, with the formal grandeur of French or Japanese prototypes. A mazelike series of stone concentric circles (made of immense granite slabs he hauled from local demolition sites) are broken by paths in mathematical progression and centered on a yin/yang symbol. The garden offers a cosmic display of flowers, vegetables, even some rare trees which grew fortuitously from seeds in the horse manure Purple bicycled daily down from Central Park.

The theoretical plan is that the garden continue to expand mathematically until "you can see it from a satellite." If Purple sometimes plays god rather than Adam, he is to some extent entitled: "It takes Mother Nature five hundred years to create one inch of topsoil; on that basis the *Garden of Eden* represents two to three thousand years of evolution." Purple also sees himself as a "mirror-image Prometheus," bringing fresh water to put out the urban fires.

According to his associate, Sheyla Baykal, the city's plan calls for "the demolition of twelve buildings, eleven of them privately owned, displacement of thirteen commercial tenants with relocation indicated for only three, and relocation of thirty-two residential tenants." Residents are also bitter about the "lower income" designation, which demands annual incomes beginning at $27,000—"a lot more money than any of us make," said neighbor Una Copley to the *Daily News* (17 July 1984). Despite endless negotiations, hearings, and press, the city has yet to reveal why, in a community blessed with all too many vacant lots, housing must be built on top of the area's sole beauty spot. Purple's lawyer has come up with a number of good arguments, among them an old English edict that makes Purple common-law owner of the land because he spent ten years improving it. His allies have succeeded in temporarily halting demolition around the garden, which remains intact at this writing.

As of 13 September [1984], a significant rescue mission had been mounted by the Storefront for Art & Architecture. Directors Kyong Park and Glenn Weiss have invited architects from all over the world to design alternative projects that include the garden. Their own proposal looked eminently reasonable, providing the same residential space plus the ready-made public art, and saving a building at 53 Stanton Street that would be better rehabbed than removed. Architectural exhibitions tend to be rather dry and heavy on detail, revealing little to the layperson about the *experience* of the spaces they describe. This show was an exception because one could take the ten-minute walk from gallery to garden and back.

The garden's message was pretty metaphysical, couched in Adam's appropriately purple prose. (Zenger is a sort of Mary Daly or "zen-vironmentalist," given to integralist puns like "huwomanimal," "the U.S. of Omerica," and "government ignoranuses.") Whatever the subtleties, the place itself spoke loud and clear for harmonious form in the midst of officially sanctioned chaos; caring work in an uncared-for space; growing things in the midst of threatened death and decay.

In most of these public artworks, the messages are multileveled, the visible wholes suggesting invisible sociocultural needs and references. Near *The Garden of Eden* there was graffiti that had a Purplish ring to it: "The Task of the Enlightened is to restore, with the tools of Creativity, what the Hateful have destroyed with their Weapons of Oppression." (N.B. *The Garden of Eden* was destroyed in 1985.)

In 1981, the then-fledgling activist artists' collective Group Material announced that it was abandoning the East 13th Street storefront in New York City where it had operated for a year. It was striking out for "the ultimate alternative space—that wall-less expanse that bars artists and their work from the crucial social concerns of the American public." Burnt out, or at least toasted, after a year of gallery-sitting, rent-paying and maintenance, bolstered by the support they had received from their mostly Hispanic community, the four survivors of the twelve-member collective declared that it was "impossible to create a radical and innovative art if this work is anchored in one special gallery location. Art can have the most political content and form, but it just hangs there silent unless its distribution makes political sense as well. . . . To tap and promote the lived aesthetic of a largely 'non-art' public—this is our goal, our contradiction, our energy."

Brave words, and true. Five years later, having swerved a bit from that primrose path, and vehemently denying rumors that Group Material was about to fold, Julie Ault, Mundy McLaughlin, Doug Ashford and Tim Rollins are taking a summer break to figure out how to get back on the True Way. While their activities in the meantime have hardly been negligible, Group Material's decision to move back into more public (if less publicized) spaces is a direct response to the current politics of the art scene, and as such reflects the dilemmas facing many exhausted cultural workers.

From its beginnings in 1979 and its year of storefront shows in 1980–81, Group Material has been known for its innovatively conceived and installed group theme shows, each a collaborative artwork with a changing number of participants. Such shows were pioneered in 1978 by another young artists' collective—Colab (Collaborative Projects), which has always used the "parasite" approach to spaces, commandeering (at times extralegally) unused spaces for "The Manifesto Show," the "Doctors and Dentists Show" and, most notoriously, "The Real Estate Show" and "The Times Square Show." What Group Material brought to the vital collaborative turmoil of 1979–81 was a clearly social, even socialist, perspective, fused with the rebellious iconoclasm and antiestablishment arrogance of their generational peers.

Their shows at the storefront were characterized by red walls and an "all-over" collection of "high" and "low" culture presented on equal terms. "Alienation" explained "our separations from society, production and nature," and was accompanied by a lecture by Bertell Ollman, "Marxist professor" at New York University and chairman of the board game "Class Struggle." "It's a Boy! It's a Girl! It's a Gender Show!" investigated "sexual freedom as a condition of society, critiqued gender roles, and questioned definitions of femininity and masculinity." "Fascere Fascis" featured "the gesture, the gaze, the stance, the class, high fashion as a dimension of the new fascist discourse." With participants like Barbara Kruger, Jenny Holzer, and Sylvia Kolbowski, these two shows between them set a precedent for later depoliticized post-modernist elaborations of such subjects.

On the less fashionable side, my favorite from Group Material's storefront era was "Arroz con Mango: The People's Choice." On New Year's Day 1981 the collective visited every apartment on the block and borrowed each family's "favorite art possession," which ranged from costume dolls to family photos to a plastic portrait of Roberto Clemente to an Abraham Walkowitz painting unearthed from the 1940s. The show was billed as "a display of the private gone public, of the not-normally-found-in-an-art-gallery, of personal choice and cultural values on one block in New York City."

In more expansive modes, this remains one impetus behind Group Material's exhibitions, epitomized in handy portable form by "MASS," a traveling piece recently shown at the New Museum. More than a hundred artists contributed works in a uniform square format that are joined to form the twelve feet by forty feet word "MASS." Through juxtaposition and unifying context, a great diversity of "signs" (including cartoons, record covers, ads) come together in a metaphor for cultural democracy: "Group Material encourages people to become involved in the making of their own society and culture."

The move away from the "security blanket" of a gallery space led to three major public projects in 1982–83: "M-5," art on the interior ad panels of a major bus line; "Subculture," a show inside the subways that was an important attempt, though the art was almost invisible given its ratio to the ads; and "Dazibaos" ("Democracy Wall"), in Union Square, modeled after Chinese Big Character posters. The red and yellow sheets juxtaposed organizational statements with local individual responses, serving to identify issues and question the meanings of "free speech."

An indoor show—"Luchar!" at the Taller Latinoamericano in 1982 was another groundbreaker. Mixing New York art with popular revolutionary culture and children's drawings from Central America, it provided a seed for the foundation of Artists Call Against U.S. Intervention in Central America, in which Group Material was fully embroiled. Its own show in that campaign, "Time Line" at P.S.1, is considered by the collective their model project: "It was good art, accessible and clear. Anybody could tell what was being said." The message was a history of U.S. intervention in Central and Latin America; a "time line" of dates and places ran around the room's upper margin while below, in a typical combination of the formal and the chaotic, were a huge variety of art and objects, including piles of coffee, bananas and sugar, like parodies of sixties "process art."

Somewhere along the way, however, Group Material got detoured into an increasingly art world context. Despite their resistance to cooptation, the times were catching up to them. Their nonchalant melange of high and low culture has become a stylistic staple of the Sohoized galleries that eventually followed Group Material to the East Village. In the last few years any number of artists have used similar materials and ideas (ads, comics, cartoons and texts borrowed from kitsch, the mass media and the graffiti-rapping-breaking cultures) without the frame of social consciousness Group Material provides.

At least in the anterooms of the avant-garde there's no longer a big deal about "is it art or not art?" The current sticking point, even at a moment when ambiguous political references are almost chic, remains "is it art or politics?" The kind of question Group Material asks— "Why is this coffee can in the same place as this painting?"—doesn't come up if art status can be conferred on the coffee can (or the beer can, *à la* Jasper Johns). But if it remains unsanctified, and it's there to make a point about hemispheric economics, the coffee can is still a problem. Group Material has been effective precisely because it continues to allow the rough edges of the social stuff to grate against the smooth edges of the art stuff. At its most abrasively populist, this approach constitutes a critical commentary on the art industry—what's in and out of it.

The real apogée of Group Material's exhibition inventions was "Americana"—a show within a show at the Whitney Museum's prestigious and trend-setting 1985 Biennial. Group Material included more artists in its small ground-floor gallery than all the rest of the grandiose national exhibition on the two upstairs floors. As usual, "Americana" was a Total Artwork, and every contributing artist was a collaborator. With characteristic disrespect for "professional" hanging methods, Group Material put the art on vertical strips of different commercial wallpapers, interspersed with cultural artifacts from the American Dream chosen for their brand name puns: Total, Wonder Bread, and Home Pride represented mass-produced, fake nourishment; Bold, All, Gain, and Cold Power became participants in the class struggle, helped along by a blender and an electric can opener. Stay Free and New Freedom maxi pads touted an unfulfilled sexual revolution and the centerpiece was a GE washer and dryer called Harvest Gold. Song titles from the Muzak tape included "You're Blind," "This Land Is Your Land," "We're Not Gonna Take It," "I Don't Wanna Play House," and "The Stripper."

The critique extended to the art. Among the collaborators were many minority artists who would probably never get into a Whitney Biennial through the front door, and well-known progressive artists like Nancy Spero who inexplicably have never been invited. "Americana" was very popular with guards and public, but the rarified art world had a little more trouble figuring it out. Accustomed to ignoring content and avoiding politics, critics tended to see the show as camp, or resurrected pop art.

Group Material's "Arts and Leisure," which just closed at The Kitchen, and may be their last show of this kind, was perhaps a revenge for such misinterpretations. Its self-referential subject was the art industry, the artist's role in the "revitalized market" of today, and art "versus" entertainment. (One participant complained that shows with political content were "not meaningful any more because all the 'possibilities' are now expressed within the market"—a loan from the Shearson concept.) The market may be revitalized but neither the art nor the ethics are showing a lot of red corpuscles. As freshman art students assiduously plan their careers and the social contradictions of gentrification versus *la gente* are visible components of the East Village scene (in SoHo they have long since disappeared beneath the boutique veneer), I wonder how long, oh lord, how long will this statement by Antonio Gramsci be timely? "The crisis consists precisely in the fact that the old is dying and the new cannot be born. In this interregnum a great variety of morbid symptoms appears."

Certain aspects of so-called post-modernism can be counted among those morbidities. Though they can also play an effective part in the dismantling of modernist pieties, fertile ideas are often sterilized by frigid theory that avoids activism and direct communication as the poisons they've always been to the art market. Activists like Group Material and Friends have invented and/or adapted post-modernist strategies of representation and appropriation. But despite common goals, the exchange rarely goes the other way. Both groups can think, but the post-modernists usually can't act.

Included in "Arts and Leisure" is a clipping from the *National Enquirer* about modern art—Miró's "squiggles and blobs,' Léger's "splotches"—headlined "Somebody Actually Paid $2.7 Million for This!" It speaks for itself because of the context Group Material provided. It doesn't need to be "rephotographed" or copied or shrouded in obscurities. Art is not just entertainment, but it doesn't *hurt* to entertain people while you're having your say.

The art world ages art and artists fast. An intrepid adolescent in 1981, Group Material had mellowed into a potent patron by 1986, though its members are still in their twenties and early thirties. The same goes for Colab, Fashion Moda, PADD, and ABC No Rio, to varying degrees. All these groups were founded around 1979 and are still miraculously alive. They are all around seven years old, and there are indications that this may be the breaking point for radical volunteer organizations as well as for marriages.

The mainstream has caught up with a few of the possibilities of social connections to art. That's fine, and we activists can consider it a victory of sorts. But it leaves us at yet another turning point, pausing for reflection, reeling under the Reagan mudslide, looking for new strategies, the next step in the development of a strong, multifaceted critical art. The spark refuses to go out. The cultural component becomes increasingly important to a disempowered and often unimaginative left. A lot of artists have one foot out the door and are weighing the advantages of homelessness. The symptoms are not all morbid. Long live Group Material in its new incarnation.

Update 1988: "Arts and Leisure" was not Group Material's "last show of this kind." As this book goes to press, the group (Now Ashford, Ault, and Felix Gonzalez-Torres) has embarked on a year-long project called "Democracy," sponsored by the Dia Art Foundation, which includes exhibitions, roundtables, and four "Town Meetings" that will deal publicly with the national crisis in Democracy.

"Welcome to America's Finest City" is San Diego's immodest slogan, touted along with its tourist-specific "Spanish Heritage." "Welcome to America's Finest Tourist Plantation" was the January 1988 version by artists David Avalos, Louis Hock, and Elizabeth Sisco. So who listens to artists, and especially to so-called political artists whose "effectiveness" is always being questioned within the mainstream? It seemed that everybody in San Diego Country listened, at least for a couple of months. Because the artists' line was not confined to a gallery, a small magazine, or even a regular street poster. Superimposed on a striking photomontage, it was affixed to the backs of a hundred city buses as a 21" × 72" poster. Advertising experts estimate that such signs are seen by 80 percent of the population. San Diego is the seventh largest city in the U.S. and January is the month of the Super Bowl, when some 80,000 visitors swell the city's rooms and heads.

   The photomontage is black and white, with a series of working hands standing out in brown. The top line of red print is largest, so after it is taken for granted, the replacement of "city" with "tourist plantation" provides the jolt. The central photo is a pair of hands, handcuffed next to a police gun in holster; it is a documentary image from a series by Sisco, and shows an "illegal" being nabbed by a border control agent after being removed from a San Diego Transit bus in 1986. The flanking photos show hands scraping a dirty dish and reaching for a doorknob over a "Maid Service Please" tag; these are posed tableaux, representing the restaurant and hotel/motel industries.

Avalos, Hock, and Sisco are, respectively, artists in residence at the Centro Cultural de la Raza, and teachers at the University of California at San Diego. Following the extraordinary media hoopla—the kind of publicity every public artist dreams of—that welcomed the bus poster to one of America's conservative strongholds, they received an award from the Mexican American Business and Professional Association "in gratitude for the work which raised the San Diego community's consciousness of the plight of the undocumented worker." This was the top layer of the artists' intentions: "If we consider the realistic rather than the mythological landscape of San Diego, then we must acknowledge that the Super Bowl could not be held here if this town did not have a tourist complex of hotels, motels, restaurants, and amusement parts. And without the undocumented worker San Diego could not have a tourist industry.''

Inflated rhetoric, righteous indignation, and some supportive if wishy-washy art criticism marked the incredible number of newspaper articles, editorials, letters to the editor, TV and radio editorials, and coverage that followed the buses. Robert L. Myers, president of KFMB radio-TV, huffed: ''We call upon those who made this ill-advised decision to rectify their mistake by removing the signs at once''; he was echoed by KCST-TV. Others blamed the media for sensationalizing the issue. The primary axe ground by the opposition was the ''bad name'' given San Diego to all those visitors annually (and royally) bilked by the tourist industry. In fact, I suspect that the least effective aspect of the art was tourist terrorism, but the poster surely put the fear of god into the economic powers that be, who didn't enjoy seeing California's lucrative Spanish heritage sullied by its less manipulable heirs.

Racist statements were made, and parried by the Chicano community. ''The hot-dog poster artists would be better with a poster thanking San Diego for accepting the Mexican overflow, resulting from the inability of its industry to support its population explosion caused by an irresponsible birthrate,'' pouted C. W. Dalton of Lakeside. ''If they do not want to be dishwashers here, let them stay home and wash dishes in Mexico. . . . I have had it up to my ears with the illegal immigrants and their 'rights'. . . . Let us face it, Mexico will never change. They will always be takers; we will always be givers,'' wrote Mary M. Gustafson of Poway. ''Someone might point out that no one forces our undocumented visitors to crawl through the fence to get here,'' reasoned David B. Dreiman of La Jolla.

Oh yeah? retorted Jesus R. Cabezuela of Chula Vista: ''The people you call 'uninvited' are, in reality, returning to the homeland of their ancestors which was stolen from them. In this case, the Anglos were both takers and givers. They took the land, then gave the Mexicans the shaft.'' Consuelo Puente de Miller, former president of the Chicano Democratic Association, rejecting the image of Mexicans as ''so many cockroaches'' pouring over the border to take American jobs, warned that ''if others don't like our color, our language, or our customs, I feel sorry for them. We are nearly half a million strong in San Diego County. We're growing stronger every day, and we aren't going anywhere.''

The racism is inspired precisely by this unavoidable fact of California's multicultural future. It's predicted that by 1990 there will be no white (or any other color) majority in the state. Not all the "invaders" are poor; Japanese investment money is so ubiquitous that Shinto rites sometimes accompany ground-breaking ceremonies in downtown San Diego. Although there was only one letter in response to the bus poster from a Chicana domestic worker—objecting to the implication that she did "slave labor"—the art does raise the specter of blanket stereotyping of all Latinos as downtrodden "aliens." While the artists could hardly have handled this complex issue in a single shot, it would make an interesting second poster, in dialogue with the first. Work against racism is necessarily half criticism and half empowerment.

The officials were a bit more circumspect than the letter writers. "I don't think it's proper," whined Phil Blair of the Super Bowl Task Force. "You want to put your best foot forward when you have a house full of guests" (paying guests, he might have added). An editor of *The San Diego Union* called the bus poster "a tasteless parody." Al Reese of the San Diego Convention and Visitors Bureau had a point he may not have meant to make: "To some extent it is an insult to the 85,000 employees in the tourist industry, implying that they are illegals or are committing illegal acts by hiring illegals."

Much of the outrage focused on the fact that the circa $8,000 tab for the posters (one letter writer with a rosy view of artists' lives said it must have cost at least $100,000) came from "public funds"; $4,600 from the NEA was funnelled through the Combined Arts and Education Council of San Diego, one of whose people said, "I'm sure the NEA grant didn't anticipate something like this, but who knows? There's freedom in the art world. Perhaps this is more license than freedom." Censorship was explored and found to be legally unsupportable: an appellate court ruling had decreed that "the mere advocacy of an ideological viewpoint on a particular social issue or legitimate governmental concern is not prohibited." (Whew. Democracy rides again.) But the transit chairman indicated that officials may be "more conscientious" in reviewing advertising material in the future. And for the time being, San Diego officialdom had to be content with boasting that they "don't shy away from controversy."

The last word on public funding came from communications professor Herbert Schiller, who wrote an editorial in *The Tribune* about the hyprocrisy of TV stations calling for censorship: "The television industry has not been shy about seeking expanded First Amendment rights for itself. Free speech for the rest of the community apparently is another matter. . . . Stations are granted operating licenses *without charge* to use a scarce and valuable public resource, the radio frequency spectrum—the air waves. This license can and often is sold for enormous sums" though there are plenty of people who consider some of the programming "offensive, biased, mindless, or without redeeming social value."

La Prensa (San Diego) also put in its two centavos worth, noting the irony of the tourist industry getting incensed about "the bad image of the fun city of San Diego": "Never mind that the local hotels and motels are gouging the unsuspecting visitor . . . that restaurants and nightclubs have jacked their prices to where local residents dare not go." (This was a casually stated and accepted fact within the controversy, supported by a local cartoon of a bus poster reading "Reserve a room and help win one for the Gyppers.") "In a fury of greed," continued *La Prensa*, "it appears that everyone is out to extract every last nickel. . . . Unfortunately, these self-sacrificing workers that work long hours daily to please the tourist industry are at the mercy of the local border patrol and the INS which constantly harasses them, beats them, and hounds them down like dogs. These workers are treated by our tourist industry as indentured servants. . . . So enjoy yourself, Super Bowl fan, and remember . . . the worker who makes your stay a pleasant one is also the most oppressed human being in America's Finest City."

Another irony was the poster's placement; undocumented workers are often "hounded" in and onto buses. Says Sisco, "We're symbolically putting the people who've been taken off back on the bus." And Avalos asks, "Is it negative to yell 'fire' in a burning building? Some people feel that speaking the truth is the most positive thing that people can do. . . . We're pleased and amazed that three artists and a hundred posters have made this kind of impact. We must have struck a nerve center."

They did, and not just in the soft underbelly of San Diego's tourist business-as-usual. The poster raised a number of issues that public and so-called political or critical or social-change art is struggling with. The bus/subway poster and the "corrected" or legitimate billboard have been popular if not proliferate art mediums for over a decade. They have been used effectively by Maria Karras and Mary Linn Hughes in Los Angeles, by Nancy Bless in Ohio, by the Artemesia Gallery in Chicago, and by Group Material and Dennis Adams in New York, among others; censorship has haunted them. In 1984, Avalos suffered the removal of his sculpture from the U.S. Courthouse Plaza in San Diego;

it depicted an undocumented worker being frisked by the *Migra* riding a Tijuana tourist donkey, and was deemed "a security risk."

Then there's the question of whether the poster is art, advertising, or politics. It doesn't matter, but the distinctions are interesting. According to a pocket dictionary, to advertise is to "make known," and its French root means "to warn." Art is "skill, profession, or craft." Okay. Politics is "the science and art of civil government." Seems we have a hybrid on our hands, which is no surprise, since much or most of the interesting art being made today is hybrid in form, content, cultural background, and—like the bus posters—intent. The artists note that in San Diego (as elsewhere), "private enterprise has papered over the space with commercial advertising," and that if the logical forum for public issues is public space, then "the first task of the public artists would be the creation of such a public space." If art in public spaces becomes "the target of this city's hostility, then public artists will increase their chances of survival by making that target a moving one."

Avalos, Hock, and Sisco also raise the issue of "cultivating a new audience"—a long-time obsession for social-change artists hoping to subvert the passive/captive experience of museums and galleries. This modest spectacle is rare in that it really did wake up a "broader audience," which is why I've concentrated here on the responses. What happens, then, when the target stops to accommodate different passengers? Since the "controversy, crisis, celebrity" (to borrow the artists' installation title) of the bus poster, it has been shown in three gallery situations, ironically framed in gold or crumpled up in a garbage can, always accompanied by its January media entourage. (There is also a videotape, for national travel.) The task was to transform its function for an art audience, so attention was diverted from its street subject to the media.

I haven't seen the installation, but presumably the poster works as art in that formalist context as well as it did on the bus line, although one defensive official turned art expert said that it was "muddled and sophomoric. It's too 'busy' to be effective." I disagree. The poster is a snazzy combination of graphic impact, layered political meaning and strong photography. Some viewers might only get the line of text, which doesn't leave them empty-headed; others, stalled in traffic behind the bus long enough to think, would start to pull in other ideas. Others may not have gotten it at all. Those who did were probably not the museum-going middle class so much as those who knew how it felt to be those brown hands.

A progressive artist's job, as Avalos, Hock, and Sisco know well, is not to sell or manipulate or decorate, not merely to compete with commercial ads for jazzy visuals and easy reading, or with high art for beauty and irony, but to produce an image that expands the public's expectations of what they may get from public forms, to provoke thought and help people look around them with fresh eyes. It's not easy. It's hard work. And it's an important way to reimagine what art means when life is not always a Super Bowl of cherries.

This is the case history of a truly activist art, a visual imagery collectively developed in response to the despair masked by smiley faces. *World War 3 Illustrated* is a comic magazine from the heart and bowels of New York's Lower East Side, which provides a microcosm for connected global struggles in Central America, in South Africa, in the Middle East . . . and in your brain. From the beginning, *WW3* has been more than a magazine, though deliberately less than a movement. The first issue appeared just as Ronald Reagan took office as the result of a mudslide. The eighth issue (early 1988) took as its theme "A Long Last Look at a Titanic." The cover is an intricate collage portrait by Aki Fujiyoshi of Reagan as a sinking ship (without the departing rats and white meese). In fact, *WW3*'s history so far has been the counter-history of the Reagan administration. In November [1988], come what may, it will enter a new phase.

The magazine was conceived by two young cartoonists during the hostage crisis in 1979. Peter Kuper said to Seth Tobocman, "Look's like there's going to be a war, so I guess we should do an anti-war magazine." The war that developed, however, was the war waged by the Reagan administration against almost everybody else, and the magazine's contents reflected a daily activism. The initial premise was "based on Marcuse's idea that a highway, a washing machine, and everything else that's built has to do with the building of the missile system, the building of the bomb shelter system," say the editors.

> We're talking about the way people live here and the way they feel here, talking about our lives. We don't want to speak from an abstracted place where they're just talking about "world issues." We want to show how that affects your housing or your day-to-day life on the streets. If we want to do an issue on doing the laundry, we can. We'll find something about washing machines that really has to do with this.

A lot of dirty water has passed under the bridge since then and a lot of dirty laundry has been hung out on public lines. But the ideologically diverse and always changing core of editors of *WW3*

(Tobocman and usually Kuper and Joshua Whalen are steady presences) is still busting ass. They not only conceive, contribute to, and produce the magazine, but devise ways to make ends meet and get it to as large an audience as possible. They hand out magazines to potential allies, spend time on college campuses and even leave copies in corporate waiting rooms, infiltrating a social sector to which they have no "natural" access. They theorize about how to set up a "functioning socialist democracy that could exist and do business in a capitalist country." But for now, only the printer gets paid. Any profits go to buy more pages, faster turnover and four-color covers.

The artist/editors of *WW3* were drawn together despite their differing backgrounds, skills, styles and politics by a deep abhorrence for the politics and the culture of the Reagan era, into which they emerged from their teens: "There was something about Reagan," they recall, "that wasn't just another Republican. It was a pervasive attitude in society, and it had to be fought on that level. It wasn't just in the government, but in how people were starting to imagine themselves. We were in our twenties, and we realized we're going to be defined as people by this period."

World War 3 began as a comic because Tobocman and Kuper were comic artists, but it became part of a wave of revival and expansion for the medium during the eighties. Comics moved beyond their traditional audience of young males from the Garry Trudeau and Gary Larson to punk zines, from Nicole Hollander to *RAW, Ripoff,* and *WW3,* into a post-neo-quasi-modernist idiom that's no longer the funnies. Reagan himself likes to be briefed with cartoons, and of course the CIA discovered the medium with Donald Duck in Latin America long before their murderous bestseller in Nicaragua. Also in the early 1980s, the art world was being temporarily revitalized by a punk-derived surge from the anarchist left, later coopted by the disastrous East Village art scene. Artist's groups, with young people in the lead, were working across the political spectrum and across race and class barriers from the South Bronx to Loisaida (Puerto Rican vernacular for the Lower East Side).

But neither the art world nor the comics world were ready for *WW3.* In 1978, Tobocman and Kuper found the underground comics still reprinting the Freak Brothers, and they were turned away by *Heavy Metal* because "our work was referential to real life and not fantasy. That kind of offended me," Tobocman recalls, "because I've been reading science fiction all my life and *all of it* was referential to real life. That's why I read it." When they did start *WW3,* it continued to fall between categories. Comic distributors said it wasn't a comic, it was just a magazine. Left distributors said it wasn't serious because it's just pictures. Finally, it was Ruth Schwartz of Mordam Records, a West Coast distributor of hardcore punk, who understood *WW3*'s crossover possibilities and has opened up its outlets to Tower Record stores across the country.

Classic, socially concerned science fiction literature and movies may be *WW3*'s direct forebears. Their ecological and social prophecies are coming to pass, and the apocalyptic vision that gives *WW3* its desperate force and unique identity is the present. Closest kin might be film, but the editors rejected the option early on because of the "oppressive process" of exploitation and financial hierarchies that govern filmmaking. "The only way to take control was to do comics. You can do them on almost no money, and by yourself, if necessary. There are issues of *WW3* that cost as little as $900 to produce."

World War 3 tries to be a resource to the "extreme left," which, they say, "is the real left." They announce demos and meetings and introduce grassroots organizations. The recent collaborations with the "New York 8" give depth and substance to the magazine's frequent antiracist contributions, just as its participation in the squatters' movement, its efforts to expose the right's agenda for the homeless, and its support of lesbians and gays have made the group a respected voice in communities far from the Lower East Side. They have taken the comic to street posters and to self help: how to do graffiti, how to do rent strikes, how to make solar panels, how to set up day care. The real message is how to start a revolution.

By 1984, it had become very clear that *WW3*'s natural constituency was first the countercultural community, and second their neighbors who were also being screwed by Reaganomics, drug traffic and gentrification. Housing was the key to many other issues. Rehab, squatting, homesteading and— increasingly—homelessness were issues shared by everybody being crowded out of this last multicultural, relatively cheap area of the city. Small shopkeepers were evicted to make way for wine bars and galleries, and landlords cut off services and encouraged arson so they could get in on the development boom. As active participants in the political struggles, *WW3* got an education of their own in the process.

WW3 differs from other "community artists"—a word they don't particularly like. Rejecting old and new left, they set out almost unconsciously to reinvent activism, avoiding the cliches of the "cultural worker" and the ambiguities of the avant-garde: "What we really set out to do in 1984 was to alter the definition of Cool."

In the process, they helped develop creative Civil Disobedience with No Business as Usual and the St. Valentine's Coalition, went to jail for postering and learned something from the European ''squatter refugees'' whose own movement had been blitzed.

WW3 has two major weapons—their smarts and their arts. The magazine is quite literally an ''organ'' on which a lot of tunes get played. Its stories go by fast (befitting the TV on which the artists were suckled) but they stick to the ribs in a way few comics do. There is a diversity of style in the ten issues [to date] that is mind-boggling and description-defying. Tobocman's graphics are a slashing barrage of black-and-white dialectics; Kuper is gentler and his autobiographical pieces about the education of an innocent are particularly convincing. Paula Hewitt's elegantly passionate drawings of women rejecting society's gift of misery move into the Käthe Kollwitz territory, and Eric Drooker's brilliant, wordless evocations of a menacing metropolis send chills down the spine. Chuck Sperry specializes in psychological politics (snakes writhing from Bud McFarlane's head, and from his Iran-bound cake and Bible); editor Joshua Whalen writes about the world from a bike-messenger's pace; and there are cameo appearances by artists like Sue Coe, Jerry Kearns and Anton van Dalen.

If fear of the future, rage about the past and alienation from the present fuel *WW3,* it is rarely righteous or cynical. One of the magazine's greatest strengths is its compassion. ''You don't have to fuck people over to survive,'' is a recurring message. It isn't even afraid of hope, poetry, emotion, and it sometimes even welcomes sentiment. One strip can border on the cute and the next may veer toward the hysterical. But beneath both is a wholehearted attempt to understand and express social conditions that many ''political artists'' theorize, rhetoricize or imagine. They hit heavy notes with a light touch. Isabella Bannerman and Robert Desmond, for example, can juxtapose photography, fat-faced little people and messages like this: ''Secrecy is a vaccine against democracy. The only secret left in the United States is that there is a real world and we're not taking very good care of it.''

In the fascism issue (#10), the contents build in an expert Möbius twist from the Holocaust to persecution of the Arabs, mediated by autobiographical reminiscences by both Kuper and Tobocman about childhood trips to Israel. In the religion issue (#5), poet/organizer Charles Frederick can offer an epic of gay Catholic childhood a few pages away from a devastating pictorialization of Jerry Falwell's ''Rapture'' speech and an array of blasphemies from all sides of the altar, executed with such freshness that the blood rises again around issues that seemed spent.

For all its global sophistication, however, *World War 3* can never escape the Dark Satanic City. Strip after strip details the nightmare of job loss, eviction, addiction, racism, rejection and violence: ''If you fuck up you're all alone.'' So they try to counter intellectual pessimism with oppositional optimism, to paraphrase Gramsci. Even in the direst tales, people make love, people give birth, people resist, people survive. *WW3* is the mirror Americans don't want to look into, the mirror that won't reply, ''We Are the Fairest of Them All.'' As everybody scrambles for the white bread, *WW3* stays home in the inner city, refusing to fight for crumbs, biting the hand that isn't feeding us and kicking ass.

Art in Public:
Conflict and Questions Today

13

Private Fantasies Shape Public Events: And Public Events Invade and Shape Our Dreams

Carol Becker

To the memory of Erica Sherover-Marcuse

Art Institute of Chicago student David Nelson's painting of Chicago's late Mayor Harold Washington in women's underwear, hung in a student exhibition in May 1988, caused a controversy with local, national and international implications. In recalling the events and analyzing their far-reaching meanings, AIC Graduate Division Chair Carol Becker brings up difficult issues that arise when weighing artists' responsibilities and artistic freedom, the First Amendment rights of individuals and those of their communities.

Becker, an educator, is critical of schools that train students to "make it in the art world" instead of teaching social responsibility for their intentions, and who indulge in promoting an iconoclasm that allows provocation merely for its own sake. Becker's analysis also treats racism, sexism and homophobia. Nelson chose to depower and degrade his subject by feminizing him. The Afro-American community in Chicago who responded to the painting objected not only on the basis of the canvas' undignified presentation of an Afro-American city official, but to its implications that Harold Washington may have been a homosexual.

In a sense, all art is public art when displayed. The content of that art always has political implications, as Nelson's traditional painting and reactions to it demonstrate. The role of the media in publicizing factions in Chicago politics through this incident brings up disturbing questions about the partnership of art in the public interest with the print and television media courted to bring efforts for social change to larger audiences.

The title of Becker's article is a quote from Charles L. Mee, Jr., from a piece about the playwright by Eileen Blumenthal, "Blitzed-out Lovers Tell a Tale for Our Time," New York Times (3 July 1988).

On 11 May 1988, the School of the Art Institute of Chicago was shaken to the core when a student painting triggered a sequence of events that fiercely engaged the city for three entire days. Rarely has a collision between the world of art and the world of politics exposed so many basic contradictions. Issues such as First Amendment rights, the limits of artistic freedom, the sanctity of the private domain, the relationship between the artist and the world at large, have become topics of public concern. Over the ensuing months the repercussions of this incident have spread throughout Chicago and throughout the national and international art community.

As chair of the Graduate Division of the school, I was involved in this incident from the beginning. After much consideration it has become clear to me that there is no simple right or wrong here, no one "truth" to be found through Cartesian analysis, no heart of the problem to be dissected, except perhaps the broken heart of the body politic. Because David Nelson's painting was conceived at a particular historical moment, it is necessary to recreate that moment and its contingencies before an analysis can be achieved.

The Chronology of Events

Day 1

On the morning of the first day, David Nelson, a graduating senior, arrived at the school at 8:00 a.m. to hang a series of paintings, his entry in the Traveling Fellowship Competition (a closed exhibition open only to the school community). At this time every year the school is transformed into a gallery for one week, while graduating students presenting work in all media compete for cash prizes. Students draw lots for location and personally select what they will exhibit. There is no prescreening.

David Nelson was lucky. He drew a prime location—a wall adjacent to the main entrance—a space no one entering the school could avoid. Nelson hung five paintings. One was a self-portrait of a confident young blond David Nelson embracing small doll-like figures representing various racial and ethnic groups. It was entitled, *I'm Sensitive and I Love All Humanity.* Close by he hung another work, which was to become known as "the painting"—a crudely executed portrait of an overweight Mayor Harold Washington dressed only in white lacy women's underwear—bra, panties, garter-belt and stockings—holding a pencil in his right hand, staring dejectedly from the canvas. The title was *Mirth and Girth.*

Before he had even completed hanging these paintings, someone had notified an alderman and the media had also been called. By 9:30 the painting was being talked about on one of the city's major black radio stations, and the staff of the *Chicago Defender* (a newspaper circulated primarily in the black community) was already in the president's office.

The painting was causing a furor. By mid-afternoon, every newspaper, TV station, and radio show was somehow involved in the ruckus. Crowds began to gather outside the school's entrance. The school's security force was kept busy prohibiting nonstudents from entering the building. A shouting match had already arisen between predominantly white art students and predominantly black members of the community. These student artists were yelling, "civil liberties," "freedom of expression," "First Amendment rights," while those from the community at large, angry that anyone would dare defame the memory of Harold Washington, were calling the students "racists."

In the meantime Tony Jones, the school's president, convened a small group of faculty, administration and staff as an ad hoc advisory group to help him determine what actions, if any, should be taken. This group crammed into the provost's office. As they deliberated, phones rang off the hook condemning the painting, and the press continued to gather in the administrative offices demanding a statement. Then suddenly the opportunity to make an academic decision was taken away as nine black aldermen, who had just marched over from City Hall, stormed the school.

Only that afternoon a resolution was introduced in the City Council which began: "Whereas, the artist, David Nelson obviously exhibits some type of demented and pathological capacities. . . . " This resolution provided justification for the aldermen's actions. It requested the removal of the painting and the withholding of city funds until it was taken down; however, it was not in any way a *mandate* for the removal of the painting by the aldermen. Nonetheless, Alderwoman Dorothy Tillman and Alderman Alan Streeter entered the school, dramatically ripped the painting from the wall with bravado and theatrics and stormed into the president's office, *Mirth and Girth* in tow. (The painting had already been damaged—a five-inch gash in one corner.)

Now eleven strong, the aldermen threatened to burn the painting right in the president's office. Luckily someone suggested that such an act might be hazardous and that it would be smarter to set fire to it outside, on the school lawn. By now the police, also locked in the president's office, had decided that the painting was "too inflammatory" to remain on the premises. It was at this point that they "arrested the painting" for having the "potential to incite a riot."

The seizure of the painting did little to abate the controversy. Crowds continued to build throughout the day. Many students who were still at the school (between the end of the semester and graduation) seemed initially concerned only with the issue of civil liberties. But soon they began to understand the complexity of the problem. Many of them found it a revelation to hear ways in which Nelson's image of Harold Washington deeply upset the black community at the school, as well as members of the black community in the city at large. They were amazed that one student's work could generate such an extreme response. Black students were torn. They were caught between their allegiance to the school, their identity as artists, and their sense that the primary contradiction of this event for them was not civil liberties but racism.

Students continued to debate among themselves and by evening, under pressure from the media to comment on the events, they drafted a simple group statement, which declared that the painting represented "the sole view of one artist" and "did not represent the collective view." And continued: "Whether or not the content of the painting was offensive, it should have been allowed to stand in public view under protection of the First Amendment rights," because such an "infringement" of "basic constitutional rights was threatening to the freedom of artists everywhere."

Day 2

Late in the evening of the first day, the school had been informed that as a result of the painting controversy, it was likely that a caucus of black state legislators would introduce a bill demanding that all state funding be withdrawn from the entire corporation, museum and school. The school was advised to act quickly. The Art Institute chartered a plane and sent a contingent of school and museum administrators, a lawyer and a student union representative to meet with the Black

Caucus to see what could be done to stop the measure, which also called for the resignation of the school's president.

While this group was in Springfield, Marshall Field V—the president of the Museum Board of Trustees—accompanied by the president and vice-president of the school, legal counsel and three other administrators, met with Mayor Sawyer, his Corporation Counsel Judson Miner, Chief of Staff Sharon Gist Gilliam, and eleven aldermen at City Hall. After many hours of grueling debate, the school promised to apologize to the city and its residents for the distress the painting had caused, and agreed not to display the painting in the future. It also promised that the school would continue its efforts to improve minority representation at all levels, with renewed dedication.

The meeting in Springfield, unlike that at City Hall, appeared to achieve a greater level of understanding on both sides. There were many rumors and misconceptions to dispel. For example, some members of the Black Caucus believed the painting had been hung in the museum among the Renoirs. Others thought it had been up on the walls for weeks and that faculty and students had seen it but had offered no criticism. The discussion made clear how little those outside the art world understood about the process of an art school. It was assumed, for example, that the school would have taken the painting down in a minute had it been of former Governor Ogilvie (who had just died) or Governor Thompson. The school's representatives assured the caucus that they had never taken a painting off the wall, no matter who was represented and no matter how compromising it might have been to any public official. The school had run into controversy before in dealing with student exhibits: live rats as part of a sculptural piece had been prohibited by the Board of Health, as had dead rats in a refrigerator, part of another installation. Mayor Daly had been portrayed as an aborted fetus. Jane Byrne and Ronald Reagan had been seen in an array of compromising postures. President Tony Jones, painted by none other than David Nelson, was shown as a suckling infant in the arms of a bare-breasted Madonna. But the school had never removed a painting or piece of artwork from the wall or from a gallery no matter how controversial its content.

Many School of the Art Institute faculty, students and staff had worked in Washington's campaigns and were great supporters of the late mayor. It was particularly painful to realize how the credibility of the entire school and museum had been implicated in this incident. In the hope of changing this perception, they joined with the Black Caucus to issue a joint statement agreeing to work together, when possible.

One issue both groups could readily agree upon was the need to increase minority representation among students, staff and faculty. The school promised to work harder to improve the numbers of minority employees at all levels and to also improve external community relations.

The school contingent returned from Springfield with a sense that some understanding had been reached, and that something of the day-to-day life and purpose of an art school had been communicated. The City Hall meeting had unfortunately not felt as encouraging. A good deal of shouting and irrational pronouncements on the part of the aldermen had left top school administrators upset and anxious about events to come.

By late afternoon, Reverend Willie Barrow of Operation PUSH appeared on national television, flanked by ten black ministers, to denounce unspecified "racist practices" at the school and to demand greater black enrollment and representation. Barrow condemned the painting incident as "the latest in a series of escalating attacks and insults against the black community." This group called for "sanctions" against the Art Institute unless it implemented a "review policy" to prevent offensive paintings from being exhibited in the future.[1]

Day 3

A day of reckoning. By now the press had had time to take various stances. Syndicated Chicago columnist Mike Royko had called those who removed the painting "Alderboobs." One journalist had labeled the entire event a "panty raid." Another had called it an "Art Raid" by an "Alderposse." For some it was a great source of humor. For most it mirrored the chilling split between the city's whites and blacks which seemed to be intensifying each day.

The story was front-page news nationally and internationally. Locally it was the *only* story. Faculty and staff had practically moved into the school to deal with the events minute by minute. Individuals from around the city called to condemn the school's publication of the full-page explanatory statements which had been agreed upon with the City Council. These callers chastised the administration for being too weak and unwilling to stand up to the aldermen. Others accused the school of somehow having "encouraged" the creation of such a painting.

For those in the administration, this was a difficult day: A decision had to be reached whether or not to proceed with graduation as planned for the next day, in spite of the bomb threats and the fact that PUSH's Reverend Barrow had called for a demonstration one thousand strong to march on the Art Institute. The school was also anticipating at least a thousand people for graduation ceremonies; many would arrive just when the PUSH demonstrators were scheduled to reach the Art Institute. The students had also called for an "Artist's Be-In" to convene at Daly Plaza: It was feared that all these groups would collide and heated interchanges occur. To assuage some anxiety, the school increased security and asked for more city protection. Graduation was to go on as scheduled. Fortunately, this turned out to be the correct policy.

The next day the school and museum were secured like fortresses: police cars, plain clothes officers and back-up forces were everywhere. Everyone was on edge. The administration knew that once graduation was over students would disperse and tensions would subside. Although the issues raised by the incident had not been resolved, it would be easier to focus on them in the summer without fear of a possible student/community confrontation.

Although there was almost palpable relief once graduation was over, there was also a deep sadness, a sense that things could never be quite the same again. The community of the school had been torn apart. It seemed there was no collective agreement as to why these events had occurred, or how they should have been negotiated. Relations between black faculty, staff, students and their white counterparts were extremely strained and self-conscious. Many Latinos, Asians and other minorities felt alienated from all sides of the issue, and met independently to discuss their positions. The school's place in the community had been seriously challenged, and the inherent contradictions of a private and elite art school located in the center of a racially diverse urban center had been exposed.

The challenge at this point was to step back, to understand what had occurred, to allow grievances to be articulated (however long that process might take) and ultimately to heal the damage that had been done. It is only now, after some time has passed, that the complexity of the events reveals itself in all its dimensions. To understand its many aspects, it is necessary to view the incident within its social context.

The Social Context

An art work is not an isolated physical phenomenon. It is a manifestation of a moment in the historical process of living.

—a South African artist

Harold Washington, Chicago's first black mayor died on 23 November 1987. Those who worked for him still refer to him lovingly as *the mayor.* He was the first person truly to crack the Machine stranglehold on city politics. To elect him, twice, required the combined forces of progressive people from every community and from every ethnic and racial group. This was a unity never before achieved in Chicago politics. It was a historic victory. But this coalition had not had enough time really to solidify. The allegiances were still precarious: Unresolved contradictions, paranoias and ancient rivalries continued to exist and then began to resurface in Chicago immediately after the mayor died unexpectedly at the age of sixty-five.

Although considerable time has passed since his death, there are many who are still in shock and mourning. Those who loved the mayor, those who worked hard to get him elected, have not forgotten him or overcome their grief. Hundreds of thousands of people walked past his open casket as he lay in state (David Nelson among them). They are still saddened by the sense of loss, which is only exacerbated by the lack of a suitable successor. Much of what Harold Washington stood for has been destroyed by divisiveness, corruption and a jockeying for power. Many have used their former closeness to him to try to win the black community to their side, while others, who were never really supportive of Washington, have misrepresented their relationship with him in order to win political power.

When the incident of the painting occurred, many were deeply upset by Nelson's work, but some *used* the incident for their own ends. They saw in it an opportunity for grandstanding, for proving themselves the true guardians of Washington's memory. It was easy to rally loyal Washington supporters around such an issue. But had these aldermen sincerely wanted to protect the mayor's memory, they could have done so in a much more useful manner. As Clarence Wilson wrote, ''Their actions changed a private, juried exhibition into a public spectacle played out in the full glare of the media and gave wide circulation and notoriety to an inept and artistically shallow work.''[2]

The incident could have been hidden from the media, dealt with quietly among leaders of the community and the school. But instead, the media was actually solicited, used to record certain figures as they marched dramatically from the school, spoils in hand. Art critic Harold Haydon said of the aldermen's behavior: "They overreacted. Harold Washington would have ignored this. He was too smart. This was a dumb thing to do."[3] The aldermen acted inappropriately, taking the law into their own hands, creating even further racial tension, and almost inciting a riot.

This incident, however, was only one among many which have caused dramatic splits between blacks and whites and between blacks and other minorities in Chicago. Prior to the conflicts around the painting, another incident had received national attention. Seemingly unrelated, the Steve Cokely affair was in fact a crucial motivating force propelling members of the black community to respond to Nelson's painting as aggressively as they did.

Steve Cokely, an aide to the acting mayor, Eugene Sawyer, made certain anti-Semitic remarks in lectures delivered at the Black Nation of Islam from August 1985 to November 1987. The gravity of his accusations shocked Jews and non-Jews alike. Among other things, he alleged that Jewish doctors on the South Side of Chicago were injecting black babies with the AIDS virus, and he later alluded to a Jewish conspiracy to "rule the world."[4] These remarks caused many to demand that Cokely be fired. It took Sawyer more than a week to make this decision. When he did, certain factions in the black community were enraged. They felt that Cokely's First Amendment rights had been violated. Any unity that had once existed between blacks and Jews had come undone.

Such unfortunate polarizations are not new to Chicago, but they now seem to occur more frequently on the national level as well. As Salim Muwakkil wrote in *In These Times:* "The *Zeitgeist* of racial intolerance has trickled down from the ruling Reaganauts to Hayden Lake, Idaho, to the college campuses, to the inner cities."[5] Eight years of Reagan had done nothing but increase tension and frustration among people who had little, if any, outlet for political expression. It also helped to cause a certain scapegoating of Jews, the most vulnerable representatives of the white power base.

The Cokely incident was only one of many indications of how tense race relations had become nationally and of how chaotic Chicago politics had become since the mayor's death. But there is no doubt that this event, which occurred only one week before the painting incident, was equated with it in the minds of some in the black community. As Alderman Streeter said when asked why he thought David Nelson painted the painting: "It's all related. I don't feel it's a coincidence.

I feel the fellow is a Jewish person who is defaming the Mayor I love. . . . ''[6] (Nelson is not, in fact, Jewish.)

During this time, there were those who reasoned: ''If Cokely was not protected under the First Amendment, if he was not permitted the right to make anti-Semitic remarks with impunity, then David Nelson should not be allowed to display a racist painting.'' The Black Caucus in Springfield even asked for the resignation of President Tony Jones, reasoning that if Cokely had been fired, then Jones should also be fired. But the analogy simply did not hold up. There was a great difference between a young student exhibiting a tasteless painting in a school competition, however racist his intent, and a mayoral aide, supposedly responsible to the Chicago community, making serious accusations against the Jewish community over a two-year period. Unfortunately, all logical thinking had fallen by the wayside. The tenor of events was captured in Alderman Streeter's assertion that, ''I don't care what the law, what the Supreme Court says, that painting will never go back up on the wall. If it does I'll tear it down myself.''[7] The ACLU lawyer defending Nelson said that the last time he had heard such a denunciation of the First Amendment was in the South during the Civil Rights campaign and it had come from irate white racists. History had come full circle.

The Issue of Iconoclasm

> No one, especially the artist, has a right to be indifferent
> to the social order.
>   —From the Manifesto of ''Los Interioristas''

The aldermen were not the only ones suffering from a myopic view of reality. David Nelson had his own subjective and less-than-lucid understanding of what was going on in Chicago. He was unnerved by a poster on sale called ''Worry ye not.'' It was an image of Jesus Christ and Harold Washington, side by side, hovering over Chicago as angels and protectors of the city. Nelson interpreted this combined image as a sacrilege. Harold Washington was mortal, not an angel or savior, thought Nelson. He wanted to pull him from the sky. For Nelson this image was particularly offensive because not only did it deify Washington but it defamed Jesus. If Washington had become an icon, Nelson was quite literally going to smash him and bring him down to earth. In an interview with the *New Art Examiner* Nelson said: ''I guess in this city there are certain deities. Washington is a deity and you can't touch him. It wasn't Washington I wanted to poke a hole in—like a balloon. It was the diety aspect . . . I'm an iconoclast, I guess I mean a person who doesn't believe in icons."[8]

A follower of Jesus Christ, Nelson admits to finding portraits of Christ within the museum collection offensive even though he is quick to state that he would never consider having them removed. In discussions he also indicated a definite uneasiness with images of gay male eroticism that had been displayed in last year's Fellowship Competition. It is not coincidental that he chose to disempower the image of Harold Washington by emasculating it. In a stereotypically homophobic manner, he insinuated that the illusion of virility people equated with Washington only concealed some type of sexual deviance.

To add to the sting, and to eliminate any question as to whether or not he was making an antigay statement, Nelson titled the painting *Mirth and Girth,* the name of a Chicago club for overweight gay men. Nelson's provocative and tasteless attempt to defame a beloved black leader prompted the *New York Times* to call the painting "savage." Michael Brenson wrote: "It is utterly unsentimental, with something of the no-holds-barred satire of 'Saturday Night Live.' Largely because of its indifference to the offense it could give, it has touched raw nerves and unleashed a storm of vindictiveness and anger."[9] It is important to note that Nelson's image does not so much depict the behavior of gay men, who do not usually dress in women's underwear, as it does transvestites or cross-dressers. It seems to be perversion that interested Nelson, but the negative power for the black community was undoubtedly primarily that it alluded to femaleness and gayness.

Nelson's decision to dress Harold Washington in women's underwear creates a provocative image which is both racist and antigay. White men have for centuries attempted to undermine black male virility. They have also attempted to negate the importance and power of black leaders, in whatever way they could. Given the history of racism, it is not surprising that black men have come to fear emasculation. Given the fact that the culture is antigay, it is not surprising that black men have come to equate one form of emasculation with gayness. It is therefore understandable that many members of the black community have become homophobic. Had this not been the case, the painting would never have received the response it did. Were Nelson not himself homophobic, he might not have painted the painting at all. Add to this complexly layered signification Nelson's portrayal of the mayor with splayed feet, an overweight body (which was one of the primary causes of the mayor's death) and a pencil, which Alton Miller (the mayor's press secretary) thought Washington had bent down to retrieve when he was actually doubled over in pain, and you can understand *why* Brenson called the painting "savage."

Many journalists writing about the painting, unwilling to think through the problem, have too readily accepted Nelson's sense of this work as iconoclasm. But this is a misnomer. Iconoclasts traditionally attempt to disempower those whose entrenched position has been oppressive to others, whose rigidly fixed and venerated image leaves no room for interpretation. There is usually a goal in mind, a need to discredit the sacredness of the image in order to liberate that which has been repressed or unspoken. In Nelson's mind Washington might have had this kind of power, but in reality he did not. As mayor, Washington doubtless had a great deal of political clout. But he had fought long and hard to win this influence, and in truth his base was always fragile at best. Although he had reached a position of personal strength, he represented a group of people—blacks, Latinos, Asians, gays, progressives—whose position in society continues to be fraught with insecurity. In the face of this fragility, it is impossible not to ask: What power was Nelson attempting to challenge? What did he think he would achieve?

Several other incidents raise questions about the nature of iconoclasm and help clarify the use or misuse of the term in relationship to *Mirth and Girth*. For example, in an exaggerated response to Martin Scorsese's *The Last Temptation of Christ,* fundamentalists tried to buy up all the prints from Universal before its release. Picket lines, protestations, and even stone-throwing turned the opening night of what might have been a small art-house premiere into a sold-out circus event. Scorcese, like Kazantzakis, from whose novel the story was adapted, was not interested in iconoclasm, although this is what he is accused of. Rather he was concerned with a demystification of the Jesus figure and an intense grappling with his trials and temptations, not as an outsider attacking the figure of Christ, but as a serious Catholic, analyzing him from within. Goddard's *Hail Mary,* in which the mother of God is presented as a beautiful gas station attendant, also received a good deal of knee-jerk criticism from those who felt Goddard's retelling of the story in a contemporary setting was sacrilege. But both filmmakers were trying creatively to rethink the traditional narrative, to add a modern, human dimension to it.

An episode in Mexico City in 1988 also has certain similarities to the painting incident. At the Museum of Modern Art in Mexico City Roland de la Rosa, a Mexican artist, displayed a montage which superimposed the face and bare breasts of Marilyn Monroe over the revered image of the Virgin of Guadalupe, who is also known as the

"National Mother," the "Mestiza Virgin," "la Guadalupana." In doing so, de la Rosa set off four months of controversy about the limits of artistic freedom. Enraged civic groups stormed the museum, demanding the artist's home address so they could "lynch him." De la Rosa became persona non grata and the museum's director was forced to resign.

In these instances Scorcese, Goddard, and de la Rosa were all working from personal visions, attempting to intersect with the collective imagination. But this effort is often misunderstood. In a July 1988 *Time* magazine interview about *The Last Temptation of Christ,* Father Morris, a Catholic priest said: "You can't be working out your private problems to the degree that it causes people to riot in the streets."[10] The Scorsese film almost caused such a response; de la Rosa's images actually did. But the concerns of these artists cannot be reduced to a discussion of their "private problems." De la Rosa, for example, was attempting to mirror the hypocrisy of Mexican culture in which pictures of la Guadalupana can be found on the walls of gas stations, side by side with glossy nudes of Marilyn Monroe and other sexual icons. Images cross over both in the imagination and in reality to become cultural oxymorons. In the confusion, mother/saint/Virgin/whore are often conflated. It is difficult to fathom what all this hysteria has been about, when in fact nothing can really damage the image of the Virgin of Guadalupe, Mary or Jesus. Their power in the collective conscious and unconscious is, for many, sacred and unshakable.

Harold Washington did not live long enough, nor had he accrued enough power, to have solidified one consistent image for people to remember him by. The black community really did believe Nelson's portrait to be slanderous and potentially damaging to his memory. And the lack of a clear sense of purpose behind the painting made it seem that much more frivolous and degrading. Needless to say, Nelson is neither Scorsese nor Goddard. His immature efforts were closer to lampooning than anything else. The painting therefore seems provocative only for provocation's sake.

Art World Narcissism

It's not a matter of right and wrong. It's freedom of expression.
—School of the Art Institute student body treasurer

It is one thing to defend an artist's right to produce any work he or she desires; it is quite different actually to approve of the subject matter of this work, or feel one must remain silent about the content even if it is offensive. Artists have a right to be critical of other artists who engage with volatile situations for no reason other than their own narcissism.

A number of years ago a New York artist displayed abstract black-and-white paintings which he called "The Nigger Paintings." Even though there was no discernible racist image in these paintings, the title of the exhibit was enough to enrage members of the art community. Protestors marching in front of Artist's Space questioned the exhibiting artist's judgment in choosing a racist title for his work. No one involved was overtly advocating censorship, but there was a push to force the artist to rethink his intention. It is not contradictory to defend the artist's right to make whatever work he or she sees fit, while at the same time encouraging the artist to be aware of the social implications of that work. If the time comes to do battle in its defense, there should be the sense that the work itself is worthy of this effort.

The art world thrives on freedom of expression and an attitude of "live and let live." Artists rarely ask each other to be accountable to any form of "good taste" or political correctness because they themselves do not want to be asked to answer for their own work in this way. The permissiveness of this world, from students with pink hair and rings in their nose, to work that is radical and innovative in form, is not easily understandable to the world outside.

Many artists themselves are often isolated from the larger human community and the issues that affect people's daily lives. Yet they like to think of their creations and their place in the order of things as progressive. They will defend, on principle, any painting, sculpture, or film deemed too radical, avant-garde, or innovative in form or content for the prevailing consciousness to readily digest. This is understandable and essential to the maintenance of artistic freedom. But in the case of "the painting," this a priori acceptance becomes problematic. The work under attack in this instance is in no way progressive; it is instead politically reactionary, homophobic, tasteless, and misguided. Yet white middle-class artists, in particular, have not seen fit to analyze the content of this painting or to speak out against it. Perhaps they fear that were they truly critical of Nelson, they might sound too much like the aldermen. Perhaps they are more comfortable hiding behind the assumed unconditional right of any artist to iconoclasm, satire, and buffoonery. Or perhaps they find it unnerving even to consider that this work could be analogous to the kind of campus racial harassment that occurred at the University of Michigan or the University of Wisconsin. And yet no matter how outrageous students may look, or how radical in form their work might be, they are still capable of producing art whose content is reactionary. Often those who understand innovation in form are not necessarily progressive in their political views, while those capable of radical analyses are often conservative in their acceptance of true innovation in form.

Beyond Polarization

> *Thinking is, indeed, essentially the negation of that which is immediately before us.*
>
> —Hegel

The real barrier to understanding the complexity of this incident is that each side feels it must choose to interpret the problem as fundamentally one of censorship or of racism. In fact one can make a case for either position. But it is only when the issue is seen as simultaneously a question of censorship and of racism that a plan of concrete action leading to resolution can be imagined.

First, it must be understood that the actions of the aldermen were in direct violation of First Amendment rights. They are legally indefensible. There is little doubt that the ACLU suit on behalf of David Nelson will be settled in Nelson's favor, in or out of court. As David Polsby, Northwestern University law professor, said on John Calloway's "Chicago Tonight Show":

> I count no fewer than five Illinois statutes, three of them felony statutes, that were violated in this case. I think Alderman Streeter puts the case exactly. The First Amendment was indeed transcended. There seems to be no argument whatsoever that the First Amendment was trampled underfoot like so much ticker tape by this vigilante action.[11]

The aldermen had no legal right to remove the painting. It is protected under the First Amendment as "visual speech." This protection is not contingent on the content of this "speech." The painting could be picketed, protested, discussed in forums to vent public criticism, but it could not be forcibly removed. Yet no matter how clearly these legal parameters are set, there are those who still believe that, given the content of the painting, such tactics were justified. Even if Nelson's actions could be seen as analogous to crying fire in a crowded theater, it would still be the responsibility of those in office to do everything they could to prevent a riot. In this case, these public officials used their official capacity to provoke one.

Although the aldermen's actions were undoubtedly illegal, their motivations must be understood. The aldermen justified their actions by calling upon a "higher moral order," which they felt themselves entrusted to enforce. Streeter and others have insisted that the First Amendment does not necessarily apply to African-Americans because they were not included in the decision-making process when the Constitution was originally drafted. Members of the black community have said that the First Amendment has not protected them from racism, inequality, economic or psychological oppression. Given these feelings, as well as the aldermen's self-prescribed commitment to upholding the image of the late Harold Washington, their actions become somewhat understandable. They were torn in their identities and felt they had to choose which loyalty to uphold. This supposed conflict of interests is in itself a consequence of racism.

Nonetheless, these leaders seriously violated their status as public officials. As long as the aldermen continue to focus on the racial slur inflicted by the painting, they needn't challenge their own actions or recognize their responsibility as elected officials to uphold the law. They also do not have to question the danger to civil liberties implicit in their attitude.

Second, like the aldermen, many white artists have also been guilty of using this incident to reinforce their personal fears. They have focused on censorship, a crucial issue, but they have polarized the problem until it has become a white/black conflict, forcing black, Latino, Asian, and Native American Indian artists in the city to choose between the importance of the issue of censorship and the concomitant issue of racism. These white artists have been unable to move intellectually and emotionally beyond their outrage that anyone would dare intrude on the sanctity of the school and make demands on artists' work. To the art world, the act of forcibly removing and consequently damaging a painting is frightening. Such actions, if allowed to continue, could ultimately result in a situation in which work of any nature, except the most neutral, would be subject to review.

At the same time that the tendencies which led to the aldermen's actions must be actively opposed, it should be recognized that the painting was extremely provocative at a time when racial tensions in the city were at an all-time high. In this sense, the painting was an extremely irresponsible act. As long as the art world continues to focus solely on the civil liberties issue, it avoids the vital questions of the responsibility of artist to the community in which he or she lives. But why does the predominantly white middle-class art world choose to avoid this questions of responsibility to a larger community outside its own parameters?

The Isolation of the Artist

To be modern is to know that which is not possible any more.

—Roland Barthes

There is a fundamental split between the internal world of the artist and the greater world outside—which makes the art world's rare encounters with the political arena that much more difficult. One strain of this problem can be traced to the nineteenth-century myth of the "romantic artist." Locked in an isolated consciousness, alienated from society, the romantic resolved to make the inner self known. Initially romanticism was progressive, liberating, representing the struggle to break with the past and to attain an ideal embodiment of a subjective emotional truth. It glorified and idealized the autonomy of the self. But a century later this tendency manifests itself as a hopeless break between the artist and the body politic. This separation has fostered anxiety, paranoia and work which has become even more cut off from its sociopolitical environment. Artists increasingly locate themselves not within a general historical context, but within a privileged dialogue with their own history. Their art refers to art which came before, and the art world has become increasingly hermetic, its discourse incomprehensible to those outside its closed system.

In the post-modern era the polarizations have become even more extreme. The artist often seems no longer to have an intelligible purpose within the culture, except to articulate the final stages of its decline. There is little dialogue with the outside, at times no longer even a tension with the inner self to spur on the dialectic. Many artists have become comfortably uncomfortable in their alienation from the larger society, and their work mirrors this resignation, blending into the existent landscape without anxiety. One cannot tell whether a work is commenting on its own exploitation, furthering that exploitation or both. There is at times no frame of reference within which to place the image, unless one is well-versed in all that is now, or once was, fashionable. The signifier has split from the signified. Meaning, which is no longer derived from a discernible context, seems hopelessly set adrift. The "aura," which Benjamin refers to as the spirituality of a work, is now too often only an afterglow of trendiness, money and success.[12]

Young artists are often well aware of the depleted condition of the art world but are unable to imagine how they might connect with a larger context. Not only are they isolated in the physical and philosophical milieu in which they exist, but they also suffer agoraphobia, fear of stepping outside this world. Often more at ease with work that stays away from the contradictions of their time than with work that engages such contradictions, they choose to make art that concerns itself primarily with formalist issues. This is unfortunately also the type of work that the art world often rewards. Ideally, as Robert Storr has written: "An artist is measured, in the first instance by the difficulty of the problem [he/she] chooses to confront."[13] But this is unfortunately rarely the case any longer. Work is often measured instead by how successful it is, or might become, in New York—how salable and collectible. When work does take a political or social stance and does reflect the temper of the times, it is either ignored or, when accepted, then absorbed—transformed into a commodity, its power diluted.

Art schools must struggle to remain aloof from these circumstances and to uphold the integrity of the creative process. They have a great responsibility to their young artists to create some island, some refuge, not isolated from the world but from the art scene—a place where real art issues are still confronted. But however much a school may try to exist outside the art world framework, students often leave feeling that what is truly important is that they make a name for themselves. It is not always clear how that name should be acquired. Both excellence and notoriety are too often seen as interchangeable paths to this same desired end. David Nelson is an example of a student seemingly unable to make these necessary distinctions.

An art school is a minisociety, a buffer between the art world and the wider culture, a place where young artists are socialized into their chosen identities. If it is successful, students learn how to think visually as well as how to execute ideas with the greatest degree of professional expertise. Schools of art should also try to train their students to think clearly, to ask themselves if their work is communicating their intention. And faculty must try to teach students to be socially responsible for their intentions.

President Tony Jones has called the School of the Art Institute a "laboratory." In this environment, some experiments are successful and others fail miserably, but all are tested. Because of the nature of visual work, success or failure must take place in a public forum. On May 11, black faculty, students and staff, in particular, were outraged by Nelson's painting. Had the outside world left the school to its own processes, it would have challenged this work and opened it to in-house discussion. But there was no time for this private process. The painting was immediately transformed into a public issue.

Administrators of the school did finally meet with David Nelson, amidst the early chaos around the painting, to discuss whether or not the response to his work was what he had intended. They hoped Nelson would recognize that the painting had gone way beyond any repercussions he might have imagined or desired, and was now actually endangering people's welfare. They hoped he would consider removing it, not because he didn't have a right to display it, but because as the artist, he had the right to control its effect. From this conversation it was clear that Nelson was unnerved and worried about his own safety. But he knew that had he removed the piece himself, he would have looked like a coward to many of his peers. He could not do it. But, in fact, had he had the courage and wisdom to take hold of the painting's effect, he would have been the sanest person in the building at that moment.

Were the art world more rigorous and more willing to hold its own to a measure of social responsibility, were it more racially and ethnically diverse, Nelson might have understood the sociopolitical situation in Chicago. He might have cared enough to think twice about his relationship to it as an artmaker. The community around him might have spurred his conscience. Had the other nonminority students understood the implications of Nelson's action in its larger context, they might not have defended him so unequivocally. Although remaining protective of Nelson's First Amendment rights, they too might have been upset at the subject of the painting and critical of Nelson's obliviousness to the historical moment. Had all these possibilities become actualities, Nelson himself might have realized what a provocative act it would be to display such a work. He might have questioned his own motivation early on, recognizing that individuality is determined, not in "isolated particularity," but in relationship to one's membership within the human community and within history.[14] Had he thought it valuable to take these considerations into account at that moment, he might have understood that his place within the larger collective was ultimately more important than either self-expression or self-aggrandizement. But Nelson, like many others, was incapable of this level of thinking. And, like many other student-artists, he believed there was no value higher than self-expression.

A Rupture in the Continuity

*The negativity everything possesses . . . is a state of priva-
tion that forces the subject to seek remedy, as such it has
a positive character.*

—Herbert Marcuse

Consciousness and dialectical thinking can only evolve in an environment willing to tackle complexity head on. They are best cultivated
where multicultural and global issues hit up against the prevailing
ideology, forcing resolution. But this ideal situation does not exist
within the art world at present. Because it is not a truly multicultural
society, it has become inbred and philosophically impoverished. Until
the demographics of the art world are transformed, instances of faulty
thinking, like the painting of *Mirth and Girth,* will continue, although
perhaps not on such a grand scale.

The situation of the School of the Art Institute of Chicago, a primarily progressive institution, is a good example of the complexity of this
problem. Like many other art schools, it is private but receives some
state and city funding and is built on Park District land. The school sits
in the middle of a city that is racially and ethnically mixed, with blacks,
Latinos, Asians, and Native Americans accounting for 57 percent of the
population. The school's minority population is, at 18 percent, better
than most learning institutions of comparable size, cost and status. And
there have been some serious attempts to increase numbers of minority students, faculty and staff over the past years, but the effect has
been less than dramatic.

The relatively small minority representation at all levels of the school
is not the result of bad faith or deliberately racist intentions on the
part of the institution; rather, it is in part due to harsh economic and
social realities. Fundamentally, it is very difficult to recruit minority ap-
plicants to a private art school. Even when the high tuition can be subsidized, as is often the case, students still need to work to pay for food,
clothing, shelter and supplies. And because they cannot work forty
hours a week and attend school at the same time, they become dependent on student loans. After four years at the BFA level, or after six,
for a combined BFA and MFA, students are usually in serious debt. And
this situation has become much worse under Reagan. "The intention
of the Reagan administration to reduce many student-aid programs and
its efforts to shift more of the burden of payment to students and their
families has seriously affected low-income students and hit minority
students especially hard."[15] At graduation, a student must begin to

pay back these loans. But unlike doctors or lawyers, artists have no guaranteed high-paying job possibilities awaiting them. There is no secure career path to follow with clear professional rewards at the other end. This is perhaps the most discouraging reality facing minority candidates. A private institution cannot alone completely repair the damage caused by a federal policy that makes it almost impossible for minorities to attend college at all.

It is even more difficult to try to compensate for the cut-backs in education that have reduced the mandatory sixty minutes of music and art per week to zero in many grade and high school curricula. There simply is not enough money to hire the necessary experts in these areas. The result is that students are not exposed to the visual arts at an early level and are therefore unable to recognize their own inclination to this vocation. If they do want to attend art school, they are then at a disadvantage when they must compete for admission or struggle to keep up with those who have already had some training in these areas.

Art schools can try to compensate for these inequities with outreach programs, but these problems have become too large to be solved with small, inadequately funded projects. There needs to be an even greater commitment to these efforts for them to be at all effective. If serious changes do not happen in the schools, there will continue to be a dearth of minority faculty in the visual arts educational system. This lack will continue to mirror itself in the general art world profile.

For these and other reasons, the School of the Art Institute has often seemed unreachable and "other." There is no doubt that the school must work to change this perception of elitism through concrete efforts. But it operates at a disadvantage in this dynamic because it is often confused with its corporate partner, the Art Institute of Chicago, a world-renowned museum, which like many other major museums, has mounted very few exhibitions reflecting the ethnic and racial composition of the city that supports it. As a result, James A. Brame, president of the Illinois Alliance of Black Student Organizations, has called the museum "a closed bastion of white male Western cultural supremacy."[16] The efforts the museum has made to transform this image have simply not been sufficient.

Had the museum and the school established stronger ties with the community sooner, these feelings might not exist and this event might not have been played out as divisively as it was. There would have been built-in avenues of trust and negotiation between the Art Institute Corporation and the community, which could have been employed to deescalate the event. The anger unleashed by the aldermen was a glimpse of the return of the repressed. It had been under the surface for some time. It is therefore not in the least surprising that the school and the museum apologized for "the painting" more than many thought necessary. This conciliatory response may well have been motivated by cumulative guilt for not having bridged these polarizations earlier.

This incident has no doubt further alienated the school, the museum and the predominantly white art world from the city at large. It has exacerbated the already existent paranoia of many artists and has increased their alienation. And it is not yet over. In spite of community organizers who try to encourage open debate on the issues involved and "unity" efforts to create multicultural events, groups predominantly white or predominantly black do continue to meet, separately, to discuss the incident. But most people involved still seem unable to exorcise their own particular anger. Both sides remain myopic, retelling the narrative in terms of "us" and "them," unaware of the narrowness of their focus, unwilling to recognize their contribution to escalating racial tension. As long as these groups are comfortable in their moral superiority, they do nothing to heal an already polarized Chicago, a city that "needs no more excuses to hate."[17]

There has been unending confusion as to the meaning of events surrounding the painting episode and a deep dissension locally and nationally as to the proper response to these events. But there *has* been consensus among many groups that the school must seize this opportunity to make some serious leaps in reaching its affirmative action goals. Internal and external task forces are at present working to build a more racially integrated art environment that attempts to reflect the demographics of the city and is more integrally connected to it. If the school can succeed in increasing the minority population, improving its overall sensitivity to include the various multicultural perspectives these efforts will bring, it may truly be one of the only art schools in the country actively committed to such values.

One can hope that these gestures will encourage a national movement committed to creating a more culturally diverse art-educational environment. Over time, such efforts will invariably affect the larger art world, which is dependent on these institutions to train the next generation of artists. If the art world does beome more accessible, artists from various ethnic and racial groups, who often retain ties to their communities as well as commitment to their own ethnic history, can help bridge the unnatural split between the art world and the larger sociopolitical framework. Their collective vision, and the imagery they create, may also help develop a less individualistic, less narcissistic sense of the place of the artist in society. However, such optimistic goals can only really be achieved on a larger scale, along with a transformation of economic and political conditions in this country.

As the immediate impact of the painting incident recedes, perhaps those involved will discover that the event has actually served to create a rupture in the continuity, dramatic enough to expose hidden contradictions and decisive enough to force an irrevocable awareness of the need for synthesis and change.

Notes

1. *Chicago Sun-Times* (14 May 1988); *Chicago Defender* (14 May 1988); *Chicago Tribune* (15 May 1988).

2. From ''Draft Statement'' written by Clarence Wilson, president of Lawyers for the Creative Arts.

3. *Chicago Sun-Times* (15 May 1988).

4. *Chicago Sun-Times* (14 May 1988), p. 4.

5. Salim Muwakkil, ''Harold Washington's Fractured Legacy,'' *IN THESE TIMES* (25 May–7 June 1988).

6. *Chicago Tribune* (15 May 1988).

7. *The Washington Post* (13 May 1988).

8. Bill Stamets, ''Theater of Power, Theater of the Absurd,'' *The New Art Examiner* (Summer 1988), p. 30.

9. Michael Brenson, Art View: ''A Savage Painting Raises Troubling Questions,'' *New York Times* (29 May 1988), p. 29.

10. *Time Magazine* (15 August 1988).

11. *Chicago Sun-Times* (22 May 1988).

12. This is a reference to Walter Banjamin's best-known essay, ''Art in the Age of Mechanical Reproduction,'' to be found in *Illuminations*.

13. Robert Storr, ''Nancy Spero: Central Issues—Peripheral Visions'' in *Nancy Spero: Works Since 1950* (Syracuse: Everson Museum of Art, 1987).

14. Herbert Marcuse, ''Science and Logic,'' from *Reason and Revolution*.

15. Reginald Wilson and Manuel J. Justiz, ''Minorities in Higher Education: Confronting a Time Bomb,'' *Educational Record* (Fall 1987–Winter 1988): 11.

16. *Chicago Sun-Times* (26 May 1988).

17. *Chicago Tribune,* Editorial (13 May 1988).

Crowding the Picture:
Notes on American Activist Art Today

Donald Kuspit

Activist artists must examine their assumptions and methods if their art is to speak effectively to its time. Otherwise, the kinds of change that activist art demands can be outmoded or even contrary to public interest.

Donald Kuspit observes that much activist art has not grappled with the complex contemporary American social situation—the isolation of the individual within the crowd. Most "political art" primarily addresses common experience, often through the techniques of mass media, and ends up as propaganda proposing new forms of slavish obedience. But contemporary loneliness can be healed only by an engagement with individual experience, encouragement to risk autonomy and transformation, and the recreation of an authentic community.

"Nonpropagandistic art," Kuspit says, "shows human catastrophe from the inside and creates the sociopolitical reality as a vehicle for an unfolding of what human beings are capable of."

Revolt today has no more content than buying a bus ticket. Any genuine attack on society today must occur on the level of abstraction. . . . The only true wrestle is with abstraction: the credo, the slogan, the symbol.
  —Harold Rosenberg, "Themes"

Politics in the United States consists of the struggle between those whose change has been arrested by success or failure, on one side, and those who are still engaged in changing themselves, on the other.
—Harold Rosenberg, "Themes"

Along this rocky road to the actual it is only possible to go Indian file, one at a time, so that "art" means "breaking up the crowd"—not "reflecting" its experience.
—Harold Rosenberg,
"The Herd of Independent Minds"

This seems a good time to analyze activist art—art that claims to be a kind of action rather than a kind of reflection. In the last decades, many American artists have joined the ranks of what was once an underdog troop. In this palace revolution that seeks to overthrow the ruling elite of formalism, even "revisions" of artistic language—experimental manipulations of the concepts and terms of high art—are considered valuable only if they serve the "higher" purpose of social change. And so where formalism offers art a certain hermetic integrity, activism promises it worldly influence and power.

But what if the proverbial choice between an art of the *vita contemplativa* and an art of the *vita activa* is no longer a valid one? What if the integrity proposed by the aesthetic position is insufficient, and the kind of change demanded by the activist approach is disingenuously inhumane? The old bifurcation of life into sectors of being and doing now seems obsolete. The traditional notion of a singular heroic identity no longer does justice to the complexity of our social relationships, nor to the subtleties of our moral situation. Today, one needs the Solomon's wisdom and stamina to create an art that synthetizes the aesthetic and activist impulses—one that addresses our humanness with depth and fullness, one that rearticulates a humanness that we feel has been obscured, even obliterated by society. A number of European artists (particularly in Germany and Italy) have risen to this challenge. In America, however, too many of our artists are settling for less, perhaps because they have not adequately recognized the rigorous demands of this enterprise.

America is above all a pluralistic society, a highly differentiated yet consummately interdependent organism. In our society, which has come to be termed the administered society, the psychopolitical tensions of class struggle, while far from irrelevant, are not all-relevant. The situation "of the 'lonely crowd,' or of isolation in the mass,"[1] as Jacques

Ellul points out, is the basic social situation today.[2] The "lonely man" is the essential man, "and the larger the crowd in which he lives, the more isolated he is."[3] This is pluralism in action, ingeniously non-disruptive for all its discontinuities. For whenever a member of this lonely crowd tries to understand, articulate, or assert his or her *individual* loneliness, he or she comes up against the overwhelming evidence of togetherness with all others in the crowd, and personal loneliness seems a fantasy. (Or a neurosis.) And whenever, conversely, the individual tries to give himself or herself over completely to the crowd's trends and passions, he or she finds this untenable, too, for the individual only reexperiences isolation within the crowd. Loneliness, then, even as it may be regarded as a sign of individuality, of separate and special selfhood and/or resistance to the crowd, is in fact only the experience that confirms the inextricable interdependence that characterizes the crowd. Loneliness is the umbilical bond to the crowd. One cannot think of mass man without thinking of the loneliness that is innate to him. To be of the lonely crowd is to feel both an irreducible isolation and an irresistible belonging.

This is why the American lonely crowd assumes an eternally melioristic society, with a perhaps nominally utopian outlook: why should the crowd work for revolution when the world, however lonely, seems to be getting better and better—or at least getting to be a better place in which to negotiate loneliness, to hide from oneself? The lonely crowd fetishizes its slack "live and let live" philosophy (be lonely and let others be lonely), believing it to be—and this is no doubt correct—preferable to the authoritarian "live and think and be like me or be destroyed by me" philosophy. But of course neither philosophy helps one realize life fully or tells why one should continue to live; and each is as full of grievances against life as the other, if more obviously so in the latter.

This is the lonely world that contemporary activist art enters into, speaks to. And such art is designed to confront rather than to console. Is the lonely crowd capable of accepting such artistic and activist urgency? Can it find the art contagious, be roused to action in the name of its cause? Can it throw off the chains of loneliness to create a community rather than a crowd?

It seems unlikely. For to inspire such response, this art must "penetrate through the common experience to the actual situation," must grasp social reality creatively, that is, "from the inside . . . as a situation with a human being in it,"[4] must wed insights to "the potency of form" that goes "beyond mere talk."[5] However, much of today's activist art plays to the common—crowd—experience, and thereby reinforces the very structures it seeks to undermine. We can look back at the social realism of the thirties as a forerunner of this. In the history-splashed panoramic murals of Thomas Hart Benton and Diego Rivera or the delineations of social suffering in the works of Philip Evergood and Ben Shahn, for example, the misery or nobility of the individual is posited as the reflection of a collective condition. Or, to put it in the terms of the lonely crowd, the individual simply echoes the voice of the crowd. A number of artists today believe they, too, are demythologizing reality, pulling back the curtain for us for a clear look at the social conditions that enslave us, define us. But just as the social realists of the thirties implicitly appropriated the big-screen techniques of the most formidable crowd-pleaser of their time—the movies—many of today's American artists mimic or employ techniques from advertising and TV. They believe this is the best way to reach the crowd—and perhaps they're right. But is it, in Rosenberg's words, the best way to "break up the crowd"? Is it the best way to move the individual to take the risk of autonomy,[6] to begin the struggle of transforming his or her own identity, a process essential to genuine social transformation?

In fact, much of today's activist art does send a message, but not the one its makers intend. Often, this art's call for social change and/or social unity relies on familiar codes, with just enough overlay of allusion to some topical situation or event to suggest political urgency. And so even viewers who may be only nominally interested in the revolutionary implications of the struggle in Nicaragua referred to in Leon Golub's paintings, for example, can feel secure in believing that in their viewing of these works they have had a political experience. The paintings' larger-than-life size, their agitated surfaces, the theatrical grandeur of their figures, who make war not love (even those who are on the same side seem to make war, perhaps in order not to have to make love), all resuggest the idea of the Hero, in whatever grotesque form. Such an idea caters to the lonely crowd, which, if it looks for salvation, looks for it in the miracle of the Great Man, be he tender or tyrannical.

Similarly, Martha Rosler's documentaries, with their apparently gritty, reportorial directness, use predetermined scenarios of misery. Rosler's intensity of focus is admirable, and she does meet a certain social reality. Her art's "factographic character," as it has been called by Benjamin Buchloh, is liberating—to a point. There's a problem, however, with her synecdochic expression of that reality. By representing a person's life with "the facts," Rosler shaves away the interior life, and the individual is flattened, once again, into cliché: "the abused woman," "the working woman," etc.

Truly creative critical art, on the other hand, can go beyond, to question not just one stereotype, or the predominant stereotype, but *all* stereotypes. In this way, the very notion of common or uniform experience—the underpinning for lonely crowd passivity—would begin to crumble. Such an art does not require a retreat from social reality, but a deeper engagement with it. Rosenberg, using war as an example, suggests the power and potential of such a deeper engagement:

> The moment an artist, ignoring the war as an external fact known to all, approaches it as a possibility that must be endured in the imagination by anyone who would genuinely experience it, he . . . arouse[s] not only hostility on the part of officials who have a stake in the perpetuation of some agreed-upon version of the war, but also a general distrust and uneasiness. For the work of art takes away from its audience its sense of knowing where it stands . . . suggests to the audience that its situation might be quite different than it has suspected, that the situation is jammed with elements not yet perceived and lies open to the unknown, even though the event has already taken place.[7]

A number of our artists today do not thoroughly scrutinize mass conceptions of political reality, but unwittingly submit to them. And more problematically, they implicitly conform to stock notions of the way social change and/or social solidarity can be achieved. The work of Hans Haacke, Barbara Kruger and Alexis Smith is to the point here. All rely on more or less familiar, easily readable images and language in a more or less tense state of juxtaposition. But after an initial surge, their art is victimized by its own media, sinks back into its sources, and what is left is the message that we can trust common experience to point the way to social transformations.

As suggested, the problem shared by many of our activist artists today lies in the way they understand—one might say in the credit they give—their viewer. At issue is whether the works of these artists engage the isolated individual within the lonely crowd in order to encourage self-awareness, independence, thoughtful examination and action, or whether these works serve as propaganda for a myth (even though an alternative one). It's a slippery question, as Ellul understands, for propaganda for an alternative myth often seems to do both:

> Just because men are in a group, and therefore weakened, receptive and in a state of psychological regression, they pretend all the more to be "strong individuals." The mass man . . . is more suggestible, but insists he is more forceful, he is more unstable, but thinks he is firm in his convictions. If one openly treats the mass as

a mass, the individuals who form it will feel themselves belittled and will refuse to participate. . . . On the contrary, each one must feel individualized, each must have the impression that *he* is being looked at, that *he* is being addressed personally. Only then will he respond and cease to be anonymous (although in reality remaining anonymous). Thus all modern propaganda profits from the structure of the mass, but exploits the individual's need for self-affirmation; and the two actions must be conducted jointly, simultaneously.[8]

What's more, Ellul makes a useful distinction between the propaganda of agitation and the propaganda of integration.[9] The propaganda of agitation

has the stamp of opposition. It is led by a party seeking to destroy the government or the established order. [It] tries to stretch energies to the utmost, obtain substantial sacrifices, and induce the individual to bear heavy ordeals. It takes him out of his everyday life, his normal framework, and plunges him into enthusiasm and adventure; it opens to him hitherto unsuspected possibilities, and suggests extraordinary goals that nevertheless seem to him completely within reach. Propaganda of agitation thus unleashes an explosive movement; it operates inside a crisis or actually provokes the crisis itself.[10]

I would argue that much of today's direct-action art lends itself to or is a species of the propaganda of agitation. It enjoys seeing all of social reality—the status quo on all fronts—as forever and completely "in crisis." As Ellul points out, the propaganda of agitation generally "can obtain only effects of relatively short duration."[11] But the "agitated" look and intention remain. What counts most, what one remembers most, about Jenny Holzer's flashing sentences on electronic message boards, for example, is their seemingly irrational relationship to one another, the digitalized fragmentation of the words themselves, their rapid movement past the eye. Disruption, structurally as well as conceptually, is the aim of Holzer's art (as it is with a number of others'). Disruption becomes an end in itself—it *is* the revolution. (And an old one at that.)

It is possible to interpret such agitational art as at once an anxious response to and rejection of what seems fated. More specifically, it may be a manic defense against oppressive fears of "death, chaos, and mystery."[12] This is not unrelated to José Ortega y Gasset's notion that the "universal pirouetting" of the modern artist can be seen as "an attempt to instill youthfulness into an ancient world."[13] But unfortunately, this universal pirouetting may be only spinning us back to the artist, not to the world.

There is another strain of activist art today that falls into the category of what Ellul calls the propaganda for integration. This art ''aims at stabilizing the social body, at unifying and reinforcing it.''[14] It accomplishes this by offering

> a complete system for explaining the world, and [providing] immediate incentives to action. We are here in the presence of an organized myth that tries to take hold of the entire person. Through the myth it creates, propaganda imposes a complete range of intuitive knowledge, susceptible of only one interpretation, unique and one-sided, and precluding any divergence. This myth becomes so powerful that it invades every area of consciousness, leaving no faculty or motivation intact.[15]

In short, this type of art calls for a new status quo—a new myth of conformity. This is what I take the work of Judy Chicago, and some of the works of May Stevens, for example, to offer. The decadent, oppressive capitalism, these works suggest, should be replaced by the wholesome new other-ism. But this is really the same old lonely crowd in new ideological clothing. The social harmony that such integration propaganda aims at can be as ruthlessly exclusive and as oppressive as the marginalizing structures it seeks to overthrow. It corresponds to the modern need ''to create and hear fables. . . . It also responds to man's intellectual sloth and desire for security.''[16] It also becomes a solution to the problem of passivity.

> The individual becomes less and less capable of acting by himself; he needs the collective signals which integrate his actions into the complete mechanism. Modern life induces us to wait until we are told to act. Here again propaganda comes to the rescue.[17]

But it is the individual struggling for autonomy[18] within the crowd that art must try to reach, cultivate, encourage, support, draw out. Goya remains an examplar for such nonpropagandistic activist art. I am speaking, particularly, of the Goya of ''*Los Desastres de la Guerra*,'' the ''*pinturas negras*'' of the Quinta del Sordo and the ''*Disparates*,'' all conceived between 1810 and 1820. With every touch, every gesture, every choice, Goya reminds us of Romanticism's discovery that life ''is not a reality which encounters a greater or lesser number of problems, but that it consists exclusively in the problem of itself.''[19] Goya's sensitivity to nuance, his transfigurations of light and dark, his leap away from the symbolic distortions of his earlier works, all make it possible for the viewer to experience horrific human catastrophes *from the inside*. In Goya, we are beyond figures of good and evil in any conventional sense: both the soldiers and their victims are miserable. The sociopolitical reality of war becomes, in these works, the vehicle for an unfolding of what human beings are capable of, what *individuals* are capable of. Without forsaking reportorial witnessing of the actual event, and yet without advocating *any* myth of man, society, or state, these works allow for freedom of insight as well as freedom of sight.

It was in a 1919 Berlin exhibition that the slogan "DADA stands on the side of the revolutionary Proletariat" was first posted.[20] And it was George Grosz and Wieland Herzfelde, John Heartfield's younger brother, who wrote:

> The pending revolution brought gradual understanding of this [social] system. There were no more laughing matters, there were more important problems than those of art; if art was still to have a meaning, it had to submit to those problems.[21]

But the anticipated revolution did *not* happen in Germany. That is no doubt why, forty years later, Hannah Höch would describe the German Dadaists' relationship with the communists as "innocent and truly unpolitical."[22] Asked whether "Dada had been, in a way, a kind of parody of a typically German *Reformbewegung*,"[23] Höch acknowledged that it had. Nonetheless, she did point out, Dada shocked people into realizing "that things could also be done differently, and that many of our unconventional ways of thinking, dressing, or reckoning are no less arbitrary than others which are generally accepted."[24]

Germany's *Neue Sachlichkeit* (New objectivity), Bernard S. Myers points out, was "another form of protest against the times . . . a bitter but dry and hard realism that is strongly emotional in character and social in content."[25] *Neue Sachlichkeit* was informed by a subliminal romantic yearning for social intimacy—"brotherhood" or "sisterhood"—as an alternative to the compulsory alienation of contractual, capitalist society. This yearning took the form of identification with one's fellow sufferer, the implicit assumption being that through such communion a new society might be forged.

In fact, both these endeavors were premised on *ressentiment*,[26] intensified by the promises of imminent revolution. This *ressentiment* has deep Romantic roots, going back at least to Shelley's assertion that "poets are the unacknowledged legislators of the world,"[27] and is a manifestation of what Abraham Maslow has called "the arrogance of creativeness."[28]

Now, with a revolution permanently pending and never arriving, a revolution permanently on hold, the seeds of German Romanticism and revolt, transplanted, have brought forth, paradoxically, a naive American "media-ated" realism. And so here, the desire to shock is what remains of German Dadaism. The major message is that everything can be done differently, which is a parody of the idea of revolution—a loss of any sense of purpose or direction. The problem is that this polymorphously perverse carnival of a world upside down, the sense of the chance character of all our engagements, becomes an enchantment in itself.

Artists like Ronnie Cutrone, Richard Hambleton, Keith Haring, Mike Kelley, Kenny Scharf and Julie Wachtel, just to name a few, revel in their abilities to shock the viewer with supposedly "unexpected" comparisons and contrasts. But who is really shocked? As I suggested earlier, though it's true that such works provide an initial ironical spark, that spark is no greater than that provided by these artists' sources—in this case, the funny papers, Saturday-morning cartoons, fifties situation comedies and detective series. In fact, the modern viewer has grown accustomed to being momentarily "jarred." So these artists, rather than effectively commenting on or critiquing this state of affairs, satisfy what has become an addiction for the lonely crowd.

Similarly, what was for *Neue Sachlichkeit* a visionary possibility now runs the risk of becoming an insidious invitation to the "one society" of the neo-*Neue Sachlichkeit*. This art, rather than suggesting how individuals might identify their real inner needs and condition, enforces common experience, crowd mentality. Much of it shows little of the emotional sensitivity to the other—little of the fellow feeling—that informed *Neue Sachlichkeit*.

Among American activist artists today, Leon Golub seems the one with the most complex yearning for community, and with the most acute awareness of its aborted character in modern society. But, as Theodor Adorno suggested, one always has to wonder whether "the artistic attitude of howling and crudeness"[29] truly denounces, or instead identifies with, the forces of social oppression. The problem with Golub's work is that it implies that there is no socially feasible alternative to the all-powerful, totalitarian figure. In his earlier paintings from the "Mercenaries" and "Gigantomachies" series, Golub seems to be struggling imaginatively with his human figures as they act out their deadly games of dominance and submission: their bodies become raw tendons of paint. But the blacks of his more recent South Africa paintings—torturers and tortured—are flattened out. Through their clothes and limbs, the surface of the canvas appears, reiterating their status as social signifiers. Rather than urgent physical presences, they become emblems of the inevitable and inescapable evil of the crowd.

Similarly, Jenny Holzer's installation for the *"Skulptur Projekte in Münster 1987"* exhibition mocks that city's memorial to the fallen German dead of World War I by amplifying the notion of the soldier as an inhuman violator. But this stereotype does not cancel out the martyr stereotype, it only tightens the stranglehold that stereotypes have on us. Holzer militantly refuses to see man *from the inside,* and thus forecloses on that possibility for the viewer as well. Let Holzer manipulate a war memorial in her own world, the one at Fifth Avenue and Sixty-Fifth Street in New York, for example, and perhaps she would be obliged to examine issues of war—and man—with more complexity, to imagine and present the "human" aspects of inhumanity.

May Stevens' work is an important example of the propaganda of feminist integration. In *Mysteries and Politics,* 1978, or her "Ordinary/Extraordinary" series, beginning in 1980, the artist has achieved something valuable. In these works, Stevens brings female characters from radically different worlds into dialogue with one another. Stevens and her viewers are surely entitled to this feminist fantasy as an ideal to strive for. But when she in effect presents femaleness as exhaustive of humanness, Stevens seems to be suggesting that only one sex should be permitted admission to this Garden of Eden. (It is incidentally worth noting that the conception of woman as the eternally enigmatic and mysterious has contributed to male inability to see woman as fully human. There is little evidence that Stevens has adequately explored the implications of this problem.)

Hans Haacke's protests of the corporate world's appropriations of culture rely on an elegant editorial selection and presentation of images to score their points, to tell us that high culture is as politically naive as business is politically clever. Haacke stands foremost among the very few artists who have had the courage to remind us of the socially oppressive realities that art enters into; his interventionary works represent an important contribution. But in his dependence on the same "distorting" techniques as those employed by corporate public relations, by choosing some "facts" and omitting others, he manipulates the viewer into accepting his version of reality. Unfortunately, however, that version of reality strips art of its multifaceted complex nature and manifestations, so that Haacke's work can be seen as social realism raised to a higher level of abstraction—with culture taking the place of the undifferentiated individual.

Many more examples of today's activist art could be presented. My point remains that a significant amount of it, so full of *ressentiment,* runs the risk of symbolizing society's arrested metamorphosis, and, simultaneously, society's lonely-crowd way of looking at things, experiencing things, (mis)understanding things. As a result, it can end up serving the purposes of what I would call "gallery leftism"—the establishment of a political identity in the art world that has an ambiguous significance in the larger world. Just as the gallery aestheticism of formalist art may have served as an attempt to "prove" that art is more likely to afford a genuine, memorable—purer—experience than nature or life, so the gallery leftism of agitation or integration serves to prove that radicalism and social criticism are purer in the art world than in the life world. But is this the vision, the goal, for which so many of our activist artists are reaching? I think not. In fact, the pretentiousness and self-privileging of either position—aesthetic or activist—is self-defeating, a betrayal of the real needs of the individual members of the lonely crowd, and a betrayal of the potential of art to meet those needs.

But we can look to the best works of the artists I have discussed in this essay, as well as to the works of a number of other artists today, to see that activist art has not reached a dead end in America. Sue Coe's renderings of social atrocities, whether grand or intimate, violent or grieving, speak from the inside of life in order to give voice to the many oppressed and miserable. With his gorgeously frightening drawings from the "Firestorm" series, 1982, Robert Morris approaches a "known" catastrophe with enormous imagination. Nancy Spero's *Torture of Women,* 1976, in its outspoken rage, in its range of gestures from delicate to savage, presents images of women in pain, but simultaneously in action. Twisted and pulled, but also buoyantly leaping and determinedly striding, they affirm multiple possibilities while acknowledging the devastating effects of oppression. Vito Acconci and Bill Viola have both used mass-media tools to promote a more complex understanding and experience of the individual human being in the social world. In Acconci's *Sub-Urb* at Artpark, 1983, the viewer/participant's intense isolation in underground "rooms," coupled with the experience of collective address as evoked by the printed, posterlike words on the walls, serves to acknowledge both the tension and the relationship between the realms of public and private. Viola produces a kind of internal Sensurround in his *Reasons for Knocking at an Empty House,* 1982, dedicated to a worker injured by a blow to the head. While the viewer faces, up close, a videotape of Viola, and while Viola swallows, breathes, while his heart beats, the earphones the viewer is wearing amplify those sounds, and one seems to be entering the body of the man who suffered that pain. And the exuberant yet elegant work of Tim Rollins and KOS asks its audience to go beyond questions of formalist eloquence to arrive at a larger definition of what constitutes effective activist artmaking.

Finally, we can also look again to the past, to David's *The Death of Marat,* 1793, as a beacon for the rich possibilities of creative activist art. David has risked a very special kind of displacement here: he has taken the fiery orator out of his familiar "crowd" context. The viewer finds Marat in the most intimate setting possible, his bath. And Marat is rendered in all his vulnerable humanness: his head, relaxed in death, bears the traces of both pain and peace; his limp hand, dropped to the floor, still clings to, but can no longer clutch, the pen. Body is not abstract here, but defined, palpable. David has stripped the scene of all the conventional codes and symbols of political struggle, the viewer and Marat "meet" one another one-to-one, yet we know we are in the presence of a powerful political picture. Intimate identification, rather than aggressive assertion, *The Death of Marat* suggests, is the mode by which one can achieve significant change, both personal and social. It is true that the activist that the artist shows us is dead. But Marat's existence, his political efforts, are all the more present as a subject for contemplation. Our hushed dialogue with David's Marat—a single, naked, dead human being—is the most radical and resonant example I know of for suggesting the human and political potential of activist art.

Notes

1. Jacques Ellul, *Propaganda: The Formation of Men's Attitudes* (first published in France, as *Propagandes,* 1962), (New York: Alfred A. Knopf, 1972), pp. 8–9.

2. See also David Riesman, *The Lonely Crowd: A Study of the Changing American Character* (New Haven: Yale University Press, 1973). The notion of the "lonely crowd" derives from Gustave le Bon's idea of the crowd, which was utilized by Freud and carried forward by Riesman and Ellul. It also involves Nietzsche's concept of "the [human] herd."

3. Ellul, p. 147.

4. Harold Rosenberg, *Discovering the Present: Three Decades in Art, Culture, and Politics* (Chicago: University of Chicago Press, 1973), p. 19.

5. Ibid., p. 53.

6. I am using "autonomy" in a modified Freudian sense, as the ability to withstand trauma from exterior as well as interior sources. David Shapiro, in his *Autonomy and Rigid Character* (New York: Basic Books, 1981), p. 16, describes autonomy as "a new kind of self-regulation . . . in the form of increasingly articulated conscious aims, and . . . a new kind of behavior, intentional, planful action—self-directed action in the proper sense." On pp. 17–18 he says that "the human sense of autonomy" derives from "active mastery of the environment." It involves an "advance in the Marxist phrase, 'from the realm of necessity to the realm of freedom.'"

7. Rosenberg, p. 19.

8. Ellul, p. 8. Lucy R. Lippard's "Some Propaganda for Propaganda," in *Get the Message? A Decade of Art for Social Change* (New York: E. P. Dutton, 1984), pp. 114–23, totally ignores these issues. Her notion of "good propaganda" (p. 116) is a contradiction in terms.

9. Ellul acknowledges that this distinction echoes Lenin's well-known distinction between agitation and propaganda proper, and the equally well-known distinction between the "propaganda of subversion" and the "propaganda of collaboration" (p. 71).

10. Ibid., pp. 71–72.

11. Ibid.

12. D. W. Winnicott, "The Manic Defence," *Collected Papers* (London: Tavistock Publications, 1958), p. 132.

13. José Ortega y Gasset, "The Dehumanization of Art," *The Dehumanization of Art and Other Writings on Art and Culture* (Garden City, N.Y.: Doubleday & Company, 1956), pp. 46–47.

14. Ellul, p. 75.

15. Ibid., p. 11.

16. Ibid., p. 148.

17. Ibid. Ellul is describing what has come to be called the "diffusion of responsibility" that occurs in the lonely crowd. There is an inability to decide to take personal responsibility for anything that occurs. See C. Mynatt and S. J. Sherman, "Responsibility Attribution in Groups and Individuals: A Direct Test of the Diffusion of Responsibility Hypothesis," *Journal of Personality and Social Psychology* 32 (1975), pp. 1111–18. See also B. Latane and J. M. Darley, *The Unresponsive Bystander* (New York: Appleton-Century-Crofts, 1970).

18. This returns us to Shapiro, who connects the "fixed purposiveness of the rigid person" (p. 75) with his or her continued emulation and identification with images of superior authority derived from the child's image of the superior authority of the adult" (p. 74). Shapiro thinks this a "miscarriage" of the development of "volitional direction and control," not its "overdevelopment." "Flexibility—not rigidity—of behavior stands at the opposite pole from the immediacy and passivity of reaction of early childhood. Flexibility—not rigidity—reflects an active self-direction. Furthermore, flexibility—not rigidity—reflects a genuinely objective attitude toward the world" (pp. 74–75). Truly creative critical art participates in the individual's autonomy. Propaganda (and the media) encourages the emulation and identification with superior authority. Ellul's discussion (p. 149) of the way the individual in the lonely crowd "feels himself *diminished*" is also worth noting in this context. "He gets the feeling that he is under constant supervision and can never exercise his independent initiative . . . he thinks he is always being pushed down to a lower level. He is a minor in that he can never act with full authority." This strongly resembles Shapiro's discussion of the difference between the rigid character and autonomy, and suggests a social rationale for it.

19. Ortega y Gasset, "In Search of Goethe from Within," *The Dehumanization of Art*, pp. 136–37.

20. Hannah Höch, quoted in Lucy R. Lippard, ed., *Dadas on Art* (Englewood Cliffs, N.J.: Prentice-Hall, 1971), p. 72.

21. Quoted in ibid., p. 81.

22. Quoted in ibid., p. 71.

23. Quoted in ibid., p. 77, Lippard, In "Dada in Berlin: Unfortunately Still Timely," *Get the Message?* pp. 67–73, sidesteps this critical recognition. She notes that the German art of the time can be distinguished from other European art "by the depth of its bitterness," then goes on to add that, ironically, "Berlin Dada art, for all its disorientation, appears more hopeful and positive" (p. 72). Thus Lippard avoids considering how the varying degrees of frustration that underlay the art of the time may nevertheless have implied an unconscious awareness of the impossibility of social revolution in the Germany of the day, as well as an unconscious recognition of the necessity of profound personal revolution as a precondition for social revolution.

24. Quoted in ibid.

25. Bernard S. Myers, *The German Expressionists: A Generation in Revolt* (New York: Frederick A. Praeger, 1966), p. 227.

26. Max Scheler, in his *Ressentiment* (New York: The Free Press of Glencoe, 1961), pp. 45–46, describes *ressentiment* as "a self-poisoning of the mind . . . a lasting mental attitude, caused by the systematic repression of certain emotions and affects which, as such, are normal components of human nature. Their repression leads to the constant tendency to indulge in certain kinds of value delusions and corresponding value judgments. The emotions and affects primarily concerned are revenge, hatred, malice, envy, the impulse to detract, and spite." None of these feelings, writes Scheler, necessarily leads to *ressentiment.* It develops "only if there occurs neither a moral self-conquest . . . nor an act or some other adequate expression of emotion . . . and if this restraint is caused by a pronounced awareness of impotence. . . . Through its very origin, *ressentiment* is therefore chiefly confined to those who *serve* and are *dominated* at the moment, who fruitlessly resent the sting of authority . . . the spiritual venom of *ressentiment* is extremely contagious" (p. 48).

27. This is the last line of Shelley's *A Defence of Poetry,* 1821. For an account of Shelley's revolutionary interests see Kenneth Neill Cameron, *The Young Shelley: Genesis of a Radical* (New York: Crowell-Collier, Collier Books, 1962).

28. Abraham H. Maslow, "Neurosis as a Failure of Personal Growth," *The Farther Reaches of Human Nature* (New York: Penguin Books, 1976), p. 39.

29. Theodor Adorno, *Aesthetic Theory* (London: Routledge & Kegan Paul, 1984), p. 327.

15

Tilted Arc: Enemy of the People?

Robert Storr

Tilted Arc, *a monumental sculpture by Richard Serra, was commissioned in 1979 by the General Services Administration at $175,000 for New York's Federal Plaza. The sculpture's placement led to immediate hostility by those who had to experience it and to a public discourse that illuminated the gulfs among artists, government patrons and the popular audience. The situation, which Robert Storr presents from beginning to end at his writing in 1985, also testifies that the convoluted process of challenging a commission is as difficult as commissioning and installing a public sculpture. The controversy underlined, as well, that site-specific sculpture is by nature never purely aesthetic but also always political.*

Serra's relationship to physical space and the audience is antithetical to that of many of the artists in this book. His work, often public, still stands apart from the social world. Serra believes, in fact, that "After the piece is created, the space will be understood primarily as a function of the sculpture."

Storr writes: "In May of 1985 Dwight Ink, the chief administrator of the General Services Administration in Washington, handed down a decision recommending the relocation of Richard Serra's sculpture Tilted Arc, *which now stands in front of the Federal Complex in downtown Manhattan. This decision followed a four-year debate over the 'appropriateness' of Serra's piece, and the importance its retention or removal would have for the future both of the GSA's Art in Architecture program and of public art in this country in general. What*

This article originally appeared in *Art in America* (September 1985). Reprinted by permission of the publisher.

follows is a description of the circumstances leading up to that judgment and some thoughts on the relation of the Serra controversy to current discussions of the politics of art in the 1980s.''
Tilted Arc was removed from Federal Plaza in March of 1989.

In 1979, in accordance with the established procedures of the General Services Administration's Art in Architecture program, Richard Serra was chosen by an independent panel of art professionals consisting of Suzanne Delahanty, Robert Pincus-Witten, and Ira Licht to offer a proposal for a sculpture to be placed in the plaza in front of the Jacob K. Javits Building on Foley Square.[1] Following extensive engineering studies and prolonged negotiations with the GSA's own design review panel, Serra's planned work, Tilted Arc, was finally approved by the then head of the GSA, Roland G. Freeman. Given the relative blandness of much public sculpture and the intransigent if not confrontational nature of Serra's art, it was a remarkable, indeed risky undertaking for both the artist and his government patrons.

For Serra's part, it would appear that the prime attraction of this commission was the very difficulty of the site offered him. Speaking to Douglas Crimp in 1980, Serra recalled:

> The Federal Building site didn't interest me at first. It's a "pedestal site" in front of a public building. There's a fountain on the plaza, normally you would expect a sculpture next to the fountain, so the ensemble would embellish the building. I've found a way to dislocate or alter the decorative function of the plaza and actively bring people into the sculpture's context. I plan to build a piece that's 120 feet long in a semi-circular plaza. It will cross the entire space, blocking the view from the street to the courthouse and vice versa. It will be twelve feet high and will tilt one foot toward the Federal building and the Courthouse. It will be a very slow arc that will encompass the people who walk on the plaza in its volume. . . . After the piece is created, the space will be understood primarily as a function of the sculpture.[2]

Though Serra had never before contended with a "pedestal" site of this kind, he had of course already made several major pieces for urban plazas. In 1977 he created Berlin Block for Charlie Chaplin in Berlin and Terminal in Bochum; the latter triggered a controversy that spilled over into the regional elections. More recently Serra built Twain, a walled enclosure for St. Louis that took eight years of negotiations; La Palmera, a concrete arc for a working-class neighborhood in Barcelona; Clara-Clara, a site-specific sculpture for Paris that was successfully moved from its planned location near the Beaubourg to a different site in the Tuileries; and the privately funded Rotary Arc, which stands in the traffic circle near the exit from New York's Holland Tunnel, about a mile from *Tilted Arc,* its federally subsidized cousin.

But if Serra's sculptures are in increasing proportion now designed for public spaces, the precarious antimonumentality of his basic aesthetic continues to be informed by the marginality and impermanence of the industrial no-man's-lands and vacant lots in which he executed much of his early work. Even *Rotary Arc* stands apart from the social world. Occupying a site seen but rarely entered or traversed by pedestrians, it slices across the axis within which it is located, rendering the surrounding whorl of buildings, driveways, crosswalks and grassy lozenges tangential to its spare sculptural sweep, while itself insisting upon its distance from and tangency to these given forms. But while *Rotary Arc* articulates a man-made but essentially uninhabited space, *Tilted Arc* stands at the heart of a heavily trafficked working environment dominated by an overbearing architectural monolith. Placed directly in the path of people largely ignorant of and for the most part alienated by modern art, *Tilted Arc* demands attention, insisting that its presence is not an adjunct or adornment of the space it occupies but the subject of that space. If David Smith's sculpture was conceived in resistance to the tyranny of architects and the bland conventions of most of public art, *Tilted Arc* was meant to actively subvert them. It is that physical polemic, aside from the arguable beauty of the piece itself, which is the work's principal virtue.

It therefore came as no surprise that when finally installed in 1981 *Tilted Arc* was greeted with marked hostility, prompting letters to the newspapers and a petition, signed by some 1,300 employees of the Federal Complex, demanding the sculpture's removal from the site it so categorically refused to "grace." *Tilted Arc* also garnered a mixed response from the art world.[3] Coming at a time when the dominant taste was shifting toward new forms of figurative painting and sculpture, it seemed to some to signal the final assimilation if not cooptation of the Minimal aesthetic by institutional culture. But government endorsement of Serra's work has not lessened its confrontational power, and contrary to expectation the furor generated by it has not died down. Rather, federal sponsorship compounded the "offense," and *Tilted Arc* became an anomalous "official" provocation dividing the art community from the public at large and the art community against itself as has no other work of recent memory.

Clearly intended to break this stalemate, GSA administrator Dwight Ink's decision to move *Tilted Arc* nonetheless involves conditions that give his judgment a distinctly Solomonic cast. The process established by Ink for the relocation requires that local GSA officers find a suitable alternative site subject to the approval of an NEA-appointed panel working in consultation with the artist. It is clear from Serra's own statements, however, that he will not cooperate in what he considers not the mere relocation of a site-specific work but its actual destruction. It is probable, and certainly to be hoped, that without his participation no museum or other reputable institution will be enlisted in this scheme. Thus it appears that while Ink has made a gesture of concession to those opposed to *Tilted Arc,* he has in fact specified terms for the resolution of the problem which dictate that the work itself will remain in place indefinitely.

The real climax of the *Tilted Arc* controversy, however, came in March [1985] in three days of hearings called by William Diamond, the New York administrator of the GSA. And if Ink's decision belongs to the history of bureaucratic diplomacy, Diamond's hearings belong to the history of the piece itself.

These hearings were not the first instance of local opposition to a GSA-commissioned work being channeled through—even instigated by—the regional hierarchy of the Federal government. In the mid-1970s a prolonged but ultimately unsuccessful campaign was waged against George Sugarman's sculpture *Baltimore Federal* by a U.S. district court judge, and in many ways the *Tilted Arc* controversy is a replay of that affair. In New York it was Judge Edward D. Re, Chief Justice of the United States Court of International Trade, who lobbied to reopen the Serra issue after three years of relative quiet, and it is obvious that Diamond's hearings were designed to orchestrate and amplify the anger that Re's efforts had brought back to the surface. Arrogating to himself the prerogative of appointing its members, Diamond created a panel consisting of three senior officers of the regional GSA administration and two outside members, Michael Findlay, vice-president of Christie's, and Thomas Levin, a lawyer and art collector.

Significantly, Diamond appointed from the art community no one whose specific concern was with public sculpture, and however sincere the participation of the last two members, it is clear that he had taken pains to assure himself a voting majority. Meanwhile, no legal basis existed for such an ex post facto move to pressure for the abrogation of a contract signed and executed between a citizen and the government. Granted, Diamond presided over the ad hoc proceedings with exemplary "fairness," extending the hearings to three days so that all who had signed up could be heard, allocating the same three minutes to each speaker, and bending the rules evenhandedly to allow key spokesmen for both sides extra time to complete their statements. But these parliamentary niceties were only camouflage for a fixed agenda.

Though claiming to have no personal grief against Serra and no intention of passing aesthetic judgment on the work itself, Diamond listened to the arguments of Serra's partisans with the ostentatious lack of enthusiasm of a bored schoolboy in French class. Then at the end of the first day, in an interview with Cable Network News, he openly declared his determination to have the sculpture removed. A professional politician using his office to speak out for the "little man" against the abuses of the Big Government of which he is in fact integrally a part, Diamond followed the by-now-familiar strategy of Spiro Agnew ("democratic" voice for the "silent majority"), and of boardroom "populist" H. Ross Perot. It was Perot who exploited the anguish of veterans to impose his own "patriotic" taste on the Vietnam War Memorial—a work which, not incidentally, owes its sculptural syntax to Serra and, like *Tilted Arc,* was thought objectionable precisely because it was open to a variety of readings.

Taking their cue from Diamond, the "little men"—and women—said much that was predictably negative and narrow. Throughout the three days of the hearings, office workers and overseers took time out from their duties and trooped in to denounce the sculpture as nihilistic and a rusted piece of junk.[4] Coming to Serra's defense was a virtual roll call of art-world personalities, an unexpected alliance which included *October* critics and their erstwhile nemesis, William Rubin of the Museum of Modern Art; Serra's peers of the 1960s such as Donald Judd and Frank Stella; and more recent "luminaries" such as Keith Haring and Tony Shafrazi, respectively the leading artist and leading dealer of the graffiti art whose authentic vernacular expression covered *Tilted Arc* itself and was cause for many of the complaints of those opposed to the Serra work. In all, this coalition of interests gave *Tilted Arc* a curiously Hans Haacke–like "provenance," which, like those Haacke has traced for Impressionist works by Seurat and Manet, encompasses the full range of the art world's social and ideological extremes.

Testimony in Serra's favor reflected a correspondingly diverse, not to say contradictory, series of perceptions and motives, and some of that testimony made for very enjoyable theater. Eliciting embarrassed laughter from Diamond and his associates, Leon Golub slyly suggested that they consider the apparently headless and decidedly bellicose bronze eagle which hung over the courtroom before any attempt was made to remove Serra's supposedly mindless and aggressive sculpture.

Meanwhile, Holly Solomon, arriving in a voluminous white fur coat, lectured the panelists on economics. "I try very hard to teach people about contemporary art," she explained, "but the bottom line is this has financial value and you really have to understand that you have responsibility to the financial community. You cannot destroy property." This spirited but "businesslike" intervention seemed an odd complement to the Marxism of other Serra supporters, but it did not appear to assuage the anger of those who saw *Tilted Arc* as nothing more than a $175,000 boondoggle.

More to the point on this score was the testimony of Serra and other GSA-commissioned artists who said that they had not only not made money on their work but had in some cases lost it—a fact confirmed by Donald Thalacker, Art in Architecture's director, in his 1980 book surveying the project's accomplishments.[5] For Serra as for Nancy Holt and others, the attraction of the program was not financial, but rather the opportunity to undertake a major work whose permanence would be guaranteed by its patrons. For these artists as well as for many of the institutional representatives who made statements on Serra's behalf—Kitty Carlisle Hart, Bess Myerson and Senator Javits among them—the issue was the trust that must be preserved between artists and the government if such programs are to succeed, and the chilling effect that censorship would have upon creative freedom in the country generally. As was several times pointed out, the "public" for the work created under Art in Architecture's aegis was national, not merely local, and the repercussion of any move to back away from GSA's commitment to the artists involved could be expected to be similarly wide-reaching. This is not an idle fear. Though George Sugarman was successful in defending his Baltimore work, Robert Murray, another Serra supporter, recently lost his fight to preserve his NEA-commissioned work in Alaska.

Meanwhile the aesthetic case for *Tilted Arc* was made by numerous curators and critics, but most persuasively by Serra himself:

> *Tilted Arc* was constructed to engage the public in dialogue that would enhance, both perceptually and conceptually, its relation to the entire plaza. The sculpture involved the viewer rationally and emotionally. A multitude of readings is possible. . . . The work through its location, height, length, horizontality and lean grounds one into the physical condition of the place. The viewer becomes aware of himself and of his movement through the plaza. As he moves, the sculpture changes. Contraction and expansion of the sculpture results from the viewer's movement. Step by step, perception of not only the sculpture but the entire environment changes.

But however clear Serra's strict phenomenological explication of *Tilted Arc,* the fact of the matter is that it has long since ceased to be and may never again be the purely abstract sculptural experience Serra intended. For both its opponents and its supporters *Tilted Arc* has become a social symbol and the rhetoric which now attaches itself to the work has a telling, sometimes grimly comic symmetry.

If to many opposed to it *Tilted Arc* represented an "iron curtain" or Berlin Wall, for Serra advocate Douglas Crimp it was no less an emblem of incipient totalitarianism.

> The view of us, the public, that is really held by those who have convened this hearing can be discerned from a passage in a letter from Chief Judge Re, who has been leading the fight to remove *Tilted Arc* since the day it was erected. . . . Judge Re writes, and I quote, "Finally, but by no means of minor importance is the loss of efficient security surveillance. The placement of this wall across the plaza obscures the view of security personnel who have no way of knowing what is taking place on the other side of the wall." Well, I would submit that it is we the public who are on the other side of this wall and it is we who Judge Re so fears and despises that he wants that wall torn down in order that we may be properly subjected to surveillance.

Crimp's fantasy of Big Brotherdom is not a purely literary conceit. As farfetched as it may at first seem, the siege mentality Crimp found manifested in Judge Re's remarks is all too real. The surreal charge that modern sculpture was a potential tool of terrorists had previously been made against Sugarman's *Baltimore Federal* and was reiterated in this case by the Federal Complex's GSA security specialist who testified that far from serving as the ideal acoustic baffle for concerts, as was later demonstrated by composer Alvin Lucier, *Tilted Arc* provided a screen for unidentified miscreants and drug pushers and might someday be used as a blast wall for bombers lurking on Foley Square.

The crux of the issue, however, was less this reciprocal paranoia than the way in which *Tilted Arc* had been used to exacerbate the already acute tensions between the public and the art community. Here Crimp was not only essentially right but eloquent.

> This hearing does not attempt to build a communality of interest in art in the public realm. Although *Tilted Arc* was commissioned by a program devoted to placing art in public spaces, that program seems now utterly uninterested in building public understanding of the art it has commissioned. This is not a hearing about the social function that art might play in our lives. Rather, it is a hearing convened by a government administrator who seems to believe that art and social function are antithetical. That art has no social function. What makes me feel manipulated is that I am forced to argue for art against some other social function. I am asked to line up on the

side of sculpture against those who are on the side of concerts or maybe picnic tables. But of course all these things have social functions. . . . It is a measure of the meager nature of our public social life that the public is asked to fight out a travesty of the democratic procedure over the crumbs of social experience.

Though Crimp's conclusions are accurate, his assertion that Serra's patrons were "utterly uninterested in building public understanding of the art it commissioned" is simplistic and wrong. Nor was Serra correct when he complained to *People* magazine, "I have the weight of government—not only their deception but their heel—on my head."[6] The "government" which was responsible for Serra's commission in the first place did not abandon him, though it might at some points have wanted to. Indeed, Art in Architecture's director Thalacker adroitly argued for him, as did a host of other elected and appointed officials committed to the support of public art.

There was in fact nothing monolithic about the political forces at work. Commissioned by federal officials in Washington but seemingly without defenders among local GSA officials, *Tilted Arc* existed in a bureaucratic power vacuum, which Diamond and his cohorts did not fail to notice. In capitalizing on its vulnerability, they were simply following the axiom of Tammany Hall boss George Washington Plunkett, who said simply enough, "I seen my opportunities and I took 'em." If there is blame to be laid at the door of Serra's patrons, it results from their having created Diamond's opportunity by allowing resentment of the work to build up unanswered, and from the fact that when they finally did come to Serra's defense they permitted their opponents to dictate the terms and the circumstances in which *Tilted Arc* was to be discussed.

The fault is not theirs alone, however. It seems to have occurred to few of Serra's most ardent allies that by failing even to *speak* to, much less *listen* to, the public that felt itself so at odds with *Tilted Arc*, they failed utterly to grasp the political reality of the situation, and so played directly into Diamond's hands. For if Crimp and Serra's attorney, Gustave Harrow, couched their remarks in terms both serious and conciliatory, much of what was said by Serra's partisans was obscure and hyperbolic, serving only to confirm the worst suspicions of those on the other side.

The testimony of Benjamin Buchloh, a scholarly and usually acute analyst of art's social subtexts, was particularly problematic in this regard. Skirting the issue of the reasons for the alienation felt by *Tilted Arc*'s adversaries while allowing that "everybody should have the right to detest contemporary art, especially art like that of Richard Serra that addresses the condition of alienation," Buchloh seemed to suggest that the transformation of such private "prejudice into public judgment or political action" was inherently reactionary. But while it is clear that such grievances or misunderstandings can be and in this case were coopted by reactionary forces, Buchloh's line of argument begs the question of what if any are the appropriate forms such collective dissatisfaction should take. Are there no terms other than outright censorship or private sufferance in which they can be expressed and rejoined?

More troubling still, Buchloh predicated his defense of Serra on a challenge to the competence of Diamond and his copanelists, who presumed to decide on a matter apparently beyond their ken. For Buchloh, this presumption placed them in "contempt" of accredited opinion in the same sense that citizens seeking to overturn the verdict of duly appointed legal experts could be found in "contempt of court." However clever as a polemical device, this analogy is double-edged. For in describing art professionals as the physicians and lawyers of aesthetics, Buchloh set up an unequal contest of clout, in effect narrowing the issue to a choice between the wisdom of the *apparatchiki* and that of the *doctoratchiki,* and in so doing seeming to confirm the impression that Serra's work represented nothing more than the taste of an artistic oligarchy. Moreover, by asserting his own authority and that of unnamed experts to declare Serra the most important sculptor of the postwar era, superior even to David Smith, Buchloh made claims for himself and Serra that in the context of the current critique of "mastery" are hard to ignore.

Further, Buchloh and others denounced Diamond's hearing by drawing historical parallels between it and the culture-bashing tribunals of Nazi Germany. To be sure, the Bitburg incident and Patrick Buchanan's ascendancy in the Reagan administration make such parallels seem less and less remote; certainly also, any official attack on art is cause for alarm, and in a worst-case scenario may be seen as a harbinger of fascism. But Buchloh's broad analogies seemed not so much a cautionary tale as the product of intellectual reflex. However odious Diamond's exploitation of popular discontent, his actions were not those of a budding commandant but of an ambitious Babbitt and experienced bureaucratic infighter. Nor were the angry but often self-effacing civil servants and aged VFW spokesmen who testified potential stormtroopers. Indeed, a few of those who expressed their discomfort with *Tilted Arc* and the process by which it had been chosen nonetheless stopped short of demanding its removal, asking instead to be given time and help to understand it.[7]

Meanwhile, if more mundane politics are to be taken into

account—and to the degree that they reveal the fissures in the "government" Serra considered to be unified against him, they *do* matter—one speaker prefaced his complaints about *Tilted Arc* by pointing out that as far as he was concerned Diamond and his GSA peers were "management'; he then explained to the members of the gallery, many of whom, on Serra's side, had left the room upon his arrival at the lectern, that far from being a blind supporter of conservatism the union he represented was currently under indictment by the Republican administration for having "illegally" organized against Reagan during the recent presidential elections.[8]

As the hearings progressed, it would seem that what rankled the naysayers was not so much the piece itself as the implication that those mystified by an intentionally disruptive presence in their midst were to blame for not embracing it, and the suggestion that as a result they were culpable for ideological crimes they had yet to commit. Confronted by a real political Other, some of Serra's supporters could not recognize it for what it was. Granted, a three-minute presentation does not permit a complex answer, but, given that limitation, it is crucial to speak in ways that do not allow for misunderstanding. In such a context it becomes all the more important not to forget that "ideology" is expressed not only in the sum of one's positions but in the tone of voice and the cultural referents one chooses to describe the world. It is time perhaps that those who have learned their politics from Benjamin, Lacan and Foucault read Saul Alinsky and other basic texts on political organization.

But if the myopia and alarmism of some of Serra's partisans were lesser irritants, the inherent contradictions in the statements of others, and the palpable contempt they expressed for the opposition were pointlessly antagonistic and self-indulgent. Indeed, the speech by the critic Clara Weyergraf, who is Serra's wife and collaborator, was, for all its ringing righteousness, stunningly wrongheaded. It was she who first announced that if *Tilted Arc* was removed she and her husband would leave the country, though this "threat" was subsequently repeated by Serra himself in numerous interviews. Given his impending retrospective at the Museum of Modern Art and his continuing ties to major New York galleries, this seemed a particularly petulant and implausible ultimatum. In the country that invented the "Love It or Leave It" bumper sticker, a "Love Me or I'll Leave You" response is a just invitation to be told to "Get Lost."

Still harder to swallow was the contempt in which Weyergraf evidently held not only her adversaries but her allies. "I was always against artists' accepting government commissions," she explained, "I always thought that art was being used as a sign to advertise liberalism.

A sign which would be ripped down when liberalism went out of political fashion. This sign is being torn into pieces right now." Nevertheless, Weyergraf actively participated in marshaling the liberal if not apolitical forces which defended *Tilted Arc,* welcoming its defenders to the podium just as Serra pumped the hand of each as they left.[9] Furthermore, it is unclear how the patronage of European governments or dealers to whom she and Serra would turn if rebuffed by the GSA is essentially different or any less precarious than that of the American art establishment.

It is perhaps unfair to tax Serra himself for the inconsistency of Weyergraf's statements or of those made by his other partisans. In fact, Weyergraf testified, "I had reservations about the Federal Plaza. Not Richard. Richard felt honored when the GSA approached him and offered him a site in New York." Moreover, it was his decision to accept the gamble of fighting for his work in the open but rigged forum created by his adversaries. Nevertheless, given his declared intent to "dislocate or alter the decorative function of the plaza," it is hard to accept his later claim that he "didn't understand what all the commotion was about," and even harder to reconcile his desire in *Tilted Arc* to "actively bring people into the sculpture's context" or his acceptance of such a commission with his statement that "trying to attract a bigger audience has nothing to do with the making of art."[10] At the root of these inconsistencies lies the fundamental paradox of Serra's thinking—a paradigm of the contradictions which continue to plague the critical debate over the relation between politics and art, the residual "radicalism" of Minimalist and anti-form art, and the supposed "conservatism" of more recent painting and sculpture. Here it is worth quoting Serra at length from a 1976 interview with Liza Bear.

> I'm not concerned with quote humanistic values on that level. If you're going to get involved, your energies are best served entering the political arena and doing it in that transitory manner. The interesting thing about abstract art is that given the basic position one assumes and the kind of experience one needs to have, the work remains free, in that it doesn't serve any ideological premise. When work ends up in museums or galleries, it can't escape from the morality implicit in those institutions. . . ; it's not independent of that larger capitalistic structure which needs close scrutiny. Well, every artist I know, to a degree—and it's to that degree that we are all more or less guilty—has to deal with these inconsistencies. There's a real trend now to demean abstract art as not being socially relevant. What you have is a return of a kind of '30s reactionary value system—the form manifests itself in various guises: entertainment as art, political writing as art, capitalism as Marxist art, documentation as art, media as art—in effect a revamped social realism or art as everything other than what I feel is essential as art experience. I've never felt, and I don't feel now, that art needs any justification outside of itself.[11]

There is no reason to suppose that Serra has changed these views, and in the present context it is a revelatory statement indeed. For in his determination to liberate art from conventions of good taste and social utility Serra glosses over the question of what if any are the specific political obligations for which artists may be held accountable. On a purely theoretical level there would seem to be none, for he assigns himself the same privileges that were claimed for the Abstract Expressionists by their liberal apologists. Looking back on and down at the Social Realism of the 1930s from an even greater distance than they, Serra describes the artist as a uniquely free individual whose work is by definition beyond ideology. Yet this is the very contention which Serge Guilbaut and others writing on the political content of the "apolitical" American abstraction in the 1950s have called into question, and if that critique is to have any meaning it must be applied not only in hindsight but in the present, and not just with respect to those artists who, like the Abstract Expressionists, make the quest for personal identity the subject of their work, but also to those, such as Serra, who arrogate to themselves a fictional freedom from historical imperatives, with the result that they regard politics as an ancillary activity.

In a genuine political critique of culture what matters is not an artist's good intentions or his background—on which score Serra is fully as much a product of Yale and the University of California at Berkeley as he is of working-class San Francisco and the steel plants in which he labored as a student—but rather the way in which art actually enters the social world.[12] Hans Haacke, for one, has made the elucidation of that process the subject of his work, and the effectiveness of his documentary outrage derives in no small measure from the sense of proportion—and humor—with which he views the ironies of his own participation in the very system he accuses. Though Serra's vision holds true to the faith of the 1960s, when, he says, it was understood that "it was your job as an artist to redefine society by the values you were introducing rather than the other way around,"[13] he has evidently gained no such sense of proportion and sees no humor in the complex structure of trade-offs upon which his own success is predicated.

Finally, for all his legitimate insistence that the integrity of Tilted Arc depends upon its preservation in its original location, what he appears to have ignored all along is that the "site" for such site-specific artworks is neither simply geographic nor purely aesthetic. It is, from the outset, political, and politics is not a matter of gestures but an ongoing, often tedious but sometimes instructive process. To make public art inevitably involves anticipating and appreciating the social impact of what one does. If one is determined not only to resist prior restraints but to win against the combined forces of conservatism and ignorance, it is not enough simply to stand on principle and react to reaction. But for all his sense of mission Serra has shown few signs that he is prepared for the hurly-burly of actual social struggle. Rather, with the exception of his formal statement to the GSA hearings, he has been content to bait his opponents, retreating from the role of "artist-hero" into that of "artist-victim," while leaving the hard work of building bridges to his lawyer and more pragmatic partisans. This failure to deal directly—much less, generously—with his least articulate but most important adversaries—that is, those who on a daily basis must live with his work—is, as much as anything, what accounts for the sourness which has tinged this debate.

The intent here is not to "blame the victim"—since the "victim" is not Serra but the *Tilted Arc* itself and, with it, the cause of public art.[14] While it is begging the question to suggest, as some at the hearing did, that the solution to the problem was to tear down the building before which *Tilted Arc* stands rather than the work itself, neither would a "prettier" or more compliant sculpture have mitigated the singular ugliness of Federal Plaza. Though not a wholly successful work, Serra's piece is nonetheless one of the most ambitious attempts by any GSA-sponsored artist to confront the premises of public sculpture, and, approached on its own terms, it is a truly impressive work. However, *Tilted Arc* should remain where it is not only for these aesthetic reasons or because removing it would set a disastrous precedent for programs such as Art in Architecture, but because it exists as a constant reminder that it is not just the public that has something to learn, but also all those who presume to speak for, and make, art in the public interest.

Insofar as *Tilted Arc* has become a symbol of this tense and ongoing standoff between artists on the one hand and their governmental patrons and popular audience on the other, it also serves to mirror the image that the art community, and in particular the art Left, presents to the world at large. In that context, if the flap over *Tilted Arc* is indeed to be taken as a test case of the "coming struggle" between reaction and progress, the rabble-rousers and the intelligentsia, then the prospects are not good. For whatever the bureaucratic or legal resolution to the issue (Serra has suggested that he will sue for an injunction to prevent the removal of the work), the crucial fact remains that *Tilted Arc*'s advocates lost the battle for the attention and sympathy of the public.

However complex or all-encompassing the radical theory of the politically minded art community has become, its praxis was revealed in this case and in others—such as the divisive fights, in recent years, over "artist housing"—to be uncertain if not wholly ad hoc. To that extent, *Tilted Arc* stands as a monument to the convergence of formalist art and "formalist" politics—a politics, that is, of theory without praxis—with the aspirations of the art falling prey to the manifest contradictions of the politics. Moreover, it is a reminder that when the interest of artists and those of a largely uninformed and hostile community collide, however self-evident the moral, social and aesthetic questions involved may seem, in practical terms the burden of proof will always fall upon art's defenders, as does the challenge to find not only the reasons but the language to make them intelligible to those for whom art is at best a decorative amenity and at worst an authoritarian imposition. The positive outcome of the debate on *Tilted Arc* is that that challenge and the cost of ignoring this lesson have been made inescapably plain.

Notes

1. The GSA Art in Architecture program was established under the Kennedy administration in 1963. Since its foundation it has commissioned over 200 works, financing them at a ration of 1/2 of 1 percent of the total construction costs of the building for which the work is planned. The Serra affair is by no means the first time that public outcry has resulted from these commissions. In 1966 the program was suspended as a result of reactions stirred by a mural painted by Robert Motherwell for the Federal Building in Boston. Restored in 1972 during the Nixon administration and placed under the directorship of Donald Thalacker, who still occupies the post, the program embarked upon a series of ups and downs of which the Serra affair is only the latest episode. In 1976 liberal Senator William Proxmire awarded the program his "Golden Fleece Award," following the erection of Claes Oldenburg's *Bat Column,* and that year its budget was cut to 3/8 of I percent of building costs. In 1977 its original budget was restored, but that same year a long controversy—eventually amicably resolved—resulted from the commissioning of Mark di Suvero's *Moto Viget* in Grand Rapids. In 1985, President Reagan gave the Art in Architecture program one of thirteen First Presidential Awards for Design Excellence.

2. *Richard Serra: Interviews Etc., 1970–1980,* written and compiled in collaboration with Clara Weyergraf (Yonkers: Hudson River Museum, 1980), p. 168.

3. *Tilted Arc*'s already voluminous press history reflects that ambivalence. Peter Schjeldahl, writing in the *Village Voice,* slammed the work when it was first installed, and current *Voice* critic Gary Indiana has been no less scathing. Michael Brenson of the *Times,* however, came to *Tilted Arc*'s defense, as did his colleague Grace Glueck, though her vote for retention was heavily qualified by questions about the GSA's selection process. Meanwhile, coverage in the *Wall Street Journal* and other New York dailies has been uniformly negative. Network TV treatment has been characterized by mockery or that sort of smug bemusement anchormen reserve for "human interest" stories about eccentric inventors.

4. The aesthetics of "rust" was one of the recurrent nuisance issues which cropped up in the hearings and in the press coverage of the issue. Once again, it is hardly adequate to simply affirm that Serra's use of industrial steel is a symbol of his solidarity with the working class when in fact the workers themselves seem consistently to miss the poignancy of that intent. Nevertheless, as the testimony made clear, the rusting of Cor-Ten steel is a self-protective process, not one of chemical degeneration. Moreover, several speakers pointed out that the green patina which covers such beloved park sculptures as the Nathan Hale statue near City Hall is nothing more or less than the result of the similar oxidation of bronze. Were it not for the graffiti scars which mar the surface of *Tilted Arc,* its rich red-brown patina would be equally beautiful and in time might come to be appreciated by those who now find it so objectionable.

5. Donald W. Thalacker, *The Place of Art in the World of Architecture* (New York: Chelsea House, 1980).

6. "A Rusty Eyesore or a Work of Art: Sculptor Richard Serra Defends His Controversial 'Tilted Arc,'" *People* (1 April 1985), p. 140.

7. In recent years efforts have been made to open the selection process to the community for which a work is commissioned, and following the Serra debate that process is being further reexamined.

8. Some sense of the larger politics and real priorities of the situation may be gleaned from the following: Over the past several years there have been numerous newspaper articles concerning working conditions in GSA-managed buildings. On June 29, 1985, *The New York Times* reported that senior officials responsible for the Federal Complex in Manhattan had waited several months before notifying employees that drinking water in the complex had been found to contain unusually high levels of lead; the test results had been obtained in February following complaints from workers. Paul Christolini, assistant regional administrator for public buildings of the GSA, was the spokesman who attempted to explain that delay. He was also a member of the Diamond panel convened in March and an ostensible representative of the interests of federal employees in the Serra matter. It would appear that Christolini considered the "danger" posed by art urgent business, whereas, based on his remarks to the *Times,* it would seem that he felt the health danger posed by possibly contaminated water was not.

9. Not only does Weyergraf hold the liberal establishment in contempt, though numerous representatives of it came to *Tilted Arc*'s defense, she has been equally scornful of the art Left with whom she might have engaged in a positive and certainly a more respectful dialogue.

   In an article titled "Holy Alliance: Feminism and Populism," published in *October* in 1981, Weyergraf dismissed the "humanism" of critics Donald Kuspit and Lucy Lippard, accusing them of acquiescence to the aesthetics of entertainment and the politics of reformism. But Weyergraf's caricature of their views is hardly an adequate basis for a critique of either populism or feminism, nor is it enough to say, as she seemed to do, that a radical art is measured by its refusal to "please" its audience. The public is not a phantom nemesis to be ignored in practice while being condescended to, if not despised, in theory, nor is public art a subsidized exercise in private virtue. However one may judge Lippard's current taste, the fact remains that she has taken the risk of exploring the possibilities for reaching out to, and engaging the imagination and concerns of, those for whom contemporary art would otherwise be alien and threatening.

Moreover, Judy Chicago, an artist whom Lippard champions and Weyergraf attacks, is not the primary and certainly not the only example of an artist who has ventured into this treacherous terrain. Whatever one may think of his entrepreneurial anarchism, Christo, for one, has long assumed the responsibility of educating his audience, incorporating not only industrial materials into his work, but the labor and technical skills of his non-artist collaborators as well. Also worth considering are the numerous and sometimes functional public works of Serra's peer and childhood friend Mark di Suvero, the "direct address" art of Barbara Kruger, the site-specific installations of Jonathan Borofsky and the programs of Creative Time, whose temporary projects for "Art on the Beach" might best be thought of as the Public Theater of sculpture.

In the context of these and other examples, Weyergraf's diatribe against "populism" is more a reflection of ideological absolutes than a consideration of the possibilities raised by artists working in an interactive relation with their audience.

10. Harriet Senie, "The Right Stuff," *ARTnews* (March 1984), pp. 52 and 55; and *Richard Serra Interviews*, p. 148.

11. *Richard Serra Interviews*, p. 63.

12. Much is made in Serra criticism of his working-class origins and his use of industrial materials and processes, and in the hearings Annette Michelson argued, "What I wish to point out . . . is the conjunction in Serra of a real concern for the notion of his work as related to that of working men in this country, as emoting from it and his concern that people working and living in the sight of their work be confronted with an art which challenges that, . . . that the office worker be presented with that same kind of challenge that the middle class and upper class art patrons have found so interesting." Though somewhat patronizingly stated by Michelson, this is a noble ambition, but once again the problem is that a bald "challenge" is not always enough, especially when it is clear that whatever motivates Serra in his art is in fact not being communicated in ways that make sense to his ostensible audience. If the burden of that misunderstanding is seen to rest only on the public, then protestations of social radicalism based on Serra's background are just an alibi for indifference.

13. Senie, "The Right Stuff," p. 55.

14. As far as the practical consequences of appearing to "blame the victim" are concerned, I would add that I have waited till now to publish this piece so as to be able to include Ink's decision and its ramifications. I emphatically do not wish to see *Tilted Arc* removed. Regarding the issue of the ugliness of the Federal Plaza site itself, there is every indication from the testimony given that little or nothing was done by those in charge of the complex to improve the location by adding seats, arranging concerts around the sculpture, or rebuilding the fountain with which it is said to conflict. Nor did anyone properly police the area so that *Tilted Arc* would not become the target of the graffiti which so offended federal employees and must certainly have upset Serra himself. Nor was any significant effort made to offer literature or organize groups to visit the work so that it might better be understood. If that failure was an oversight on the part of the Art in Architecture program, it would seem that local officials responsible for *Tilted Arc*'s upkeep and their employees' well-being were more than happy to cut the work loose, permit-

ting it to drift in a sterile architectural no-man's-land so that it would come to be seen as the cause for the plaza's lack of amenities and progressive deterioration.

All otherwise unattributed quotations are taken from transcripts of the Diamond hearings published by the GSA.

16

Fractured Space

Suzanne Lacy

Suzanne Lacy presents a discussion of processes and issues surrounding the creation of a public artwork based on her own practice. Lacy's considerations may seem wholly foreign to traditional public art as expressed by the Serra controversy or the General Services Administration. Certainly she is far from her beginnings as a studio artist and from most studio art making today.

Lacy believes that as an artist she is a member of a society whose involvement is integral to her method and critical dialogue rather than, as Serra maintains, a creator of society. And, she cautions, ''Artists who adopt the rationale that they passively 'reflect' society manage thereby to position themselves as universalists divorced from responsibility for values while still receiving society's accolades for their individualistic expressions.'' In contrast to studio art, public artworks rely from their inception on acknowledgment within their environments and from their audiences.

Lacy examines the danger of coopting authentic content when performance is presented as spectacle, and of the role of media in regard to performance, tableau and monument. Sensation and novelty can produce aesthetic sensibilities antithetical to the ethical decisions that Lacy wants to make with regard to her subject, participants, agencies involved and audience. With mentor Allan Kaprow, she believes that ''artmaking [is] a metaphorical ground for the examination of public, private, and mutual accountability.''

A Contemporary Tableau

In 1987, along with collaborators Susan Stone, Anne Bray, Willow Young, and Carol Heepke, I directed *The Dark Madonna,*[1] the final

THE DARK MADONNA
Suzanne Lacy, 1987
A tableau of women in white was shrouded in black as night fell and as women in black gathered to talk about racism. Staged in the University of California's Franklin Murphy Sculpture Garden.
(Photo courtesy Susan R. Mogul)

performance of a three-part, year-long work exploring women's inter-racial relationships through the Madonna metaphor. The performance took place in the noteworthy Franklin Murphy Sculpture Garden at the University of California at Los Angeles. The audience of approximately two thousand arrived at dusk; in the remnants of the day they saw fifty "sculptures," individual or grouped women, dressed in white and posed motionless on pedestals. As the sun set on their still figures, voices from speakers hidden in trees related these women's experiences with racism.

At the precise moment when light gave way to dark, several barely perceptible figures in black darted through the garden, throwing black cloth over the white garments. Other "sculptures" slowly dropped outer garments to reveal black underneath. Within seconds the light tableau was gone.

From four corners of the garden fifteen groups of black figures with hand-held flashlights wound their way through the garden, and the dark tableau began. The soundtrack changed to voices of women struggling to overcome their anger and distrust. One after another these groups settled to the ground, huddled over their flashlights and began to talk about race. Ribbons surrounding the garden were cut, allowing the audience and their flashlights to flood the tableau stage. The performance dissolved into real time discussion.

Art in the Public Interest: Whose Voice?

I think a lot of senility comes from the fact that nobody asks you anything. Nobody includes you in the social ceremonials. Nobody asks you to speak. Pretty soon you lose your memory.

—Meridel Le Seuer

Discussions about art in public places are held largely by a class of critics and artists who ignore aspects of a complex and often highly politicized heritage. Questions of aesthetics, largely sculptural in nature, dominate the critical dialogue, with community involvement evaluated as an appendage of, rather than integral to, the critique. Contemporary criticism has no means to evaluate the meaning attributed by participants or viewers to their experience, perhaps because this experience is not deemed relevant.

Mass media, on the other hand, packages and commodifies such experience under the duplicitous guise of egalitarianism, leaving us with the bitter taste of inauthenticity and manipulation. In the contemporary spectacles of media and art, who is speaking? What is to be believed? The difficulty in locating an authentic voice is a condition growing out of alienation from personal experience and a confusion of authorship. Our first task in this situation is to develop a language that allows the experience of large numbers of people into public art and the dialogue that surrounds it.

Who is speaking in *The Dark Madonna*? What did the Black, Latina, white, American Indian, and Asian Pacific women in the performance feel was noteworthy in their experience, fitting material for a work of art? To begin to develop language appropriate to public art, we will need to consider how the complete process of preparation and exhibition is integral to the work—educating the community, working within the mass media stream, locating the work in its place, recruiting assistants and performers and networking with social institutions. *The Dark Madonna* was a process that began with a well-attended conference on historical and anthropological interpretations of the Black Madonna images in various ethnic cultures. Next, a series of small group discussions culminated in audiotaping sessions to provide the raw material for the soundtrack which would accompany the performance broadcast on loudspeakers during the performance. This process included linking with multiple ethnic communities and exploring racial controversy, even within the project. The performance was the culmination of this process, the public presentation of the year's engagements.

Equally important to process is context, i.e., how work is situated within the life of a community and society. Works of public art enter a preexisting physical and social organization. How the work relates to, reinforces or contends with forms of expression of that community is a question that contributes to the critical dialogue. The Franklin Murphy Sculpture Garden's collection includes approximately seventy works. Of those on display, fifty-four are by men, and five by women. In the garden the voices of women—old women, Black women, Asian women, disabled women, women with children, pregnant women— as a self-representing group are seldom heard. The irony of *The Dark Madonna* was to invade this realm with the actual bodies and experiences of women of color, relating the tableau form, with its populist and antiheroic heritage, to the sculptures. It was a framing calculated to comment upon established conventions at that site and to alter its meaning temporarily.

Considering process and context as aspects of the actual work does not eliminate discussion of its aesthetic impact, but simply returns to it a fullness of expression implied in the term ''public art.'' A more difficult area to grapple with critically is that of accountability and ethics.

An inevitable component of going public with art is what happens with or to an audience. How responsible is an artist for the reactions to his or her work? How does the work contribute to public debate, our sense of ourselves, our social agenda? Public art offers the opportunity, if not the mandate, to reintroduce a discussion of ethics into the art world discourse, made more urgent by the presence of mass media's incursion into meaning and morality. It is in this discussion that we address the question of authorship, for in the social as well as aesthetic intentionality the artist's gaze is discerned. How he or she will arrange the elements of the tableau to reveal meaning, to inspire an alignment of value or an attitude of questioning, is a measure of the artist's ethics and beliefs.

To consider carefully the public nature of art is to undertake an analysis of art making that highlights issues of audience, context, and meaning. I am arguing not for some presumptive theory that encompasses all of public art, but for exploration. The problem is that the dialogue surrounding public art is too closely circumscribed; by asking more far-ranging questions, we can consider not only public art but perhaps the very nature of art in our contemporary situation.

The Performance Culture: A Dilemma

It has been well described,[2] this society of the spectacle, this fractured space of urban dispersion and physical alienation, of a hyperreal surround that disconnects and recontextualizes our experiencing. The contemporary stage for spectacle is the mass media; but its language of signs and symbols penetrates to include the stage of the public mind.

Spectacle is the total manipulation of images within the context of certain social conditions. The commodity system, with its predisposition toward material objects and the increased demand for sensation and novelty, hypnotizes and directs the viewer's gaze into an illusory relationship with the thing observed. Metaconditioning is the result of the spectacle society; its anonymous aim, to perpetuate itself.

Notice how performance is implicated as a tool of the spectacle society; how social display, amplified by media, begins in the act of performance. An actress performs as a housewife who is fanatically drawn to the use of her air freshener; a candidate's acceptance speech is evaluated later by newscasters to determine the effectivness of his performance; a small child demands a favorite cereal in the same self-conscious tones heard on Saturday morning television; the president of a small Latin American country is aware how crucial is his self-presentation on American television. A battle is staged; an election is staged; a wedding is staged; a demonstration is staged. According to Bonnie Marenca, "the growth of the media and communication in the evolution of society has made Theatricalism into the twentieth century political/art form: it subsumes both ideology and individuality as our way of being in the contemporary world."[3]

In such a context, is authentic experience possible? What is to be believed as real, what prerehearsed and prescribed? Was the opening of the Summer Olympics in Los Angeles in 1986 an embodiment of a shared spirit of human interrelatedness, cutting across the boundaries dividing countries—or a spectacular tableau of commodified sentiment, skillfully devised to draw in the most skeptical observer?

Perhaps the single largest influence on our present art situation is that of mass media, the surround of electronic communications that increases our notion of scale, audience, and potential impact. In this expanded but depersonalized context we are able to imagine an audience numbering not in the thousands but the millions, with work whose scale is limited only by the boundaries of technology and our ability to pay for it.

Artists operate within the media context of hidden authorship. Barthes describes Diderot's conception of the tableau as a "pure cut-out segment with clearly defined edges, irreversible and incorruptible; everything that surrounds it is banished into nothingness, remains unnamed, while everything that it admits within its field is promoted into essence, into light, into view."[4] A tableau is a framing device, a way of structuring reality for the viewer. As such, it is a conceived strategy, an authored opinion of reality. Such intentional framing is inherently political. "In order to tell a story, the painter has only an instant at his disposal, the instant he is going to immobilize on the canvas and he must thus *choose* it well" (emphasis mine).[5] Theater, and we might extend the observation to the performance culture, is "that practice which calculates the place of things *as they are observed*; if I set the spectacle here, the spectator will see this; if I put it elsewhere, he will not, and I can avail myself of this masking effect and play on the illusion it provides."[6] Thus the politically engaged and authored tableau is what Diderot calls a "pregnant moment" in which the historical meaning and political surround of the represented action can be read at a glance.

In the space of contemporary media, the tableau, disguised as such, is enacted. The authorship of the tableau is hidden by the very pervasiveness of its expression and a calculated disconnection of the author to the work. In this anonymous climate, reality is created by a seeming inevitability of image, word, and apparent meaning, as in the days after the final Dukakis-Bush debate before the November 1988 election, when a seemingly inevitable decline in Dukakis' popularity was reflexively analyzed by media makers in terms of their own role in creating the situation.

This reality is reinforced by popular notions of a true, static, and fixed history, which exists in spite of media's continuous restructuring. Arlene Raven cites Reagan's appearance at the Bitberg cemetery as an example: "His silent gesture . . . was powerful enough to make him an interpreter and transformer of history. His action redefined the meaning of the Holocaust by renaming victims and perpetrators of its crimes."[7]

Tableau, the framing of reality, is embedded in contemporary society by the rituals and performances surrounding it. The tableau of Reagan's appearance was made real by dual rituals: the memorialization that took place in the German cemetery, and the ritual of an audience, seated in living rooms, linked by imagination to a world of event-substantiating observers. The framed picture of reality represented in the tableau is reinforced by the processional of meaning that surrounds the media event, and by this performance it is commemorated into our current notion of history.

Monuments and Public Art

Performance and tableau act together in the public space to create a monument of meaning. Monument, the concrete expression of our collective remembering and shared values, is "the device by which communities enter" themselves into the stream of history.[8] Much of contemporary art is the monument to an individual's self-expression. Is it not curious how—in the spectacle society, with its elongated audience reach, staggering scale, and confusion surrounding authenticity of individual experience—we come to question the relationship between monument and art?

The tableau recognized by Diderot was one in which an individual authored a representation of reality; however, turn-of-the-century tableau and pageant makers[9] put these representations to work in what they saw as the public interest. For several decades tableaux were linked with notions of collective truth and human advancement. Yet before World War II Michael Klein pointed to a new kind of tableau which "in addition to its ability to project moral and ethical beliefs, could now also be a vehicle for framing individual philosophies, personal myths, and experience of the artist."[10]

In the decade after the war, the Abstract Expressionists, according to Arlene Raven, "took the form and scale of public murals and made the larger painting surface the vehicle for expressing one man's loneliness . . . [and] the tableau could now be drained of its social roots."[11] Today individual expression in the arts has become pervasively impersonal and, divorced of accountability for meaning, *appears* to be a larger social expression. Artists who adopt the rationale that they passively "reflect" society manage thereby to position themselves as universalists divorced from responsibility for values while still receiving society's accolades for their individualist expressions.

The contradictions in this position are exposed to scrutiny when we enter the space of public art. Inherent in the phrase is a clash of intentions that is fertile ground for the exploration of the nature and purpose of art making. "Public" conjures up lofty ideals of collective expression and common good, such as those claimed by proponents of community theater; in today's culture this is seen to compete with private expression.

It is as intriguing as it is inevitable that once we have entered public space we question the relationship between monument and sculpture, newscast and video art, spectacle performance and produced mass media event. Are John Malpede's performances with the skid row group Los Angeles Poverty Department related to the media spectacle Hands across America? Is Maya Lin's Vietnam Memorial related to Richard Serra's "Tilted Arc"? Are Ant Farm's *Amarillo Tapes* (productions while in residence at a New Mexico television station) related to CBS news coverage?

In an exhibition at New Langton Arts Gallery in San Francisco in August 1988[12] monuments, memorials, and public artworks were exhibited by a mixture of artists and architects. In a politically charged panel discussion, the artists' fundamental assumptions and values were questioned. The public nature of the works and the intention of their makers to go beyond individual expression gave rise to the possibility of an aesthetic critique united with political intentions and social effects.

On that panel I proposed a model to deconstruct common elements of public art works:

MODEL FOR ELEMENTS IN PUBLIC ART

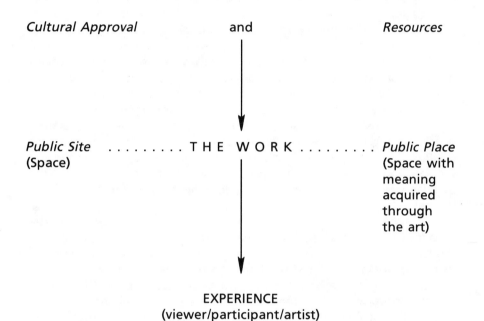

Cultural Approval   and   *Resources*

Public Site . . . . T H E W O R K . . . . *Public Place*
(Space)   (Space with
                                               meaning
                                               acquired
                                               through
                                               the art)

EXPERIENCE
(viewer/participant/artist)

(Rituals of preparation,
consecration and observation)

Public . . . . MEANING . . . . Private
(Shared)   (Personal)

Cultural Approval and Resources

Whereas a work of individual art executed in the studio needs approbation only after its creation in order to move into an exhibition space, a public artwork must rely from its very inception on some degree of cultural approval. That is, for a work to be made in the public sector (except for extremely transient and guerilla works), it must enter a negotiating process with those who represent that sector. These negotiations can be complex and lengthy, as well as involving hundreds of people, as in Christo's *Running Fence.* Other art exists through tacit community agreement, as with an often-commandeered billboard on the side of Galeria de la Raza in San Francisco's Mission District. Nevertheless, a process by which the values inherent in the proposed work are aligned to some degree with those in the immediate community is the underlying factor predisposing placement of the work.

In some instances, artists take this negotiation to be an opportunity for expanding the effectiveness of their work and educating the public to its political and aesthetic intentions. Others go further and see this education as a structural component of the work itself—the social processional, one might say, leading to the unveiling of the tableau.

One measure of cultural approval is a very pragmatic one: the amount of resources dedicated to a work's execution. It is possible to infer an estimation of society's values from the resources awarded to its public works. Amalia Mesa-Bains, on the New Langton Arts Panel, pointed out that often artists whose political views represented women and minorities seemed to create more transient and smaller-scale works, a factor she attributed to resources and values rather than artistic vision.

In America, governmental resources awarded to public art are growing with Percent for Arts Programs and other forms of grants. The Art in Public Places category of the National Endowment for the Arts sets the standards for recognition and resource allocation of public art, thereby shaping concepts of the field. Funding is based, in large part, on a traditional sculptural model, albeit with a token concern for community. The NEA has the paradoxical but inevitable position of being both the major proponent for the development of public art and its limiting factor in the conceptualization of what is appropriately public. In light of the previously cited concern by Amalia Mesa-Bains, the agency's emphasis on the permanence of a work is troublesome and not in keeping with the ephemeral, transitory and performative character of our society or much of our contemporary art. The diversion of resources from impermanent and process-oriented work continues to direct our attention away from the very issue of community interest and the role of the public in art making that called this granting body into being.

Site

The first condition for either individually authored artworks or representative monuments is a public site—one prepared, through community education or preexisting significance, to take on heightened meaning as a result of the work placed there. In the case of monuments, a committee or agency determines the need and secures the sites appropriate to the social cause to be commemorated. Likewise, for publicly situated artworks, a committee or individual, often the artist, acts on behalf of the cause of "art" to secure a site.

In the very recent past we've seen a shift in artists' use of public space, from what may be termed the "plunk theory" of public art to the "chat-them-up theory." In the former method, a site is secured and a sculpture installed, thereby making it accessible to the masses. At a few very notable times, those masses responded negatively, although often it was merely with indifference, thus giving rise to the second theory. If Richard Serra, for example, had practiced this "chat-them-up" procedure, he might not have created the same dense controversy with his rusted steel work that bisected a New York City plaza. Serra's defense of individual artistic expression is at ever-increasing odds with the rise of interest in public and site-specific art, yet it remains an example of the major ethical polarity in the tension between self-representation and public representation.

In this second form of public art, artists work with the community; that is, in varying degrees they try their models out on the community, work with architects and city planners and are somewhat receptive to public feedback, as long as individual artistic expression is not compromised. Public art of this ilk attempts to interface traditional sculptural forms with the existing environment so that the audience "buys into" the work.

Coincident with both of these methods for procuring public sites has been a method of commandeering public space by unauthorized placement of work. This longstanding tradition of public art (frequently temporary because of its content and limited access to resources) is related to street theater, surreptitious postings and graffiti. Political convictions are frequently revealed in the subject matter, materials used and means of distribution.

Increasingly, we see examples in a variety of media of artists who center their inquiry on social processes.[13] Although generally these artists retain primary aesthetic control, the creative input of the community is discernible and plays a major role in locating the work and shaping the final presentation. Such artists function like community organizers as well as creative directors, developing sophisticated strategies for the coalescence of a variety of experiences, values and notions of appropriate forms. The securing, indeed often the choice, of sites for such work frequently comes out of or is incorporated into the rationale of the work.

However the site is secured, at some point before, during or after the placement of the work, significance is achieved and relationship— between work and site—occurs.[14]

Experience

The work of art (or monument) thus arrives in its public place, negotiated through the choice and significance of the site, cultural approval (or at least acceptance) and allocated resources. However much interaction may have already taken place, at its installation or performance and thereafter, we shall assess the response of the viewers/participants as a predicating condition of the work's meaning. It is in the space of the relationship between work and public that that experience takes place.

Yet here the dilemma stated previously becomes evident: How are we to gain access to that experience and, once having done so, believe in it? In an impasse that is an outcome of the media spectacle, we are left with extreme skepticism about the availability of authentic experience to the experiencer. Robert Morgan expresses this skepticism directly: "There is no way that we can isolate the situation of the spectacle apart from our lives; we can only be alert to the phenomenon and to the type of behavior which it implies; a sort of aggressive nonaction and a relatively mindless pursuit toward the deference of meaning."[15] Throughout the literature one finds references to the seeming inevitability of enforced passivity and voyeurism in the relation of the spectator to the spectacle.

We reinforce our own passivity when we unwittingly apply the preconditions of the media spectacle—the demand for constantly renewed novelty and increasing sensation—to sensibilities not sustained by ethical decisions. Novelty, or uniqueness, is taken as proof of authenticity. For example, we are drawn to support causes and candidates in what we suspect might be media manipulation of our emotional states, and our dilemma is confounded when we find ourselves needing ever newer information to continue the belief structure. Pervasive cynicism, which appears to be the only free-will response to society's spectacle, is the result of disbelief in experience, our own and anyone else's.

This skepticism infiltrates, even dictates, content in art making and art theory. It is an impasse, if not of our own making, at least one to which we contribute. According to Johannes Birringer, "The current hysteria of theory has itself assumed a fantasmatic character and thus contributes to the further abstraction or the denial of the decaying material conditions in the midst of the fictitious environments."[16]

Meaning

When thousands of visitors arrive to stand, each year, before Maya Lin's Vietnam Veterans Memorial, with its seeming unending scroll, a powerful ritual of naming is enacted, individual experiences occur and collective meaning is generated. The controversy surrounding the work's creation was but the awareness that such generation of meaning would take place and that it might have political implications. It is quite possible that no one knew for sure exactly what the nature of that meaning would be; rather, it was the knowledge that a relationship *would* occur among the work, its place and the viewer. It was the fear of unmediated, unpredictable, authentic experience, for out of such response ethics are sharpened, and action might ensue.

The first mandate for attributing meaning to a work of public art is to recognize that meaning-making is a shared activity between artist and observer. To the degree that participation takes place, experience will be evoked. When art arrives at its public site ready for a fresh and unexpected encounter, it posits the relationship among the artist, the observer and the temporal community that occurs via the artwork as the primary source of energy. Clearly this approach demands a leap of faith, a belief that nonmediated voices can be heard, felt deeply and trusted.

An essential and predisposing condition for such a relationship to develop is the artists' assumption of authorship. This encompasses not merely who did the work, but what point of view is expressed. The contemporary tableau makes ethical and aesthetic positions available to the viewer who enters the engagement, and it is our task now to develop a language to assess this exchange.

If art making is meaning-making in its deepest sense, then art criticism is the description and pursuit of that meaning. Meaning will be found not simply within the aesthetics of physical form. Process, relationship, the positioning of the work relative to popular culture, the artists' beliefs and values—even, perhaps, the very way an artist lives life—all might be considered in an expanded inquiry. As Allan Kaprow stated, "Art is a weaving of meaning making activity with any or all parts of our life . . . what is at stake now is to understand that of all the integrative roles art can play, there is none so crucial to our survival as the one which serves self knowledge."[17] In the fractured space of our contemporary surround, integration is a rejuvenating act, and art making a metaphoric ground for the examination of public, private and mutual accountability.

Notes

This article was written with the support of California College of Arts and Crafts, "Making Space: A Conference on Women's Creativity" sponsored by the Focused Research Program in Gender and Women's Studies at the University of California at Irvine, and "Making Space," an exhibition and lecture series at the Presentation House Gallery in Vancouver, B.C. Thanks to Zante River for manuscript preparation, and to my dear friend Moira Roth for editing assistance.

1. *The Dark Madonna* (Suzanne Lacy, 1985–86) was sponsored by the Wight Art Gallery at the University of California at Los Angeles, under the directorship of Dr. Edith Tonelli. The soundtrack for the performance was composed by Susan Stone.

2. Among them I have consulted the works of Bonnie Marenca, Robert Morgan, and Arlene Raven.

3. Bonnie Marenca, *Performing Arts Journal* 10, no. 3 (1987): 25.

4. Roland Barthes paraphrasing Denis Diderot, "Diderot, Brecht and Eisenstein," *Image-Music-Text* (New York: Hill and Wang, 1977), p. 70.

5. Ibid., p. 73.

6. Ibid., p. 69.

7. Arlene Raven, "Commemoration: Public Sculpture and Performance," *High Performance* 8, no. 2 (1985): 37–38. Over the past several years Arlene Raven and I have exchanged ideas on the tableaux and pageant movement, its American history and contemporary implications. Her article in *High Performance* is a significant contribution to this evolving exploration and raises several interesting questions.

8. From an exhibition statement for "Monument and Memorial, An Exhibition and Public Forum on the Place and Forms of the Monument," curated by Nayland Blake for the New Langton Arts Gallery, San Francisco, August 1988. The show included works by Thomas Lucian Chytrowski, Michael Larson, Suzanne Lacy, Rudy Lemcke, Amalia Mesa-Bains, Richard Posner and Gretchen Bender.

9. During the last half of the nineteenth century, an obsession developed in parlors across America. After dinner entertainment with friends and family consisted of the enactment of elaborately staged, costumed and choreographed tableaux, whose themes ranged from fairy tales to religious allegories. Tableaux were seen as a way for "everyman" and woman to theatricalize their lives and paint great masterpieces with their bodies.

Because of their graphic and didactic nature, these tableaux often made moral, religious or social statements, representing charity, greed and so on. They were a way for people to affirm belief systems in a rapidly changing society. We might say these were aspirational and populist works, though their platitudinous nature is somewhat humorous to us today.

Along with this instructive and entertaining diversion there developed a pageant, or civic theater, movement that captured the sensibilities of tableaux makers and framed these as extravagant public theater. Cooperation among people of greatly varied backgrounds, socialization of foreigners into the American Way, the formation of a common and shared history, the perpetuation of belief systems and values— these were some of the goals of the community theater movement.

More than a few of these theater works were created with a radical end in mind, such as the Patterson Silkworkers Strike (1914), which was an actual strike transplanted into Manhattan by John Reed and his friends in order to capture media attention. The Woman's Peace Pageant (1913) featured Greek chariots, performers in togas, an operatic aria and hundreds of children with balloons, calling attention in the streets of Washington, D.C., to politics and World War I.

10. Michael Kelin and Robert Stearns, "Tableaux," *Tableaux, Nine Contemporary Sculptors,* Catalogue of the Contemporary Arts Center (Cincinnati, Ohio, 1982), p. 7.

11. Arlene Raven, p. 38.

12. See note 9.

13. One of the contemporary ironies for ethnic and other artists who have been working in communities for years is the continued devaluing of "community art" within a context of heightened interest in public art. The lack of recognition of aesthetic issues posited by the work of such artists rings all the more hollow as better established artists adopt content and sometimes forms of this work and, with more resources at their disposal, are hailed as models.

14. In an unpublished manuscript, Jeff Kelly describes this relationship as a transformation from site into place, which he suggests occurred during the sixties, partially as a result of the investigation by Abstract Expressionists of spaces first within, then outside, the canvas, gallery and studio; and during the seventies when, "At some moment . . . we crossed an important threshold—we moved, at least in our attitudes, beyond sites and into places. In the same way the terms 'earthworks' and 'site' were buried in the material and perceptual conditions of minimalist sculpture, so the term 'place' was implicit in what might be called the working conditions of sites. Emerging at first in artists' statements and NEA brochures about public art, 'place' soon required more rigorous definition by artists and critics who suspected—and whose personal experiences told them—that it meant something very different to be in a place than to be on-site."

15. Robert Morgan, "Performance and Spectacle in the Post-Industrial Age," unpublished manuscript (1988), p. 6.

16. Johannes Birringer, unpublished manuscript (1988), p. 2.

17. Allan Kaprow, "The Real Experiment," *Artforum* 25 (December 1985): 42.

Art in Public Places: Seattle

Matthew Kangas

Matthew Kangas reviews government-sponsored public art in Seattle over a period of thirty years. His focus on publicly approved projects without political or social impetus provides a contrast for the artistic explorations in the public domain that are discussed in the greater part of this book. His approach also makes clear the relationship between public art and changing times—the arrival or departure of new populations, civic and historical events, the creation of institutions, the turnover of ideas for bringing public art into existence—as manifested in one city.

The imposition of an artwork in a public setting, even within Seattle's acclaimed public art program, is never, according to Kangas, without a "glitch." In Nine Spaces, Nine Trees, for example, Robert Irwin failed to anticipate the effect of Seattle's annual nine months of rain. Puddles formed underneath the sculpture and became insurmountable barriers to foot travel between building and sidewalk.

Seattle's highly designed environment in the 1990s has been created partly by artists. But public works must now be maintained by the city at a massive expense. Artists accommodated the generous system by behaving professionally and being "repaid handsomely." In so doing, they may have unwittingly set a precedent for future public creators never to dare challenge the status quo. Such a stance is a far cry from the idealism that motivates most artists working in the public interest.

Introduction

Because the forms of art have evolved and diversified so dramatically in the last several decades, there is a disparity

> between contemporary artistic practice and public expec-
> tations of what art should look like.
> —John Beardsley, Art in Public Places, 1981

The extraordinary understatement above puts a brave face on a conflict-fraught activity, government-sponsored public art paid for by federal, state, city or county funds. For every success story—and I will argue Seattle is the biggest success story of all—there is a failure, a glitch, a fiasco or a tragedy related to choice or the subsequent imposition of an artwork in a public setting. Long after the authoritarian exercise of Renaissance or baronial patronage, public art administrators daily tread on shards of broken glass in efforts to ameliorate urban spaces, be true to artists' intentions for their work and appease often ignorant and occasionally enlightened politicians and citizen-member commissions.

The Seattle story could not have occurred everywhere. A youthful city history, an ambitious postwar generation of builders and managers, a setting of great natural beauty and a group of highly skilled public servants wanting a challenge all came together at the right time, around 1973, to put into motion programs matched at the county and state levels and resulting in literally hundreds of permanent and temporary projects to serve art in the public interest.

By and large, the public is pleased: With one or two notable exceptions discussed below, the ''disparity'' referred to above has been smoothed over by a mixture of careful community participation and preparation, a sensitivity to attaining the best possible work for the appropriate site and a civic consensus that paying for and supporting such art is the right thing to do.

The concatenation of circumstances that got the respective state, city and county arts commissions rolling built up over a period of two decades or more: As the city of Seattle grew, citizens from older American cities moved to the Pacific Northwest, bringing a sense of hope and reform, of caution and culture, which combined gradually through members' groups composed of artists, collectors and political activists whose policy recommendations eventually became law.

Part of a growing national trend, too, the programs, once in place, remained attentive to change and were flexible enough to reflect artists' own evolving philosophies about their roles in the civic environment. Thus, for example, the shift from stationary abstract-object sculpture to collaborative design teams occurred at the same time that the damaged idealism of the 1960s found channels for involvement among a small group of educated artists moving to Seattle in the mid-1970s. A plethora of projects ensued, aided by funding from the National Endowment for the Arts, which matched or supplemented local budgets.

Lest this sound too good to be true, the individually sited pieces and the design team collaborations also generated frequent controversy, especially from artists themselves, many of whom felt shut out by the new breed of professional public artists better attuned to what the cultural administrators wanted next, and better able to supply it, whether nebulous planning proposals, "objective" jury-panel participation or low-profile "site-integration" art wherein the art might be barely noticeable at all.

These dissenting artists' concerns were met head on by the commissions and staff persons who judiciously set up clever programs for purchases of "portable works" on an annual basis, for temporary performance-art or installation projects, even though by charter, none of them could officially commission nonpermanent works. Other funding sources were found. There was in Seattle, it seemed, something for everyone.

Nevertheless, the sheer volume of works by now completed, the amount of funds involved now and in the near future and the prospect of a variety of enormous projects contemplated through the end of the century have led a number of artists to concentrate on exclusively issue-oriented art, executed or installed in the public arena. Their projects are not the main focus of this essay, though they are dealt with briefly below because of the stark and humble contrast to the publicly approved achievements currently underway or planned. Rather, it may be more helpful and instructional to review the Seattle situation, remarkable because of an almost complete *absence* of politically or socially generated public art, in order to set into relief the explosion of artistic practice explored in the rest of this book.

Since the mainstream projects, given their skillful adaptation and evolution to society's needs, show no sign of slowing down, short of radical demolition legislation, Seattle's public art must be examined in light of how the artistic styles they represent reinforce or dispute Beardsley's notion of "disparity between contemporary artistic practice and public expectations." It may also be possible to determine whether Seattle has sought a "middle way" between vanguard taste and the philistines waiting beyond the gate. Either way, a chronological review citing the major legislations and what they led to will set the stage for the less conventional work under discussion in this book.

1960–1972: Fountains and a Fair

Though there was definitely public art in Seattle before 1960, much research remains to be done on that spotty, earlier era. The first public statue, a bust of the city's namesake, Chief Sealth, was installed at Pioneer Square, now a historic landmark district, in 1909. James A. Wehn, the artist, followed with a full-length bronze of the Suquamish chief three years later. Long before that, the shorelines and Indian villages were filled not with totem poles—those carvers lived farther to the north on Vancouver Island—but with long houses containing baskets woven of cedar bark.

Important downtown construction did not seriously begin until as late as the 1930s, twenty to thirty years after the reconstruction of Pioneer Square, which was initially destroyed in the Great Fire of 1889.

During the Depression, the New Deal administration of Franklin D. Roosevelt set up in Seattle, as elsewhere, make-work projects for artists. Under the direction of Robert Bruce Inverarity, another artist, newly arrived midwesterner Mark Tobey, along with other local artists—Kenneth Callahan (later the city's first art critic) and painter William Cumming—participated in the easel program. Few monuments were built except, for example, the murals by Jacob Elshin, a Russian emigré, at the University District post office. Few accounts of the period exist, though Cumming's memoir, *Sketchbook,* details the shattered political idealism and the warm personal relations among the group during the Depression.[1]

Across the city, construction projects such as hospitals, clinics and University of Washington buildings developed in the succeeding decade, but little thought was given to integrating art and architecture or even to making a place for an appropriate artwork after the building was finished. Seattle Art Museum founder Richard E. Fuller preferred to grace the exterior of his 1932 Bebb and Gould-designed *art deco* structure with Ming tomb guardian figures and two Chinese stone camels. Dudley Pratt, a university sculpture professor, provided bas-relief glazed terra cotta friezes for parts of the new university medical school, for Doctors Hospital (later Virginia Mason) clinic on First Hill and for the electrical engineering department on campus, the latter designed by Paul Thiry, the area's leading International-style architect, who would play an important role in designing the 1962 World's Fair tract.

A few years before the fair, the first really important work of art in a public place during the modern period, the *Fountain of Wisdom* (1960), was built at the new main branch of the Seattle Public Library.

The artist, George Tsutakawa, had been born in the U.S. but was sent to Japan for schooling as a boy. His return to the U.S. for higher education was followed by the beginning of World War II, during which he was a language expert for the U.S. Army.

His studies at the University of Washington School of Art in the preceding years firmly established him as a modernist,[2] and three crucial visits by Alexander Archipenko for seminars at the School of Art left a lasting impact on Tsutakawa's style. Though many critics and curators[3] have traced the Asian origins of the artist's hallmark stacked-volume forms, specifically to the Tibetan wayside shrines of piled rocks or *obos*, Archipenko's example was far more important and stood Tsutakawa in good stead for the next forty years. Put simply, the reversing of concave and convex forms so common to the Russian's cubo-constructivist imagery found an enthusiastic echo in the Japanese-American artist's evocation of nature and geometry. *Fountain of Wisdom* splashes water from three tiers of curved steel petal or hollow-sphere forms and spills into an oval pond filled with flat Pacific coast stones collected by Tsutakawa's children and transported inland to the library's grand entrance on Fifth Avenue. The curved forms contrast perfectly with the raked perpendicularity of the five-story modernist glass and steel building, and the sound of rushing water further echoes Seattle's saltwater and freshwater surroundings. The age of fountains was under way.

Without describing them all, it is important to note that, at this stage, there developed a healthy competition for fountain commissions between public and private builders, and Tsutakawa became the beneficiary of both. Whether a fountain (now destroyed) at the Northgate shopping mall or a memorial to prominent architect Floyd Naramore or to the *Seattle Post-Intelligencer* reporter Bobbi McCollum, Tsutakawa's fountains were scattered across the city, then throughout the nation, and finally coming full circle, into Japan. They set the stage for the acceptance of abstract-object sculpture, which they resembled when the water was turned off, and they emphasized the special nature of Eastern and Western art-style influences on Seattle, which had previously been thought the exclusive province of Westerners like Tobey and Morris Graves.[4]

Century 21 was the smallest international exposition ever organized (seventy-two acres) and the only one to make a profit. Again, the World's Fair architecture, such as the Coliseum, the craft center, the modern art pavilion, all designed by Paul Thiry, are worthy of an entire retrospective analysis of their own. Suffice it to say, ample arrangements were made for fountains, and Thiry himself designed two ungainly works built of solid concrete. A performing arts center was built for the international musical and theater troupes that visited during the fair. This complex forms the core of Seattle Center, converted from the fairgrounds after the event, and the eventual home of the Seattle Arts Commission.

A central circular pit lined in pebbled concrete with elaborate spray nozzles, the International Fountain was the result of a worldwide competition won by three young Japanese architects. A kind of self-contained *son et lumière,* the fountain had a complicated music-programming and lighting system.

The fountain mentality, which reached its apex during the fair, was a double-sided issue for public art and a phase or vogue for the city rather than a long-lasting commitment. Leading steel and bronze sculptors were increasingly being invited to create single-site works—so long as a plumbing system could be hooked up and the waterworks turned on. Thus, Everett DuPen's largest public commission, the fair's *Creation of Man,* sat on a pool of water beside the Coliseum and squirted at intermittent intervals. Similarly, another Yale man, James FitzGerald (1910–73) embarked on a series of spouting abstract-expressionist bronzes after the success of *Northwest Fountain,* which graces the courtyard of the fairgrounds' resident theater playhouse.

It was as if the city could not make a commitment as a whole to nonfunctional, nonfountain public art. Even the only mural, a Venice-constructed glass mosaic by Paul Horiuchi, had to perform double duty as the stage backdrop for a moated amphitheater near the base of the Space Needle.

The only truly imaginative use of such constraints almost appeared to be a satire or parody of the city's fountain fixation. Jacques Overhoff, working for the fair's landscape architect Lawrence Halprin, designed and built an extraordinary assemblage of twirling sprinklers, faucets and pipes situated in the reflection pool directly beneath the Space Needle. Rapidly dubbed ''Plumber's Nightmare'' by a delighted public, the officially untitled work was never completely installed with all its possible appurtenances and, victim to the city's growing ''sophistication'' during the 1970s, was dismantled and eventually replaced by Alexander Lieberman's 120-foot-long *Olympic Iliad.* The parts for Overhoff's daring antifountain remain in storage.

By the end of the decade, 1969, the new Seattle-Tacoma International Airport was completed. The idea to include major works of art came from one of the participating architects, Gerald Williams of The Richardson Associates, and the results are still impressive today, long after many other airports such as San Francisco, Dallas and Atlanta have repeated the concept. Apart from the fact that it is one of the most compact and efficient airports in the world, with a minimum of walking or awkward staircases, Sea-Tac also used some of the first poured-concrete, circular-ramp parking garages.

Essentially a long curved rectangle with spokes leading out to satellite terminals, the main area was divided in half length-wise. Nearest the parking garage side, airline ticket counters and baggage handlers run the entire length. Parallel to that, near the satellite spokes, a series of quiet lounges, giftshops, newsstands and restaurants honeycomb the other side. It was in this area that the artworks were sited. The sense of pleasant surprise at seeing art upon arrival was one goal, and an ameliorated environment for those awaiting either arrivals or departures was the other.

Thus, a Frank Stella painting from the *Protractor* series has a prominent position, while a black wall by Louise Nevelson nestles darkly in an adjacent lounge. A seventy-five-foot-long Op art mural, *Spectrum Delta II* by Francis Celentano, embraces another lounge wall, although it is punctuated—or marred—by two structural posts before it. The centerpiece of the collection, *Central Plaza Sculpture* by Robert Maki, is a combination of gray-painted, angled aluminum walls, which symbolically create a shelter space appropriate to the airport's architectural meaning and typical of Maki's softened, human approach to geometry. Other works by Alden Mason, Jonn Geise and Chris English, as well as two stained-glass windows by Dick Weiss added in 1988, complete the collection.

A few years before, in 1967, the federal government, through the newly formed National Endowment for the Arts, established the Art in Public Places grant program. Under the initial stewardship of visual arts program head Henry Geldzahler, Seattle became the second city after Grand Rapids, Michigan, to receive a grant.[5] Within two years, coinciding with the Sea-Tac project, Isamu Noguchi's *Black Sun* (1969) joined the Ming Tomb guardians and stone camels in front of the Seattle Art Museum. Thus was begun a series of mostly black, single-site sculptures that would increasingly dot the city as noticeably and repeatedly over the next decade as the fountains had during the preceding one.

First, however, the mechanisms—legal, civic, and bureaucratic—had to be put into motion. Building on recommendations by a citizens arts-activist group, Allied Arts of Seattle, and an artists' coalition, The Artists Group (TAG), Mayor Wes Ulhman created the appropriate agency, Seattle Arts Commission, first headed by John Blaine. Executive-appointed, unpaid citizen members made up the first commission and were soon joined by a few professional staff members, including former Seattle Art Museum employee Anne Focke, who would go on to found the city's first alternative contemporary art space, *and/or*.

By 1973, Seattle joined Baltimore, Philadelphia and Honolulu by passing landmark 1 percent legislation. One percent of all civic capital construction budgets and bond issues would go to art. A parallel King County arts commission also passed a 1 percent law and was in turn followed one year later, 1974, by state arts commission legislation calling for 1/2 percent to be devoted to art. The state became one of the few to include a percentage of public school construction budgets for art as well.

It soon became clear to the young Seattle Arts Commission that not all the monies generated by municipal works projects originating chiefly in the city light and water departments could or should reasonably be spent on outdoor art. Today there are four categories of visual arts expenditure: the portable works collection; specific single-site commissions; the architect and artist design teams; and the latest, "special projects," a hybrid between design-team collaborations and specific-site commissions. Over the next decade, portable works purchases led to a collection, routinely circulated through city-owned buildings, of over two thousand paintings, photographs, sculptures, craftworks and other objects in a variety of media. Though the spotlight of attention has gone to outdoor commissions, it could be argued that the biggest safety valve for defusing art community dissatisfaction over the fewer and larger commissions has been the annual purchase awards (sometimes totalling $100,000 to $200,000) of smaller works for city offices and department headquarters. Not restricted to Seattle resident artists alone, the collection also includes works by former Seattle or Washington state residents such as John Cage, Chuck Close, William T. Wiley, Merrill Wagner and Michael Lucero.

1973–1984: The Plaza vs. the Planners

Under the guidance of art in public places coordinator Patricia Fuller and her successors Richard Andrews, Lyn Kartiganer and Diane Shamash, Seattle developed the concept of a collaborative process between architects and artists that would later become a model for the nation.[6] Partly growing out of the idealism of certain artists whose faith in reform or revolution had been shattered by the late 1960s, the artist-design team program provided a mode of reentry into mainstream society and a way to have a tangible impact on the political and municipal environment. Though it would be a long time before the traditional abstract-object or, to put it more crudely, the "plaza plop" approach, wore out, the golden age of public art in Seattle actually became a cooperative program between both visions, the monolithic and the dispersed. Instead of bringing in the artists after the architects had "done their damage," the argument went, why not invite them at the beginning to see how they could *influence* the entire outcome?

Viewlands/Hoffman hydroelectric power receiving substation, built for City Light, was the pilot project for the architect-artist collaborations and, in many respects, this award-winning job remains the most successful and nationally acclaimed. Artists Sherry Markovitz, Andrew Keating and Buster Simpson worked with architects Hobbs/Fukui and David Rutherford over a three-year period to plan, create and decorate a two-square-block area in a northern working-class neighborhood. In a way, the artists arrived too late to have all the influence they would have desired, but the trio nonetheless transformed an unremarkable building project into a sightseeing attraction by adopting a comical pastel color scheme, or "mass palette," as Keating described it, and, among other things, commissioning sixty wind vanes by an elderly Grand Coulee, Washington, couple, Emil and Veva Gehrke, to be displayed in a cyclone-fence-enclosed sculpture garden. In 1988, the three returned to the site, courtesy of the arts commission, to repaint, restore and rearrange the centerpiece of the neighborhood and the diamond in the crown of the city's design-team innovations.

Less fortunately, the next substation, Creston-Nelson, though a beautiful high-tech contrast to Viewlands/Hoffman, was built in an even worse neighborhood near the city's southern limits and has fallen victim to a rare occurrence in Seattle, the vandalism of public art. Sculptors Clair Colquitt, Merrily Tompkins and Ries Niemi created whimsical structures such as a monumental mosaic head of Nikola Tesla, the electricity-coil theorist and inventor, a giant stacked totem of tinted concrete outlet plugs, and an aluminum bench tracing the breakdown of electric power from dam to domestic consumers. All three have been seriously damaged, repaired, reinstalled and subsequently revandalized.

Though a spate of remodeling projects on fire stations, libraries, and police stations generated several design-team collaborations during the early 1980s, none attained the power of Viewlands/Hoffman or Creston-Nelson, perhaps because they involved preexisting structures. And a county project, the new downtown jail by architects Naramore, Bain, Brady & Johanson, was radically scaled down after a public uproar over the prospective $600,000 out of $60 million that theoretically could have been spent on art. Instead, two attractive but rather tame projects grace the exterior entrance, the only area eventually allotted for art. Martha Schwartz' *Jailhouse Garden* was finally dedicated in 1987, joining Benson Shaw's *Torus, Torum II* (1984), a cast-concrete relief mural of interlocking geometric patterns which unhappily reminded many of chains.

Once Richard Andrews joined the SAC staff as art in public places coordinator, Fuller's design team darlings took a backseat to a revival of single-site, abstract-object sculpture by artists of mostly national repute. With the exception of Andrews' National Oceanographic and Atmospheric Administration (NOAA) sculpture park at Sand Point, billed as a design-team project but hardly collaborative in the original Seattle sense, high modernism seemed to make a comeback with five major works. Not equally successful in siting or internal aesthetic content, the metal or stone works epitomize the impersonal plaza style. Abstract-modern sculpture seems to have many lives, like Dracula, and is definitely in Seattle's near future as well.

After the success of the Noguchi at Volunteer Park, another piece by the artist was arranged, this time by the General Services Administration (GSA) for the Second Avenue entrance to the new Federal Office Building. *Landscape of Time* (1975) is far less successful because the architect Fred Bassetti insisted on integrating the five stones into an Italianate brick paving-stone sidewalk, thereby robbing the piece of any autonomy.

A similar problem occurred with Lloyd Hamrol's *Gyrojack* (1979), built with NEA funds as the pendant in an urban minipark at Third Avenue and Bell Street. Rather than siting the stacked, poured concrete circular ramps on a platform or plinth of its own, the architect John Ullman planted grass around half of it to ''wed'' it to the rest of the park. Though it has been used as a stage for contemporary dances, *Gyrojack*'s home, Regrade Park, had to be closed and remodeled in 1987 because it had become the exclusive province of poverty-level, alcoholic native peoples.

Shortly before the Hamrol dedication, another work encountered difficulty. It was *Adjacent, Against, Upon,* installed at the new Myrtle Edwards Park by Michael Heizer. The public outcry over the Heizer piece, fueled and stirred by daily newspaper columnists rather than art critics, was sudden, brutal and troubling.[7] Three large stones, quarried in the Cascade Mountains, were placed adjacent, against and upon polygonal concrete plinths in a thin shoreline park setting on Elliott Bay, north of the Pike Place Market and waterfront area. The shock may have had more to do with the scale and the strength of the piece than with any inherent hostility toward public art because, by 1980, television commentators were comparing it favorably with newer works, and within ten years it became one of the most popular works of art in public places within the city.

Less harmonious though definitely assertive, *Black Lightning* (1981) by the late Ronald Bladen, was another pet project of Andrews'. One more black-painted steel work, a zig-zag on two stunted vertical posts, *Black Lightning* bluntly commands the space before the Flag Plaza Pavilion at Seattle Center and is a forbidding sight in midwinter. During the rest of the year, it seems oddly placated by banks of flowering impatiens with dozens of daisies beyond. The only site relation which might save the piece from itself is the proximity of the Coliseum, where heavy-metal rock concerts frequently give *Black Lightning* a perfectly appropriate setting and appearance. On those evenings, it resembles the necklaces or leather-jacket decorations of the concert-goers waiting in line next to it.

Not surprisingly, Richard Andrews went on to head the visual arts program for a few years at the National Endowment for the Arts. He was so successful at raising money for his Seattle projects that he became a natural candidate for running the national program and further implementing his own views on the collaborative team approach. Before he left Seattle, however, he oversaw two other projects which were mixed successes, *Nine Spaces, Nine Trees* (1983) by Robert Irwin and the sculptures at NOAA by Siah Armajani, Scott Burton, Doug Hollis, Martin Puryear, and George Trakas.

If the major development of the 1973–84 period was the shift from "plaza plop" art to artist-design teams, it could be argued that the Andrews position came right down the middle between the two "extremes." Avoiding the immersion approach of the artists on Viewlands and Creston but sidestepping the insensitive plunking down of one work in one plaza, Andrews sought out a happy politically acceptable medium (which he subsequently took to Washington, D.C.). It could be that, in order to get the job done, this was necessary. It also could be that the kind of artist needed to successfully run the gauntlet of planners and architects did not yet exist in sufficient numbers.[8] Either way, the original impetus of the design-team notion was modified at NOAA, just as the older concept of the stationary, monolithic object in a plaza was challenged in the Irwin work.

Even though Robert Irwin spent a great deal of time contemplating the needs of the unattractive space at the old Public Safety Building, he neglected to appreciate one constant in the Seattle setting: rain. Nine months out of the year, city streets are wet, causing the puddles underneath *Nine Spaces, Nine Trees* to become enormous barriers between the building and the sidewalk. And even though Irwin put a great deal of consideration into the blue color of the cyclone fencing, that hue is not enough to overshadow the prisonlike aspect of the nine enclosures. The cement-potted plum trees he chose bloom only for a brief period each year and do not sufficiently transform the piece into something beyond its grudging and grim structure. Viewed from the window of the mayor's office on the twelfth floor of the municipal building across the street, *Nine Spaces, Nine Trees* has a bland, ordered quality. Seen from the ground on a dark afternoon of pelting rain, it is an utter failure, the arrogant and ugly stepchild of the art in public places collection.

As the NOAA project began, George Trakas claims to have "saved" the shoreline blackberry bushes from being torn out by the landscape architects, but that seems to be the extent of any artist's influence on the firm of Jones and Jones.[9] It was probably unrealistic to expect that five such busy and nationally established artists would be willing to attend as many meetings as local team artists like Andrew Keating, Buster Simpson, Barbara Noah, or Carolyn Law did in their various efforts to influence the course of the overall design structures.

Settling for half a loaf, the NOAA artists selected sites, drew up their plans, left town, returned for the building phase, oversaw the completion in some cases, were feted locally and left once again. As Barbara Swift, the landscape architect chosen to refurbish Regrade Park, pointed out in the only remotely critical assessment of the project, "the artists entered the project too late to produce a finely integrated effort."[10]

Since the total NOAA setting adjacent to Lake Washington and Magnuson Park covers over four hundred acres, one might have hoped for some startling and innovative collaborations. A mirror-faced administration building, sleek and technocratic, looks out onto the water, with four of the sculptures near the shoreline in sight and one, a cement berm by Martin Puryear, next to the other end of the building. Unfortunately, grassy slopes have been substituted for the urban plaza. Swift denies any relationship between the landscape forms and the artworks,[11] drawing attention to how siting and grading could have been more sensitively dealt with in the resulting artworks.

Scott Burton's *Viewpoint* features stone chairs on a gridded plinth, a "drawing room without walls"[12] elevated above the connecting path and punctuated with planters that contain flowers, shrubs, and trees that have barely survived the lakeside weather. Far from site-related, *Viewpoint* does not even take native vegetation into account but remains securely on the drawing board, environmental only in the sense of an opened-up domestic interior.

Trakas built *Berth Haven,* a wood and steel swimming dock, into something so functional as barely to seem art. More amusingly, the artist swears he returns annually to personally scrape seagull droppings from the rusted steel surfaces, so deep is his commitment to the site.[13]

Armajani seemed to confuse fresh water with salt water, affixing metal-letter phrases about the sea and whaling from Herman Melville's novel *Moby-Dick* onto the sides of two bridges over drainage ditches, or "swales." As Swift noted, "the [drainage] swales should have been more clearly articulated during the site grading to provide the sense of movement and passage."[14] Armajani's legendary dependency upon texts did not rescue *NOAA Bridges* from banality. Nor does the piece fulfill his vaunted exhortation to "begin a search for a cultural history."[15]

Only Doug Hollis' *A Sound Garden* took full advantage of object, function and unique site. Rising on a natural knoll, with both Armajani's bridges in sight, *A Sound Garden* conjures up a twenty-first-century entertainment, the creation of random musical sounds through the hollow columns of rotating metallic wind vanes. One approaches via a special triangular-brick paving path and perches on any of the steel mesh benches. Depending upon the velocity of the wind, the music whines or drones, whistles or screams. In a city where bad weather plays such an important role in everyday life, Hollis captured a positive spinoff effect of the constant rain or wind. Looking back at the grim, technocratic-looking building while the wind music plays creates an eerily appropriate sensation, like something out of Godard's film *Alphaville,* or Truffaut's *Fahrenheit 451.*

At the same time Andrews arranged a humbler but subtly effective project, the *First Avenue Tree Planting,* in Belltown, the city's disappearing artist quarter. A collaborative venture between the original design-team pilot project member Buster Simpson, Jack Mackie and two architects, Deborah Rhinehart and Paul Rhinehart, it is situated between the Pike Place Market to the south and Denny Way to the north. Belltown was long an area of merchant seamen's hotels, trade union headquarters, small manufacturing concerns, and by the 1970s, storefronts converted into artists' studios. Many of the city's leading younger artists like Simpson and Keating lived there for many years before being forced out by higher rents and the many condominium towers that now dot the neighborhood.

Andrews assembled local and NEA funds to allow Simpson and his colleagues to combine varied deciduous and evergreen trees planted on the sidewalks of First with Simpson's symbolic street furniture alongside. After several years of growth, the trees are peculiarly impressive. They act both as a legacy of the earlier artists' presence in the neighborhood and as a living reminder that cities need growing things, not just tall buildings sprouting up all over the place.

Drawing upon resources at a sandstone quarry in Wilkerson, Washington, Simpson brought down from the mountains large, barely hewn chunks of stone to be transformed in some cases into steps leading to nowhere in front of demolished buildings, mock classical columns on their sides to be used as benches for Metro transit stops, and in a variety of other ways. This was an extension of many earlier guerrilla art projects throughout the late 1970s and early 1980s, such as his Post Alley self-watering planters in the Market, his ingenious cherry tree birdfeeder using the "last cherry tree in Belltown," and a myriad of other barely perceptible constructions. Together, the projects transformed the street architecture of the area and gave it a unique character. Simpson's genius or "instant archeology" is one of the true assets to emerge out of the public art explosion and it was to Andrews' credit that he found a way to let the artist leave his imprint in a more enduring manner. It was also a way to bring art in public places to a low-income neighborhood frequented by the homeless and transient, two of Simpson's favorite audiences.

At the other extreme, up-scale consumerism, one project in the Seattle Arts Commission's special projects category, *Euphonic Metaphors II* (1981) by James Hirschfield, extended an earlier temporary project he did for *and/or.* Thin fishing line filament was stretched in planes at varying heights in an indoor space. The adaptation to a corporate lobby space, the atrium at Rainier Bank Tower, was a striking contrast to the plain white cube at *and/or.* Both were highly successful at radically altering a given interior with minumum material intrusion. The grand piano in the three-story atrium is often played by people passing through either to the building's offices or to the surrounding boutiques. Far from Simpson's beloved homeless, Hirschfield's yuppies encountered elegant, dematerialization of space, and illusionistic patterning depending upon the height of the viewer and the reflection of light on the taut filament. For both Simpson and Hirschfield, the aesthetic intervention involved already existing architectural structures. One artist chose the rough-and-tumble clutter of the urban street; the other moved indoors to offset or screen out the consumerist ambiance. Both turned their backs on the abstract-object in favor of the natural, the temporal, the evanescent visual experience, and the lower profile. In light of what was to come in the next few years, the memory of both their works attained a poetic delicacy and ecological frailty not likely soon to be equalled.

EUPHONIC METAPHORS II
James Hirschfield, 1981
Temporary installation at Rainier Bank Tower Atrium sponsored by Seattle City Light
1% for Art.
(Photo copyright © 1981 by Dick Busher)

1985–1988: Confronting the Changing Urban Scene

When Richard Andrews left Seattle to head the visual arts program at the NEA until 1987, his successors Lyn Kartiganer and Diane Shamash inherited a bundle of giant projects that are still underway today. Before reviewing the three major undertakings of this period—the Metro transit tunnel, Westlake Center and the state convention center—it is worth remembering how the portable works collection evolved for both the city and county commissions. Instead of putting out an annual call for photography one year, ceramics the next, and fiber the following, for example, both bodies independently decided to institute senior honors programs to commission major works from established artists. Amounts vary between $12,000 and $25,000 and will be raised as the programs progress. So far, the county has made awards to well-known figures like university painters Alden Mason and Boyer Gonzales, former Clyfford Still protege William Ivey and Guy Irving Anderson. Ceramist Robert Sperry has also been a recipient. Each artist chose his or her own site within a building owned by the county.

The city commission honors program began with a special project to supplement portable works already installed in the Seattle Opera House by Northwest masters like, again, Guy Irving Anderson, Mark Tobey, Morris Graves, and university modernists like Walter F. Isaacs, Wendell Brazeau, and Howard Kottler. Dedicated in 1986 were a nineteen-foot lobby painting, *Sargasso Stir* by Lois Graham; a pair of carved wooden reliefs near elevators by Jack Chevalier; a porcelain figure tableau depicting local artists by Patti Warashina; and a multipartite painting by Michael Spafford based on the Wallace Stevens poem "Thirteen Ways of Looking at a Blackbird." Each artist again chose his or her own setting within the building.

The first civic improvement bond allowed for the construction of a downtown tunnel in which diesel transit busses manufactured in Italy will convert to electric trolleys and stop at five major stations: Convention Place, Westlake Center, University Street, International District, and Pioneer Square. Beginning at the entry to the downtown area, busses will leave Interstate Highway 5 and enter near the newly completed Washington State Trade and Convention Center. At the first Metro station will be a series of integrated works such as a waterwall by Jack Mackie, above-ground marquee structures by Alice Adams and another work by Maren Hassinger. Next, passengers will ride to the core of the city's shopping precinct, Westlake Center. Below ground, three Seattle painters, Fay Jones, Gene Gentry McMahon, and Roger Shimomura, have designed figurative-narrative enamel-on-steel murals which reflect the commercial cacophony of the boutiques and department stores out-side. The subsequent stop will be near the new Robert Venturi-designed Seattle Art Museum, due to be completed in 1991. Vicki Scuri has designed wall and floor patterns which serve as a backdrop for light work sculptures by Robert Teepie and Bill Bell. Finally, at the International Station, two poems by Laureen Mar will be etched in stainless steel and placed on crossbeams of the trellis walkways.

Initial planning with architects was done by Mackie, Adams, Scuri, Kate Ericson and architect/graphic designer Sonya Ishii. Other artists involved in such elements as "electronic light works, . . . an Origami wall, and street improvements (such as entry gates, planter boxes, tree grates, and street clocks)"[16] are Garth Edwards, Jim Garrett, Brian Goldbloom, Virginia Paquette, Susan Point, H. Ramsay, Dyan Rey, Laura Sindell, and William Whipple. Completion is expected by 1990.

After over twenty years on the drawing board, Westlake Center, a privately developed shopping mall with an adjacent pocket park, was ultimately built by the Rouse Corporation, a fate Seattle had previously avoided but which had already befallen other American cities like Boston and Baltimore. One man, visionary architect, urban planner, and Market preservationist Victor Steinbrueck (1909–1985) fought for years for a completely open downtown central square park like Union Square in San Francisco—and lost. Mayor Charles Royer, a former television news anchorman, eventually called in Rouse who constructed a twelve-story office building at the north end with an indoor boutique mall below and a triangular park designed by landscape architects Hanna/Olin of Philadelphia at the south, Pike Street, end. Alice Aycock and Dennis Adams are providing spot decoration and amelioration for the remodeled Alweg monorail terminal near the boutiques.

At the other end, Robert Maki had a far greater impact on the designers for what is left of Steinbrueck's dream, the park between Pine and Pike. Over a period of years with successive plans being vetoed by the City Council, Hanna/Olin finally followed sculptor Maki's sug-gestions and the design was approved in 1986. It features a "water-wall," paving stone sidewalks in a Salish Indian weaving pattern, and Maki's seven-part dispersed red granite sculpture, *Westlake Star/Seven Hills.*

Farther uptown, the state convention center—a largely windowless concrete bunker bordering on Lawrence Halprin's Freeway Park which covers Interstate 5—was designed by The Richardson Associates, ar-chitects of Sea-Tac airport. Under the supervision of art in public places coordinator for the state, Sandra Percival, an extraordinary range of indoor and outdoor projects will come to fruition by the end of the

1980s. So ingrained is the site-integration idea by now that well-known artists like Jackie Ferrara and Jenny Holzer are designing, respectively, a lobby tile floor and a message sign for the escalator corridor.

Composer David Mahler has assembled *Centennial Bell Garden* to honor the state's one-hundredth birthday in 1989 by bringing together one church bell from each of the thirty-nine counties in the state, electronically wiring them to play at intervals and installing them along a walkway facing Pike Street. Coming full circle, Buster Simpson has devised *Seattle George,* a living ivy effigy of the state's namesake, George Washington, as a twenty-eight-foot-high entry portal connecting the south, window-side of the building to Freeway Park.

With all this construction, torn-up streets and maddening traffic rerouting, few people except artists like Glenn Weiss and Gerard Albanese noticed that the available downtown low-income housing in Seattle had shrunk from sixty thousand to six thousand in less than a decade. As a result, Nine One One director Weiss followed up a 1987 summer project, "Homes for Art"[17] (repeated in summer 1988)—artist installations in or on suburban homes—with a searing indictment of the city's development policies of "build and neglect," disregarding the homeless. During a week in November 1987 "Home Street Home" drew attention to the plight of the dispossessed with spray-painted slogans, sidewalk stencils, wheat-pasted accusatory posters, instigated street actions, and other activities. Creating temporary movable street sculptures, many of the artists attempted to protest the ongoing, massively dislocating construction projects discussed above, as well as recent landmark legislation (first in the nation) banning "aggressive panhandling" and the sales of fortified wines such as MD 20/20 and Thunderbird in downtown convenience stores regularly patronized by indigents. Media response was instantaneous and extensive.

Weiss and other artist participants like photographer Albanese and performer Susan Galligan had struck a raw nerve in the neverneverland of successful public art. It could be openly argued that while artists were benefiting from the bonanza, some people, mostly anonymous, were actually being hurt. By raising the issue, they built on the earlier "subliminal" art projects of Simpson in Belltown and expressed a sensibility of discomfort, unease, and anguish as the young city on Puget Sound prepared to gear up for the final decade of the century.

1991–2000: Endings and Beginnings

Although "Home Street Home" came as a rude shock to many, its sobering message may have been undermined in part by its very topicality. A permanent work built a few years before, *Veterans Lobby* (1982–1985) by Richard Posner, stands a better chance of sneaking political content into the realm of art in the public interest. In a remarkable sleight-of-hand, Posner made a glass entry wall or "glass hearth" for the new wing of the Veterans Administration Hospital on Beacon Hill. As one enters the vestibule, the 900-square-foot cast-glass wall appears to be a comforting burning fireplace. But as one leaves, the image viewed is of marching soldiers. Playing off the "swords to ploughshares" idea, Posner managed to comment on the war-related injuries treated at the VA and to instill a sincerely sympathetic domestic image of the burning hearth. The GSA paid for the work and there was not one whiff of outrage or outcry.

Peggy Holmes, the county's coordinator, is overseeing an enormous overhaul and expansion of the low-income public hospital Harborview Medical Center, which will continue until 1998. Phase One involves Vicki Scuri's exterior tire-tread patterns in cast, custom-form concrete for the five story Boren Avenue garage. Holmes is also anticipating a ten-year master plan to decide how to use vast unspent sums generated by the Kingdome. Though works were originally installed by Jacob Lawrence and Michael Spafford, among others, veteran local artist-planners Mackie, Ishii, and Hirschfield are seeking new sites within the 67,000-seat structure. A 225-acre county sculpture park near Sea-Tac airport is another possibility for county-owned land. It could build on the example of the nearby gravel-pit-turned-earthwork by Robert Morris, *Untitled* (1979).

As if the mega-projects of the late 1980s in downtown Seattle had not satiated the area's craving for public art, five future undertakings will insure frantic activity through the year 2000 at least. After a $400,000 feasibility study by Disney Imagineering calling for a $380 million revamping of Seattle Center, city council members are undecided about the former fairgrounds' fate. A new symphony hall at the very least seems assured, with the land recently donated, and existing per cent laws promise an elaborate role for art. Another likelihood is a municipal gallery to display or house the portable works collection, expected to grow to three thousand by 1999.

An international sculpture festival scheduled for 1991, *à la* Muenster or Documenta at Kassel, should bring thousands of visitors to Seattle to inspect extant public art as well as over thirty new permanent and temporary works specially commissioned for the occasion. Planned to coincide with the new Seattle Art Museum opening, the festival will highlight a single work chosen to sit before the museum's front door at the corner of First Avenue and University Street. Close to $1 million has been raised from public, museum, and private sources for the new museum sculpture and the festival as a whole.

Where does this leave us? Seattle will have a highly designed environment for which artists will share credit or blame. With the festival ahead, it seems the city has come almost full circle from fountain to abstract-modern object, to post-modern subliminal or dispersed, to artist-designed doorknobs and seats, and back to single-site works planned for celebrating the new museum. By the way, museum architect Venturi threatened to walk off the project if anything remotely resembling an artist design team was advocated for the museum. Finally, the crushing weight of all this art will require massive maintenance funds.

Will there be a backlash? None yet seems in sight but it could be that, in their rush to accommodate a generous system, public artists on the Seattle projects have set in motion a model for the artist's role in society during the next century: cooperate, collaborate, behave professionally, and thou shalt be repaid handsomely. It seems a long way from Duchamp's *Fountain* or Rodin's *Burghers of Calais* or art's idealistic challenging of the status quo with which the century began.

Notes

1. William Cumming, *Sketchbook: A Memoir of the Northwest School* (Seattle, Wash.: University of Washington Press, 1985).

2. T. Gervais Reed, "George Tsutakawa: An Introduction/A Conversation on Life and Fountains," *Journal of Ethnic Studies* 4, no. 1 (1976).

3. Bruce Guenther, *Documents Northwest: George Tsutakawa* (Seattle, Wash.: Seattle Art Museum, 1986).

4. Actually, earlier artists like Fujii, Kenjiro Nomura, and Kamekichi Tokita had painted in the style of Cézanne and other early modernists but their achievements were largely overlooked because of World War II and their subsequent and premature deaths related to experiences in the internment camps.

5. John Beardsley, *Art in Public Places: A Survey of Community-Sponsored Projects Supported by the National Endowment for the Arts.* Edited by Andy Harney (Washington, D.C.: Partners for Livable Places, 1981), p. 20.

6. See my "Artists on the Design Team: 3 Seattle Projects," *Art Criticism* 1, no. 3 (1981).

7. Beardsley, p. 79.

8. Nancy Joseph, "Artists on Design Teams," *Seattle Arts—Newsletter of the Seattle Arts Commission* (November 1983).

9. Conversation with author, Bellingham, Washington (August 20, 1987).

10. Barbara Swift and Robert Wilkinson, "The NOAA Artwork Program: Exploring Cultural History on a Shoreline Site," *Landscape Architecture* (Fall 1988).

11. Ibid.

12. Ibid.

13. Conversation with author, Bellingham, Washington (August 20, 1987).

14. Swift and Wilkinson.

15. Julia Brown, ed., *Siah Armajani* (Yonkers, N.Y.: The Hudson River Museum, 1987).

16. Jim Hirschfield and Larry Rouch, *Artwork/Network/A Planning Study for Seattle: Art in the Civic Context* (Seattle, Wash.: Seattle Arts Commission, 1984).

17. ''Seattle Homes are Homes for Art,'' *Seattle Arts—Newsletter of the Seattle Arts Commission* (September 1987).

18

Forward in an Aftermath: Public Art Goes Kitsch

Michael Hall

What has been the effect of the climate of permissiveness of the 1980s on public artworks? Michael Hall looks at the condition of public art today by focusing on recent public art activity in Detroit, an American city with its own art world microcosm.

The easy but indifferent reception of any and all efforts out-of-doors as public art has compromised artists' intentions and the artistic meanings of their works. Postmodernism has affected contemporary public art by accepting artworks and gestures based on imitation. And kitsch, claims Hall, is a system of imitation. The new kitsch in public can be commissioned or grassroots. But "we don't notice works of kitsch in the environment." Kitsch is easily assimilated.

For Hall, public art "in the aftermath" must be both original and dialectical. The alternative to kitsch is still art.

In June 1985, the city of Detroit initiated legal proceedings to resolve citizen complaints against an environmental "junk" sculpture assemblage built and maintained by a Detroit street artist named Rosetta Burke.[1] Three months earlier, in March, a regional arts administrator in New York had convened a hearing to consider citizen complaints against a steel site sculpture designed and installed in a Manhattan plaza by artist Richard Serra.[2] Almost a year later, in March of 1986, the City of Detroit dispatched a fleet of dump trucks and front-end loaders to Mrs. Burke's residence. For the next two hours, city workers proceeded to demolish and remove her two-block-long *Paradise*. Three months after this, the General Services Administration in Washington, D.C., constituted a panel to "relocate" Serra's federally commissioned 120-foot-long *Tilted Arc.*

By the end of August 1987, an aging Rosetta Burke had been placed in a foster home far from the house she had lived in amidst the assemblages she sometimes referred to as "a catalogue of the professions of man." Her neighbors felt themselves well rid of her "catalogue." To them, it had been only a nuisance and a health hazard. Sanitation Department administrators barely recall its removal. In the same summer, an embittered Richard Serra was denied the appeals and suits he had filed to block his *Arc's* removal. Government officials had become convinced that the New York public perceived the structure more as an eyesore and an obstruction than as a work of art. Serra and his supporters from the art world argued vainly that the *Arc* was an innovative piece of sculpture sited to aesthetically challenge the viewers moving past it in the plaza.

Somewhere in a swirl of events, bracketed by the Burke and Serra affairs, an era passed. Street art in the state, and state art in the streets, had reached limits that would radically reformulate the politics, aesthetics and, indeed, the whole concept of public art in America at the end of the century. In this aftermath, a certain hollowness seemed to ring in Sam Hunter's confident 1985 proclamation that "In the seventies the triumph of the new public art was firmly secured."[3] In this same aftermath, the popular adage about beauty being in the eye of a beholder broadened to embrace David Hume's contention that it exists in the *mind* of the beholder.[4] "Seeing" in the late 1980s (at least as it pertains to the perception of public art) has inclined almost everyone to reexamine the mythopoetic concept of the "popular mind." New claims of "triumphs" are now tempered by rethought social expectations and reformulated political strategies.

A look at the condition of public art today should begin with a survey that can be focused and put in the perspective of a post Burke/Serra milieu. For such a focus, I suggest an inspection of recent public art activity in Detroit. As a study model, Detroit is, in many ways, a typical American city, complete with its own American art world microcosm. Despite critic Robert Pincus-Witten's reference to the Detroit art scene as "Islands in the Blight,"[5] there is much transpiring in Mrs. Burke's hometown to illustrate poignantly the forward position of public art in the aftermath.

In a decaying neighborhood on Detroit's east side, a thirty-four-year-old black artist has begun transforming abandoned houses and vacant lots with sculpture installations and architectural embellishments fashioned from discarded tires, oil drums, furniture and toys expressionistically polychromed with bright enamel paints. The artist, Tyree

Guyton, was recently featured in an issue of *People* magazine, where he was heralded as "the Rembrandt of refuse, the Giotto of junk."[6] *People* photographed Guyton (paintbrush in hand) in front of one of his works and splashed a caption over the photo proclaiming that this artist "transforms trash into murals and crack houses into ghetto galleries."[7] Tyree's family and neighbors speak out strongly in favor of his right to engage in the activity they call his "self-expression." Since the media began spreading the story of the social importance of what he has done, Guyton reports that he has been invited to recreate his Heidelberg Street facelift in several urban neighborhoods far from Detroit. New Morning, Mrs. Burke.

Downtown, Detroit's Transportation Corporation recently inaugurated its People Mover Monorail System. The system's elevated tram traverses 2.9 miles of track connecting thirteen stations dotted around the city's central business district. Riders need wait only about three minutes between trains. The futuristic stations where they wait are festooned with murals and sculpture for their viewing pleasure. In all, fifteen artists (some local, some from out of town) were commissioned to produce the artworks for the People Mover stations. Their activities were funded by a broad coalition of private donors, corporate sponsors, arts institutions, government agencies and the Transportation Corporation itself. Installed without protest and, as of yet, ungraffitied, the art in the stations has encouraged Michigan public art advocates to be optimistic about the future of similar projects now being proposed for other architectural sites throughout the state. New Morning, Mr. Serra.

Finally, on a traffic island where the main north-south avenue bisecting Motown intersects the main east-west boulevard overlooking the river that separates the United States from Canada, Detroiters view a new civic monument. Sculptured by Robert Graham, the piece is an homage to the city's great boxing champion, Joe Louis. The work was presented as a gift to the people of Detroit by *Sports Illustrated* magazine. The monument heroically commemorates Louis' knockout punch in the form of a gargantuan bronze forearm and fist suspended by cables in a structural pyramid. Like some great four-ton battering ram, the fist thrusts horizontally out toward cars passing between it and the riverfront. Up the street, an earlier commemorative statue titled *The Spirit of Detroit* sizes up the new heavyweight on the block. New morning, Gutzon Borglum—but then, the sun never really sets over your Mount Rushmore, does it?

Something is surely going on. Detroit's new morning dawns in the midst of a hiatus. Outrage, complaint, hearings, controversy, even plain old skepticism, are all suspended in the ambiance surrounding current public art installations. Things unthinkable in the old order don't even raise an eyebrow in the new. Imagine: A lone street artist sets up shop as a city planner and launches a major neighborhood revitalization without even so much as an environmental impact study. More incredibly, an army of academy-trained sculptors and painters descend on a city's tram stations to transform them into an Alhambra of ceramic, bronze and neon, while a gaggle of corporations line up to pay them to do it principally because one determined taste maker insists that it's a good thing to do. Wildest of all, a popular sports journal throws a bronze right jab into the midsection of a city in a fixed fight paid off in monopoly money. Something, it seems, moves in the land to gather all manner of art productions and to contextualize them blithely as public art. In this context, they become fixed in a homogenized social perception altogether indifferent to the creative motivations and aesthetic dispositions of artists or, for that matter, to the meaning and cultural usefulness of any given project as art.

What, we ask, precipitates this new climate of accepting indifference? Could we finger simple lack of public interest? This seems doubtful given the traditional American habit of social/political activism. Fatigue then; perhaps some malaise has infected a public exhausted from too many art skirmishes on the aesthetic frontiers opened by state and federal funding over the past two decades. Unlikely again, given the American "never say die" temper. Preoccupation with other issues? Maybe, but again, there is ample historic evidence to show that even with a host of distractions, Americans monitor their culture with a vigilant compound eye that is difficult to divert or blind.

If we look beyond the obvious, a more plausible and provocative answer offers itself. The new public art may simply have evolved into a panstylistic form of kitsch. If this is the case, Detroit's new art would fail to elicit response precisely because, as Harold Rosenberg stated in 1959, kitsch art for the sensibility has "that arbitrariness and importance which works take on when they are no longer noticeable elements of the environment."[8] Perhaps inadvertently emulating current trends in product design. Today's artists and the public have collaborated in the invention of "user friendly" art—an art that need only be consumed to have been useful.

The bibliography on kitsch, though small, is, nonetheless, filled with serious and considered speculations. Cultural observers writing on kitsch concern themselves with objects and activities generated in what they identify as "systems of imitation"—systems in which gestures are produced that displace meanings and transform syntaxes. As the term "kitsch" applies to objects per se, it refers less to things that might be tacky or tasteless than to things typified by a certain bogus character. The kitsch object is not always easy to identify for it has a life of its own and engages all of us in various social, intellectual and sensory relationships. Kitsch is principally differentiated from art because, unlike art, it exists in a realm "which does not accept the nature of things in the light of their critical or revelatory attributes, but to the extent which they cover and protect, relieve and console."[9] With this in mind, we can seriously ask whether or not the whole enterprise of public art may have slipped into the condition of kitsch. In this condition, the new shaping of the public environment would leave that environment essentially shapeless.

The political implications of public art as kitsch are problematic. One of the fundamental assumptions in the concept of public art is that art has a message. Consequently, public art sponsors, expecting the art they support to carry a message, frequently turn to kitsch to accomplish their purposes. The problem, as Hermann Broch pointed out in 1933, is that "we cannot say that all art which contains a message is kitsch, although the system of imitation—as represented by kitsch—is well suited to being subordinated to extra-artistic purposes."[10]

Traditionally, Americans have been rather smug on the subject of kitsch, believing that it infects the art of totalitarian regimes rather than that produced by democracies. In 1939, Clement Greenberg stated that "the main trouble with avant garde art and literature, from the point of view of fascists and Stalinists, is not that they are too critical, but that they are too 'innocent,' that it is too difficult to inject effective propaganda into them, that kitsch is more pliable to this end."[11] Greenberg, of course, was right, but the world of 1939 was not the world today—a world where kitsch infects artlike productions far more subtle than heroic Nazi statuary. The contemporary problem entails an assessment of kitsch as a system of imitation in an art world where art has been given the permission to imitate not only other art but a host of non-art gestures all based on imitation—in short, the art of the world we call "postmodern."

The present argument need not digress into a defense or a condemnation of postmodernism—ample discourse on this subject already exists. What we should note, however, is that postmodernism in art and architecture grew out of a socioaesthetic permission that is very specific to our present time in history. Postmodernism, as critique, as style, and as a mode of thought, permeates contemporary culture. Hence, it affects the condition of contemporary public art.

Fermenting in the postmodern brew, there is a form of intellectual bricolage that proceeds logically from certain philosophical and linguistic deconstructions of late modernism. By disecting and bisecting modern culture, linguists and critics isolated a veritable storehouse of signs ready to be recycled in new syntactic systems. Once modernism had been outmoded as a primitive syntax (and accordingly set aside), its grammar melded into a larger historic archive essentially available to us all as a reference. This may not have necessarily been untimely or inappropriate. Late modernist public art had become predictable and ripe for retirement. Its successor, however, runs the gamut. Liberated from its historic base, postmodern public art risks losing its power to engender wonder (and anxiety) in favor of becoming simply absurd, "because what is missing is precisely that power of meaning that the syntactic system gives to the true work of art."[12] In the present moment, public art (in fact, all art) risks becoming kitsch if it proceeds from circumstances where "there is no new formative act in the system of imitation; the irrational is not clarified, the cognitive aspect is still confined to the sphere of the finite, and there is only a substitution of one rational definition for another rational definition."[13]

In the new "art speak," then, who is formulating the new grammar? It would be easy to hint at dark schemes plotted out by political necromancers and entrepreneurs. It would be equally easy to inveigh against an emerging new fascism, where public kitsch signals the last stage of a cultural disintegration. Let's not! Without becoming skeptics or Pollyannas, we could accept the new kitsch as a sign of a time. The signs are there—it is the times that need looking at. Who in our time is buying and selling systems of imitation—and why? The answer is that we all are. We all participate in a culture that has grown rich transferring and appropriating ideas, strategies and technologies. We should not, then, be surprised to find "single elements or even whole works of art 'transferred' from one status and used for a different purpose from the one for which it was created."[14] Such transference is commonplace in our media world. In film, the "real" character of an actor is always eclipsed by some set of superficial characteristics created by a director and edited into the imitation that becomes the screen character. It is certainly not by chance that in our time Ronald Reagan became "the first professional actor selected by corporate media interests to represent its interests to become ruler of a nation."[15]

Faithful to this paradigm, the art world imitates the real world. In the postmodern period, Bauhaus design transforms into corporate trademarks, the alienated Abstract Expressionist painter transforms into an official culture hero, and Pop superstar Andy Warhol deliberately inverts the historic humanist posture of the artist with his statement,

"I want to be a machine." The trend is not new. Dan Graham documents the almost immediate 1950s media assimilation of the Abstract Expressionist espousal of art as self-expression divorced from explicit social content. "Although the artist still believed that the meaning of his work was determined solely by his uncompromised, subjective intuition, market and media forces were, in fact, giving the work a different meaning—a meaning which was beyond the artist's control."[16] Today, the imitations and transferences Graham describes have accelerated to levels unknown and unimagined in Jackson Pollock's time and in their acceleration and convolution have spawned the new kitsch.

Consider the Detroit model again. All the players are in place and Detroit's game is "The Game." To find the common kitsch denominator in Detroit's new array of public art is to find the commonality in that which otherwise overlaps only coincidentally. In a nutshell, Detroit's contemporary street art and state art all conform to panstylistic norms of imitation—imitations of art, politics and history. We would find this pattern consistent throughout the United States today.

Tyree Guyton's Heidelberg Street assemblages transform in all three arenas. Despite his somewhat novel use of tires, doors, toys and mannequins, Guyton, as a sculptor, replicates a form of assemblage now at least half a century old. He learned well the modern design and sculpture lessons taught in the art school he attended. In its orthodoxy, his expression is neutralized both by internal flaccidity and by the external social forces determined to exploit its familiarity and malleability. A certain soft-core "Keinholtzian" look typifies a Guyton assemblage but, unlike a Keinholtz, a Guyton is neither threatening nor potent—politically or aesthetically. A stroll down Heidelberg Street (despite the rawness of Detroit's East Side) recalls a stroll down the main street of Disneyland. Guyton, like Disney, delights, entertains and beguiles with his fantasy facades.

Nonetheless, "crack house to fun house" is something that city hall is not going to miss a chance to exploit politically. In a recent memo, the director of the Detroit City Planning Commission requested that the director of the city's Department of Buildings and Safety rescind its order to destroy one of Guyton's made-over houses. The memo declared that the house should no longer be slated for demolition as an abandoned building because an artist had "made the house a work of art."[17] Can one bureaucrat convince another that the maintenance of an "Arte Povera" Magic Kingdom can precipitate social reforms? The answer is probably "yes," especially in a political vacuum where any stand-in for innovation is worth a shot. Plus, after all, Guyton's

ASSEMBLAGE AT 3670 HEIDELBERG STREET
Tyree Guyton, 1988
Wood, found objects, and paint. Detroit, Michigan.
(Photo by Michael Hall)

labors come to the city essentially free and demolition moratoriums themselves can always be rescinded.

Beyond art and politics, Guyton's work has reached the academic world. A scholar involved with Afro-American history has cited the constructions on Heidelberg in defense of his argument that Kongo visual culture survived American slavery. Guyton's repeated incorporation of tires in his assemblages presumably evokes an ancient circular Kongo cosmogram. His painted triangles and crosses are interpreted similarly. Insofar as they imitate various Kongo signs, Guyton's marks and structures will have an audience of historians ready and able to displace them for their own needs. As vernacular witness to the popular acceptance of assemblage as sculpture, as social/political activism and as academic argument on the transgenerational transplantation of culture, the bricolage on Heidelberg Street seems to be a triumph. Alas, wherever Tyree Guyton's art is of concern, we find syntactic displacements that indelibly bear the mark of kitsch.

And what of the art in the People Mover stations? Like the Heidelberg promenade, it also becomes an Adventure Land for the senses—this time with a twist of Epcot Center hi-tech thrown in. It too intertwines history, art and politics in a matrix of imitation, but this time under the umbrella of formal commission. The concept for the People Mover project came from a prominent citizen-cum-arts-booster who turned a private vision into a civic cause. Her campaign began at city hall and then proceeded into the community where corporations, private patrons and several arts councils were persuaded to contribute the $2.5 million necessary to commission and install the station murals and sculpture. The realized People Mover projects demonstrate that guerrilla art promotion is as effective in high places as it is on Heidelberg Street.

For the People Mover's Michigan Avenue station, sculptor Kirk Newman produced fourteen bronze relief figures depicting people caught in the hectic crush of commuter life. With their hats askew and their briefcases flying, Newman's businesspeople race to catch their trains. His cast of characters jostle and tumble up and down the wall alongside the escalator leading from the street to the elevated station platform. The success of this work may be in its whimsical quality as caricature, but today's real commuters and city dwellers experience urban life as something fraught with stress and anxieties that have little to do with merely catching trains. In an anxious world, Newman trivializes angst. He finds his art "People Mover acceptable" precisely because it imitates rather than expresses the tensions of a time.

ON THE MOVE
Kirk Newman, 1987
Bronze. Michigan Avenue Station—The People Mover,
Detroit, Michigan.
(Photo by Michael Hall)

NEON FOR THE GREEKTOWN STATION
Stephen Antonakos, 1987
Multicolored free form neon. Greektown Station—The People Mover,
Detroit, Michigan.
(Photo by Michael Hall)

At the Greektown station, Stephen Antonakos bedecked the concourse between the waiting platform and a shopping/restaurant complex with several groups of calligraphic multicolored neon shapes. Antonakos, a formalist with a Minimalist bent, conceived his project with the sculptural clarity and surety of design that has typified his work for three decades. Nonetheless, his creation seems to fall victim to client suitability overkill. A Greek-American is tapped for the Greektown station commission. His neon work is selected to grace an environment already saturated with flashing lights and glitz. Ambitious and costly ($150,000 plus), the Antonakos piece unfortunately loses its confrontational bite in a physical and political ambiance where both ideas and forms are subsumed into a kitsch pastiche.

Finally, we turn to the Financial District station where Joyce Kosloff has installed an enormous ceramic tile mural that covers the main interior of a two-story structure. Kosloff developed her mural around a huge letter "D" (for Detroit) and various images of bears and bulls (the principal symbols of stock market fluctuation). Entwined through these motifs, she depicted a bestiary of animal and plant forms derived from early illuminated manuscripts and from various Arts and Crafts architectural details found on many early twentieth-century Detroit buildings. Ironically, Kosloff's kitsch histories and histrionics are lost to their audience. Viewers can get no farther than ten feet back from her mural and thus never see it in its entirety. As a consequence, the work neither decorates nor instructs as its creator and sponsors had intended. One Michigan Arts Council administrator, discussing the project's shortcomings, lamented, "We should have understood better what the model we looked at was telling us."[18]

As pseudo-angst, ethnic politics, and intellectual pandering neutralize the critical and revelatory aspects of these three productions, related displacements nudge the other twelve People Mover projects into the realm of kitsch. Responsibility for this must be put squarely on the shoulders of the movers and shakers who conceived and directed the project and on the artists who accepted the commissions. Theirs was a not-so-veiled vision of an art for the masses. Hence, a production of public works relatively bereft of psychic tension. Art expected to become a part of a city's daily life becomes answerable to Harold Rosenberg's charge that "if art becomes an extention of daily life it

---

D FOR DETROIT
Joyce Kozloff, 1987
Glazed ceramic. Financial District Station—The People Mover, Detroit, Michigan.
(Photo by Michael Hall)

loses itself; it becomes a commodity among commodities, kitsch.''[19] The contemporary corporate and governmental preference for the imitation over the original was succinctly expressed in a recent statement made by the city attorney from the Detroit suburb of Farmington Hills. Clarifying his position on a public art matter, the attorney said, ''We don't want to leave art work to the imagination.''[20] Public art conforming to this expectation must go kitsch.

Across the boards it has. Downtown, the Joe Louis Monument steps forward to take its place at the high heroic end of the spectrum of public kitsch in Detroit. In some ways, the Louis *Fist* could have initiated rather than closed this discussion. As an imitation in a high history, it is a kitsch classic. It harkens to a model fully certified in a mature cultural tradition (Michelangelo to Rodin) and it achieves kitsch status exploiting and aping that tradition.

The Fist appeared on the Detroit stage seemingly by magic. Backstage, however, a lot of strings must have been pulled to bring off the illusion. The monument came as a gift sponsored by *Sports Illustrated* magazine to commemorate the centennial of the Detroit Institute of Arts. A now-replaced director of the Institute and members of his staff proposed three sculptors as candidates for the commission. *Sports Illustrated* tapped Robert Graham from among the three, and the project was launched. A ''special committee'' made up from the Joint Museum Collections Committee, the Founder's Society Board and the Arts Commission approved the Institute's accession of the piece. Graham requested that his monument design not be made public until the ''gift'' was in place. The committee demurred.

The Institute subsequently turned to city hall for the clearances and technical assistance necessary to erect the piece downtown. A white art and financial establishment creating a monument to a black folk hero in Detroit walks several thin lines to its ''public art'' goal. *The Fist* prevailed and was unveiled and dedicated with speeches and official fanfare in October of 1986.[21] The new director of the Detroit Institute of Arts, inheriting *The Fist* as a fait accompli, welcomed it to the city's collection with the following words:

> The outstretched arm and fist of Robert Graham's Monument to Joe Louis speaks about strength and the search for personal achievement. It is at once specific in

---

MONUMENT TO JOE LOUIS
Robert Graham, 1986
Bronze, 24' × 24' × 6'. Detroit, Michigan.
(Photo by Michael Hall)

its reference to the great boxer and universal in its symbolism honoring the human potential in us all.

I cannot imagine a more appropriate gift from SPORTS ILLUSTRATED than this monument to Joe Louis. The arm, with its show of strength and perserverance, is a synonym for Detroit and symbolizes its Renaissance spirit because it is the work of a contemporary sculptor with acknowledged roots in the classical past.[22]

Such bogus sociology and art criticism inflects most of the official pronouncements on the Louis Monument to date. Perhaps artificiality and insincerity are all that the piece can elicit—kitsch begets kitsch. Certainly, the critical dialogue on *The Fist* supports Clement Greenberg's 1939 contention that "Kitsch is vicarious experience and faked sensations."[23] *Sports Illustrated* now sponsors an annual Joe Louis Award to recognize Detroit athletes. Miniature versions of the monument are given to the award winners. Somewhere between business and art, the monument and its replicas join Philadelphia's "Rocky" statue in a sports kitsch no zone.

In the post Burke/Serra aftermath, it has become difficult to know an original from an imitation and almost impossible to place an original directly into public space. Kitsch like *The Fist,* however, need not be the only consequence of this dilemma. A public art that is both public and art is not impossible. As an alternative to kitsch, there is art—art that would not be interesting if it were not elusive and art that would not be engaging if it were not, at times, confounding. The course to kitsch is blind, but sightedness is only a matter of paying attention. Sightedness in the aftermath is about looking in unlikely places and, perhaps, listening to unlikely artists with other ideas.

An impressed concrete roller built by Los Angeles sculptor Carl Cheng is the kind of unlikely thing we might consider. We would find Cheng's roller on its unlikely storage pad on the beach at Santa Monica, California. The twelve-foot-wide, fourteen-ton drum we find is the result of a public art effort that took some six years to instigate and realize. Cheng regards his art as a tool and sees American life as something to be tangibly marked by the instruments he creates as an artist. Six years become part of his latest work.

The roller activates in a piece Cheng calls *Walk on L.A.* Once a month the City of Santa Monica sends workers out to hitch a large tractor up to the roller and drag it up and down the beach near the city's historic arcade pier. The impressions on the roller's surface leave a print in the sand as the tractor moves along. At close inspection, the print left behind is a relief map of a city complete with miniature freeways, houses, sports arenas and traffic jams. A sprawling sand castle metropolis up and down the beach is formed in a few hours. Almost

WALK ON L.A.
Carl Cheng, 1988
Concrete and steel, 9′ × 12′. Santa Monica, California.
(Photo by Michael Hall)

as quickly, the print is erased—absorbed into the life of the beach. Gulls track through it, kids build onto it and adults laugh gleefully as they "stomp" the minigridlocks they know too well at full scale.

Cheng's is a gentle and generous art. He likes the engagements his printed city elicits from its viewers. He likes the give-and-take in the process that required him to map his own way through city hall and a dozen councils enroute to having his "Santa Monica Art Tool" commissioned. Cheng even looks forward to maintaining his piece over the years and to training the succession of tractor drivers that will pull it down the beach in the future. Carl Cheng's public is "work-a-day," and his concept of public art demands a creative response to contemporary social structures of work and play. Cheng's populism is sophisticated and authentic. He doesn't believe public art is about intimidation *or* condescension. Rather he expects his art to be an original dialectical engagement of a public life in which the private musings of artists become an active part. He sums it up best himself: "I'm inspired by philosophical questions about man being a part of nature. . . . It's an artist's job to think up stuff. . . . People have always debated what is art. That is the beauty about art, it makes people think."[24]

Original dialectical responses preclude kitsch. Public art in the aftermath might consult a quirky sand map on the Santa Monica beach if it wants to rechart its course. A tide of kitsch need not wash away public art's historic expectation to be both original and dialectical—and, in the process, to become (dare we say it?) beautiful.

Notes

1. See John McAleenan, "Her 'Art' Adored, Deplored," *The Detroit News* (25 June 1985), sec. A, pp. 1, 4.

2. See Sherrill Jordan, ed., *Public Art Public Controversy: The Tilted Arc on Trial* (New York: A.C.A. Books, 1987), pp. 47–56.

3. Sam Hunter, "The Public Agency as Patron," in Dorothy C. Miller and Sam Hunter, eds., *Art for the Public* (New York: The Port Authority of New York and New Jersey, 1985), p. 35.

4. See David Hume, "Of the Standard of Taste," *Essays Moral, Political and Literary* (Oxford: Oxford University Press, 1963), p. 234.

5. Pincus-Witten, Robert, "Detroit Notes: Islands in the Blight." *Arts Magazine* (February 1978): 137–43.

6. Brad Darrach and Maria Leonhauser, "Scene." *People* (15 August 1988), p. 58.

7. Ibid., p. 58.

8. Harold Rosenberg, *The Tradition of the New* (New York: Horizon Press, 1959), pp. 264–65.

9. Vittorio Gregotti, "Kitsch and Architecture," in Gillo Dolfles, ed., *Kitsch: The World of Bad Taste* (New York: University Books, 1969), p. 276.

10. Hermann Broch, "Notes on the Problem of Kitsch," in *Kitsch: The World of Bad Taste*, p. 68.

11. Clement Greenberg, *Art and Culture: Critical Essays* (Boston: Beacon Press, 1961), p. 19.

12. Broch, p. 75.

13. Broch, p. 76.

14. Gillo Dolfles, ed., *Kitsch: The World of Bad Taste*, p. 17.

15. Dan Graham, "The End of Liberalism (Part II)," in Peter D'Agostino and Antonio Muntadas, eds., *The Unnecessary Image* (New York: Tanam Press, 1982), p. 40.

16. Ibid., p. 38.

17. Tyree Guyton, personal communication, October 1988. A copy of the memo from the director of Detroit's City Planning Commission dated September 30, 1988, was sent to Guyton. As of the date of my conversation with the artist, the Department of Buildings and Safety had not responded to the Planning Commission's request and, thus, the house at 3670 Heidelberg Street remains on the city's demolition list.

18. Craig Carver, personal communication, September 1988. Carver is the director of the Michigan Council for the Arts Individual Artist Program. The Michigan Council provided some "seed money" for the People Mover project, and Carver was personally involved with the screening process that reviewed artist proposals to determine which ones would ultimately be commissioned for the various People Mover stations.

19. Rosenberg, p. 267.

20. Joanne Maliszewski, "Ordinance on Artwork: Pending Law Could Force Sculpture's Removal," *Farmington Observer* (Michigan) (6 October 1988).

21. Several people knowledgeable on the subject of the Louis Monument provided information and thoughts on the project and its implementation. Among them were: Davira Taragin, curator of Decorative Arts at the Detroit Institute of Arts; Joy Hakanson Colby, art critic for the *Detroit News*; and Carol Campbell, executive to the mayor of the city of Detroit.

22. Samuel Sachs II, "A Work in Progress," in *Monument to Joe Louis* (New York: Time, Inc., 1986), n.p.

23. Greenberg, p. 10.

24. Jay Goldman, "Roll 'Em!" *Los Angeles Times* (24 March 1988), pp. 1 and 10.

Contributors

CAROL BECKER is the chair of the Graduate Division of The School of the Art Institute of Chicago. She has her doctorate of philosophy in literature from the University of California, San Diego. She is also a professor of liberal arts. Her book *The Invisible Drama: Women and the Anxiety of Change,* published by Macmillan, was released last year. She writes about issues concerning women, politics, art, popular culture and the place where these intersect.

LINDA FRYE BURNHAM was the founding editor of *High Performance* magazine. She is a contributing editor to *The Drama Review* and a staff writer for *Artforum.* In January 1989 she cofounded, with Tim Miller, a performance art space in Los Angeles.

EVA SPERLING COCKCROFT is a muralist, painter, arts activist, writer, and photographer. Aside from "La Lucha Continua," other recent murals include "Homage to Revolutionary Health Workers," Leon, Nicaragua (1981), "Homage to Seurat: La Grande Jatte in Harlem," New York (1986) and "The Changing Face of Soho," Broadway/Lafayette Subway Station, New York (1988). She was active with the Peoples Painters (1972–74), Cityarts Workshop (1981–82), Artists for Nuclear Disarmament (1982), Political Art Documentation Distribution (1983–87), an organizer of Artists Call and Art Against Apartheid and has directed the community mural group, Artmakers, Inc., since 1983. She is an author of *Toward a People's Art,* an analytical book about the mural movement published in 1977, and many articles about art and society including "The United States and Socially Concerned Latin American Art" which appeared in the Abrams book, *The Latin American Spirit.*

STEVEN DURLAND is the editor of *High Performance* magazine. As a writer, sculptor and performance artist, he has lectured and presented work throughout the United States as well as Canada, Ireland and England.

WENDY FEUER has been Director of the Metropolitan Transportation Authority's Arts for Transit Office since its inception in 1985. The office was created to integrate the performing and visual arts into the metropolitan region's mass transit systems. Among other programs, she oversees a Percent for Art Program that is part of the MTA's multibillion-dollar rebuilding initiative. Before coming to the MTA, she worked for the New York State Assembly developing artists' rights, historic preservation and sports legislation. Her professional career has been dedicated to improving the built environment on both policy and programmatic levels. She has a masters degree in art history from the University of North Carolina, Chapel Hill.

GUILLERMO GÓMEZ-PEÑA, interdisciplinary artist/writer, has lived and worked on the border region of San Diego–Tijuana since 1983, where he coedits the bilingual interdisciplinary arts magazine, *The Broken Line.* His project, ''Borders, Myths and Maps,'' explores U.S.-Mexico relations, border mythologies and cultural topography with the use of multiple mediums: performance, audio art, book art, experimental poetry, critical writings, photography and multimedia altars. Gómez-Peña is a founding member of the binational *Border Arts Workshop* and is a regular contributor to Mexico's national newspaper, *La Jornada,* and to the North American national radio show, *Crossroads.*

MICHAEL HALL was born in southern California in 1941. He graduated Phi Beta Kappa from the University of North Carolina in 1962 and completed his M.F.A. in sculpture at the University of Washington in 1964. He is currently head of the Sculpture Department at the Cranbrook Academy of Art in Bloomfield Hills, Michigan. As a sculptor, critic, and American folk art collector, he lectures widely on the subject of American culture.

As an artist Hall has participated in major group shows throughout America. His twenty-two solo exhibitions have been well documented and catalogued. Hall has received numerous prizes and awards including a Guggenheim Fellowship, a National Endowment for the Arts Fellowship and two Michigan Council for the Arts Creative Artists Grants. A book of his compiled lectures and essays was published in 1988 by UMI Research Press.

ROBIN HOLLAND was born in Yonkers, N.Y., in 1952. She received a B.A. in literature and creative writing from the State University at Binghamton (Harpur College) in 1974. Photographing professionally since 1980, she concentrates on portraiture and art. Her photos have been extensively published in magazines and newspapers such as *The*

Village Voice, The New York Times, New York Magazine, USA Today, The Philadelphia Inquirer Magazine, Manhattan, inc., L.A. Style, 7 Days, Savvy, Vanity Fair, Elle, Film Comment and *Newsweek.*

MATTHEW KANGAS is chief visual arts critic for *Seattle Weekly.* Former art critic for PBS-TV affiliate, KCTS-9, he also writes for *Art in America, American Craft, American Ceramics* and *Art Criticism.* He was born in Seattle in 1949 and graduated from Reed College and Oxford University.

DONALD KUSPIT, professor of art history and philosophy at the State University of New York at Stony Brook, received the Frank Jewett Mather award for distinction in art criticism, presented in 1983 by the College Art Association. In addition to holding two Ph.D.'s—one in philosophy from the University of Frankfurt and one in art history from the University of Michigan—he is the author of five books on criticism, two of poetry, and over 500 articles. His books of criticism include *Clement Greenberg: Art Critic* (1979); *Leon Golub: Existentialist/Activist Painter* (1985); *The Critic Is Artist: The Intentionality of Art* (1984); *Louise Bourgeois* (1988); and *The New Subjectivism* (1988). His numerous articles have appeared in such journals as *Artscribe, Arts Magazine, C Magazine, Contemporanea, Wolkenkratzer, Artforum,* where he is a staff member, and *Art in America,* where he is a contributing editor. He is also the editor of *Art Criticism.*

SUZANNE LACY, currently dean of fine arts at the California College of Arts and Crafts, is an internationally known performance artist whose work includes large scale performances on social themes and urban issues. Lacy has published articles in *Performing Arts Journal, High Performance* and *Artweek.* She has exhibited in the Museum of Contemporary Art in London, the Museum of Modern Art in San Franciso and the New Museum in New York. Lacy's work has been reviewed in *Artforum, The Drama Review, Media Arts, High Performance, L.A. Times, Village Voice,* and numerous books.

LUCY R. LIPPARD is a writer and activist who has published thirteen books on contemporary art and one novel. Her interest in public art has led her to make performances, flyers, comics, political street theatre and demonstration art, as well as to write about them and to work with artists' groups concerned with a variety of public art forms. Among her books are *Overlay: Contemporary Art and the Art of Prehistory* (Pantheon, 1983) and *Get the Message? A Decade of Art for Social Change* (Dutton, 1984). She is currently at work on a book about contemporary art and the crosscultural process.

ARLENE RAVEN is an art historian writing criticism in New York for the *Village Voice* and a variety of art magazines and academic journals. She is the New York editor of *High Performance,* a member of the editorial board of *Genders* magazine, and general editor of the series "Art on the Edge" for UMI Research Press. Her selected essays were published as *Crossing Over: Feminism and Art of Social Concern* (UMI Research Press, 1988). She was an editor and contributor to *Feminist Art Criticism: An Anthology* (UMI Research Press, 1988), winner of the Susan Koppelman Award by the Women's Caucus of the Popular Culture Association/American Culture Association for the best anthology published in 1988. *Exposures: Women and Their Art* was published by NewSage Press in 1989. Raven was a founder of the Women's Caucus for Art, the Los Angeles Woman's Building and *Chrysalis* magazine. She has lectured nationally and taught at California Institute of Arts, The Maryland Institute, Parsons School of Design, UCLA, University of Southern California, and The New School for Social Research. Recipient of two NEA art critics fellowships and an honorary Doctor of Humanities degree from Hood College, she has curated exhibitions for a number of institutions, including the Baltimore Museum of Art and the Long Beach Museum of Art. Raven studied at Hood College, George Washington University, and Johns Hopkins University, and holds an M.F.A. in painting and M.A. and Ph.D. degrees in art history.

PHYLLIS ROSSER has been a contributing editor to *Ms.* magazine for the past fifteen years. She is currently director of her own consulting firm, The Equality in Testing Project. She has had numerous articles on arts in education and testing reform published in *Ms.* and other magazines. Her article on the National Endowment for the Arts' Artists-in-Schools Program, "A is for the Arts: A Revolution in the Schools" (*Ms.,* 1976), was read into the *Congressional Record.* Her pioneering work on sex bias in the Scholastic Aptitude Test has focused national attention on the fact that females' average scores are approximately sixty points lower than males' even though they receive higher average grades in all subjects in high school and college. She is currently writing a major report on sex bias in standardized testing under a Federal Department of Education grant from the Women's Educational Equity Act Program and has testified before Congress on sex bias in the Scholastic Aptitude Test. She is also a sculptor who has had two one-woman shows at the Ceres Gallery in New York City. Her feminist art criticism appears in *Women Artists News* and regularly in *New Directions for Women.*

MOIRA ROTH, now Trefethen Professor of Art History, Mills College, Oakland (previously she taught at the University of California, San Diego), is a feminist art historian and critic. She studied at the London School of Economics and Washington Square College, New York University, and received her Ph.D. at the University of California, Berkeley. She has written extensively on performance art, women's art, and contemporary art in general. Her writings include "The Aesthetic of Indifference" (*Artforum,* November 1977), "Visions and Re-Visions" (*Artforum,* November 1980), *The Amazing Decade: Women and Performance Art in America, 1970–1980* (Los Angeles, Astro Artz, 1983, editor and contributor), "Suzanne Lacy: Social Reformer and Witch" (*The Drama Review,* Spring 1988) and "Diggings and Echoes" (in *Autobiography: In Her Own Image,* Intar Gallery catalogue, 1988). Currently she is working on a nationwide research project with women artists of color.

ROBERT STORR is a painter and critic living in New York. A contributing editor to *Art in America* as well as a member of the Editorial Board of the CAA's *Art Journal,* Storr has been Boston editor of the *New Art Examiner* and is a frequent contributor to *Art Press* (Paris) and *Parkett* (Zurich and New York). He has also written for the *Village Voice, New York Newsday, Arts Magazine* and *The Harvard Advocate,* and conducted interviews for the Video Data Bank of Chicago. He is the author of books on Philip Guston and Louise Bourgeois, coauthor of a monograph on Chuck Close and has written major catalogue essays on Ellsworth Kelly, Nancy Spero, Louise Bourgeois, Dorothea Rockburne and Betty Goodwin. Storr has taught widely and has spoken at institutions around the country, including the Museum of Modern Art, the Whitney Museum, the Guggenheim Museum, the Neuberger Museum, the Museums of Contemporary Art in Chicago and Houston, Harvard, New York University, Princeton, U.C.L.A., University of Texas and many others.

JUDY COLLISCHAN VAN WAGNER (Ph.D., University of Iowa; M.F.A., Ohio University) is director of the Hillwood Art Gallery, Long Island University, C. W. Post Campus, where she initiated and supervises the university's extensive Public Art Program. She is a free-lance art critic writing for *Arts* magazine and is the author of numerous catalogue essays and two books, *Women Shaping Art: Profiles of Power* (on women art critics and dealers), Praeger 1984, and *Contemporary Women Drawers,* Hudson Hills Press, 1990. She serves as cochair of the Visual Artists panel for the New York State Council on the Arts.

JEFF WEINSTEIN writes a weekly column about the theory and practice of consumerism for the *Village Voice*, where he is also senior editor in charge of art criticism. He is author of *Life in San Diego*, a novel, and the Pushcart Prize–winning story ''A Jean-Marie Cookbook.'' Weinstein has published articles about art, fashion, food, literature, television and sexual politics for *Art in America, In These Times, The Advocate* and *The Village Voice,* and his collection of essays about food in the eighties, *Learning to Eat,* was recently published by Sun & Moon.

Bibliography

Compiled by
Judy Collischan Van Wagner

Books

Anderson, Wayne. *American Sculpture in Process: 1930–1970*. Greenwich, Connecticut: New York Graphic Society, 1975.

Bach, Ira J., and Mary Lackritz Gray. *A Guide to Chicago's Public Sculpture*. Chicago: University of Chicago Press, 1983.

Banfield, Edward C. *The Democratic Muse: Visual Arts and the Public Interest*. New York: Basic Books, Inc., 1984.

Barnett, Alan W. *Community Murals: The People's Art.*New York: Cornwall Books, 1984.

Barthes, Roland. *The Eiffel Tower and Other Mythologies*. New York: Hill and Wang, 1979.

Beardsley, John. *Art in Public Places*. Washington, D.C.: Partners for Liveable Places, 1981.

_____. *Probing the Earth: Contemporary Land Projects*. Washington, D.C.: Smithsonian Institution Press, 1977.

Benjamin, Walter. *Illuminations*. New York: Schocken, 1969.

Bitterman, Eleanor. *Art in Modern Architecture*. New York: Reinhold Publishing Corporation, 1952.

Clapp, Jane. *Art Censorship*. Metuchen, New Jersey: The Scarecrow Press, 1972.

Cockcroft, Eva, John Weber, and Jim Cockcroft. *Toward a People's Art: The Contemporary Mural Monument*. New York: E. P. Dutton & Co., 1977.

Cork, Richard. *Art beyond the Gallery in Early 20th Century England*. New Haven: Yale University Press, 1985.

Cruikshank, Jeffrey L., and Pam Korza. *Going Public: A Field Guide to Developments in Art in Public Places*. Amherst, Massachusetts: Arts Extension Service and the National Endowment for the Arts, 1988.

d'Harnoncourt, Anne. *Celebration, Buildings, Art, and People*. Washington, D.C.: United States General Services Administration, 1976.

Diamonstein, Barbaralee, ed. *Collaboration: Artists and Architects*. New York: Watson-Guptil Publications, Whitney Library of Design, 1981.

Dorfles, Gillo, ed. *Kitsch: The World of Bad Taste*. New York: University Books, 1969.

Douglas, Nancy E. *Public Plazas, Public Art, Public Reaction.* Monticello, Illinois: Vance Bibliographies, 1983.

Elsen, Albert E. *Rodin's Thinker and the Dilemmas of Modern Public Sculpture.* New Haven: Yale University Press, 1985.

Feld, A. M. O'Hare, and J. M. D. Schuster. *Patrons Despite Themselves: Taxpayers and Arts Policy.* New York: New York University Press, 1983.

Fleming, Ronald Lee, and Renata von Tscharner. *Place Makers: Public Art That Tells You Where You Are.* New York: Hastings House Publishers, 1981.

Freeman, Robert, and Vivienne Lasky. *Hidden Treasures: Public Sculpture in Providence.* Providence, Rhode Island: Rhode Island Bicentennial Foundation, 1980.

Fried, Frederic, and Edward V. Gilou, Jr. *New York Civic Sculpture.* New York: Dover Publications, 1976.

Fuller, Patricia. *Five Artists at NOAA: A Casebook on Art in Public Places.* Seattle: Real Comet Press, 1985.

Fundaburk, Emma Lila, and Thomas G. Davenport. *Art in Public Places in the United States.* Bowling Green, Ohio: Bowling Green University Popular Press, 1975.

Gayle, Margot, and Michele Cohen. *The Art Commission and the Municipal Art Society Guide to Manhattan's Outdoor Sculpture.* New York: Prentice Hall Press, 1988.

Goheen, Ellen R. *Christo: Wrapped Walk Ways.* New York: Harry N. Abrams, 1978.

Goldwater, Robert J. *What Is Modern Sculpture?* New York: Museum of Modern Art, 1969.

Goode, James M. *Open-Air Sculpture of Washington: A Comprehensive Historical Guide.* Washington, D.C.: Smithsonian Institution Press, 1974.

Graham, Dan. "The End of Liberalism (Part II)." In *The Unnecessary Image,* edited by Peter D'Agostino and Antonio Muntadas, 36–41. New York: Tanam Press, 1982.

Greenberg, Clement. *Art and Culture: Critical Essays.* Boston: Beacon Press, 1961.

Greenberg, David, Kathryn Smith, and Stuart Teacher. *Big Art: Megamurals and Supergraphics.* Philadelphia: Running Press, 1977.

Haas, Richard. *An Architecture of Illusion.* New York: Rizzoli International Publications, 1981.

Harris, Stacy Paleologos, ed. *Insights/On Sites: Perspectives on Art in Public Places.* Washington, D.C.: Partners for Liveable Places, 1984.

Hartford, Huntington, *Art or Anarchy? How the Extremists and Exploiters Have Reduced the Fine Arts to Chaos and Commercialism.* New York: Doubleday, 1964.

International Union of Public Transport. *Revue: Metro Art.* April 1987–January 1988, pp. 253–301.

Jewett, Masha Zakheim. *Coit Tower.* San Francisco: Viking Press, 1977.

Jordan, Sherrill, ed. *Public Art Public Controversy: The Tilted Arc on Trial.* New York: A.C.A. Books, 1987.

Krauss, Rosalind E. *Passages in Modern Sculpture.* New York: Viking Press, 1977.

Krier, Rob. *Urban Space.* New York: Rizzoli International Publications, 1979.

Lamont, Corliss. *Freedom Is as Freedom Does.* New York: Horizon Press, 1956.

Larson, Gary O. *The Reluctant Patron: The United States Government and the Arts, 1943–1965.* Philadelphia: University of Pennsylvania Press, 1983.

Lederer, Joseph, and Arley Bondarin. *All around the Town: A Walking Guide to Outdoor Sculpture in New York City.* New York: Charles Scribner's Sons, 1975.

Lennard, Suzanne, H. Crowhurst and Henry L. Lennard. *Livable Cities: Towards Criteria for Public Art.* Southhampton, N.Y.: Center for Urban Well-Being, 1987, pp. 89–96.

Lippard, Lucy R. *Get the Message? A Decade of Art for Social Change.* New York: E. P. Dutton, 1984.

_____. *Overlay: Contemporary Art and the Art of Prehistory.* New York: Pantheon Books, 1983.

_____. *Six Years: Dematerialization of the Art Object.* New York: Praeger Publishers, 1973.

Lipse, Mike. *Places as Art*. New York: Publishing Center for Cultural Resources, 1985.

Loeffler, Carl E., ed. *Performance Anthology: Source Book for a Decade of California Performance Art*. San Francisco: Contemporary Arts Press. 1980.

Lynch Kevin. *The Image of the City*. Cambridge: MIT Press, 1979.

_____. *What Time Is This Place?* Cambridge: MIT Press, 1972.

Maldonado, Tomás. *Design, Nature, and Revolution: Toward a Critical Ecology*. New York: Harper and Row, 1972.

Marcuse, Herbert. *The Aesthetic Dimension: Toward a Critique of Marxist Aesthetics*. Boston: Beacon Press, 1978.

_____. *Reason and Revolution*. Boston: Beacon Press, 1969.

Marling, Karal Ann. *Wall-to-Wall America: A Cultural History of Post-Office Murals in the Great Depression*. Minneapolis: University of Minnesota Press, 1982.

Massachusetts Bay Transportation Authority. *Arts on the Line: A Public Art Handbook*. Cambridge, Mass.: Massachusetts Bay Transportation Authority, 1987.

McKinzie, Richard D. *The New Deal for Artists*. Princeton, New Jersey: Princeton University Press, 1973.

McNulty, Robert H., Leo Penne, and Dorothy R. Jacobson. *The Economics of Amenity: Community Futures and Quality of Life*. Washington, D.C.: Partners for Livable Places, 1985.

Miles, Don C., Robert S. Cook, and Cameron B. Roberts. *Plazas for People*. New York: New York City Department of City Planning, 1978.

Miller, James E., Jr., and Paul D. Herring. *The Arts and the Public*. Chicago: University of Chicago Press, 1967.

Ministere des Communications Services des Relations publiques. *L'Art dans le metro*. Brussels: Ministere des Communications, 1982.

Mooney, Michael M. *The Ministry of Culture: Connections among Art, Money and Politics*. New York: Wyndham Books, 1980.

Mulcahy, Kevin V., and C. Richard Swain, eds. *Public Policy and the Arts*. Boulder, Colorado: Westview Press, 1982.

Nawrocki, Dennis Alan. *Art in Detroit Public Places*. Detroit: Wayne State University Press, 1980.

Nelson, Doreen. *Transformations: Process and Theory*. Santa Monica, California: Center for City Building Educational Programs, 1984.

Netzer, Dick. *The Subsidized Muse: Public Support for the Arts in the United States*. Cambridge: Cambridge University Press, 1978.

O'Connor, Francis V., ed. *Art for the Millions: Essays from the 1930s by Artists and Administrators of the WPA Federal Art Project*. Greenwich, Connecticut: New York Graphic Society, 1973.

_____. *The New Deal Art Projects: An Anthology of Memoirs*. Washington, D.C.: Smithsonian Institution Press, 1972.

Overmyer, Grace. *Government and the Arts*. New York: W. W. Norton & Co., 1939.

Page, Clint, and Penelope Cuff. *Public Sector Designs*. Washington, D.C.: Partners for Livable Places, 1984.

Park, M., and G. Markowitz. *Democratic Vistas: Post Offices and Public Art in the New Deal*. Philadelphia: Temple University Press, 1984.

Perlman, Bernard B. *One Percent Art in Civic Architecture*. Baltimore: RTKL Associates, 1973.

Purcell, Ralph. *Government and Art: A Study of the American Experience*. Washington, D.C.: Public Affairs Press, 1956.

Raine, Nancy. *Arts on the Line: A Public Art Handbook*. Cambridge: Cambridge Arts Council, 1987.

Raven, Arlene. *Crossing Over: Feminism and Art of Social Concern.* Ann Arbor: UMI Research Press, 1988.

_____. "Freeze Frames and a Still Whisper: Two Performances by Suzanne Lacy." In *DOC*U*MEN*TIA,* edited by f-stop Fitzgerald. San Francisco, Los Angeles and New York: Last Gasp of San Francisco, Post Contemporary Publications, Astro Artz, 1987.

Redstone, Louis G. *Art in Architecture.* New York: McGraw-Hill Book Co., 1968.

Redstone, Louis G., and Ruth R. Redstone. *Public Art: New Directions.* New York: McGraw-Hill Book Co., 1981.

Restany, Pierre, and Bruno Zevi. *SITE: Architecture as Art.* New York: St. Martin's Press, 1980.

Robinette, Margaret. *Outdoor Sculpture: Object and Environment.* New York: Watson-Guptill Publications, Whitney Library of Design, 1976.

Rosen, Nancy. *Ten Years of Public Art: 1972–1982.* New York: Public Art Fund, Inc., 1982.

Roth, Moira. "Autobiography, Theatre, Mysticism and Politics: Women's Performance Art in Southern California." In *Performance Anthology: Source Book for a Decade of California Performance,* edited by Carl Loeffler and Darlene Tong. San Francisco: Contemporary Arts Press, 1980.

_____, ed. *The Amazing Decade: Women and Performance Art in America, 1970–1980.* Los Angeles: Astro Artz, 1983.

Sachs, Samuel, ed. "A Work in Progress." *Monument to Joe Louis.* New York: Time, Inc., 1986.

Schwartz, Myra E. *Annotated Bibliography on Art in Public Places.* Monticello, Illinois: Vance Bibliographies, 1984.

Schwartzman, Allan. *Street Art.* Garden City, New York: Dial Press, 1985.

Scruggs, Jan C., and Joel L. Swerdlow. *To Heal a Nation: The Vietnam Veterans Memorial.* New York: Harper & Row Publishers, Inc., 1985.

Sky, Allison, ed. *On Site V.P. (Visual Pollution).* New York: SITE, 1971.

Soderstom, Goran, ed. *Art Goes Underground.* Stockholm: City of Stockholm, 1988.

Sommer, Robert. *Street Art.* New York: Links Books, 1975.

Sonfist, Alan, ed. *Art in the Land.* New York: E. P. Dutton, 1983.

Spies, Werner. *The Running Fence Project—Christo.* Rev. ed. New York: Harry N. Abrams, 1980.

Strom, Marianne. *Metro-Art Dans Les Metro-Poles.* Brussels: Generale de Banque, 1987.

Thalacker, Donald W. *The Place of Art in the World of Architecture.* New York: Chelsea House Publishers, 1980.

Thompson, Lynn, ed. *Artwork/Network: A Planning Study for Seattle: Art in the Civic Context.* Seattle: Storefront Press, 1984.

vanBruggen, Coosje, R. H. Fuchs, and Claes Oldenburg. *Claes Oldenburg: Large Scale Projects, 1977–80.* New York: Rizzoli, 1980.

Wainwright, Nicholas B., ed. *Sculpture of a City: Philadelphia's Treasures in Bronze and Stone.* New York: Walker Publishing Co., 1974.

Whyte, William H. *The Social Life of Small Urban Spaces.* Washington, D.C.: The Conservation Foundation, 1980.

Catalogues

Architectural Art: Affirming the Design Relationship: A Discourse. New York: American Craft Museum, 1988.

Artists and Architects: Challenges in Collaboration. Cleveland, Ohio: Cleveland Center for Contemporary Art, 1985.

Art in the Environment. Boca Raton, Florida: Boca Raton Museum of Art, 1976.

Art for the Public. Essays by Sam Hunter and Dorothy Miller. New York: The Port Authority of New York and New Jersey, 1985.

Art in Public Places and Contemporary Sculpture in a Rural Community. Big Rapids, Michigan: State College Office of the Arts, 1979.

Art for Whom? London: Great Britain Arts Council, 1978.

Artpark: The Program in Visual Arts. Lewiston, New York: Artpark, 1974, 1976, 1977.

Auping, Michael. *Common Ground: Five Artists in the Florida Landscape.* Sarasota, Florida: John and Mable Ringling Museum of Art, 1982.

Bach, Penny Balkin. "Choreography and Caution: The Organization of a Conservation Program." In *Sculptural Monuments in the Outdoor Environment.* Philadelphia: Pennsylvania Academy of Fine Arts, 1985.

_____. *Form and Function: Proposals for Public Art in Philadelphia.* Philadelphia: Pennsylvania Academy of Fine Arts and Fairmount Park Art Association, 1982.

Berger, David. *Private Visions/Public Spaces.* Bellevue, Washington: Bellevue Art Museum, 1987.

Beyond the Monument. Essay by Gary Garrels. Cambridge: MIT Committee on the Visual Arts, 1983.

By the People, For the People: New England. Introduction by Charles H. Sawyer and essay by Edith A. Tonelli. Lincoln, Massachusetts: De Cordova Museum, 1977.

Cathcart, Linda L. *Other Realities—Installations for Performances.* Houston, Texas: Contemporary Arts Museum, 1981.

Citywide Contemporary Sculpture Exhibition. Toledo: Toledo Museum of Art, 1984.

Cruikshank, Jeffrey L., and Pam Korza. *Going Public: A Field Guide to Developments in Art in Public Places.* Amherst, Mass.: Arts Extension Service, 1988.

Davies, Hugh Marlais. *Artist and Fabricator.* Amherst, Massachusetts: University of Massachusetts at Amherst, 1975.

Davies, Hugh M., and Ronald J. Onorato. *Sitings.* La Jolla, California: La Jolla Museum of Contemporary Art, 1986.

Doezoma, Marianne, and June Hargrove. *The Public Monument and Its Audience.* Cleveland: Cleveland Museum of Art, 1977.

Drawing In Situ. Essay by Judy Collischan Van Wagner and organized by Carol Becker Davis. Brookville, New York: Hillwood Art Gallery, Long Island University, 1986.

Earthworks: Land Reclamation as Sculpture. Seattle: Seattle Art Museum, 1979.

The Empire State Collection: Art for the Public. Foreward by Mario M. Cuomo and introduction by Irving Sandler. Albany: Empire State Plaza Art Commission, 1987.

Environmental Art Projects: 1981. Morristown, New Jersey: Morristown Museum of Arts and Sciences, 1981.

Gunter, Virginia. *Earth, Air, Fire, Water: Elements of Art.* Boston: Museum of Fine Arts, 1971.

Insight/On Site. Essay by Tiffany Bell and organized by Carol Becker Davis. Brookville, New York: Hillwood Art Gallery, Long Island University, 1988.

Kardon, Janet, Lawrence Alloway, Nancy Foote, and Ian McHaig. *Urban Encounters: Art, Architecture, Audience.* Philadelphia: Institute of Contemporary Art, 1981.

Lacy, Suzanne. "Mass Media, Popular Culture, and Fine Art: Images of Violence Against Women." In *Social Works.* Edited by Nancy Buchanan. Los Angeles: Los Angeles Institute of Contemporary Art, 1979.

Maltz, Russell. *Pool.* Brookville, New York: Long Island University, 1980.

Mecklenburg, Virginia. *The Public as Patron: A History of the Treasury Department Mural Program Illustrated with Paintings from the Collection of the University of Maryland Art Gallery.* College Park: University of Maryland, 1979.

Miller, Dorothy C. *U.S. Government Art Projects: Some Distinguished Alumni.* New York: Museum of Modern Art, 1963. Mimeo.

Monumenta. Introduction by Sam Hunter and essays by Hugh M. Davies and Sally E. Yard. Newport, Rhode Island: Monumenta Newport, Inc., 1974.

The Muralist and the Modern Architect. New York: Kootz Gallery, 1950.

Naudé, Virginia Norton, ed. *Sculptural Monuments, In an Outdoor Environment.* Philadelphia: Pennsylvania Academy of Fine Arts, 1985.

Nawrocki, Dennis Alan, and Thomas J. Holleman. *Art in Detroit Public Places.* Detroit: Wayne State University Press, 1980.

Neubert, George. *Public Sculpture/Urban Environment.* Oakland, California: Oakland Museum, 1974.

New York/Chicago: WPA and the Black Artist. Organized by Ruth Ann Stewart. New York: The Studio Museum in Harlem, 1977.

Nierengarten-Smith, Beej. *Laumeier Sculpture Park.* St. Louis, Missouri: Laumeier Sculpture Park, 1986.

Nordland, Gerald. *Controversial Public Art: From Rodin to di Suvero.* Milwaukee: Milwuakee Art Museum, 1983.

O'Connor, Francis V. *Federal Art Patronage: 1933 to 1943.* College Park: University of Maryland Art Gallery, 1966.

Park, Marlene, and Gerald E. Markowitz. *New Deal for Art: The Government Art Projects of the 1930s with Examples from New York City and State.* New York: Gallery Association of New York State, 1977.

Poetry Must Be Made by All! Transform the World! Stockholm, Sweden: Moderna Museet, 1969.

Public Art in Chinatown: Sculpture, Drawings, Models, Plans. Essays by John Yau, Kyong Park, Peter Kwong and organized by Robert Lee. New York: Asian American Arts Centre, 1988.

Public Art at Lehigh University—The Muriel and Philip Berman Sculpture Collection. Bethlehem, Pennsylvania: Lehigh University Art Galleries, 1987.

Raven, Arlene. *At Home.* Long Beach, California: The Long Beach Museum of Art, 1983.

_____. *RAPE.* Columbus, Ohio: The Ohio State University Gallery of Fine Art, 1985.

Riedy, James L. *Chicago Sculpture.* Urbana, Illinois: University of Illinois Press, 1981.

Rose, Barbara. *Sculpture off the Pedestal.* Grand Rapids, Michigan: Grand Rapids Art Museum, 1973.

Roth, Moira. *Barbara Smith.* San Diego, La Jolla: University of California, 1974.

_____. "Character, Costume and Theater in Early California Performance." In *Living Art.* Vancouver, Canada, 1981.

_____. *Jo Hanson.* San Diego, La Jolla, San Francisco: University of California and San Francisco Museum of Art, 1975.

_____. "Jill Scott: The Home-Coming." In *Jill Scott: Work 1975–1980,* 1981.

_____. *Joyce Shaw: The Lady and the Bird.* Los Angeles: University of Southern California, 1976.

_____, introd. *Exchanges of Sources: Expanding Powers.* Organized by Rebecca Ballenger, 1983.

Schwartz, Joyce Pomeroy. *Artists and Architects: Challenges in Collaboration.* Cleveland: Cleveland Center for Contemporary Art, 1985.

Sculpturesites. Amagansett, New York: Roger Wilcox, 1982.

Sites and Solutions: Recent Public Art. Reading, Pennsylvania: Freedman Gallery, Albright College, 1985.

Stearns-Phillips, Daydre. *Western's Outdoor Museum.* Bellingham, Washington: Western Washington University, 1979.

Taylor, Joshua C. *Across the Nation: Fine Art for Federal Buildings, 1972–79.* Washington, D.C.: National Museum of American Art, The Smithsonian Institute, 1980.
Van Wagner, Judy Collischan. *Public Art Program, Long Island University.* Brookville, New York: Hillwood Art Gallery, Long Island University, 1989.
The Ways of Wood. New York: Organization of Independent Artists, Inc., and Queens College, 1984.
Weintraub, Linda. *Land Marks.* Annandale-on-Hudson, New York: Bard College, 1984.

Articles

Acconci, Vito. "Public Space: The Street and the Park." *Stroll* (April/May 1988): 50–51.
Adams, D., and A. Goldbard. "Tough Times." *Heresies* 6 (1987): 41–44.
Alloway, Lawrence. "Monumental Art at Cincinnati." *Arts Magazine* 45 (November 1970): 32–36.
_____. "One Sculpture." *Arts Magazine* 45 (May 1971): 22–24.
_____. "Public Sculpture for the Post-Heroic Age." *Art in America* 68 (October 1979): 9–11.
_____. "The Public Sculpture Problem." *Studio International* 184 (October 1972): 122–25.
"Architecture and Public Spaces." *The Public Interest* 74 (Winter 1984).
Art in America (issue devoted to public art in Europe) 75 (September 1987).
"Art in the Environment." Essays by A. L. Harney, A. O. Dean, H. H. Hitchcock and W. Seale. *AIA Journal* 65 (October 1976): 33–61.
Artner, Alan G. "Debate Rages: Can Public Art Be Recalled?" *Chicago Tribune,* 8 March 1985.
_____. "Public Sculpture, Always an Imposition?" *Chicago Tribune,* 19 May 1985.
Ashton, Dore. "Unconventional Techniques in Sculpture." *Studio International* 170 (1965): 22–25.
"Atomic Energy and Stellar Energy, Panels Designed by U. H. Ellerhussen, Century of Progress Exposition, 1933," *Design* 35 (October 1933): 12–12a.
Baker, A. T. "Shaping Water into Art." *Time,* 12 September 1977.
Baker, Elizabeth C. "Mark di Suvero's Burgundian Season." *Art in America* 62 (May–June 1974): 59–63.
Balfe, Judith H., and Margaret J. Wyszomirski. "Public Art and Public Policy." *The Journal of Arts Management and Law* 15 (Winter 1986).
Beardsley, John. "Paradigms in Public Sculpture." *The Public Interest* (Winter 1982): 24–27.
_____. "Personal Sensibilities in Public Places." *Artforum* 19 (Summer 1981): 43–45.
Berman, G. "Abstractions for Public Spaces." *Arts Magazine* 56 (June 1982): 81–86.
Billiter, B. "Simon Rodia's Incredible Towers," *ARTnews* 78 (April 1979): 92–96.
"Blames Public for Frog and Faun School." *Art Digest* 5 (1 March 1931): 7.
Bloc, A. "Artist in the Landscape: The Role of the Artist in Modern Architecture." *Studio* 169 (February 1965): 50–55.
Bloom, J. "Changing Walls: Art for the People and the People as Artists." *Architectural Forum* 138 (May 1973): 20–27.
Boettger, Suzaan. "Scenes from a Marriage: Public Art and the Public." *The Museum of California* (July 1982): 11–13.
Bongartz, Roy. "Where the Monumental Sculptors Go." *ARTnews* 75 (February 1976): 34–37.
Brooks, Rosetta. "Tim Rollins + K.O.S. (Kids of Survival)." *Artscribe* (May 1987).
Brown, Milton W. "New Deal Art Projects: Boondoggle or Bargain." *ARTnews* 81 (April 1982): 82–87.

Burnham, Linda. "Tracking a New Wave of Socially Committed Art." *American Theatre* 5 (1988): 39–40.

_____. "Up the Revolution." *High Performance* 10 (1987): 12.

_____. "What Price Social Art?" *High Performance* 9 (1986): 8.

_____. John Malpede, and Elia Arce. "LAPD, Skid Row and the Real Deal." *High Performance* 43 (1988): 21–27.

Cameron, Dan. "The Art of Survival: A Conversation with Tim Rollins and K.O.S." *Arts Magazine* (June 1988).

Carpenter, Edward K. "Urban Art." *Design and Environment* (Summer 1974): 17–27.

Carter, Malcolm N. "The F. D. R. Memorial." *ARTnews* 77 (October 1978): 50–57.

Celant, Germano. "Artspaces." *Studio International* 190 (1975): 114–23.

Clancy, Frank. "Lawyers Team Up to Fight for the Homeless." *Los Angeles Times,* 18 September 1986.

Clay, Grady. "Vietnam's Aftermath: Sniping at the Memorial." *Landscape Architecture* 72 (March 1982): 54–56.

Cleary, F. "Art in the Subway." *Sculptural Review* 33 (Summer 1984): 9.

Crimp, Douglas. "Richard Serra's Urban Sculpture." *Arts Magazine* 55 (November 1980): 118–23.

Cumbow, Robert C. "Public Art/Private Vision." *Arts Line* 3 (May 1985).

Danto, C. "Perspective: On Public Art and the Public Interest." *ARTnews* 86 (October 1987): 208.

Danto, Arthur C. "Public Art and the General Will." *The Nation,* 28 September 1985.

Davis, Douglas. "Public Art: The Taming of the Vision." *Art in America* 62 (May–June 1974): 84–85.

Dean, Andrea O. "Art in the Environment." *AIA Journal* (October 1976): 40–43.

_____. "Bunshaft and Noguchi: An Uneasy but Highly Productive Architect-Artist Collaboration." *AIA Journal* (October 1976): 52–55.

_____. "Grand Rapids Becomes a Showplace of the Use of Sculpture in Public Places." *AIA Journal* (October 1976): 40–43.

Denvir, B. "Icons in Public Places." *Art and Artists* (October 1982): 32.

Devree, Howard. "Sculptors out of Doors." *Magazine of Art* 31 (May 1938): 308.

Dimitrijevic, N. "Meanwhile, In the Real World." *Flash Art* (May 1987): 44–49.

Dixon, Jenny. "Public Domain." *American Craft* 48 (June/July 1988): 62–67.

_____. "Resolving the Polarities in Public Art." *PLACE* (January 1983): 1–5.

Dornberg, John. "Art Vandals: Why Do They Do It?" *ARTnews* 86 (March 1987): 102–9.

Dubin, Zan. "Freeway Mural: A Lady Is Waiting." *The Los Angeles Times,* 22 January 1987.

Durant, Mark. "Art, Life and the Edge." *Artweek,* 9 March 1988.

Durland, Steve. "Hot Shorts." *High Performance* 8 (1985): 411–12.

Duval, P. "Murals, a Political Art." *Royal Architectural Institute of Canada Journal* 26 (January 1949): 9–11.

"Earthworks, Earthwords." *The Seattle Sun,* 18 September 1979.

"Earthworks Revisited: From Smithson to Simpson." *The Arts—Newsletter,* October 1982.

Eckart, Wolf von. "The Malignant Objectors." *The Public Interest* (Winter 1982): 22–24.

Eisner, Elliot W. "The Primacy of Experience and the Politics of Method." *Educational Researcher* 17 (June/July 1988): 15–20.

Esterow, Milton. "How Public Art Becomes a Political Hot Potato." *ARTnews* 85 (January 1986): 75–79.

"Fair as a Patron of Art: Cross-Section of Sculpture and Murals." *ARTnews* 38 (May 25, 1940): sup 14–15.

"The Farm Project." *Artweek,* 12 September 1981.

Feuer, Wendy. "Down the Tube: A Rapid View of Underground Art." *Stroll* (June/July 1988): 84–89.

Filler, Martin. "The Magic Fountain." *Progressive Architecture* 59 (November 1978): 86–87.

Fleming, L. "Private Sector/Public Art." *ARTnews* 82 (December 1983): 112.

Fleming, Ronald Lee. "The Meaning of Place." *The Public Interest* (Winter 1982): 27–30.

Foote, Nancy. "Monument—Sculpture—Earthwork." *Artforum* 18 (October 1979): 32–37.

Forgey, Benjamin. "It Takes More Than an Outdoor Site to Make a Sculpture Public." *ARTnews* 79 (September 1980): 84–89.

_____. "A New Vision: Public Places with Sculpture." *Smithsonian* (October 1975): 51–57.

_____. "The Perils of Street Sculpture: Ed McGowin and the Marring of Inscape." *The Washington Post,* 13 February 1985.

_____. "When Plain Is a Plus: Baltimore's Smashing Pearlstone Park." *The Washington Post,* 20 July 1985.

Fox, Mary Jo. "Outcasts." *Los Angeles Weekly,* 27 June–2 July, 1986.

Franz, Gina. "How Public is Public Sculpture?" *The New Art Examiner* (February 1980).

Freedman, Doris. "Public Sculpture." *Design and Environment* (Summer 1974): 19.

Freeman, Allen. "Extraordinary Competition: The Winning Design for the Vietnam Memorial and Other Entries." *AIA Journal* (August 1983): 47–53.

Freeman, Patricia. "Skid Row Acting Troupe Makes the Street Its Stage." *Los Angeles Herald Examiner,* 10 September 1986.

Freudenheim, S. "Under the Singing Eucalyptus Tree." *Artforum* 26 (April 1988): 24–30.

Friedman, Mildred, ed. "Site: The Meaning of Place in Art and Architecture." *Design Quarterly* 122 (1983).

Fritz, C. "O! Deliver Us from Cranks and Prudes." *Sculptural Review* 34 (Winter 1935–36): 9.

Frost, R. "Sculptors on Park Avenue." *ARTnews* 36 (April 16, 1938): 13.

Furst, H. "What the Public Should Know about Art," *Colour* 3 (March 1931): 12–14.

Galloway, D. "The Perils of Public Sculpture." *Art in America* 75 (December 1987): 37–39.

Geibel, Victoria. "Architecture + Art . . . A Fine Romance?" *American Craft* (June/July 1988): 26–33.

Gilbert-Rolfe, Jeremy. "Capital Follies." *Artforum* 17 (September 1978): 66–67.

Glueck, Grace. "Art in Public Places Stirs Widening Debate." *The New York Times,* 23 May 1982.

_____. "Art for Whose Sake?" *Continental Airlines EXTRA* (December 1982): 51–55.

_____. "Redefining the Whole Relationship between Art and Society." *ARTnews* 79 (October 1980): 58–63.

_____. "What Part Should the Public Play in Choosing Public Art?" *The New York Times,* February 1985.

Goldberg, R. "Performance—Art for All?" *Art Journal* 40 (Fall/Winter 1980): 369–76.

Goldin, Amy. "The Esthetic Ghetto: Some Thoughts about Public Art." *Art in America* (May–June 1974): 30–35.

Goldstein, Richard. "The Pandemonium of Public Art." *The Village Voice,* July–August, 1981.

Gortazar, Fernando Gonzalez. "Sculptures as 'Vitalizing Elements' in Superficial Urban Settings." *Landscape Architecture* 66 (1976): 512, 534–36.

Gutheim, F. A. "Architecture, Art, Life; Model for a Community Center, Collaborative Enterprise." *Magazine of Art* 30 (May 1937): 306–9.

Haigh, Ann. "Art and Animation Enliven Europe's Subways." *PLACE* (December 1982): 4–6.

Hall, Michael D. "Art in Public: It May Be Public, but Is It Art?" *Boston Review* (June 1988): 5–6, 21–22.

Harney, Andy. "Expanding the Dialogue on Public Art." *PLACE* (September 1981).

_____. "The Proliferating One Percent Programs for the Use of Art in Public Buildings." *AIA Journal* (October 1976): 35–39.

Harrison, Helen A. "Subway Art and the Public Use of Arts Committee." *Archives of American Art Journal* 21 (1981): 3–12.

Hawthorne, D. "Does the Public Want Public Sculpture?" *ARTnews* 81 (May 1982): 56–63.

Heath. T. "Pensive Turtle." *Artscanada* 31 (Autumn 1974): 74–75.

Hitchcock, Henry Russell, and William Seale. "How Nebraska Acquired a State Capitol Like No Other." *AIA Journal* 65 (October 1976): 56–61.

Hochfield, S. "The Moral Rights (and Wrongs) of Public Art." *ARTnews* 87 (May 1988): 143–46.

"Hotel Art." *ARTSLine,* March 1984.

Howett, Catherine M. "Landscape Architecture: Making a Place for Art." *Places* 2 (1985): 52–60.

_____. "The Vietnam Veterans Memorial: Public Art and Politics." *Landscape* (April 1985): 1–9.

Hughes, Kathleen A. "Street People Find a Home in the Theater." *The Wall Street Journal,* 22 July 1986.

Hutchinson, P. "Earth in Upheaval, Earth Works and Landscapes." *Arts Magazine* 43 (November 1968): 19.

Huxtable, Ada Louise. "Public Sculpture—A City's Most Pervasive Art." *The New York Times,* 15 September 1974.

Johnson, Kathryn. "Government Art: Beauty or Eyesore?" *U.S. News & World Report,* 23 September 1985.

Johnston, Jill. "Hardship Art." *Art in America* 72 (September 1984): 176–79.

Kent, Corita. "Art at 90 Miles an Hour (Gaily Striped Storage Tank for Boston Gas.)." *ARTnews* 75 (November 1976): 18.

Kent, Sarah. "Bronx Break." *Time Out,* 23–30 September 1987.

Kepes, Gyorgy. "The Artist as Environmentalist: A Proposal." *Ekistics* (1972): 372–74.

Kiesler, Frederick J. "Notes on Architecture as Sculpture." *Art in America* 54 (May 1966): 57–68.

Kramer, Hilton. "Sculpture Is Having a Coming-Out." *The New York Times,* 19 February 1978.

_____. "Visual Noise (Isn't Public Sculpture Better Thought of as Litter on a Large Scale?)" *Art and Antiques* (May 1988): 111–12.

Krauss, Rosalind. "Sculpture in the Expanded Field." *October* 8 (Spring 1979): 31–44.

Lacy, Bill N. "New Guidelines for Federal Architecture." *Art in America* 60 (September–October 1972): 19.

Lacy, Suzanne. "The Bag Lady." *Block* 7 (1982): 32–35.

_____. "The Greening of California Performance: Art for Social Change—A Case Study." *Images & Issues* (Spring 1982): 64–67.

_____. "Learning to Look: The Relationship between Art and Popular Culture Images." *Exposure* 19 (1981): 8–15.

Lacy, Suzanne, and Leslie Labowitz. "Evolution of a Feminist Art: Public Forms and Social Issues." *Heresies* 2 (Summer 1978): 76, 78–85.

Lacy, Suzanne, and Lucy R. Lippard. "Political Performance Art: A Discussion by Suzanne Lacy and Lucy R. Lippard." *Heresies* 5 (1984): 22–25.

Larson, Kay. "The Expulsion from the Garden: Environmental Sculpture at the Winter Olympics." *Artforum* 18 (April 1980): 36–45.

_____. "Public Sculpture II: Provisions for the Paradise." *Artforum* (Summer 1981): 37–42.

_____. "Shooting for the Sun." *The Village Voice,* 12 November 1979.

Levine, Edward. "Artists in Society." *The Public Interest* (Winter 1982): 31–34.
Lewis, J. A. "Baltimore: People Sculpture: Objections Overruled (Environmental Sculpture for the Plaza of Baltimore's New Federal Courthouse and Office Building)." *ARTnews* 75 (December 1976): 83–85.
_____. "Modern Medicis for Public Art." *ARTnews* 76 (April 1977): 37.
Linker, Kate. "Public Sculpture: The Pursuit of the Pleasurable and Profitable Paradise." *Artforum* 19 (March 1981): 64–73.
_____. "Public Sculpture II: Provisions for the Paradise." *Artforum* (Summer 1981): 37–42.
Lippard, Lucy R. "Art and Politics: Questions on a Politicized Performance Art." *Art in America* 72 (October 1984): 39–41.
_____. "Complexes: Architectural Sculpture in Nature." *Art in America* (January–February 1979): 86–97.
_____. "Gardens: Some Metaphors for a Public art." *Art in America* (November 1981): 136–50.
Loeb, Barbara. "Ways of Looking: The Setting, the Audience, the Artwork." *Seattle Arts* (May 1984).
Marlin, William. "Sprucing Up a City." *Saturday Review* (7 February 1976): 50–52.
Mather, B. F. "Decoration on a Large Scale; Woman's Week Exposition at Municipal Auditorium, Minneapolis." *Design* 39 (March 1938): 20.
Mathews, Jane De Hart. "Art and Politics in Cold War America." *American Historical Review* 81 (October 1976): 762–87.
Mayer, Rosemary. "Performance and Experience." *Arts Magazine* 47 (December 1972): 33–36.
McCoy, Garnett. "Poverty, Politics, and Artists." *Art in America* (August–September 1965): 88–107.
Meadmore, Clement, Edward Fry, and Barbara Rose. "Symposium on Three Dimensions." *Arts Magazine* 49 (January 1975): 62–65.
Miss, Mary. "On a Redefinition of Public Sculpture." *Perspecta* 21 (1984): 52–69.
"Murals, Murals, in Every Post Office, but What Do They Express?" *Art Digest* 9 (September 1935): 7–8.
Navaretta, Cynthia. "Public Sculpture and the Question of Functionalism." *Women Artists News* 12 (June 1987): 19–20.
Noah, Barbara. "Cost-Effective Earth Art." *Art in America* (January 1980): 12–15.
Nochlin, Linda. "The Paterson Strike Pageant of 1913." *Art in America* 62 (May–June 1974): 64–68.
_____. "The Realist Criminal and the Abstract Law." *Art in America* 61 (September–October 1973): 54–61.
O'Doherty, Brian. "Context as Content, Part III." *Artforum* 15 (November 1976): 38–44.
_____. "The Eye and the Spectator, Part II." *Artforum* 15 (April 1976): 26–34.
_____. "The Grand Rapids Challenge." *Art in America* 62 (January–February 1974): 78–79.
_____. "Inside the White Cube: Notes on the Gallery Space, Part I." *Artforum* 15 (March 1976): 24–32.
_____. "Public Art and the Government: A Progress Report." *Art in America* 62 (May–June 1974): 44–49.
"Performance." *Studio* 192 (July 1976): 2–68.
"Philadephia: Sculpture of a City." *National Sculpture Review* 25 (Spring 1976): 8–15.
Phillips, Patricia C. "'Tilted Arc' Hearing Forum: Something There Is That Doesn't Love a Wall." *Artforum* 23 (Summer 1985): 100–1.
Pidgeon, M. "Political Street Art in Santiago." *Studio* 185 (April 1973): 160.
Princenthal, Nancy. "Art in the Subways." *Industrial Design* 31 (November/December 1984): 38–39.

_____. "On the Waterfront." *Art in America* 75 (April 1987): 210–11.

"Public Art Works." *College Art Association Newsletter* 12 (Winter 1987/88).

"Public Sculpture." Essays by J. Rees, P. Ferriday, and T. Crosby. *Studio* 184 (July 1972): 9–47.

Raven, Arlene. "Commemoration: Public Sculpture and Performance." *High Performance* 8 (1985): 3, 36–40.

_____. "Doing and Making Good: Art in the Public Interest." *The Village Voice*, 3 May 1988.

_____. "Here Comes the Neighborhood." *The Village Voice*, 5 July 1988.

_____. "The L Word (Jerri Allyn's *The Lesbian Bride*)." *The Village Voice*, 4 August 1987.

_____. "Not a Pretty Picture: Can Violent Art Heal?" *The Village Voice*, 17 June 1986.

_____. "Serving Food for Thought." *High Performance* 10 (1987): 64–68.

_____. "A Woman's Place." *Daily News Magazine, The New York Daily News*, 17 July 1988.

Rees, Jeremy. "Public Sculpture." *Studio International* (July–August 1972): 10–15.

Rees, Jeremy, and T. Stokes. "Public Sculpture?" *Studio* 185 (February 1973): 46–47.

"Reexamination of Public Art." Essays by A. Goldin, M. Trachtenberg, B. O'Doherty, D. Shapiro, E. C. Baker, L. Nochlin, A. Topping, D. Davis. *Art in America* 62 (May 1974): 30–44, 55–74, 84–85.

"Restuarant Renaissance: Rise of the Midwest Mural." *ARTnews* 48 (April 1949): 53.

Reynolds, Patrick T. "The Threat to Outdoor Art." *Historic Preservation* 36 (June 1984): 34–39.

Robbins, Corinne. "New York: 'Public Sculpture in Public Places.'" *Arts Magazine* (Summer 1967): 50–51.

Robinson, Walter. "Art and the Law: Moral Rights Comes to New York." *Art in America* 71 (October 1983): 9.

_____. "Art + Life = Artists' Performances." *Art in America* 69 (January 1981): 15.

Rose, Barbara. "Public Art's Big Hit." *Vogue* (July 1977): 118.

_____. "Shall We Have a Renaissance?" *Art in America* 55 (March–April 1967): 30–39.

Rosler, Martha. "Private and the Public: Feminist Art in California." *Artforum* 16 (September 1977): 69–74.

Rosser, Phyllis. "A is for the Arts: A Revolution in the Schools." *Ms.* (May 1976).

_____. "The Town That Kids Built: Games That Teach Children a New Way of Thinking." *Ms.* (November 1979).

Roth, Moira. "Allan Kaprow, An Interview by Moira Roth." *Sun and Moon* (Fall 1978).

_____. "Art in a Community Context." *High Performance* 9 (1986): 42–46.

_____. "An Interview with Linda Montano." *High Performance* (December 1978).

_____. "An Interview with Lynn Hershman." *Journal of the Los Angeles Institute of Contemporary Art* (January/February 1978).

_____. "An Interview with Pauline Oliveros." *New Performance* 1.

_____. " An Interview with Town Artist, David Harding." *High Performance* 9 (1986).

_____ "Performance—Art in 1980's: A Turn of Events." *Studio International* 195 (June 1982): 16–24.

_____. "Robert Smithson on Duchamp, an Interview." *Artforum* (October 1973).

_____. "A Star Is Born: Performance Art in California." *Performing Arts Journal* 12 (Spring 1980).

_____. "Suzanne Lacy: Social Reformer and Witch" and "Selected Bibliography" and "Chronology." *The Drama Review* (Spring 1988).

_____. "Suzanne Lacy's Dinner Parties." *Art in America* (April 1980).

_____. "Toward a History of California Performance: Part I." *Arts Magazine* (February 1978).

_____. "Toward a History of California Performance: Part II." *Arts Magazine* (June 1978).

_____. "Visions and Re-Visions: A Conversation with Suzanne Lacy." *Artforum* 19 (November 1980): 42–45.

Scherer, M. A. "What Happened to Our Art?" *The Capital Times* [Madison, Wisconsin], 6 May 1985.

Schwartzman, Allan. "Bugs in the System." *The Print Collector's Newsletter* 15 (March/April 1984): 9–11.

Scott, Nancy. "Creating a Stage for the Homeless to Perform." *San Francisco Examiner*, 24 January 1988.

_____. "Politics on a Pedestal." *Art Journal* 38 (Spring 1979): 190–96.

"Sculptures for Bored Bankers at the Bowery Bank, New York." *Progressive Architecture* 46 (December 1965): 136–41.

"Sculpture on the Streets." *Architectural Review* 143 (March 1968): 209–12.

"Sculpture in the Sun." *Art Digest* 12 (May 1, 1938): 12.

"Seat and Read at and/or." *WestArt* [Auburn, California], 12 October 1979.

Senie, Harriet. "The Right Stuff." *ARTnews* 83 (March 1984): 50–59.

_____. "Urban Sculpture: Cultural Tokens or Ornaments to Life?" *ARTnews* 78 (September 1979): 108–14.

Shapiro, David. "Sculpture as Experience: The Monument That Suffered." *Art in America* 62 (May–June 1974): 55–58.

Sherin, Kerry. "The Empire State Plaza Collection." *Capital Region* (March 1987): 29.

Sinclair, Stephen. "When Art Meets the Community." *NEA Cultural Post* (March–April 1980): 1, 8–9.

Slavin, Maeve. "Art and Architecture: Can They Ever Meet Again?" *Interiors* 139 (March 1980): 78.

Solnit, R. "A New Place for Art: Art as Place." *Artweek* 18 (5 September 1987): 21.

Sommer, Robert. "People's Art." *AIA Journal* 58 (December 1972): 29–34.

Sonfist, Alan. "Natural Phenomena as Public Monuments." *Tracks 3* 1–2 (Spring 1977): 44–47.

Sorell, V. A. "From the Studio into the Street." *Art Journal* 39 (Summer 1980): 286–87.

Stalker, Douglas, and Clark Glymour. "The Malignant Object: Thoughts on Public Sculpture." Replies by Wolf von Eckardt, John Beardsley, Ronald Lee Fleming and Edward Levine. *The Public Interest* (Winter 1982): 3–36.

Stein, C. "Challenge: Sculpture in Public Places." *Sculpture Review* 32 (Spring 1983): 21–23.

Stevens, C. "Private Visions, Public Art." *Print* 41 (September/October 1987): 106–13.

Stevens, Mark, Mary Hager, and Maggie Malone. "Sculpture Out in the Open." *Newsweek*, 18 August 1980.

Storr, Robert. "*Tilted Arc:* Enemy of the People?" *Art in America* 73 (September 1985): 73, 90–97.

Stroll (The Magazine of Outdoor Art and Street Culture). New York: Creative Time (published twice a year).

Tacha, Athena. "Rhythm as Form." *Landscape Architecture* 68 (May 1978): 196–205.

Tarzan, Deloris. "Art, the Public and Public Art." *The Seattle Times*, 21 September 1980.

_____. "Hot Debate over Expenditure." *The Seattle Times*, 22 September 1980.

Tighe, Mary Ann. "Di Suvero in Grand Rapids: The Public Prevails." *Art in America* 65 (March–April 1977): 12–15.

Tomkins, Calvin. "The Art World: Like Water in a Glass." *The New Yorker*, 21 March 1983.

_____. "Tilted Arc." *The New Yorker*, 20 May 1985.

_____. "The Urban Capacity." *The New Yorker*, 5 April 1982.

Trachtenberg, Marvin. "The Statue of Liberty: Transparent Banality or Avant-Garde Conundrum?" *Art in America* 62 (May–June 1974): 36–42.

Tuchman, Phyllis. "Sculptors Mass in Toronto." *Art in America* 66 (September–October 1978): 15–16.

"Underground Art (in Toronto's Subway)." *ARTnews* 74 (October 1975): 126.

"Unique Cocktail Lounge, Murals and Fittings All of Rubber, Hotel Portage, Akron, Ohio." *Architecture and Engineering* 124 (March 1936): 58–60.

Viladas, Pilar. "Art for Whose Sake?" *Progressive Architecture* 66 (April 1985): 29.

Vrchota, Janet. "Grand Rapids Case Study." *Design and Environment* (Summer 1974): 28–31.

Vrchota, Joliene. "Urban Art Portfolio." *Design and Environment* (Summer 1974): 32–35.

"Wall, Exhibition at Bertha Schaeffer Gallery." *Arts and Architecture* 75 (March 1958): 20–21.

"War Murals for Victory." *Art Digest* 18 (July 1944): 15.

Welsh, Anne Marie. "Malpede Piece Shows Street Smarts." *San Diego Union,* 16 May 1988.

Welzinbach, Michael. "Fine Art vs. Public: 'Tilted Arc,' Other Works Perplexing to Audience." *Washington Times,* 21 June 1985.

Westbrook, John. "Places of the Art." *PLACE* (September–October 1986).

Wilmouth, Charles. "Raw and Beautiful." *San Diego Gay Times,* 20 May 1988.

Winerip, Michael. "Computerized Billboard Brightens up Times Square with Art-of-the-Month." *The New York Times,* 26 August 1983.

Wines, James. "Public Art and Private Gallery." *Art in America* (January–February 1970): 74–75.

Reports, Special Publications and Unpublished Documents

Allen, Jerry, "How Art Becomes Public." In *Public Art Collection Portfolio.* King County, Washington: King County Arts Commission, 1985.

Allocation for Art for Public Facilities: A Model Act. Washington, D.C.: National Assembly of State Arts Agencies, 1984.

The Art Program of Rockefeller Center and Its Contributing Artists. New York: Rockefeller Center, Inc., 1972.

Arts on the Line: Eight Year Report. Boston: Massachusetts Bay Transportation Authority, 1986.

Association of the Bar of the City of New York, Committee on Art Law. *Commissioning a Work of Public Art: An Annotated Model Agreement.* New York: Volunteer Lawyers for the Arts (distributed by American Council for Arts), 1985.

Design, Art, and Architecture in Transportation. Washington, D.C: U.S. Government Printing Office, 1977–80.

Downtown Art in Public Places Policy. Los Angeles: Los Angeles Community Redevelopment Agency, 1985.

Green, Dennis. *% for Art: New Legislation Can Integrate Art and Architecture.* Denver, Colorado: Western States Art Foundation, Inc., 1976.

Halprin, Lawrence, and Associates. *Environmental Criteria for the California State Capital Plan.* Sacramento: California Department of General Services, 1968.

Harrison, Helen A. "Social Consciousness in New Deal Murals." Unpublished Masters thesis. Case Western Reserve University, 1975.

Inserts. New York: Public Art Fund, 1988.

Land Use and Transportation Plan for Downtown Seattle. Seattle: City of Seattle, Land Use & Transportation Project, 1985.

McDonald, William F. *Federal Relief Administration and the Arts: The Origins and Administrative History of the Arts Projects of the Works Progress Administration.* Columbus: Ohio State University Press, 1969.

Murphy, Levy, Wurman. *Penn's Landing: Philadephia's Urban Waterfront.* Philadelphia: Old Philadelphia Development Corporation, Penn's Landing Corporation, 1975.

O'Connor, Francis V., ed. *Federal Support for the Visual Arts: The New Deal and Now.* 2nd ed. Greenwich, Connecticut: New York Graphic Society, 1971.

Redevelopment Authority, City of Philadelphia. *Annual Report, 1975.* Philadelphia: Redevelopment Authority, 1975.

Redevelopment Authority, City of Philadelphia. *City Art.* Philadelphia: The Fine Arts Program of the Redevelopment Authority, City of Philadelphia, 1979.

Rockefeller, David, Jr. *Coming to Our Senses: The Significance of the Arts for American Education.* American Council for the Arts in Education: Special Project Panel Report, 1977.

Rockwood, Lynda K. *Documentation for Public Art Collections.* Olympia, Washington: Washington State Arts Commission, 1982.

Rubenstein, Erica Beckh. "Tax Payers' Murals." Unpublished Ph.D. dissertation.

Sandler, Irving. *A Report on Public Art to the Chairman of the National Endowment for the Arts.* Washington, D.C., 1973. Mimeo.

Senie, Harriet. "Studies in the Development of Urban Sculpture 1950–1975." Unpublished Ph.D. dissertation, New York University, 1981.

Solomon, Jay. *Art in Architecture Program.* Washington, D.C.: U.S. General Services Administration, 1977.

Special Commission on Art in State Buildings. *A Program to Integrate Art and State Buildings.* Lansing, Michigan: Report of the Special Commission on Art in State Buildings to Governor William G. Milliken, 1978. Mimeo.

U. S. General Services Administration. *Art in Architecture Program.* Washington, D.C.: U. S. General Services Administration, 1979.

U. S. Department of Transportation. *Design, Art, and Architecture in Transportation.* Washington, D.C.: U. S. Government Printing Office, 1977–80.

Index

Other DA CAPO titles of interest